THE MESSAGE OF MATTHEW

Blessings

Rocco A. Errico

12-12-91

Other books by the author:

THE ANCIENT ARAMAIC PRAYER OF JESUS
LET THERE BE LIGHT — The Seven Keys
TREASURES FROM THE LANGUAGE OF JESUS
CLASSICAL ARAMAIC — Elementary Grammar Book One

THE MESSAGE OF MATTHEW
AN ANNOTATED PARALLEL ARAMAIC-ENGLISH
GOSPEL OF MATTHEW

Annotated and translated from
the Peshitta-Aramaic text by
ROCCO A. ERRICO

Noohra Foundation, Publisher
18022 Cowan Street, Suite 100B-G
Irvine, California 92714

THE MESSAGE OF MATTHEW: *An Annotated Parallel Aramaic-English Gospel of Matthew.* Copyright © 1991 by *Rocco A. Errico*. All rights reserved. Printed in the United States of America. No part of this book may be used or reproduced in any manner whatsoever without written permission except in the case of brief quotations embodied in critical articles and reviews. For information, address Noohra Foundation, 18022 Cowan St. (Ste. 100B-G), Irvine, CA 92714.

First Edition, 1991

ISBN: 0-9631292-0-1

CONTENTS

A Word from the Translator — vii

Acknowledgments — ix

Introduction — xi

    THE ARAMAIC LANGUAGE
        A Brief History
        Matthew, Mark, Luke and John in Aramaic - their value
        The Aramaic Script and Text of Matthew
        Judaism and the Semitic Customs of the Times

Abbreviations

THE MESSAGE OF MATTHEW

    Chapters 1-28. English Translation and Annotations — 1

    Chapters 1-28. Aramaic Text - Eastern Script — A - 1

Appendix 1: Preface from the Aramaic Dictionary by Mar Touma Oddo (abridged) — 123

Appendix 2: The Aramaic letters, vowels and their English equivalents — 129

Bibliography — 131

A WORD FROM THE TRANSLATOR

In 1970 I began lecturing in various Faiths throughout the United States and Canada on the Syro-Mesopotamian (Aramaic) cultural background of Holy Scripture which was based on the Aramaic-Peshitta texts of the Hebrew Bible and the New Testament, the Aramaic language of Jesus and on the history and Semitic customs and manners of the Near East. During years of lecturing I received numerous requests for a parallel Aramaic-English New Testament (especially for the teachings of Jesus) showing the meanings of Aramaic words and explaining the cultural-religious customs of Jesus' day.

It gives me great pleasure to fulfill these requests by presenting the first annotated, parallel Aramaic-English Gospel of Matthew. The intention of this annotated translation is to carry the reader into the Semitic world in which the Scriptures were born. The simplicity, directness and typical eastern transparency and manner of delivery becomes evident when one reads the text of this "Shemitic dialect." This work is not intended as a critical treatment of the Gospel although there are references made to the latest biblical critical materials available during the preparation of this manuscript. My desire is to underscore the human Jesus in his own Aramaic-Hebrew culture, religion and atmosphere. The risen Christ, in his spiritual nature, belongs to the entire human family in every generation and in every age; but in his own incarnation, he was an Easterner – a son of the Near East. When one begins to understand the rich cultural and religious philosophy of the Syro-Mesopotamian people of the Bible, along with its Judaic context the Gospel takes on new meaning for the reader. Dr. Abraham Rihbany, a Lebanese minister and author puts this idea so succinctly in his book *THE SYRIAN CHRIST*, pp. vi-vii, 4-6, and 12:

> In the Gospel story of Jesus' life there is not a single incident that is not in perfect harmony with the prevailing modes of thought and the current speech of the land of its origin. It is most natural, then, that Gospel truths should have come down to the succeeding generations – and to the nations of the West – cast in Oriental moulds of thought, and intimately intermingled with the simple domestic and social habits of Syria. The gold of the Gospel carries with it the sand and dust of its original home. . . . I know that the conditions of life in Syria of to-day are essentially as they were in the time of Christ, not from the study of the mutilated tablets of the archaeologist and the antiquarian, . . . but from the simple fact that, as a sojouner in this Western world, whenever I open my Bible it reads like a letter from home. Its unrestrained effusiveness of expression; its vivid, almost flashy and fantastic imagery; its naive narrations; the rugged unstudied simplicity of its parables; its unconventional portrayal of certain human relations; as well as its all-permeating spiritual mysticism, . . . might all have been written in my primitive village home, on the western slopes of Mount Lebanon some thirty years ago. . . . The need of the Western readers of the Bible is, in my judgment, to enter sympathetically and intelligently into the atmosphere in which the books of the Scriptures first took form: to have real intellectual, as well as spiritual, fellowship with those Orientals who sought earnestly in their own way to give tangible form to those great spiritual truths which have been, and ever shall be, humanity's most precious heritage.

I am indebted to my mentor, the late Dr. Geroge M. Lamsa, Bible translator and Eastern theologian, who, for ten years, taught me the ancient Aramaic language and gave me "eastern eyes" to see the sacred writings from their Semitic perspective; to understand the eastern customs, metaphors, mysticism and psychology behind the teachings and narratives. It has been my intent throughout my four years of a labor of love on this present volume to share Matthew's joyful message (celebration) of Jesus' Semitic teachings from his own native tongue, culture and religion.

October 14, 1991

ACKNOWLEDGEMENTS

I am deeply grateful to and appreciative of the following individuals who supported and encouraged this work of the Message of Matthew: The Rev. Fr. Michael J. Bazzi, L.S.T., specialist in the Aramaic language both ancient and modern, pastor of St. Peter's Chaldean Catholic Church of San Diego; a native of the Near East from Telkepe, Iraq, whose mother tongue is Aramaic. I am indebted to him for the many hours he spent going over my English translation of the Aramaic Peshitta Text and for the insightful suggestions he made concerning the biblical customs of the Near East. Also to Mr. Louis Khodabakhsh (Coda), a native Assyrian and expert in the classical Aramaic language for reviewing and correcting my typed manuscript of the Aramaic Peshitta text of Matthew, and for his kind permission to reprint his translation of the Preface (see appendix I) to the Aramaic Dictionary by Mar Touma Oddo.

Concerning the English portion of the manuscript: Many thanks to the Rev. Richard L. Hill, Vice President of the Noohra Foundation whose constant practical imput and constructive suggestions to keep on adding more annotations helped shape the book in its present form. Also to the Rev. Ann D. Milbourn for typing the first draft of the English portion of my translation and annotations, and for her final editorial suggestions; to Ms. Carol Marshall who continually and carefully made sure the comas and syntax were in good order; and to Mr. Richard Boal, Ms. Nell E. Clement, Ms. Sue Edwards, Mr. and Mrs. A. Kling and to all the members of the Noohra Foundation whose continual support has made this work possible.

My special thanks to Mr. Daniel MacDougald, Jr. for his kind permission to use in the cover design of this book selected passages from the tenth century C.E., Khaboris manuscript of the New Testament scribed in ancient Estrangela Aramaic.

NOTE: The ancient Aramaic symbol ⳨ which appears on the two title pages of this book is a Near Eastern scribal abbreviation of the name of God *"Yah"* for *"Yahweh."* This name was revealed to Moses on Mt. Sinai, Ex. 3:14. Some of the Eastern scribes employed this symbol to indicate that the writings or the manuscripts were of a sacred nature. In 1970 the Noohra Foundation stylized this symbol ⳨ with a sunburst as its logo.

INTRODUCTION

ܠܫܢܐ ܐܪܡܝܐ
THE ARAMAIC LANGUAGE

A Brief History

The Aramaic language made its historical appearance toward the end of the second millennium B.C.E., in Mesopotamia - the fertile crescent of the ancient Near East. Gradually, at the onset of the first millennium B.C.E., the written and spoken forms of the Aramaic tongue began making inroads throughout Near Eastern lands. It was the language of the Arameans, Assyrians, Chaldeans, Hebrews and Syrians.

Historians tell us that the term Aramaic ܐܪܡܝܐ is derived from Aram, ܐܪܡ. According to Hebrew Scripture, Aram was the grandson of Noah.[1] Aramaic is a Semitic (more precisely - Shemitic) language.[2] The word Aram - ܐܪܡ is formed from an Aramaic noun and adjective: Araa, ܐܪܥܐ meaning earth, land, terrain and Ramtha, ܪܡܬܐ meaning high. The fertile valley, Padan-Aram (Mesopotamia)[3] was the territory in which the descendants of Aram dwelt and in which Aramaic developed and remained pure. In the course of time, because of the practicality of its alphabet and simplicity of style in writing and speaking, it attracted all classes of people, goverment officials, merchants and writers. Thus, by the 8th century B.C.E., Aramaic became the common tongue (lingua franca) among the majority of Semitic clans and was the major language from Egypt to Asia Minor to Pakistan. It was employed by the great Semitic empires, Assyria and Chaldea (Babylon). It was also the language of the Persian (Iranian) government in its Western provinces. This Semitic tongue continues to be spoken and written in today's world by a variety of Chaldean, Assyrian and other Semitic communities in the Near and Middle East, Australia, the United States and elsewhere. These communities regulary speak the Aramaic language at home, in their social, political, domestic meetings and in their religious worship - liturgy.

Biblical as well as secular history records the various expulsions of the twelve tribes of Israel from their homeland to Assyria and Chaldea. Historically, the two most important exiles are: In 721 B.C.E., the Assyrians took the ten Northern tribes of the House of Israel captive to Nineveh and scattered them throughout Mesopotamia (Northern Iraq, Afkanistan and Pakistan). These warring conquerors repopulated Northern

---

1 Gen. 10:22
2 The term "Shemitic" is derived from the name "Shem," the son of Noah. See Gen. 5:32. The expression "Semitic" applies not only to various Semitic dialects but to all the descendants of Shem: the Akkadians, Arameans, Assyrians, Chaldeans, Hebrews and Arabs.
3 The land is also called Beth Nahreen - ܒܝܬ ܢܗܪܝܢ - the land between the rivers.

Israel with some of their own people and other Semitic clans who spoke Aramaic in its Assyrian dialect. (Eastern Aramaic was divided into two dialects, the Northern vernacular spoken in Assyria and the Southern vernacular spoken in Chaldea – Babylon.) These new inhabitants of the northern sector of Palestine intermarried with the remnant of Israelites that were left behind by the invading armies of Assyria. The descendants of these mixed marriages came to be known as Samaritans. The second exile: In 587 B.C.E., Nebuchanessar, the Chaldean king, deported the remaining two tribes of the House of Judah, the southern kingdom of Israel to Babylon.

Then in 539 B.C.E., Cyrus, the ruler of Persia (Iran) conquered the great city of Babylon and ended the Chaldean empire. The Persian king granted freedom to the exiled Jews who were living in Babylon. They could now return to Palestine under the protection of the Persian power. By this time, the Jewish people who returned to their homeland were speaking the Southern dialect of Aramaic. Therefore, during the first century in Palestine, the people of Judea spoke in the Southern dialect of Aramaic. But in Galilee, Jesus, his disciples, followers and contemporaries spoke in the Eastern, Northern dialect of Aramaic.[4] It is interesting to note that the manner of speech, the phraseology, the idioms and the orientation in the four gospels (Matthew, Mark, Luke and John) are vividly and distinctively Aramaic. The constant repetitions are characteristic of Eastern speech. Such phrases as, ܐܡܝܢ ܐܡܝܢ ܐܡܪ ܐܢܐ ܠܟܘܢ – Amen, amen, amar'a lkhon, "Truly, truly, I say to you," or "In those days," "And it came to pass," "And he said to them," are peculiarly Aramaic. Hebrew was spoken in some areas of the Holy Land, but there is some discussion among present day scholars as to its widespread use during the first century C.E.

Alexander the Great had conquered the Near East in 330 B.C.E., and after his death in Babylon, four of his generals divided the Near Eastern lands among themselves. Palestine became a part of that division. The Greeks were Gentile pagans who despised the religion of the Jews. They persecuted and killed the Jews unmercifully. But in 66 B.C.E., Pompey, the famous Roman general and statesman, conquered Eastern Asia Minor, Syria and Palestine and put them under the rule of the Romans. In the time of Jesus, there were ten cities known as the Decapolis. These cities were located east and northeast of the Jordan River as far as Damascus and were independent of Galilee and Judea. The majority of their inhabitants were Gentiles and it is believed that Greek was the predominant language. Therefore, the Greek tongue was also known in Palestine.[5] Be that as it may, the first century evidence clearly indicates that Aramaic was the most common language used throughout Palestine.[6] The message of Jesus of Nazareth was proclaimed and taught all over Palestine, Lebanon, Syria and Mesopotamia in the Eastern

---

4 Mk. 14:70.
5 See DO YOU KNOW GREEK? – How Much Greek Could the First Jewish Christians Have Known? by J. N. Sevenster. Leiden: E. J. Brill 1968.
6 See "The Languages of Palestine," pp 29-56, A WANDERING ARAMEAN, Collected Aramaic Essays by J. Fitzmyer.

Aramaic language. Aramaic remained the common language of the Near East until the 7th century C.E.; then Arabic gradually began to supplant Aramaic. Nonetheless, the Christians of Mesopotamia (Iraq), Iran, Syria, Turkey and Lebanon kept the Aramaic tongue alive domestically, scholastically and liturgically. In spite of the pressure of the ruling Arabs to speak Arabic, Aramaic is still spoken today in its many dialects, especially among the Assyrians and Chaldeans. It is known as Syriac but this is a misnomer. Syriac is the Greek term for Aramaic.[7]

Another important aspect of the Aramaic language was its use as the major tongue for the birth and spread of spiritual and intellectual ideas in and all over the Near East. According to the research and opinion of an outstanding Aramaic and Arabic scholar, Professor Franz Rosenthal who, in the Journal of Near Eastern studies, states: "In my view, the history of Aramaic represents the purest triumph of the human spirit as embodied in language (which is the mind's most direct form of physical expression) over the crude display of material power . . . Great empires were conquered by the Aramaic language, and when they disappeared and were submerged in the flow of history, that language persisted and continued to live a life of its own. . . The language continued to be powerfully active in the promulgation of spritual matters. It was the main instrument for the formulation of religious ideas in the Near East, which then spread in all directions all over the world. . . The monotheistic groups continue to live on today with a religious heritage, much of which found first expression in Aramaic."[8]

Matthew, Mark, Luke and John in Aramaic – Their Value

In the last two centuries, there has been great interest and much work accomplished in understanding and realizing the importance of the Aramaic language and in an Aramaic approach to the four Gospels[9] by many outstanding American and European scholars. Some have maintained that the Aramaic phrases, or "Aramaisms," in the four gospels and in the first half of the book of Acts were not written by bilingual authors who were thinking in Aramaic and wrote in coarse Greek, but that these "Aramaisms" were direct translations from original Aramaic documents no longer extant. Needless to say, there is much dispute over this theory. Most literary critics consider this theory of the Aramaic origins to be "revolutionary." Nonetheless, as far as New Testament studies are concerned, many scholars believe it to be a "refreshing contribution" for the following reasons: 1. It is based on sound philology. 2. It does not lead into the involved study of interior sources or documents. 3. It clarifies many difficult passages. 4. It projects the written sources to a period very close to the time of Jesus of Nazerth.

---

7 See "The Aramaic Language," THE NEAR EAST IN HISTORY, Philip K. Hitti. For a detailed account of the language see appendix 1, "Preface of the Author" from THE ARAMAIC DICTIONARY by Mar Touma Oddo, an abridged translation from Aramaic by Mr. Louis Coda.

8 F. Rosenthal, "Aramaic Studies during the past thirty years", in *Journal of Near Eastern Studies* (Chicago – 1978), pp 81-82.

9 Among the Aramaic speaking people the gospels of Matthew, Mark, Luke and John are called the "four-fold joyful message (Gospel) of Christ."

Biblical experts today employ the theory to support a plausible hypothesis that the Greek sources behind the gospels in Greek came from Aramaic documents and not just from oral traditions in Aramaic.[10]

Regardless of how one may theorize, a translation based on the Aramaic text of the gospels is helpful in many ways, such as: 1. Aramaic specialists tell us that the Aramaic language used in the Peshitta Eastern text[11] is almost identical to that which was actually spoken by Jesus. 2. The Aramaic words left in the Greek text of the Gospels were translated into Greek, but in the Aramaic text, there are no such translations.[12] 3. The strong flavor and character of the Semitic world becomes more apparent from Aramaic syntax and use of Eastern figures of speech than from Greek syntax and use of words. 4. Semitic plays on words found in the Aramaic gospels as in the Hebrew Bible could not be preserved in the Greek. 5. It enables us to perceive more clearly Jesus and his teachings in the context of his own language, people and time. 6. It clarifies many Semitic terms of speech which in Greek become obscure.

The Aramaic Script and Text of Matthew

Papias, Bishop of Hierapolis in Asia Minor, early 2nd century, says that Matthew wrote the *logia* (discourses, oracles, sayings) in Hebrew, that is, in the Aramaic used by the Jewish people of that time. Matthew's gospel was undoubtedly written in the secular Aramaic script (Aramaic square letters): א, ב, ג, ד, ה, ו, ז, ח, ט, י, כ, ל, and so forth. In fact, the alphabet used in writing all traditional texts of the Hebrew Bible is more precisely Aramaic than Hebrew. The Aramaic "square shaped" letters (see above examples) were employed in Hebrew papyri and parchments in the second and first

---

10 See THE NEW WESTMINISTER DICTIONARY OF THE BIBLE, "Gospel" - edited by Henry Snyder Gehman, Princeton Theological Seminary.

11 The official text of the Bible among Syriac-speaking (Aramaic-speaking) Christian lands. This particular text is venerated by all Christians in the Near East and India, by Eastern Christians (Assyrians and Chaldeans), Catholics and non-Catholics. Its originality and authority are upheld by all ancient churches of the East. Peshitta means "simple," "pure," "original" or, as applied to the text, "current." "The Aramic verb ܦܫܛ, P'shat, signifies *to unfold, spread out* that which was folded up, so that it can be seen in its true form, dimensions and character. Thus, the participle ܦܫܝܛܐ, Peshitta, means *spread out, not involved, folded up, simplex, not duplex;* or, as applied to a translation, *explicit, free from ambiguities, direct, simple and easy to understand.* This is precisely the style or character of the venerable Peshitta text." - Rev. Dr. James Murdock, Professor of Ecclesiastical History, Syriac New Testament.

12 For example Mt. 27:46, the Greek text says, "And about the ninth hour, Jesus cried out in a loud voice and said: Eli, Eli, lema sabachthani; that is, God of mine, God of mine, Why have you forsaken me?" Whereas the Aramaic text says, " And about the ninth hour, Jesus called out in a loud voice and said: Oh, God, Oh God, For what a purpose You have kept me!" Errico translation. The expression in the Greek "that is" means that it is translating the Aramaic phrase left in the Greek manuscript. In the Aramaic text, the phrase "that is" is not present.

centuries B.C.E. and are attested as the normal alphabet for writing Hebrew from that time to our present day. According to Rabbinic sources, Ezra, the great Jewish leader, priest, scribe, wise student and teacher of the Torah, had chosen the secular Aramaic script for the writing of the Torah instead of the ancient Hebrew letters. Beginning with the Babylonian captivity Aramaic as the popular language had been slowly and gradually replacing Hebrew; therefore the change in script was meant to facilitate the study of the Torah by the people.[13] Rabbinic tradition has held Ezra in very high esteem and has placed him second only to Moses. Under his leadership, Ezra brought a very large remnant of the common people, priests, Levites, singers, porters and temple servants *(Nethinites)* from Babylon to Jerusalem in the seventh year of the reign of Artaḥshisht, King of Persia (Iran), 458 B.C.E.[14]

In the annotations of this book, when a specific scriptural word or phrase is defined and explained, I used both the Aramaic Eastern classical script and the square shaped letters with English transliterations. For example, Mt. 6:13, footnote 18, the Aramaic word for "evil," "error" "mistake" is written: (1) ܒܝܫܐ - eastern classical script, (2) בישא - square script and is pronounced *Beesha* - English transliteration. I employed the classical script for reading the Aramaic text of Matthew and not western Syriac commonly used by scholars because the classical has only six letters which differ in shape from the very old Estrangela letters. Estrangela - ܐܣܛܪܢܓܠܐ is the ancient form which was used by scribes in writing the gospels before classical Aramaic came into use. It derived its name Estrangela from two Aramaic words ܣܛܪ, star, "to write" and ܐܘܢܓܠܝܘܢ, awangaleeon, "gospel." The Aramaic script of Matthew appears on the right page and is paginated as A - 1, A - 2, etc. The "A" represents the Aramaic language. Thus "A - 1" means page 1 of the Aramaic text of Matthew. The corresponding English translation appears on the left page and is paginated in the usual manner.

The Aramaic Peshitta text of both the Hebrew Bible and the New Testament is highly venerated in the East and is considered the only authorized text. As far as the New Testament is concerned, eastern tradition among the Aramaic speaking Christians teaches that the Peshitta text was written in the early era of Christianity by an unknown scribe or scribes. In the west there has been a great deal of debate and controversy as to the date and by whom the work was accomplished. Most New Testament scholars claim that the present Aramaic Peshitta text is a translation of a very early Greek manuscript which is no longer extant.[15] This certainly does not devalue the Aramaic Peshitta text but increases its importance. There are also those who claim that the Peshitta text of the

---

13 See "Exile and Return," ANCIENT JUDAISM, Irving M. Zeitlin, pp 258-280.
14 Ezra 7:1-10
15 THE EARLY VERSIONS OF THE NEW TESTAMENT, Bruce M. Metzger, "Problems concerning the Date and Textual Affinities of the Peshitta New Testament," pp 56-63.

of the New Testament does not depend on a Greek source.[16] It is also interesting to note that the Peshitta texts from the various centuries do not differ from one another as do the Greek texts. Eastern church scribes exercised extreme care in their transcription of ancient New Testament documents.

The translation of THE MESSAGE OF MATTHEW is based on a 6th century (possibly 7th century) Peshitta Aramaic Manuscript of the New Testament (Estrangela script). This document is without chapters and verses[17] so I utilized the Eastern Aramaic Peshitta-classical script which was printed in 1950, Mosul-Bagdad edition, Iraq, for the order of chapters, verses and for the addition of vowel points. My occasional translation of a verse from the Hebrew Bible is from the published Masoretic Hebrew Text, Biblia Hebraica, Stuttgartensia 1983.

Judaism and the Semitic Customs of the Times

In the last two decades, there has been many new writings on the sociological and religious traditions of first century Palestinian Judaism which have aided in reexamining, reconstructing and resolving many social and historical New Testament problems. These recent and insightful findings from the Dead Sea Scrolls and other archaeological treasures are especially enlightening for understanding the religio-social context during the lifetime of Jesus. I have included some of these views in the annotations.

The everyday psycho-social and domestic customs in the annotations are based on ten years of in-depth studies of the ancient biblical Aramaic culture, psychology, philosophy and symbolism of the Near East with Dr. George M. Lamsa, Bible translator, a native Assyrian whose mother tongue was Aramaic; and on the works of the late Dr. Abraham M. Rihbany, also a native of the Near East, from the province of Mount Lebanon; and on my continual research in the Near Eastern biblical history and Aramaic-Hebrew culture. In regard to the authenticity of these customs,[18] the following is a quote from Dr. W. A. Wigram, noted British scholar, who lived among a surviving remnant of a once powerful nation - the Assyrians in Northern Iraq. (It is interesting to note that Dr. Lamsa was born and reared among these people who practiced the ancient Near Eastern Biblical customs.) The descendants, largely mixed with the blood of the ten northern tribes of the House of Israel, still live, think and speak as did the people among whom Jesus was born and to whom he taught his message:

---

16 NEW TESTAMENT ORIGIN, George M. Lamsa, "Origin of New Testament text," pp 50-56. "It was natural for the disciples of Jesus and for the evangelists to be inspired to preach and write in their own tongue, Aramaic. They recorded for their own people what their Master had preached to them in Aramaic. . . " p. 52. See also pp 81-88, "The Eastern Text," "The Peshitta Text."

17 The Bible was divided into chapters in the 13th century C.E. in Europe and in the 15th century the chapters were divided into verses.

18 See p. vii "A Word from the Translator" especially Dr. Abraham Rihbany's remarks on the everyday biblical customs.

We have now traced the history of a strange nation, from very early days to what is practically our own time-up to, in fact, the eve of the Great War (World War 1) . . . A strange survival in an isolated corner of the world, these last representatives of the ancient Assyrian stock have hitherto *kept up the most primitive of Semitic customs to an extent that can hardly be paralleled elsewhere,* even in Mesopotamian marsh districts. One thing is certain, that the Assyrians boast with justice that they alone of all Christian nations still keep as their spoken language what is acknowledged to be the language of Palestine in the first century, and that therefore they alone among Christian nations, if we except a few villages that may still exist in Lebanon, use regularly the language of Christ.[19]

It was only natural that this old Semitic stock (Assyrians), living where nothing had ever occurred to disturb their habits of life, *should keep up the old Semitic customs. They still lived, or did live until the change of the great war brought about an alteration, the life of the Old Testament.* Bible customs, or those we call such, were, of course, not peculiar to the Hebrew, but were the *common heritage of all the stock to which he belonged and a part of the atmosphere of the land.*[20]

In conclusion, I feel the following quote aptly gives us a genuine insight into the mental, social and psychological attitudes of the Aramaic speaking people and Near Eastern peoples in contrast to Western systematic applications and attitudes toward religion in general.

As is well known to church historians, the Syrian Christians of the Semitic stock have had very little to do with the development of the "creeds of Christendom." Theological organization has been as foreign to the minds of the Eastern Christians as political organization. They have always been *worshipers* rather than *theologians, believers* rather than *systematic thinkers.* Their religious thinking has never been brought by them into logical unity, nor their mysticism into full metaphysical development.

The Oriental (Easterner) has been a lender in religion and a borrower in theology. The course of religion ran from the East to the West, the course of theology ran from the West to the East. Had it been left to itself, it is certain that the Christianity of Palestine never would have built up such a massive structure of doctrine as the Athanasian Creed.[21] Wherever the great doctrinal statements of our religion may have originated, - whether in Rome,

---

19 THE ASSYRIANS AND THEIR NEIGHBORS, W. A. Wigram, pp 177, 181. However, it must be stated that not only the Assyrians but also over one million Chaldeans and Syrians speak and use regularly the language of Jesus. It is also interesting to note that in 1950 a community of Jews who had immigrated from Iraq to Israel spoke Aramaic.
20 Ibid., p. 185.
21 A profession of faith widely used in Western Christendom but not in the East. The date of the Creed is disputed. However some authorities hold that it was composed after 428 C.E. It basically covers two main doctrines - The Trinity and The Incarnation. It also embraces anathemas. Today, its use has been restricted or abandoned completely.

Constantinople, Antioch, or Alexandria, - *their essential parts were Greek and Roman, and not Oriental (Eastern).*

The Christian Church had its simple origin with a group of Jewish followers of Jesus Christ in Palestine, but it had its marvelous expansion and organization among the "Gentiles." In Palestine the faith of the Church may be said to have been instinctive, but among the Gentiles and under Greek and Roman influences that faith became highly reflective. *Faith in God the Father, and in his Son (by anointing) Jesus Christ, and love of the brethren, constituted the simple creed of the Palestinian Christians....* The creed of the theologians consists of many "articles"; the creed of Christ only of two, - "Love the LORD thy God with all thy heart, and thy neighbor as thyself." I prefer Christ's creed.[22]

ܕܘܘܡܘ ܠܚܟܝܡܐ ܒܠܚܘܕܘܗܝ܂ ܥܘܒܕܢܐ ܕܝܢ ܢܥܦܐ ܡܥܒܢܐ ܠܟܠܟܘܢ ܐܡܝܢ܂ ܓܥܕܘܗܝ ܕܡܪܢ ܢܥܦܐ ܡܥܒܢܐ ܒܝܕ ܚܠܓܝܢ ܐܡܝܢ ܀

Now God is the only wise one. Praise to Him through Jesus the Messiah throughout the ages! Amen! The loving-kindness of our Lord Jesus the Messiah be with all of you. Amen! Rom. 16:26-27.

May the loving, guiding and awesome Presence of God continue to nourish and enlighten our hearts and spirits always. Peace be with us all.

---

22 THE SYRIAN CHRIST, Abraham M Rihbany, pp 404-406, 410.

ABBREVIATIONS

KJV	King James Bible
N.T.	New Testament
Gen.	Genesis
Ex.	Exodus
Lev.	Levitcus
Num.	Numbers
Deut.	Deuteronomy
Josh.	Joshua
1 Sam.	1 Samuel
2 Sam.	2 Samuel
1 Ki.	1 Kings
2 Ki.	2 Kings
1 Chron.	1 Chronicles
2 Chron.	2 Chronicles
Neh.	Nehemiah
Ps.	Psalms
Prov.	Proverbs
Ecc.	Ecclesiastes
Isa.	Isaiah
Jer.	Jeremiah
Ezek.	Ezekiel
Dan.	Daniel
Hos.	Hosea
Jon.	Jonah
Mic.	Micah
Mal.	Malachi
Mt.	Matthew
Mk.	Mark
Lk.	Luke
Jn.	John
Heb.	Hebrews
Rev.	Revelation
B.C.E. (B.C.)	Before the Common Era
C.E. (A.D.)	Common Era

THE HOLY GOSPEL

OF OUR LORD

JESUS THE MESSIAH

THE MESSAGE

OF MATTHEW

ܟܬܒܐ ܕܬܫܥܝܬܐ

ܕܡܪܝ

ܝܘܚܢܢ ܒܪ ܙܥܒܝ

ܚܣܝܐ

ܕܐܪܒܝܠ

THE MESSAGE OF MATTHEW

Chapter 1

THE ANCESTRY OF JESUS

1. The ancestral[1] record[2] of Jesus the Messiah, the son of David,[3] the son of Abraham.[4]

2. Abraham fathered[5] Isaac; Isaac fathered Jacob; Jacob fathered Judah and his brothers;

3. Judah fathered Parz and Zarh from Tamar,[6] Parz fathered Hezron; Hezron fathered Aram;

4. Aram fathered Aminadab; Aminadab fathered Nehson; Nehson fathered Salmon;

5. Salmon fathered Boaz from Rahab; Boaz fathered Obed from Ruth; Obed fathered Jesse;

---

1 A document which listed ancestors was very important to Eastern people. One of the many Near Eastern styles of beginning a book was to open with a genealogical table. This fact is evidenced by the numerous recorded genealogies throughout the Bible. Matthew's genealogy is divided into three sections, each with fourteen generations. Section one: Abraham to King David, section two: Solomon to Yokanyah, section three: Shelathel to Jesus. The names in the first two sections can be found in 1 Chron. 1:34-3:24 of the Greek text of the Hebrew Scriptures known as the SEPTUAGINT. The third section lacks one name. See verse 17, footnote 10.

2 ܟܬܒܐ, כתבא, Kthawa, - *scroll, book, record, roll*. The first and second chapters of Matthew serve as a foreword to his gospel. It is believed by the majority of New Testament experts that Chapters 1 and 2, which are referred to as the Infancy Narrative, first appeared on a separate scroll which was not originally a part of Matthew's book. These scholars also tell us that verses 18-25 were completely independent in origin from the genealogical table (verses 1-17). The title of the book is THE MESSAGE OF MATTHEW. The word "message" comes from the Aramaic term ܟܪܘܙܘܬܐ, כרוזותא, Karozootha and is usually translated into English as "gospel." But the word means *message, preaching, proclamation*. The root of the word in Aramaic is ܟܪܙ, כרז, Kraz - *to be proclaimed, announced, preached, publicly taught, celebrated*. These writings were a declaration or a form of "preaching" by Matthew. It is likely that an Eastern scribe named the document THE MESSAGE OF MATTHEW after he had edited and compiled all the scrolls into book form. See "Authorship and Date" p. A - 1.

3 The term "son of David" is a royal, messianic title. The bearer of this title was to be the final successor of King David and was to restore Israel as a free and sovereign nation.

4 "Son of Abraham" is a broader and less restrictive title than "son of David." A "son of Abraham" was to bless all nations and not just Israel. See Gen. 12:1-3. In other words "son of David" is more nationalistic in its implication but "son of Abraham" is more universal.

5 ܐܘܠܕ, אולד, Awlid, - literally means *to give birth, generate, beget*, hence *to father*.

6 The episode of Judah and Tamar, Gen. 38:6-30.

AUTHORSHIP AND DATE

THE GOSPEL OF MATTHEW, according to Eastern tradition, was the preaching and writings of the Apostle Matthew and in its original form was written in Aramaic. A few scholars of the New Testament credit Matthew with having written the sayings and deeds of Jesus while his lord was teaching, preaching and healing throughout Galilee. They also suggest that the gospel was in circulation among the newly formed communities of believers about 12 to 20 years after the Resurrection. However, at a later date these original writings were collected and compiled by an eastern scribe (editor or copyist) who inserted additional material such as Jesus' ancestral record, infancy narrative and other information. Modern scholars of the New Testament are in disagreement as to the author of the gospel of Matthew and propose that the gospel made its appearance somewhere between 75 and 90 C.E.

Many New Testament experts hold the theory that Mark was the first gospel and not Matthew. They posit that our present gospel of Matthew may be a copy of Mark's gospel with modifications or that it comes from early Aramaic collected sayings of Jesus known as Q (Quelle, a German word meaning "Source"). On the other hand, there are scholars who think that the Apostle Matthew may have been the original author not only of his own gospel but that his material formed the basis for the writings of Mark and Luke, assuming he gathered the teachings of Jesus together in a collection similar to Q. See Mt. 9:9, footnote 8, "Matthew" and Mt. 7:29, footnote 17, the section on the sayings of Jesus. For further information on the various opinions, see JESUS AND THE JUDAISM OF HIS TIME, Irving M. Zeitlin, "Who was the First Evangelist?" pp 85-98.

6. Jesse fathered King David; David fathered Solomon from the wife of Uriah;[7]

7. Solomon fathered Rhebam; Rhebam fathered Abiyah; Abiyah fathered Asa;

8. Asa fathered Jehoshapat; Jehoshapat fathered Yoram; Yoram fathered Oziyah;

9. Oziyah fathered Yotham; Yotham fathered Ahaz; Ahaz fathered Hezakyah;

10. Hezakyah fathered Mnashay; Mnashay fathered Amon; Amon fathered Yoshiyah;

11. Yoshiyah Yokanyah and his brothers in the Babylonian exile.

12. Then after the Babylonian exile Yokanyah fathered Shelathel; Shelathel fathered Zurbabel;

13. Zurbabel fathered Abiod; Abiod fathered Elyakem; Elyakem fathered Azor;

14. Azor fathered Zadok; Zadok fathered Akin; Akin fathered Eliyod;

15. Eliyod fathered Eliazar; Eliazar fathered Mathan; Mathan fathered Jacob;

16. Jacob fathered Joseph, the husband of Mary of Whom was born Jesus,[8] who is called the Messiah.[9]

---

7 I.e., Bathsheba. Take note that it says "wife of Uriah" and not *wife of David*. See 2 Sam. 11:1-27.

8 Some N.T. interpreters suggest that the 16th verse originally must have read that "Joseph begat Jesus" pointing out the fact that the entire genealogy would be valueless without stating the fatherhood of Joseph. Usually, the Sinaitic Aramaic text is quoted as evidence which reads, ܝܥܩܘܒ ܕܝܢ ܐܘܠܕ ܠܝܘܣܦ. ܝܘܣܦ ܗܘ ܕܡܟܝܪܐ ܗܘܬ ܠܗ ܡܪܝܡ ܒܬܘܠܬܐ ܐܘܠܕ ܠܝܫܘܥ ܕܡܬܩܪܐ ܡܫܝܚܐ. "Jacob fathered Joseph. Joseph, to whom the Virgin Mary was betrothed, fathered (begat) Jesus who is called the Messiah." - Errico translation. However, most textual critics believe the above quotation to be a paraphrase of the reading preserved in the Curetonian Aramaic (Syriac) manuscript or is an imitation of the preceding pattern in the genealogy. In the East, the Sinaitic, Curetonian and many other such Aramaic texts are of late origin and are not considered authentic texts but revisions. They are rejected and are not used as sacred literature. Be that as it may, there is also a verse in the gospel of John (1:45) in all Aramaic and Greek texts of the New Testament which says, "Philip found Nathanael, and said to him, We have found that Jesus, *the son of Joseph, of Nazareth*, is the one concerning whom Moses wrote in the law and the prophets." See also Mt. 13:55; Lk. 4:22; Mt. 2:23, footnote 12, Nazareth.

9 ܡܫܝܚܐ, משיחא, Msheeha - *Messiah, the Anointed, the Appointed one*. The term "Messiah" is a title and not a proper name. (Greek form is *CHRISTOS* - Christ.) Jesus was called the Anointed One. According to Hebrew Scripture, kings, priests and prophets were anointed with consecrated oil into their respective offices - Ex. 28:41; Lev. 4:3, 5, and 16; 1 Sam. 2:10, 35; 1 Ki. 19:16. The kings of Israel were known as the "LORD'S anointed ones." David called King Saul the "LORD'S Anointed (Messiah-Christ)." See 1 Sam. 24:6; also "The Messianic Expectation" p. A - 2.

ܘ: ܐܝܫܝ ܐܘܠܕ ܠܕܘܝܕ ܡܠܟܐ. ܕܘܝܕ ܐܘܠܕ ܠܫܠܝܡܘܢ ܡܢ ܐܢܬܬܗ ܕܐܘܪܝܐ.

ܙ: ܫܠܝܡܘܢ ܐܘܠܕ ܠܪܚܒܥܡ. ܪܚܒܥܡ ܐܘܠܕ ܠܐܒܝܐ. ܐܒܝܐ ܐܘܠܕ ܠܐܣܐ.

ܚ: ܐܣܐ ܐܘܠܕ ܠܝܗܘܫܦܛ. ܝܗܘܫܦܛ ܐܘܠܕ ܠܝܘܪܡ. ܝܘܪܡ ܐܘܠܕ ܠܥܘܙܝܐ.

ܛ: ܥܘܙܝܐ ܐܘܠܕ ܠܝܘܬܡ. ܝܘܬܡ ܐܘܠܕ ܠܐܚܙ. ܐܚܙ ܐܘܠܕ ܠܚܙܩܝܐ.

ܝ: ܚܙܩܝܐ ܐܘܠܕ ܠܡܢܫܐ. ܡܢܫܐ ܐܘܠܕ ܠܐܡܘܢ. ܐܡܘܢ ܐܘܠܕ ܠܝܘܫܝܐ.

ܝܐ: ܝܘܫܝܐ ܐܘܠܕ ܠܝܘܟܢܝܐ ܘܠܐܚܘܗܝ ܒܓܠܘܬܐ ܕܒܒܠ.

ܝܒ: ܡܢ ܒܬܪ ܕܝܢ ܓܠܘܬܐ ܕܒܒܠ. ܝܘܟܢܝܐ ܐܘܠܕ ܠܫܠܬܐܝܠ. ܫܠܬܐܝܠ ܐܘܠܕ ܠܙܘܪܒܒܠ.

ܝܓ: ܙܘܪܒܒܠ ܐܘܠܕ ܠܐܒܝܘܕ. ܐܒܝܘܕ ܐܘܠܕ ܠܐܠܝܩܝܡ. ܐܠܝܩܝܡ ܐܘܠܕ ܠܥܙܘܪ.

ܝܕ: ܥܙܘܪ ܐܘܠܕ ܠܨܕܘܩ. ܨܕܘܩ ܐܘܠܕ ܠܐܟܝܢ. ܐܟܝܢ ܐܘܠܕ ܠܐܠܝܘܕ.

ܝܗ: ܐܠܝܘܕ ܐܘܠܕ ܠܐܠܝܥܙܪ. ܐܠܝܥܙܪ ܐܘܠܕ ܠܡܬܢ. ܡܬܢ ܐܘܠܕ ܠܝܥܩܘܒ.

ܝܘ: ܝܥܩܘܒ ܐܘܠܕ ܠܝܘܣܦ ܓܒܪܗ ܕܡܪܝܡ ܕܡܢܗ ܐܬܝܠܕ ܝܫܘܥ ܕܡܬܩܪܐ ܡܫܝܚܐ.

THE MESSIANIC EXPECTATION

In the hearts and minds of the people of Israel there burned a strong desire and dream for a peaceful and joyful future. This dream for a better future was the Messianic concept and vision inspired by their prophets. The pre-exilic prophets had hoped and worked for their nation to cleanse itself morally and become a guide among all the nations. According to Isaiah's vision, Israel, having cleansed itself, would then be ruled by a king from the family of David. Under the wise and powerful leadership of this King, justice, peace, compassion and national contentment would reign and abound.

However, after Israel's exile and return to their homeland, known as the Second-Temple Era, the Messianic concept gradually changed. Now the emphasis of salvation began to shift from the destiny of the nation to the individual. The first glimpse of this idea is seen in the teaching of the resurrection envisioned by the prophet Daniel. (Dan. 12:1-3, about 167-165 B.C.E.) The Messianic idea underwent more modification. Malachi predicted that Elijah would appear and prepare the way for the Messiah - a human, earthly Messiah endowed by the God of Israel with the necessary powers to lead the people in the paths of peace and justice. More and more writings began to appear transforming the earlier Messianic ideas. The Messiah would be a powerful militant and political leader destroying the enemies of God and His people. He would be a supernatural Messiah. The expectation of the coming of the Messiah was so high and prevalent among the people during the Roman occupation that it gave rise to many false messiahs. These pretenders led the people into violent attacks against the Romans but they and their followers were very quickly crushed by the iron hand of Rome.

17. Thus all these generations from Abraham until David are fourteen generations; and from David until the Babylonian exile are fourteen generations; and from the Babylonian exile until the Messiah are fourteen[10] generations.[11]

18. Now[12] the birth of Jesus, the Messiah, was in this manner: When Mary his mother was promised[13] to Joseph, before they lived together,[14] she was found pregnant by the Holy Spirit.

19. Now Joseph her husband was devout,[15] and he did not want to disgrace her; so he was thinking he might set her free secretly.[16]

20. Then while he was thinking about these things, the messenger of the LORD appeared to him in a dream[17] and said to him: Joseph, son of David, do not be afraid to take Mary, your wife, because that which is conceived in her is from the Holy Spirit.

---

10 The construction of the three sections of "fourteen" generations is artificial and was accomplished through the omission of names. It is believed that it was purposely recorded to correspond to the numerical value of King David's name which in Aramaic and Hebrew (דוד, ܕܘܝܕ,) is spelled with the consonants DWD דוד, ܕܘܝܕ, - D is 4, W is 6, D is 4 = 14.

11 Verse 17 concludes the genealogy section. The scribe included the ancestral names: 1) to prove Jesus was the promised Messiah as a descendant of the royal family of David, 2) to trace his lineage back to Abraham, 3) to refute any slander concerning Jesus' birth.

12 This section (verses 18-25) is completely separate in origin from the genealogy which precedes it. See footnote 2.

13 ܡܟܝܪܐ, מכירא, Mkheera, usually translated as *betrothed, promised, engaged* but its root meaning is *to barter, to bargain, to purchase* Evidently, the amount of the dowry had been settled and given to Mary's family according to the Near Eastern custom; therefore, Mary and Joseph were regarded as married. The social practice for a marriage is usually done through a matchmaker who approaches the parents of the prospective bride with a group of town elders. (Sometimes the parents make the arrangements without a matchmaker.) The dowry is decided by the social standing, weight, health and beauty of the bride. However, the most essential factor tends to be the physical stamina of the woman. Once all of this is settled, the dowry paid and preparations made for the wedding, the bride becomes the wife and property of her husband.

14 I.e., before he took her home with him. See verse 24, footnote 23.

15 ܟܐܢܐ, כאנא, Kena - *a just, pious, devout, righteous, gentle individual*. In other words, one who reveres God and follows the commandments (Torah).

16 Joseph was contemplating a divorce without a public hearing.

17 The Aramaic word ܚܠܡܐ, חלמא, ḥelma means *dream*. It comes from the root ܚܠܡ, ḥlm - *to dream*. This same root word is used for the Hebrew and Arabic word "dream". It is interesting to know that "ḥlm" also means *to heal, make whole, sound, well, restore*. Easterners believe that God's guidance and revelation can come through dreams. Therefore, they put a great deal of trust in dreams of angelic messages and visitations. See "Dreams and Visions" p. A - 3.

ܝܙ: ܟܠܗܝܢ ܗܟܝܠ ܫܪ̈ܒܬܐ ܡܢ ܐܒܪܗܡ ܥܕܡܐ ܠܕܘܝܕ ܫܪ̈ܒܬܐ ܐܪܒܥܣܪ. ܘܡܢ
ܕܘܝܕ ܥܕܡܐ ܠܓܠܘܬܐ ܕܒܒܠ ܫܪ̈ܒܬܐ ܐܪܒܥܣܪ. ܘܡܢ ܓܠܘܬܐ ܕܒܒܠ ܥܕܡܐ
ܠܡܫܝܚܐ ܫܪ̈ܒܬܐ ܐܪܒܥܣܪ.

ܝܚ: ܝܠܕܗ ܕܝܢ ܕܝܫܘܥ ܡܫܝܚܐ ܗܟܢܐ ܗܘܐ. ܟܕ ܡܟܝܪܐ ܗܘܬ ܡܪܝܡ ܐܡܗ ܠܝܘܣܦ
ܥܕܠܐ ܢܫܬܘܬܦܘܢ. ܐܫܬܟܚܬ ܒܛܢܐ ܡܢ ܪܘܚܐ ܕܩܘܕܫܐ.

ܝܛ: ܝܘܣܦ ܕܝܢ ܒܥܠܗ ܟܐܢܐ ܗܘܐ. ܘܠܐ ܨܒܐ ܕܢܦܪܣܝܗ. ܘܡܬܪܥܐ ܗܘܐ
ܕܒܛܠܝܐܝܬ ܢܫܪܝܗ.

ܟ: ܟܕ ܗܠܝܢ ܕܝܢ ܐܬܪܥܝ. ܐܬܚܙܝ ܠܗ ܡܠܐܟܐ ܕܡܪܝܐ ܒܚܠܡܐ ܘܐܡܪ ܠܗ: ܝܘܣܦ
ܒܪܗ ܕܕܘܝܕ. ܠܐ ܬܕܚܠ ܠܡܣܒ ܠܡܪܝܡ ܐܢܬܬܟ. ܗܘ ܓܝܪ ܕܡܬܝܠܕ ܒܗ ܡܢ
ܪܘܚܐ ܗܘ ܕܩܘܕܫܐ.

DREAMS AND VISIONS

Dreams and visions play a major role in the lives of Eastern people, especially among the lives of the Hebrew people. For instance when God revealed himself to the patriarchs and prophets, He usually did so through dreams and visions. However, dreams and visions were not the only means for spiritual guidance and communication.

We are told in Numbers 12:6 the following: "And the Lord said to them, Hear now my words: If you are prophets I, the Lord, will reveal myself to you in a *vision* and will speak to you in a *dream*." Aramaic text, Errico translation. When King Solomon prayed for wisdom, the scribe who chronicled the King's reign reports, "In Gibeon the Lord appeared to Solomon *in a dream* by night and God said, Ask that I shall give thee." 1 Ki. 3:5, KJV. "For God speaks once; he does not speak a second time; through a *dream* and through a *vision* of the night, when sleep falls upon men, while in deep slumber upon the bed, then he opens the ears of men . . . " Job. 33:14-16, Aramaic text, Errico translation. The recorded appearances of God and angels in the Hebrew Bible usually occurred in the minds and hearts of the people while they were sleeping or in a deep trance.

Dr. Abraham Rihbany, commenting on dreams and visions, states, "I do not know how many times I heard it stated in my native land and at our own fireside that heavenly messengers in the forms of patron saints or angels came to pious, childless wives, in dreams and visions, and cheered them with the promise of maternity." THE SYRIAN CHRIST p. 12. See Mt. 1:20, footnote 17, "Dream."

21. Then she will give birth to a son, and you shall name[18] him Jesus[19] indeed he shall bring his people back to life[20] from their sins.[21]

22. This then all occurred so that what was said by the LORD through the prophet might be fulfilled:

23. Lo, a virgin shall become pregnant and shall give birth to a son, and they shall call him Ammanuel,[22] which is interpreted: Our-God-with-us.

24. Then when Joseph woke up from his sleep, he did as the messenger of the LORD had commanded, and he took his wife home[23] with him.

25. And he did not know her until she gave birth to her firstborn son; then she named him Jesus.

---

18 It may also be translated as "she shall name . . ." instead of "you shall name . . ." But because of the context, the pronoun "you" is preferable.

19 ܝܶܫܽܘܥ, יֵשׁוּעַ, Eshoa or Eeshua – *Yahweh saves, Savior, Deliverer*. Hebrew form – *Yehoshua*. In Scripture the name appears in the shortened form *Yeshua (Joshua)*. Scholars suggest that the name "Jesus" originally and more precisely means *Yahweh, help!* It is interesting to note that the name "Jesus" was a popular and common name in Palestine during the first Century.

20 The Aramaic verb ܚܝܐ, חיא, Hyah means *to save, live, revive, resuscitate, recover, bring back to life*. There is a play on words in the Aramaic text with the name Jesus (Yahweh saves) and the verb Hyah (saves). " . . . and you shall name him *Yahweh saves* indeed he shall *save* his people from their errors (sins)."

21 ܚܛܗܐ, חטהא, Htaha, root meaning *to miss;* hence, *sin, error, mistake*.

22 ܥܡܢܘܐܝܠ, עמנואיל, Ammanuel, – *God with us*. See Isa. 7:14. Why was Jesus never called or referred to by the name Ammanuel? Evidently the scribe is telling us that the son of Mary and Joseph is to be named "Jesus" (see verse 21, footnote 18) but at the same time their son will be the fulfillment of the Ammanuel (God with us) prophecy because he will be the bearer of the Divine Presence (In Hebrew – *Shekinah*.) among the people. The prophecy of Isaiah (7:14) has to do with a political problem and not with the birth of the Messiah. However, the gospel writer is placing a spiritual emphasis on the prophecy in regard to Jesus.

23 The Aramaic phrase ܘܕܒܪܗ ܠܐܢܬܬܗ, ודברה לאנתתה, literally rendered is: *"and he took his wife."* or *"and he took charge of his wife."* The added expression "home with him" is implied. See footnote 14.

ܟܐ: ܬܐܠܕ ܕܝܢ ܒܪܐ. ܘܬܩܪܐ ܫܡܗ ܝܫܘܥ ܗܘ ܓܝܪ ܢܚܝܗ ܠܥܡܗ ܡܢ
ܚܛܗܝܗܘܢ.
ܟܒ: ܗܕܐ ܕܝܢ ܟܠܗ ܕܗܘܬ ܕܢܬܡܠܐ ܡܕܡ ܕܐܬܐܡܪ ܡܢ ܡܪܝܐ ܒܝܕ ܢܒܝܐ:
ܟܓ: ܕܗܐ ܒܬܘܠܬܐ ܬܒܛܢ ܘܬܐܠܕ ܒܪܐ. ܘܢܩܪܘܢ ܫܡܗ ܥܡܢܘܐܝܠ. ܕܡܬܬܪܓܡ
ܥܡܢ ܐܠܗܢ.
ܟܕ: ܟܕ ܩܡ ܕܝܢ ܝܘܣܦ ܡܢ ܫܢܬܗ. ܥܒܕ ܐܝܟܢܐ ܕܦܩܕ ܠܗ ܡܠܐܟܗ ܕܡܪܝܐ. ܘܕܒܪܗ
ܠܐܢܬܬܗ.
ܟܗ: ܘܠܐ ܝܕܥܗ ܥܕܡܐ ܕܝܠܕܬܗ ܠܒܪܗ ܒܘܟܪܐ. ܘܩܪܬ ܫܡܗ ܝܫܘܥ.

AN EASTERN PERSPECTIVE ON CONCEPTION AND BIRTH

The following quotes are not a critical examination of the birth story from a rational "Western" point of view nor should it be understood as an attempt to "prove" the narrative. But rather these comments from a native Syrian reflect the typical eastern, spiritual attitude toward human reproduction and birth.

To us every birth was miraculous, and childlessness an evidence of divine disfavor. From this it may be inferred how tenderly and reverently agreeable to the Syrian ear is the angel's salutation to Mary, "Hail, thou that art highly favored, the Lord is with thee; blessed art thou among women! - Behold thou shalt conceive in thy womb and bring forth a son." Lk. 1:28, 31. A miracle? Yes. But a miracle means one thing to your Western science, which seeks to know what nature is and does by dealing with secondary causes, and quite another thing to an Oriental, (Easterner) to whom God's will is the law and gospel of nature. The Oriental does not try to meet an assault upon his belief in miracles by seeking to establish the historicity of concrete reports of miracles. His poetical, mystical temperament seeks its ends in another way. . . . But the story of Jesus' birth and kindred Bible records disclose not only the predisposition of the Syrian mind to accept miracles as divine acts, without critical examination, but also its attitude toward conception and birth, - an attitude which differs fundamentally from that of the Anglo-Saxon mind. . . . . Back of all these social traits, and beyond the free realism of the Syrian in speaking of conception and birth, lies a deeper fact. To Eastern peoples, especially the Semites, reproduction in all the world of life is profoundly sacred. It is God's life reproducing itself in the life of a man and in the living world below man; . . . . THE SYRIAN CHRIST, pp 20-25.

Chapter 2

THE VISIT OF THE MAGI

1. Now when Jesus was born in Bethlehem¹ of Judea in the days of King Herod,² Magi³ came from the East to Jerusalem,

2. And they were asking: Where is the King of the Jews, who has been born? Because we have seen his star⁴ in the East, and we have come to pay homage to him.

3. Then King Herod heard about it and became disturbed and all Jerusalem⁵ with him.

4. And he gathered all the chief priests and scribes of the people and kept asking them just where the Messiah will be born?

5. Then they answered: In Bethlehem of Judea for so it is written by the prophet,

6. Even you, Oh Bethlehem of Judea! You were not the least among the kings of Judah for out of you shall come forth the king who shall shepherd my people Israel.⁶

7. Then Herod secretly called the Magi and learned from them at what time the star had appeared to them.

---

1 A small town about six miles south of Jerusalem, in the state of Judea. Bethlehem was well known as the seat of the family of David. See Ruth 1:1, 4:11; 1 Sam. 16:1; Mic. 5:2.

2 Herod the Great, an Idumaean, became governor of Galilee in 47 B.C.E., then in 40 B.C.E., Antony and Octavius made him the king of Judea. Herod was also a friend of Julius Caesar.

3 ܡܓܘܫܐ, מגושא, Mghoosheh. These men were Chaldean priests who were schooled in the art of magic and enchantments and in astronomy and astrology. They were fire and sun worshippers, soothsayers, fortune tellers and the scientists of their day. The gospel scribe does not tell us how many Magi were present. Early Eastern tradition tells us that there were 12 Magi. In later Christian traditions the number became three because of the three gifts (verse 11). They also became known as kings which was based on Ps. 72:10 and Isa. 49:7.

4 Easterners believe that every human being has his/her star in heaven which holds the secret of his/her destiny and watches over him/her. When a person is kind, it is said that "his star is attractive." When two people care for each other "their stars are in harmony." This particular star symbolized the Messiah and the peace and assurance his kingdom was to bring on earth. See Num. 24:17.

5 The expression "all Jerusalem," i. e., "the entire city of Jerusalem" is a scribal embellishment. It is written in this manner so the reader or listener will not forget. It is done to make an impression. Eastern writers when stressing an event or a teaching use certain words and expressions such as "all," "entire," "Never was there such a time, nor will there ever be" and so forth. See Mt. 8:32, footnote 22, 13:34, footnote 7; 24:21 and Mk. 1:33.

6 See Mic. 5:2.

ܡܬܝ ܒ: ܒ.

ܒ: ܟܕ ܕܝܢ ܝܫܘܥ ܐܬܝܠܕ ܒܒܝܬ ܠܚܡ ܕܝܗܘܕܐ. ܒܝܘܡܝ ܗܪܘܕܣ ܡܠܟܐ ܐܬܘ
ܡܓܘܫܐ ܡܢ ܡܕܢܚܐ ܠܐܘܪܫܠܡ.

ܓ: ܘܐܡܪܝܢ. ܐܝܟܘ ܡܠܟܐ ܕܝܗܘܕܝܐ ܕܐܬܝܠܕ. ܚܙܝܢ ܓܝܪ ܟܘܟܒܗ ܒܡܕܢܚܐ. ܘܐܬܝܢ
ܠܡܣܓܕ ܠܗ.

ܓ: ܫܡܥ ܕܝܢ ܗܪܘܕܣ ܡܠܟܐ ܘܐܬܬܙܝܥ ܘܟܠܗ ܐܘܪܫܠܡ ܥܡܗ.

ܕ: ܘܟܢܫ ܟܠܗܘܢ ܪܒܝ ܟܗܢܐ ܘܣܦܪܐ ܕܥܡܐ. ܘܡܫܐܠ ܗܘܐ ܠܗܘܢ ܕܐܝܟܐ
ܡܬܝܠܕ ܡܫܝܚܐ.

ܗ: ܗܢܘܢ ܕܝܢ ܐܡܪܘ. ܒܒܝܬܠܚܡ ܕܝܗܘܕܐ. ܗܟܢܐ ܓܝܪ ܟܬܝܒ ܒܢܒܝܐ:

ܘ: ܐܦ ܐܢܬܝ ܒܝܬܠܚܡ ܕܝܗܘܕܐ. ܠܐ ܗܘܝܬܝ ܒܨܝܪܐ ܒܡܠܟܐ ܕܝܗܘܕܐ. ܡܢܟܝ
ܓܝܪ ܢܦܘܩ ܡܠܟܐ ܕܗܘ ܢܪܥܝܘܗܝ ܠܥܡܝ ܐܝܣܪܐܝܠ.

ܙ: ܗܝܕܝܢ ܗܪܘܕܣ ܡܛܫܝܐܝܬ ܩܪܐ ܠܡܓܘܫܐ. ܘܝܠܦ ܡܢܗܘܢ ܒܐܝܢܐ ܙܒܢܐ ܐܬܚܙܝ
ܠܗܘܢ ܟܘܟܒܐ.

THE STAR

The story of "The Star of Bethlehem" agrees so easily and beautifully with eastern thought and temperament. Easterners believe the heavens reveal the glory of God and the stars tell many wondrous things to the entire human family. (See Ps. 19:1-4, p. 6, footnote 7.) The ancient song writer also sings of the omniscience of God in Psalm 147:4-5, "He tells the number of the stars; he calls them all by names. Great is our LORD, and of great power: his understanding is infinite." In the East, stars are seen as messengers of good and evil, objects of the highest ideals or the "crudest superstitions." Every community has a "stargazer" who can read an individual's fortune and who can "arrest" an absent person's star and learn whether things are going well or ill for him or her. Israel, at times, put too much trust in the stargazers of their day. See Isa. 47:13-14. "Beyond all such crudities, however, lies the sublime and sustaining belief that the stars are alive with God. . . . the beautiful story of the star of Bethlehem, indicates that to the Oriental mind the "hosts of heaven" are no masses of dust, but the agencies of the Creator's might and love. So the narrative of the Nativity sublimates the beliefs of the Orientals about God's purpose in those lights of the firmament, by making the guide of the Wise Men to the birth place of the Prince of Peace a great star. . . . " THE SYRIAN CHRIST, pp 36-37.

8. And he sent them to Bethlehem and said to them: Go and diligently inquire about the little boy, and when you have found him, come, report to me that I may go and pay respect to him.

9. Now when they had heard from the king, they went away; and behold that same star which they had seen in the East was going before them,[7] until it came and stood over where the little boy was.

10. Then when they saw the star, they rejoiced exceedingly with tremendous joy!

11. And they entered the house and saw the little boy with Mary his mother; and they fell down and adored him; then they opened their treasures and offered him gifts[8] of gold and myrrh and frankincense.

12. Now it was revealed to them in a dream that they were not to return to Herod; so they went to their own country by another route.

THE FLIGHT INTO EGYPT

13. And when they had departed, the messenger of the LORD appeared in a dream to Joseph and said to him: Rise up, take the little boy and his mother, and flee to Egypt and stay there until I tell you because Herod is about to look for the little boy so that he might destroy him.

14. Then, during the night, Joseph rose up, took the little boy and his mother and fled to Egypt.

15. And he stayed there until the death of Herod so that what was declared by the LORD might be fulfilled, which said: From Egypt I have called my son.

---

[7] The Magi were guided by the star, that is, its position directed them. In those ancient days, and even today in areas where the compass is unknown, travelers depend on the stars as one would on a compass. Eastern people consider the stars as guides and companions, the wondrous display of God's power, wisdom and glory. *"The heavens tell the story of God's glory and the firmament manifests his handiwork. Day after day pours forth speech and night after night declares his understanding. There is no speech, also no words whose sound is unheard. Their joyful message has gone out throughout the land and their words to the end of the world. Above the sun, among the heavens (literally, among them) he pitched his tent."* Ps. 19:1-4, Aramaic text, Errico translation. See "The Star" p. A - 5.

[8] When a male infant is born, relatives, friends, neighbors and strangers "parade" into the house, even on the day of birth, to bring presents and congratulate the parents on the divine gift which is now in their keeping. It was because of this custom the Magi who were strangers were permitted to enter the house with gifts.

ܚ: ܘܫܕܪ ܐܢܘܢ ܠܒܝܬܠܚܡ. ܘܐܡܪ ܠܗܘܢ: ܙܠܘ ܒܥܘ ܥܠ ܛܠܝܐ ܒܚܦܝܛܘܬܐ.
ܘܡܐ ܕܐܫܟܚܬܘܢܝܗܝ. ܬܘ ܚܘܐܘܢܢܝ ܕܐܦ ܐܢܐ ܐܬܐ ܐܣܓܘܕ ܠܗ.

ܛ: ܗܢܘܢ ܕܝܢ ܟܕ ܫܡܥܘ ܡܢ ܡܠܟܐ ܐܙܠܘ. ܘܗܐ ܟܘܟܒܐ ܗܘ ܕܚܙܘ ܒܡܕܢܚܐ
ܐܙܠ ܗܘܐ ܩܕܡܝܗܘܢ. ܥܕܡܐ ܕܐܬܐ ܩܡ ܠܥܠ. ܡܢ ܐܝܟܐ ܕܐܝܬܘܗܝ ܛܠܝܐ.

ܝ: ܟܕ ܕܝܢ ܚܙܘܗܝ ܠܟܘܟܒܐ. ܚܕܝܘ ܚܕܘܬܐ ܪܒܬܐ ܛܒ.

ܝܐ: ܘܥܠܘ ܠܒܝܬܐ. ܘܚܙܘܗܝ ܠܛܠܝܐ ܥܡ ܡܪܝܡ ܐܡܗ. ܘܢܦܠܘ ܣܓܕܘ ܠܗ.
ܘܦܬܚܘ ܣܝܡܬܗܘܢ ܘܩܪܒܘ ܠܗ ܩܘܪܒܢܐ ܕܗܒܐ ܘܡܘܪܐ ܘܠܒܘܢܬܐ.

ܝܒ: ܘܐܬܚܙܝ ܠܗܘܢ ܒܚܠܡܐ ܕܠܐ ܢܗܦܟܘܢ ܠܘܬ ܗܪܘܕܣ. ܘܒܐܘܪܚܐ ܐܚܪܬܐ ܐܙܠܘ
ܠܐܬܪܗܘܢ.

ܝܓ: ܟܕ ܕܝܢ ܐܙܠܘ ܐܬܚܙܝ ܡܠܐܟܐ ܕܡܪܝܐ ܒܚܠܡܐ ܠܝܘܣܦ ܘܐܡܪ ܠܗ: ܩܘܡ ܕܒܪ
ܠܛܠܝܐ ܘܠܐܡܗ. ܘܥܪܘܩ ܠܡܨܪܝܢ. ܘܗܘܝ ܬܡܢ ܥܕܡܐ ܕܐܡܪ ܐܢܐ ܠܟ. ܥܬܝܕ
ܗܘ ܓܝܪ ܗܪܘܕܣ ܠܡܒܥܝܗ ܠܛܠܝܐ ܐܝܟ ܕܢܘܒܕܝܘܗܝ

ܝܕ: ܝܘܣܦ ܕܝܢ ܩܡ ܕܒܪܗ ܠܛܠܝܐ ܘܠܐܡܗ ܒܠܠܝܐ. ܘܥܪܩ ܠܡܨܪܝܢ.

ܝܗ: ܘܗܘܐ ܬܡܢ ܥܕܡܐ ܠܡܘܬܗ ܕܗܪܘܕܣ. ܕܢܬܡܠܐ ܡܕܡ ܕܐܬܐܡܪ ܡܢ ܡܪܝܐ
ܒܢܒܝܐ ܕܐܡܪ: ܕܡܢ ܡܨܪܝܢ ܩܪܝܬ ܠܒܪܝ.

16. At that time when Herod realized that he had been insulted[9] by the Magi, he became very furious; so he sent word and had all the little boys of Bethlehem, and all its surroundings, murdered, those who were from two years and under according to the time that he had inquired from the Magi.

17. Then was fulfilled what was spoken by Jeremiah the prophet who said:

18. A voice was heard in Ramtha, much weeping and wailing, Rachel crying over her sons, and she could not be consoled because they live no longer.[10]

THE RETURN FROM EGYPT AND ON TO NAZARETH

19. Now when Herod the king died, the messenger of the LORD appeared in a dream to Joseph in Egypt.

20. And he said to him: Rise up and take the little boy and his mother and go to the country of Israel because those who were wanting the little boy's life are dead.

21. So Joseph rose up and took the little boy and his mother and came to the land of Israel.

22. But when he had heard that Archelaus[11] was king in Judea in the place of his father Herod, he was afraid to go there; so it was revealed to him in a dream that he should go to the land of Galilee.

23. And he came and lived in a town named Nazareth[12] so that what was said by the prophet might be fulfilled that he shall be called a Nazarene.

---

9 ܒܙܚ, בזה, Bazaḥ means *to treat with contempt, scorn, ridicule, insult, mock, disgrace.*
10 See Jer. 31:15.
11 Archelaus was the oldest son of Herod and thus received a double portion of the inheritance which included the province of Judea. His authentic title was Ethnarch. Each of his brothers, Antipas and Philip, received one portion and the title Tetrarch; Antipas ruled Galilee and an area east of the Jordan, and Philip ruled Gaulonitis and Trachonitis and other provinces.
12 A small village in Southern Galilee, about sixteen miles southwest of Tiberias, a little north of the Great Plain of Esdraelon. Most scholars believe that Jesus, more than likely, was born in Nazareth in Galilee. (However this is not certain.) He was called a Nazarene, his adherents Nazarenes and the Roman inscription on his cross stated that he was of Nazareth. According to the gospel of John, Jesus' origin had been questioned, " . . . but others said: Is it possible that the Messiah should come from Galilee? Does not the scripture say that the Messiah shall come from the seed of David and from Bethlehem, the town of David? So the people were divided over him." Jn. 7:41-43. John also tells us in Chapter 1, verse 45, " . . . We have found that Jesus, the son of Joseph, *of Nazareth*, is the one concerning whom Moses wrote in the law and the prophets." New Testament experts also suggest that Bethlehem as the birthplace of Jesus is more theological than historical. See Mt. 1-2, p. A - 7.

THE INFANCY NARRATIVE
Mt. 1-2.

The Infancy Narrative found in Matthew, chapters 1 and 2, is understood not as a biographical tradition but as a "religious" tradition, that is, a theological approach to the messiahship of Jesus of Nazareth. Each episode that occurs in these two chapters has been subjected to much historical and scholastic investigation and is recognized as a "theological prologue" to the Gospel. For a thorough treatment on this topic see THE FORMULA QUOTATIONS IN THE INFANCY NARRATIVE OF MATTHEW by George M. Soares Prabhu, Rome: Biblical Institute Press. Also see "Son of God and Virgin Birth; Jesus, Son of Joseph; Virgin Birth in Philo," pp 213-222, JESUS THE JEW by Geza Vermes.

It it also interesting to note that the term "Nazarene" in verse 23 "he shall be called a Nazarene" is used as a figure of speech. It refers to Jesus' consecration and dedication to God and the Torah.

Chapter 3

THE APPEARANCE OF JOHN THE BAPTIZER

1. Now in those very days[1] John the Baptizer came and he was preaching in a deserted region[2] of Judea,

2. Proclaiming: Return to God![3] The kingdom of heaven[4] has arrived!

3. Because this is he of whom it was said by the prophet Isaiah: A voice which cries in the desert, Make ready the highway of the LORD and level His paths![5]

4. At that time John was clothed in camel's hair and fastened around his loins were leather belts[6] and his food was locusts[7] and wild honey.

5. Then Jerusalem and all of Judea and all the countryside around Jordan were coming to him.

6. And they were being baptized by him in the river Jordan, confessing their sins.

7. When he saw many of the Pharisees and Sadducees[8] coming to be baptized, he said to them: Oh brood of poisonous snakes! Who warned you to escape from the anger that is coming?

---

1 This phrase refers to Mt. 2:23, i.e., while Jesus was living in Nazareth.
2 ܚܘܪܒܐ, חורבא, Ḥorba - *a desert, plain, wilderness, waste place.* Uninhabited areas or plains with ample water and vegetation are also called Ḥorba. In this passage Ḥorba means an uninhabited area which was used for pastoral purposes by sheep-raising people.
3 ܐܬܘܒ, תוב, Tow - *to turn, return;* Semitic meaning *Return to God!* See p. A - 9, "Repentance."
4 The phrase "kingdom of heaven" is another way of saying "kingdom of God." In those days the religious authorities avoided uttering the word "God" because of its sacredness. They substituted the word "heaven" for "God," hence, the term "kingdom of heaven" is used throughout the gospel of Matthew instead of "kingdom of God." See Mt. 5:3, footnote 5, "Kingdom."
5 See Isa. 40:3.
6 This style of attire was the sign of the office of a prophet. See 2 Ki. 1:8; Zech. 13:4. John patterned his ministry in the same mode as the prophet Elijah. See also Mt. 11:8, footnote 6.
7 ܩܡܨܐ, קמצה, Qamṣeh, - *locusts or roots (wild root vegetables, possibly carrots or parsnips).* Certain varieties of locust were considered clean and edible, others unclean.
8 The Pharisees and Sadducees were two of the major sects of the Jews during the Second Temple period. The word ܦܪܝܫܐ, פרישא - Preeshah, "Pharisee" means *the separate one or the separatist.* The Pharisees were very strict in their observance of the twofold Torah, the written and the oral law, and taught the doctrine of the resurrection. It was a very large group and had many pious members. See "The Pharisees" p. A - 8. The Sadducees were a smaller group but were more influential politically since their membership was from the aristocratic families of priests. See "The Sadducees" p. A - 9.

THE PHARISEES

The so-called "sect" of the Pharisees was truly a widespread socio-religious movement within Judaism. Its aim was not a political one. The movement gave birth to most of the outstanding Torah scholars in Judaism. Its recorded historical appearance takes us back to the time of the revolt of the Maccabees in 168 B.C.E. (Maccabee means the "hammerer.") See the Apocrypha Books 1 and 2 Macc. for the history of the Jewish uprising against the Hellenizing policy which the Seleucid Syrian king, Antiochus Epiphanes, was attempting to force on Palestine. The actual revolt was for the most part provoked by the high priests who had lost favor with the pious masses of Jews (known as the Hasidim) because of their scandalous actions both politically and religiously, the final straw being the act of offering swine's blood to Zeus on the altar of the temple. The Jews needed new leadership and the large company of devout was ready with highly honored scribes, Torah scholars and teachers. The behavior of these new leaders made their opponents nickname them "Pharisees" - "Separatists."

The principle idea of the movement was to follow the Torah (Law) not only as it is laid out in the five books of Moses, Genesis to Deuteronomy, but to adhere to their forefathers' interpretation of those writings - the "Torah" - from the time of Ezra and Nehemiah and the return from Babylon. Thus, the pious created the oral law, "the tradition of the fathers" which in the gospels is called "the tradition of the Elders." They believed in God's omnipotence, human responsibility, free will and the resurrection of the dead. The gospel writers tell us that the Pharisees did not associate with anyone who did not keep the rigorous and demanding standards of purity which they had set and interpreted from the twofold Torah - the written and oral law.

8. So, bear fruits[9] that are worthy[10] of returning to God.

9. And do not expect and say to yourselves that we have a father, Abraham, because I am telling you that God is able from these stones to raise up children for Abraham.[11]

10. And, behold, the axe is already placed by the root of the trees; thus every tree which does not yield good fruits shall be cut down and thrown into the fire.[12]

11. I am baptizing you with water for the act of turning to God; but he who is coming after me is more powerful than I, he whose shoes I do not deserve to remove,[13] he shall baptize you with the Holy Spirit and with fire.[14]

12. He whose winnowing shovel[15] is in his hand, and he cleans his threshing; and the wheat he gathers into his barns and the straw he burns in the fire that never goes out.

THE BAPTISM OF JESUS

13. Then Jesus came from Galilee to the Jordan to John that he might be baptized by him.

---

9 Practice good deeds which go beyond good intentions and are characteristic of a true turning to God.

10 ܫܘܝܢ, שׁוין, Shawein, from the root word ܫܘܐ, שׁוא, Shwa - *to be even with, to be equal to, to deserve, to be worthy, to be consistent with.* "So, practice good deeds that are consistent with returning to God." See p. A - 9, "Repentance."

11 Just being a descendant of Abraham alone cannot bring salvation to Israel. John the Baptizer declares that God can make children (i.e., create a new nation) for Abraham from anyone or even from stones. Every individual must turn to God to be a true descendant of Abraham.

12 Fruit trees are very highly valued especially when crops are poor. Easterners plant fruit trees and depend on them for their living. When a fruit tree does not bear edible fruit or is dying, it is immediately cut down and used for kindling. New fruit trees are planted in their stead. Until the turn of the 20th century, trees which provided shade and aesthetic beauty were not prized and sometimes were cut down and burned for fuel.

13 Proverbial saying. I am less than a servant; I cannot even remove his shoes from his feet. John, the Baptizer, used this Eastern expression to exalt the Messiah and to divert the attention of the crowds away from himself; i.e., he humbled himself.

14 "Fire," symbolic of purification and cleansing. Fire also is indicative of the Presence of God. In this passage, fire represents the power of the Holy Spirit which cleanses the inner being. Water cleanses the physical body; the Spirit cleanses the heart and mind (soul).

15 A shovel which was used to winnow grain, that is, to separate or eliminate the chaff from the grain. Once grain has been threshed by oxen on the open floor, it would be winnowed by throwing it up with large wooden forks or shovels against the evening breeze, which blew away the chaff (straw), while the heavier grain fell on the ground in a heap. The chaff was then used for fuel and the grain gathered into the barns.

ܚ: ܥܒܕܘ ܗܟܝܠ ܦܐܪܐ ܕܫܘܐ ܠܬܝܒܘܬܐ.

ܛ: ܘܠܐ ܬܣܒܪܘܢ ܘܬܐܡܪܘܢ ܒܢܦܫܟܘܢ: ܕܐܒܐ ܐܝܬ ܠܢ ܐܒܪܗܡ. ܐܡܪ ܐܢܐ
ܠܟܘܢ ܓܝܪ: ܕܡܫܟܚ ܐܠܗܐ ܡܢ ܗܠܝܢ ܟܐܦܐ ܠܡܩܡܘ ܒܢܝܐ ܠܐܒܪܗܡ.

ܝ: ܗܐ ܕܝܢ ܢܪܓܐ ܣܝܡ ܥܠ ܥܩܪܐ ܕܐܝܠܢܐ. ܟܠ ܐܝܠܢܐ ܗܟܝܠ ܕܦܐܪܐ ܛܒܐ ܠܐ
ܥܒܕ. ܡܬܦܣܩ ܘܢܦܠ ܒܢܘܪܐ.

ܝܐ: ܐܢܐ ܡܥܡܕ ܐܢܐ ܠܟܘܢ ܒܡܝܐ ܠܬܝܒܘܬܐ. ܗܘ ܕܝܢ ܕܒܬܪܝ ܐܬܐ ܚܣܝܢ ܗܘ
ܡܢܝ. ܗܘ ܕܠܐ ܫܘܐ ܐܢܐ ܡܣܐܢܘܗܝ ܠܡܫܩܠ. ܗܘ ܢܥܡܕܟܘܢ ܒܪܘܚܐ
ܕܩܘܕܫܐ ܘܒܢܘܪܐ.

ܝܒ: ܗܘ ܕܪܦܫܐ ܒܐܝܕܗ ܘܡܢܩܐ ܐܕܪܘܗܝ. ܘܚܛܐ ܢܟܢܫ ܠܐܘܨܪܘܗܝ. ܘܬܒܢܐ ܢܘܩܕ
ܒܢܘܪܐ ܕܠܐ ܕܥܟܐ.

ܝܓ: ܗܝܕܝܢ ܐܬܐ ܝܫܘܥ ܡܢ ܓܠܝܠܐ ܠܝܘܪܕܢܢ ܠܘܬ ܝܘܚܢܢ ܕܢܥܡܕ ܡܢܗ.

THE SADDUCEES

According to the Jewish historian, Flavius Jospehus, the movement of the Pharisees represented the pious people but the sect of the Sadducees stood for the affluent. The Sadducess had governed the Jewish state from the time of the Persian period and were formed from the wealthy lay and priestly aristocracy. The Semitic term Sadducees, ܙܕܘܩܝܐ, זדוקיא, zadokayeh - "righteous ones" is derived from the name of the faithful priest Zadok, who ministered to King David in Hebron after the death of King Saul. See 2 Sam. 8:17; 1 Chron. 12:23-28. Zadok's descendents had held the high priestly office in Jerusalem since the time of Solomon. It was the priestly upper classes who were in charge of political affairs during the Hellenistic period. The high priest with other priests had formed and directed the Jewish high council which eventually became the Sanhedrin. It was the Sadducees who named the Hasidim - the pious who opposed the corruption in the priesthood - "Pharisees," that is, "Separatists." See p. A - 8, "The Pharisees."

REPENTANCE

The Aramaic word ܬܝܒܘܬܐ, תיבותא, Tyawootha is usually translated as "repentance" but it refers to the action of turning or returning. The Hebrew word Shuvu, "repent" also means "return," the idea being one must return to God and His covenant. According to widely attested Jewish sources "Returning to God, His covenant and the practice of good works brings salvation." John the Baptizer proclaimed both good works and returning to God. See Mt. 3:2, footnote 3; 3:8, footnotes 9, 10.

14. But John stopped him, saying: I need to be baptized by you, yet you have come to me?

15. Then Jesus answered and said to him: Let it be for now; for thus it is necessary for us so that all justice[16] may be fulfilled; and then he let him.

16. Now when Jesus was baptized, as soon as he came up from the water, the heavens were opened to him and he saw the Spirit of God descending like a dove and it came upon him.[17]

17. And behold, a voice from heaven was saying: This is my son,[18] the beloved![19] I am delighted with him![20]

---

16 Authentic piety - ܟܐܢܘܬܐ, כאנותא, Kenootha, - *justice, devoutness, righteousness, godliness.* An ethical justice based on the Torah. See Mt. 1:19, footnote 15; Mt. 5:6, footnote 8; Mt. 5:10, footnote 14. Jesus did whatever was necessary for a just life because he was one with the Father. See p. A - 10.

17 The "dove" is used metaphorically to indicate the Holy Spirit. It also is used to signify meekness and purity as well as peace, harmony and tranquility. In the Near East when describing a humble and gentle individual, it is said, "He is so meek that a bird will not fly away from him." The Spirit's descent upon Jesus not only refers to his anointing as Messiah, his approval and empowerment by God for the mission (Acts 10: 37-38), but also to his meekness and humility.

18 In the Aramaic language and Semitic culture, the term ܒܪ ܕܐܠܗܐ, בר דאלהא, Bar dalaha, *God's son, God's child* has many meanings and may refer to: 1. an orphan, 2. a meek young man, (in contrast, a meek older man is often called "a man of God.") 3. a peacemaker, 4. a good, kind or pious individual, 5. the Messiah. In this usage it is a Messianic title and means *God's beloved one.* The word "son" is used subtly in the Aramaic language because it infers "likeness," "resemblance" and "to be in the image of." Hence, "son of God" signifies "like God" or "God-likeness." (See Mt. 4:4, footnote 6 - for additional shaded usage of the term "son.") The meaning of "son of God" depends on context. See Mt. 5:9, footnote 13. (It is interesting to note that Israel was also called "God's son" - Hos. 11:1.) This "special" sonship in Hebrew Scripture and in the New Testament does not refer to a "physical-divine" sonship but rather to a spiritual relationship between God (Spirit) and the individual designated as "son." Sonship, then, is a spiritual relationship between God and a human being which is based on love, respect and doing the will of the father (God). When Easterners called someone "son" or "my son" it was their way of showing affection and meant "beloved." In the above verse (17) "my son" refers to the Messiah. See Mt. 26:63, where the high priest uses the Messianic title, " . . . tell us if you are the Messiah, God's son?" The Apostle Simon calls Jesus, the Messiah, the "son (beloved) of the living God." See Mt. 16:16. According to the synoptic gospels, Jesus was God's son by the "anointing" of God. "You are the Messiah-Christ, (the Anointed), the son of the living God!" The psalmist too refers to the Messiah, the Anointed, as "God's son" for he says, "I will declare the decree: the LORD hath said unto me, Thou art my son: this day have I begotten thee." Ps. 2:7; KJV. (According to rabbinic interpretation this verse refers to the king of Israel who was anointed of God.) The word "begotten" is used figuratively. The Jewish concept of the Fatherhood of God has always been spiritual.

19 "The beloved" was another title used for the Messiah. See above - footnote 18.

20 The joy of a father delighting in his son who was faithfully revealing His will. See p. A - 10.

ܝܕ: ܗܘ ܕܝܢ ܝܘܚܢܢ ܟܠܐ ܗܘܐ ܠܗ ܘܐܡܪ ܐܢܐ ܣܢܝܩ ܐܢܐ ܕܡܢܟ ܐܬܥܡܕ
ܘܐܢܬ ܠܘܬܝ ܐܬܝܬ.

ܝܗ: ܗܘ ܕܝܢ ܝܫܘܥ ܥܢܐ ܘܐܡܪ ܠܗ: ܫܒܘܩ ܗܫܐ. ܗܟܢܐ ܓܝܪ ܝܐܐ ܠܢ ܕܢܫܠܡ
ܟܠܗ ܟܐܢܘܬܐ. ܘܗܝܕܝܢ ܫܒܩܗ.

ܝܘ: ܟܕ ܥܡܕ ܕܝܢ ܝܫܘܥ ܡܚܕܐ ܣܠܩ ܡܢ ܡܝܐ. ܘܐܬܦܬܚܘ ܠܗ ܫܡܝܐ. ܘܚܙܐ
ܪܘܚܐ ܕܐܠܗܐ ܕܢܚܬܐ ܐܝܟ ܝܘܢܐ ܘܐܬܬ ܥܠܘܗܝ.

ܝܙ: ܘܗܐ ܩܠܐ ܡܢ ܫܡܝܐ ܕܐܡܪ: ܗܢܘ ܒܪܝ ܚܒܝܒܐ. ܕܒܗ ܐܨܛܒܝܬ.

JESUS' BAPTISM

The baptismal occurrence reflects Jesus' anointing as Messiah, his genuine humility, devotion to God and indentification with his people. He would do whatever was just, that is, whatever was authentically devout in carrying out the will of God, such as being baptized by John. "Then Jesus answered and said to him: Let it be for now; for thus *it is necessary for us so that all justice (devoutness) may be fulfilled;* and then he let him." Mt. 3:15. Through submission to John's baptism, Jesus also indentified himself with the people and showed his solidarity with them as he did many times by eating meals with sinners and associating with those of "questionable reputation." See p. 10, footnotes 16 and 17. "The heavens were open *to him*" means Jesus received a revelation. When "he saw" the Spirit of God descend like a dove, in that moment, Jesus knew and felt that he was anointed by God for his role and mission as Messiah. The spiritual anointing was Jesus' own vision and experience. However, scholars propose that the message of the heavenly voice, "This is my son, the beloved! I am delighted with him!" was a public, objective manifestation.

THE FATHER-SON RELATIONSHIP

In the Eastern culture the relationship between a father and a son is extremely important and precious. In the gospels, it focuses on faith and trust. The traditions of the family are carefully obeyed and carried out by the son. A son, out of a loving bond with his father, faithfully does his father's wishes (will). John, in his gospel, reveals more fully the Near Eastern father-son relationship theme between Jesus and God. His expressions "only begotten," "in the bosom of the Father," etc., are Aramaic metaphors and need to be understood as such. See Jn. 1:14,18; 5:19-23, 26, 37, 43; 10:34; 14:28. Jesus not only knew that God was his Father but that He was the Father of all races. Futhermore, he told his disciples that God rejoices, like a concerned parent (father), when he sees his children who had gone astray returning home. See the parable of the Prodigal Son, Lk. 15:11-32. In verses 16 and 17, Matthew describes a psychic happening; the Father approves and acknowledges His son, the beloved, with whom He is so utterly delighted. This episode is in perfect harmony with the mystical soul expression of the East.

CHAPTER 4

THE TEMPTATION OF JESUS

1. Then Jesus was guided by the Holy Spirit[1] to the wilderness[2] so that he might be tested[3] by the adversary.[4]

2. And he fasted forty days and forty nights;[5] then finally he became hungry.

3. And he who tests approached and said to him: If you are God's son, command that these stones may become bread.

4. Then he answered and said: It is written that it is not by bread alone a human being[6] lives but by every word that comes from the mouth of God.[7]

5. Now then the adversary led him to the holy city *(Jerusalem)* and put him on the pinnacle of the temple.

---

1 I.e., guided by an inner, spiritual and powerful impulse. See p. A - 11 "The Trial in the Desert."

2 ܡܕܒܪܐ, מדברא, Madhbra – *desert, wilderness*. There is an Aramaic play on words between the verb "guided" *DBR* and the noun "wilderness" *MDBR*.

3 ܢܣܐ, נסא, Naseh, root meaning *to weigh, try out, prove, to test one's self*. Holy men, or anyone who aspires to leadership, are generally tested and must endure trials. All ancient literature is full of such episodes. See Ps. 11:5 and Abraham's testing – Gen. 22:1, "And after these things it happened that God tested (tempted) Abraham . . . "

4 ܐܟܠܩܪܨܐ, אכלקרצא, Akelqarṣar, – *an accuser, slanderer, adversary*. The root meaning *to gnaw, ridicule*. This word is usually interpreted as the devil or satan. Jesus was engaged in an internal struggle externalized as the adversary (satan). See Mt. 6:13, footnote 18.

5 Moses had fasted on the mountain for forty days. Now the Messiah, as the new lawgiver and leader of Israel, was to undergo the same process as Moses; therefore, he fasted forty days before beginning his mission. See Ex. 34:28, and Elijah 1 Ki. 19:8. (Easterners believe forty is a holy number.)

6 ܒܪܢܫܐ, בר-נשא, Bar-nasha is a compound noun. ܒܪ, בר, bar, means *son* and ܐܢܫܐ, אנשא, Nasha, means *man, humankind, human being*. Linguistically, it is improper to translate the Aramaic term Bar-nasha as "the son of man." Yet, many translators have rendered this term literally. For instance, in numerous translations Mt. 4:4 has been rendered, "man cannot live etc." Then in another passage, Mt. 16:13, the exact same Aramaic term is translated as "son of man." In both of these passages Bar-nasha should read as either "man" or "human being." In Aramaic when the word ܒܪ, Bar, "son" is joined to other words, they change meaning. There are many such examples: ܒܪܐܒܐ, בר-אבא, Barabbas (father's son) but it means *resembles his father*; ܒܪܐܓܪܐ, בר-אגרא, Bar-Agara (son of the roof top) – *lunatic*; ܒܪܙܘܓܐ, בר-זוגא, Bar-Zauga (son of the yoke) – *friend, companion*; ܒܪܗܝܠܐ, בר-הילא, Bar-Ḥila (son of power) – *soldier*; and ܒܪܝܘܠܦܢܐ, בר-יולפנא, Bar-Yolpana (son of learning) – *disciple*. Thus, ܒܪܢܫܐ, בר-נשא, Bar-nasha (son of man) – *man, human, human being*.

7 See Deut. 8:3. Jesus refused to demonstrate the miracle asked by the adversary. Throughout the gospel Jesus responded only to those who asked in faith. See Mt. 12:38-39, 16:1-4, 27:39-42.

THE TRIAL IN THE DESERT

Once Jesus had been baptized by John and anointed by God as Messiah, he had to fast and retreat to the desert so that he could decide his future. He must test himself to see how he would present himself in his new role and ministry. Moses and Elijah were in the wilderness when the God of Israel had appeared to them and counseled them for their future work. See Exodus, Chapter 3, 1 Kings 19:8-17 and Mt. 4:2, footnote 5. Jesus, surrounded by the quiet and mystical radiance of the desert, communed with the spiritual forces which were moving and working within him. He was to face an inner struggle with dark forces (adversary) which would try to deter him from fulfilling his mission. There was no better place for this to happen than in the desert. See Mt. 4:1 and 4:11. At night the vast star-filled heavens appear to be a glorious, decorated canopy stretched out over the desert floor radiating a soft light and flooding the earth with peace and harmony.

By going through the three temptations Jesus knew that: 1) He would not "turn stones into bread," that is, resort to signs or magic so that he might prove he was the Messiah. He would nourish his people with the word of God. He would heal and perform miracles only in response to faith. 2) He would not purposely put himself in danger and expect God to save him because he was the Messiah. 3) He refused material wealth and power. God alone was to be served and worshipped. God is the true possessor of heaven and earth and all the kingdoms of this world. When the ordeal in the desert was over, Matthew tells us angels approached Jesus and kept ministering to him. The Aramaic word for "angel," מלאכא, Malakha means *messenger, minister, counselor, emissary*. See Ps. 104:4, Heb. 1:7. The angels, that is, God's "messages or thoughts" were supporting and strengthening Jesus after his struggle with negative forces was over. He was hearing from his Father's emissaries. Notice that verse 11 says "were serving him" which means they kept waiting on him and giving him support.

6. And he said to him: If you are God's son, throw yourself down; because it is written He will command His messengers concerning you and on their hands shall they carry you that your foot may not stumble against a stone.[8]

7. Jesus said to him: It is also written, you shall not test the LORD your God.[9]

8. Again the adversary led him to a very high mountain and showed him all the kingdoms of the world and their splendor.[10]

9. And he said to him: I will grant you all these things if you will fall down and kneel before me.[11]

10. Then Jesus said to him: Go away, satan, because it is written that you shall kneel before the LORD your God and you shall worship Him only.[12]

11. Right then the adversary left him. And behold, messengers (angels) approached and were serving him.

THE PUBLIC MINISTRY OF JESUS IN GALILEE

12. Now when Jesus heard that John had been arrested, he departed to Galilee.

13. And he left Nazareth and came to live in Capernaum[13] along the seaside within the boundaries of Zabulon and Napthali,

14. So that it might be fulfilled what was spoken by the prophet Isaiah, who said:

15. Oh land of Zabulon, Oh land of Napthali road of the sea, the crossing of Jordan, Galilee of the gentiles!

16. The people who are sitting in darkness saw a tremendous light,[14] and those who are sitting in the region and in the shadows of death, light has dawned upon them![15]

---

8 See Ps. 91:11-12.
9 See Deut. 6:16 and p. A - 11, "The Trial in the Desert."
10 "Splendor" refers to material power and wealth.
11 "kneel before me," "worship me" or "submit to me."
12 "Worship Him only" or "work, serve Him only." See Deut. 6:13.
13 "Capernaum" - the village of Nahum which is located on the northwest shore of the Lake of Galilee.
14 The "light" was symbolic of the Messiah and his teaching. According to rabbinic literature, one of the names of the Messiah was "Light."
15 See Isa. 9:1-2.

ܘ: ܘܐܡܪ ܠܗ: ܐܢ ܒܪܗ ܐܢܬ ܕܐܠܗܐ. ܫܕܝ ܢܦܫܟ ܠܬܚܬ. ܟܬܝܒ ܓܝܪ ܕܠ
ܡܠܐܟܘܗܝ ܢܦܩܕ ܥܠܝܟ. ܘܥܠ ܐܕܝܗܘܢ ܢܫܩܠܘܢܟ. ܕܠܐ ܬܬܩܦ ܒܟܐܦܐ
ܪܓܠܟ.
ܙ: ܐܡܪ ܠܗ ܝܫܘܥ: ܬܘܒ ܟܬܝܒ ܕܠܐ ܬܢܣܐ ܠܡܪܝܐ ܐܠܗܟ.
ܚ: ܬܘܒ ܕܒܪܗ ܐܟܠܩܪܨܐ ܠܛܘܪܐ ܕܪܡ ܛܒ. ܘܚܘܝܗ ܟܠܗܝܢ ܡܠܟܘܬܐ ܕܥܠܡܐ
ܘܫܘܒܚܗܝܢ.
ܛ: ܘܐܡܪ ܠܗ: ܗܠܝܢ ܟܠܗܝܢ ܠܟ ܐܬܠ ܐܢ ܬܦܠ ܬܣܓܘܕ ܠܝ.
ܝ: ܗܝܕܝܢ ܐܡܪ ܠܗ ܝܫܘܥ: ܙܠ ܠܟ ܣܛܢܐ. ܟܬܝܒ ܓܝܪ ܕܠܡܪܝܐ ܐܠܗܟ
ܬܣܓܘܕ. ܘܠܗ ܒܠܚܘܕܘܗܝ ܬܦܠܘܚ.
ܝܐ: ܗܝܕܝܢ ܫܒܩܗ ܐܟܠܩܪܨܐ. ܘܗܐ ܡܠܐܟܐ ܩܪܒܘ ܘܡܫܡܫܝܢ ܗܘܘ ܠܗ.
ܝܒ: ܟܕ ܫܡܥ ܕܝܢ ܝܫܘܥ ܕܐܫܬܠܡ ܝܘܚܢܢ. ܫܢܝ ܠܗ ܠܓܠܝܠܐ.
ܝܓ: ܘܫܒܩܗ ܠܢܨܪܬ. ܘܐܬܐ ܥܡܪ ܒܟܦܪܢܚܘܡ ܥܠ ܝܕ ܝܡܐ ܒܬܚܘܡܐ ܕܙܒܘܠܘܢ
ܘܕܢܦܬܠܝ.
ܝܕ: ܕܢܬܡܠܐ ܡܕܡ ܕܐܬܐܡܪ ܒܝܕ ܐܫܥܝܐ ܢܒܝܐ ܕܐܡܪ:
ܝܗ: ܐܪܥܐ ܕܙܒܘܠܘܢ ܐܪܥܐ ܕܢܦܬܠܝ ܐܘܪܚܐ ܕܝܡܐ ܥܒܪܗ ܕܝܘܪܕܢܢ ܓܠܝܠܐ
ܕܥܡܡܐ.
ܝܘ: ܥܡܐ ܕܝܬܒ ܒܚܫܘܟܐ ܢܘܗܪܐ ܚܙܐ ܪܒܐ. ܘܐܝܠܝܢ ܕܝܬܒܝܢ ܒܐܬܪܐ ܘܒܛܠܠܝܗ
ܕܡܘܬܐ ܢܘܗܪܐ ܕܢܚ ܠܗܘܢ.

17. From that time[16] Jesus began to preach and to say: Turn to God! Because the kingdom of heaven has arrived!

18. Now while he was walking along the seashore of Galilee, he saw two brothers, Simon, who was nicknamed Peter[17] and his brother Andrew, who were throwing nets into the sea, for they were fishermen.

19. And Jesus said to them: Follow me and I will make you become fishers of people.

20. So they immediately left their nets and went after him.[18]

21. And when he passed on from there, he saw two other brothers, Jacob,[19] the son of Zebedee and his brother John in a boat with Zebedee their father; and they were repairing their nets. And Jesus called them.

22. Then they immediately left the boat and their father; and they went after him.

23. And Jesus was traveling all over Galilee and was teaching in their meeting places[20] declaring the joyful assurance of the kingdom and healing all pain and disease among the people.

24. And his reputation was heard all over Syria,[21] so they brought him all those who were badly afflicted with various illnesses and those who were suffering from severe pains and insanity and the epileptics[22] and the cripples; and he healed them.

25. Thus huge crowds went after him from Galilee and from the ten cities[23] and from Jerusalem and from Judea and from across the Jordan.

---

16 That is, from the time when Jesus had heard John had been arrested, see verse 12.

17 ܟܐܦܐ, כאפא, Kepa is an Aramaic nickname and means *stone, rock*. See Mt.10:2, footnote 4.

18 The call of disciples by a holy teacher or prophet is usually done in this manner (verses 19-22). This was the ancient custom. See 1 Ki. 19:19-20, the calling of Elisha.

19 ܝܥܩܘܒ, יעקב, Yaqob. See Mt. 10:3, footnote 5.

20 ܟܢܘܫܬܐ, כנשתא, Kenooshtha, *a meeting place*. "Synagogue" is derived from the Greek word SYNAGOGE - *gathering, assembly*. The Kenooshtha was the public Jewish meeting place for non-sacrificial worship. See "The Synagogue" p. A - 13.

21 A contrast is made here between Galilee and (Gentile) Syria. Jesus' fame had spread north and northeast of Galilee. See Mt. 8:28-29. The maniacs of Gardara had heard of Jesus' reputation.

22 ܒܪܐܢܫܐ, בר־אנרא, Bar-Agara, literally, *lunatic*. See Mt. 4:4, footnote 6, Bar-Agara. At that time people believed that there was a connection between certain mental disorders, epilepsy and the moon. Thus, any time the moon was full, people expected epileptic seizures to occur.

23 The ten cities (Decapolis) were located east and northeast of the Jordan River as far as Damascus and were independent of Galilee and Judea. The majority of their inhabitants were Gentiles. This is the first encounter the Gentiles had with Jesus who was announcing the universal kingdom to the world.

THE SYNAGOGUE

The Hebrew phrase Ohel Moed, *tent of meeting*, more closely approximates the meaning of the Greek word *SYNAGOGE*. Most scholars believe that the synagogue originated in Babylon during the exile. Some biblical experts consider 2 Chron 17:9, "And they (Levites) . . . went about throughout all the cities of Judah and taught the people," as a possible clue to the beginning of the synagogue as an institution. Then again, Ezek. 11:15-16 is usually cited as the first hint to the origin of the synagogue because of the Hebrew words *Mikdash Meaht*, translated as "little sanctuary." See also Ezek. 14:1 and 20:1. Be that as it may, when the synagogue did appear, it was an assembly and form of ceremonial worship where prayer, confession and fasting were practiced but no animal sacrifice. As the institution developed, scriptural passages were read and interpreted during the gatherings. The concept of the one universal God was promoted and maintained at synagogue meetings. See Mt. 4:23, footnote 20.

CHAPTER 5

THE SERMON ON THE MOUNT

1. Now when Jesus saw the crowds, he ascended the mountain;[1] and when he sat down, his disciples approached him.

2. And he opened his mouth[2] and was teaching them saying:

3. Delighted[3] are those who surrender to God,[4] for theirs is the kingdom[5] of heaven!

4. Delighted are the wailing ones,[6] for they shall be consoled!

5. Delighted are the meek,[7] for they shall inherit the land!

6. Delighted are those who hunger and thirst for justice,[8] for they shall be full!

7. Delighted are the compassionate,[9] for compassion shall return to them!

---

1 Matthew states that Jesus' discourse was given on a mountain. The entire scene is meant to correlate with that of Moses and the giving of the Law on Mount Sinai. See Ex. 19:1 and p. A - 14.

2 "Opened his mouth" - this phrase should not be understood literally. It is a Semitic idiom meaning "to speak." The same idiom is found in Ps. 38:13 but in the Psalm it means "not to speak."

3 ܛܘܒܝܗܘܢ, טוביהון, Toowayhon. The word for "blessed" in Aramaic is ܒܪܟ, ברך, barekh. Toowayhon means *happy, content, blissful, delighted, fortunate.* "Delighted" suggests great happiness, prosperity and abundant goodness.

4 ܡܣܟܢܐ ܒܪܘܚ, מסכנא ברוח, Miskaneh brooh, literally *poor in spirit.* This Aramaic idiom refers to those who let God guide them in everything; those who are humble and rely totally on God and not upon material things. God is always faithful, but material things come and go. In other words, God is "top priority" in their lives. According to rabbinic sources, in Judaism of the last two centuries B.C.E., the term "poor" had practically become a synonym for "pious" or "saintly." "Poor in spirit" is used with a specialized meaning and not just in the sense of those who possess nothing.

5 ܡܠܟܘܬܐ, מלכותא, Malkootha, - *kingdom* comes from the root ܡܠܟ, מלך. malkh which signifies *counsel, advice.* See also Mt. 3:2, footnote 4.

6 ܐܘܝܠܐ, אוילא, Aweleh, - *mourners, wailing ones.* Those who were wailing were crying out and deeply grieving over their social and political conditions and longed for the establishment of God's kingdom and His justice. Only God could bring them comfort and consolation. See Ps. 126:5; Isa. 61:2-3.

7 ܡܟܝܟܐ, מכיכא, Makeekheh, - *meek, lowly, humble.* The meek or humble are those who are yielding, pliable, flexible and unassuming. See Gen. 13:15; Ps. 37:11,22.

8 ܟܐܢܘܬܐ, כאנותא, - *justice, goodness, righteousness.* See Isa. 51:1; Ps. 36:10; Mt.3:15, footnote 16.

9 ܡܪܚܡܢܐ, מרחמנא, Mraḥmaneh, - *merciful, compassionate.* from the root ܪܚܡ, רחם, *to love, delight in, to be kind, friendly.* The compassionate were those who performed deeds of mercy, a form of practical compassion.

ܡܬܝ: ܗ.

܂ܒ ܟܕ ܚܙܐ ܕܝܢ ܠܟܢܫܐ ܠܓܝ̈ܙܐ ܣܠܩ ܠܛܘܪܐ. ܘܟܕ ܝܬܒ. ܩܪܒܘ ܠܘܬܗ ܬܠܡܝ̈ܕܘܗܝ.

܂ܓ ܘܦܬܚ ܦܘܡܗ. ܘܡܠܦ ܗܘܐ ܠܗܘܢ ܘܐܡܪ:

܂ܕ ܛܘܒܝܗܘܢ ܠܡܣܟܢ̈ܐ ܒܪܘܚ. ܕܕܝܠܗܘܢ ܗܝ ܡܠܟܘܬܐ ܕܫܡܝܐ.

܂ܗ ܛܘܒܝܗܘܢ ܠܐܒܝ̈ܠܐ. ܕܗܢܘܢ ܢܬܒܝܐܘܢ.

܂ܘ ܛܘܒܝܗܘܢ ܠܡܟܝ̈ܟܐ. ܕܗܢܘܢ ܢܐܪܬܘܢ ܠܐܪܥܐ.

܂ܙ ܛܘܒܝܗܘܢ ܠܐܝܠܝܢ ܕܟܦܢܝܢ ܘܨܗܝܢ ܠܟܐܢܘܬܐ. ܕܗܢܘܢ ܢܣܒܥܘܢ.

܂ܚ ܛܘܒܝܗܘܢ ܠܡܪ̈ܚܡܢܐ. ܕܥܠܝܗܘܢ ܢܗܘܘܢ ܪ̈ܚܡܐ.

THE TEACHING ON THE MOUNT
An Overall View

This very important section of the gospel of Matthew (Chapters 5 - 7) contain the basic teachings of Jesus -- known variously as "The Sermon on the Mount," "The Constitution of the Kingdom of God" and "The Messianic Torah." Knowing the Semitic idioms, language, religious and cultural context of Jesus' teaching is necessary to understand much of the Master-Teacher's sayings. These utterances express his own distinct views, interpretation of the Torah (written law) and his deviation from some of the traditions of the times (oral law). Jesus' emphasis on meekness, justice, peace, purity of heart, compassion, love of self, of neighbor, of enemy and devotion to God through a practice of authentic piety is in perfect harmony with the spirit and heart of Hebrew Scripture, its sages, prophets and song writers (Psalmists). His magnetic presence and powerful words reached into the souls and ignited the hearts of his disciples, followers and people. There is no doubt Jesus' teaching was meeting the needs of those who longed for the kingdom of heaven with its genuine justice. He pronounced joy, that is, delight on the poor, the mourners, the humble, the seekers of justice, the merciful and those who were persecuted for the sake of justice. He encouraged doing good works based on the time-honored values found in Holy Scripture. He had the deepest respect for the Torah and came to fulfill it even though his critics thought otherwise. "Do not imagine that I have come to nullify the law (Torah) or the prophets. I have not come to nullify but to fulfill." See Mt. 5:17-20. Jesus taught his disciples to practice the spirit of the Law by helping them to see beyond the traditions of the elders and man-made rules and regulations. Faith, prayer, giving, fasting, healing, forgiveness and more are all a part of Jesus' sound and practical ethics recorded in these three chapters.

8. Delighted are those who are pure in their hearts,[10] for they shall see God![11]

9. Delighted are the peacemakers,[12] for they shall be called the children of God![13]

10. Delighted are those who are persecuted for the sake of justice,[14] for theirs is the kingdom of heaven![15]

11. Delighted are you when they taunt you and persecute you and are saying every kind of vicious word against you falsely because of me.

12. At that very moment be joyful and be exceedingly glad, for your payment is abundant in heaven;[16] for in the same manner they persecuted the prophets who were before you.

13. You are the ones who are the salt of the earth! Now if that salt be flavorless, with what will it be salted? It will be worth nothing, except that it be thrown outside and be stepped on by people.[17]

14. You are the ones who are the light of the world![18] A city that is built on a mountain cannot be hidden.

15. And they do not light a lamp and put it under a bushel but on a lampstand so that it shines to all those who are in the house.

16. Thus, let your light shine in the sight of the people so that they may see your good deeds and may praise your Father who is in heaven.[19]

---

10 Idiom: "pure heart" – *a sincere, contrite individual*. A clear heart and mind perceives God.

11 The verb ܢܚܙܘܢ, נחזון, Niḥzon may be translated in the present or future tense, "they see God," or "they shall see God." To see God is "to know" the everpresent Divine Presence, i.e., God's immanence. See Ps. 17:15.

12 ܥܒ̈ܕܝ ܫܠܡܐ, עבדי שלמא, Awdey shlama, literally – *peace-doers*. The work of peacemakers was to bring reconciliation among quarreling people. ܫܠܡܐ, שלמא, – *peace*, comes from the root ܫܠܡ, שלם, Shlm and means *to submit, surrender, finish, come to an end*.

13 Literally "sons of God;" i.e., those who are "like-God". Another name for God is "Peace," thus "children of God" connotes "children of Peace," "like-Peace." We are told that King Solomon was the first King of Israel to be called "son of God." His name means "Peaceable."

14 Kenootha – *justice, a form of godliness*. Authentic piety based on God's laws. See footnote 8 and Mt. 3:15, footnote 16..

15 See 1 Pet. 3:14; Acts 5:41.

16 Idiom – Your reward is assured.

17 See Mk. 9:50; Lk. 14:34.

18 See Isa. 49:6 and p. A – 15 "Light."

19 "Father who is in heaven" was in general use among the Jews in the first century C.E.

ܣܐ: ܛܘܒܝܗܘܢ ܠܐܝܠܝܢ ܕܕܟܝܢ ܒܠܒܗܘܢ. ܕܗܢܘܢ ܢܚܙܘܢ ܠܐܠܗܐ.

ܣܒ: ܛܘܒܝܗܘܢ ܠܥܒܕܝ ܫܠܡܐ. ܕܒܢܘܗܝ ܕܐܠܗܐ ܢܬܩܪܘܢ.

ܣܓ: ܛܘܒܝܗܘܢ ܠܐܝܠܝܢ ܕܐܬܪܕܦܘ ܡܛܠ ܟܐܢܘܬܐ. ܕܕܝܠܗܘܢ ܗܝ ܡܠܟܘܬܐ ܕܫܡܝܐ.

ܣܕ: ܛܘܒܝܟܘܢ ܐܡܬܝ ܕܡܚܣܕܝܢ ܠܟܘܢ. ܘܪܕܦܝܢ ܠܟܘܢ. ܘܐܡܪܝܢ ܥܠܝܟܘܢ ܟܠ ܡܠܐ ܒܝܫܐ ܡܛܠܬܝ ܒܕܓܠܘܬܐ.

ܣܗ: ܗܝܕܝܢ ܚܕܘ ܘܪܘܙܘ. ܕܐܓܪܟܘܢ ܣܓܝ ܒܫܡܝܐ. ܗܟܢܐ ܓܝܪ ܪܕܦܘ ܠܢܒܝܐ ܕܡܢ ܩܕܡܝܟܘܢ.

ܣܘ: ܐܢܬܘܢ ܐܢܘܢ ܡܠܚܗ ܕܐܪܥܐ. ܐܢܗܘ ܕܝܢ ܕܡܠܚܐ ܬܦܟܗ. ܒܡܢܐ ܬܬܡܠܚ. ܠܡܕܡ ܠܐ ܐܙܠܐ. ܐܠܐ ܕܬܫܬܕܐ ܠܒܪ ܘܬܬܕܝܫ ܡܢ ܐܢܫܐ.

ܣܙ: ܐܢܬܘܢ ܐܢܘܢ ܢܘܗܪܗ ܕܥܠܡܐ. ܠܐ ܡܫܟܚܐ ܕܬܛܫܐ ܡܕܝܢܬܐ ܕܥܠ ܛܘܪܐ ܒܢܝܐ.

ܣܚ: ܘܠܐ ܡܢܗܪܝܢ ܫܪܓܐ ܘܣܝܡܝܢ ܠܗ ܬܚܝܬ ܣܐܬܐ. ܐܠܐ ܥܠ ܡܢܪܬܐ. ܘܡܢܗܪ ܠܟܠ ܐܝܠܝܢ ܕܒܒܝܬܐ ܐܢܘܢ.

ܣܛ: ܗܟܢܐ ܢܢܗܪ ܢܘܗܪܟܘܢ ܩܕܡ ܒܢܝܢܫܐ. ܕܢܚܙܘܢ ܥܒܕܝܟܘܢ ܛܒܐ ܘܢܫܒܚܘܢ ܠܐܒܘܟܘܢ ܕܒܫܡܝܐ.

LIGHT

The Aramaic word for "light" ܢܘܗܪܐ, נוהרא, Noohra, when used metaphorically also means *teaching, enlightenment, brilliance, intelligence*. In the East, good and pious people are called the light of the world. Light also represents the presence of God. Faith, forgiveness, humility, meekness, peace, compassion, justice, love and purity of heart are the "light" of the human soul and must shine in the world. When good works are done in the power of the aforementioned "light," God is glorified and the human family sees that the kingdom of God has truly arrived! Thus, Jesus said to his disciples, "You are the light of the world . . . let your light shine in the sight of people so that they may see your good deeds and may praise your Father who is in heaven." The disciples were to carry out and act upon the teaching of their lord.

17. Do not imagine that I have come to nullify the law (Torah) or the prophets. I have not come to nullify but to fulfill.

18. For I truly tell you that until heaven and earth shall pass away, not even a yodh[20] or a line shall pass away from the law (Torah) until all shall be fulfilled.

19. Now anyone who merely analyzes[21] one of these small commandments and teaches the people so, he shall be regarded as least in the kingdom of heaven; but anyone who practices and teaches, he shall be regarded as great in the kingdom of heaven.

20. For I tell you that if your devoutness[22] does not surpass that of the scribes and Pharisees, you shall not enter the kingdom of heaven.

21. You have heard[23] that it was said to those who were before you: You shall not murder; and anyone who murders deserves the judgment of the court.

22. But I am saying to you that anyone who is angry with his brother for no reason deserves the judgment of the court; and anyone who says to his brother, you are worthless![24] deserves the judgment of the congregation; and anyone who says, you are stupid[25] is sentenced to Gehenna of fire.[26]

23. If, then, it happens that you may be offering your sacrifice upon the altar and right there you remember that your brother holds something of a grudge against you;

24. Leave your sacrifice right there on the altar and go, first thing, be reconciled with your brother; and then come, present your sacrifice.

25. Become reconciled with your accuser immediately while you are on the road with him, lest your accuser hand you over to the judge, then the judge hand you over to the jailer and you shall be thrown into prison.

---

20 Yodh, ܝ - יֹד, the smallest letter in the Aramaic and Hebrew alphabets.

21 ܫܪܐ, שׁרא, Shra, literally means *to untie, make something unbinding*; also *to analyze*. Jesus admonished those who taught the law with great detail but who did not practice what they taught. See Mt. 23:2-7.

22 ܟܐܢܘܬܟܘܢ, כאנותכון, Kenoothkhon - *your goodness, uprightness, devoutness*. A genuine piety, and godliness founded on God's laws. The disciples of Jesus are encouraged to practice the inner meaning and not just the outward observance of the Torah. The ways of practice follow verse 20.

23 "You have heard," has the meaning "you have received a tradition."

24 ܪܩܐ, רקא, Raqa, literally *You are spit*. An extremely insulting remark, it means one is worthless as spit, despicable, contemptible, good-for-nothing.

25 ܠܠܐ, ללא, Lila. Another insulting but antiquated Aramaic word which implied great stupidity. This is a very offensive remark.

26 "Gehenna of fire" or "Hell fire" is an Aramaic idiom: Mental anguish and torment; regret, destruction.

܀܂ ܀܀܀

26. And truly I say to you, you will not come out of there until you have paid the last small coin.

27. You have heard that it was said: You shall not commit adultery.

28. But I am saying to you that anyone who looks at a woman so that he may desire her, right then commits adultery in his heart.

29. If, then, your right eye causes you to stumble, tear it out and throw it away from you[27] because it is better for you that one of your members perish than your entire body fall into Gehenna.[28]

30. And if your right hand causes you to stumble, cut if off and throw it away from you; because it is better for you that one of your members perish than your entire body fall into Gehenna[29]

31. It has been said that anyone who divorces his wife shall give her divorce papers.

32. But I am saying to you that anyone who divorces his wife, except in the case of adultery, makes her commit adultery; and anyone who marries a woman who is separated and not divorced commits adultery.

33. Again, you have heard that it has been said to those who were before you that you shall not lie in your oaths, but you shall entrust your oaths to the LORD.

34. Yet I am saying to you: You shall not swear[30] at all; not by heaven, for it is the seat of God;[31]

---

27 "Tear out the eye and throw it away" is an idiom and means "stop the habit that leads you to destruction."

28 ܓܗܢܐ, נגהא, Gehenna - an idiom: *torment, destruction*. See p. A - 17 "Hell Fire - Gehenna."

29 See above footnotes 26 and 27. None of these Aramaic expressions should be understood literally.

30 Swearing in the name of God, holy men, sacred places and things is an integral element in Eastern Semitic speech, "For men swear by one who is greater than themselves; and in every dispute among them, the true settlement is by oaths (swearing);" Heb. 6:16. Scripture is full of examples of swearing in the name of God, - Gen. 21:23-24, Rom. 9:1. The writers of Holy Scripture tell us that the LORD God also took oaths (swore), - see Gen. 22:16, Isa. 62:8, Heb. 3:11 and 6:13. In a very natural and spontaneous manner an Eastern speaker will turn his eyes and lift his hands toward heaven and say, "By God, what I said is right and true!" or "Let God witness to the truth of my words!" Apparently, swearing had lost its original sacredness and had become meaningless. Jesus encouraged direct, truthful and straightforward conversation without the need of swearing. "But let your words be: Yes, yes, or no, no; anything more than these is from a deceiver." Mt. 5:37. See also James 5:12.

31 Isa 66:1.

ܗܐ: ܘܐܡܝܢ ܐܡܪܢܐ ܐܢܐ ܠܟܝ: ܕܠܐ ܢܦܩܬ ܡܢ ܬܡܢ. ܗܠܟܡܐ ܕܬܦܪܥܢ ܐܚܪܝܐ ܐܣܪܢܐ.

ܗܘ: ܫܡܥܬܘܢ ܕܐܬܐܡܪ: ܕܠܐ ܗܓܘܪ.

ܗܙ: ܐܢܐ ܕܝܢ ܐܡܪܢܐ ܐܢܐ ܠܟܘܢ: ܕܟܠ ܡܢ ܕܚܐܪ ܐܢܐ ܒܐܢܬܬܐ ܐܝܟ ܕܝܕܥܠܗ. ܡܢܬܪܐ ܓܪܗ ܒܠܒܗ.

ܗܚ: ܐܝܢ ܕܝܢ ܥܝܢܟ ܕܝܡܝܢ ܐܢ ܡܓܕܠܐ ܠܘܟ ܐܣܘܪܗ ܘܫܒܩܗ ܡܢܟ. ܦܝܫ ܠܘܟ ܓܪܬ ܕܚܕܟܐ ܡܢ ܗܕܡܟ. ܘܠܐ ܟܠܗ ܦܓܪܘܟ ܢܦܠ ܒܓܗܢܐ.

ܗܛ: ܘܐܢ ܐܝܕܘܟ ܕܝܡܝܢ ܐܢ ܡܓܕܠܐ ܠܘܟ. ܩܛܘܥܗ ܚܕܪܗ ܘܫܒܩܗ ܡܢܟ. ܦܝܫ ܠܘܟ ܓܪܬ ܕܚܕܟܐ ܡܢ ܗܕܡܘܟܝ. ܘܠܐ ܟܠܗ ܦܓܪܘܟ ܢܦܠ ܒܓܗܢܐ.

ܠܐ: ܐܬܐܡܪ: ܕܡܢ ܕܫܪܐ ܐܢܬܬܗ. ܝܗܒ ܠܗ ܟܬܒܐ ܕܦܘܪܟܐ.

ܠܒ: ܐܢܐ ܕܝܢ ܐܡܪܢܐ ܐܢܐ ܠܟܘܢ: ܕܟܠ ܡܢ ܕܫܪܐ ܐܢܬܬܗ ܠܒܪ ܡܢ ܡܠܬܐ ܕܙܢܝܘܬܐ. ܥܒܕ ܠܗ ܕܬܓܘܪ. ܘܡܢ ܕܢܣܒ ܥܒܝܩܬܐ. ܓܐܪ.

ܠܓ: ܗܘܒ ܫܡܥܬܘܢ ܕܐܬܐܡܪ ܠܩܕܡܝܐ: ܕܠܐ ܬܕܓܠ ܒܡܘܡܬܘܟ. ܡܫܠܡܬ ܕܝܢ ܠܡܪܝܐ ܡܘܡܬܘܟ.

ܠܕ: ܐܢܐ ܕܝܢ ܐܡܪܢܐ ܐܢܐ ܠܟܘܢ: ܠܐ ܬܐܡܘܢ ܣܟ. ܠܐ ܒܫܡܝܐ ܕܟܘܪܣܝܐ ܗܘ ܕܐܠܗܐ.

HELL FIRE
Gehenna

The name "Gehenna," *Gei Hinnom* in Hebrew, is derived from the infamous valley of Ben Hinnom, southwest of Jerusalem (Jer. 19:2). After the fall of the northern kingdom of Israel, Assyria made the southern kingdom of Judah pay tribute. In 2 Chron. 28, we are told that the Judean King Ahaz (735-715 B.C.E.) took some of the precious silver and gold ornaments of the Temple to appease the King of Assyria. Ahaz worshipped and offered sacrifices to idols. In the valley of Hinnom in Jerusalem the King condemned his son to the flames as a sacrificial offering to pacify the gods. It was because of these horrible atrocities and practices that the valley, *Gei Hinnom*, became a Hebrew term for hell. During the time of the New Testament, the Hinnom Valley became a place to burn rubbish and the bodies of plague victims. Jesus used the Aramaic term "Gehenna" or "Gehenna fire" (verses 22, 29, 30) idiomatically to indicate deep regret, mental suffering, torment or destruction. These words should not be taken literally. This inner, psychological condition is a result of making grave insulting remarks against one's brother (verse 22) or practicing certain habits that are destructive (verses 29-30).

35. Not by the earth, for it is a footstool under His feet,[32] also not by Jerusalem, for it is the city of the great king.

36. Likewise you shall not swear by your head, because you are not able to create in it one single strand of hair, black or white.

37. But let your words be: Yes, yes; or no, no; anything more than these is from a deceiver.

38. You have heard that it has been said: An eye for an eye, and a tooth for a tooth.[33]

39. Yet I am saying to you that you shall not resist an evildoer,[34] but anyone who slaps you on your right cheek, turn to him the other also.[35]

40. And anyone who wants to sue you and take away your linen garment, leave him your robe also.[36]

41. Anyone who forces you into service for one mile, go with him two.[37]

42. Anyone who asks from you, you give to him; and anyone who wants to borrow from you, do not refuse him.[38]

43. You have heard that it was said, that you shall be friendly to your neighbor[39] and hate your enemy.[40]

---

32 Isa. 66:1.
33 Ex. 21:24; Lev. 24:20; Deut. 19:21.
34 ܒܝܫܐ, בישא, Beesha: *a doer of wrong, a troublemaker.* See p. A - 18 "Beesha-Evil and Its Many Subtle Shades of Meaning."
35 Idiom: Do not augment, escalate the difficulty or problem. "A soft answer turns away wrath." Pr. 15:1. Verses 38 and 39 are not a prohibition against self-defense but rather a remedy against strife and vengeance. Jesus encourages peace and harmony in human relationships.
36 This expression must not be taken literally. It means that it is better to lose something little and have peace than to quarrel and lose something greater.
37 Many times in the East, individuals are forced into carrying burdens for ruling officials, armies and powerful leaders. It is better to comply willingly and freely than to resist the imposition and create worse hardships for one's self. The less resistance the better the chance for quick release from the enforced task.
38 Learn to share what you have with others. See Lev. 25:35. There is an Eastern saying, "Do not refuse your neighbor's request for tomorrow you may be in want."
39 ܩܪܝܒܐ, קריבא, Qareewa, - *kinsman, relative, neighbor.*
40 Lev. 19:18; Lk. 6:27.

[Aramaic text omitted - 9 numbered verses]

BEESHA-EVIL AND ITS MANY SUBTLE SHADES OF MEANING

The Aramaic word ܒܝܼܫܵܐ, בישא, Beesha - *evil* comes from the root word ܒܐܫ, bish - *to displease, to harm, to be evil, to seem bad, to err, to be worse, to afflict, to be mistaken, to be unripe, to be unfortunate.* Thus, the word Beesha as a noun, adjective or adverb has literally scores of various meanings. The following are just a few of its shaded denotations and implications: *bad, ugly, error, cruel, mistake, malignant, rotten, unripe, immature, unfortunate, unlucky, wicked, wrong, diseased, incorrect, the evil one (a satan, one who will mislead), culprit, deceiver, troublemaker* and so forth. For instance, the prophet Jeremiah in his vision sees two baskets of figs, one basket with good figs and the other with evil figs (bad, unripe) Jer. 24:1-2. In Mt. 7:17, Jesus refers to good trees (healthy) and bad trees (sick or unhealthy), good fruits (excellent) and bad fruits (inedible). But, most importantly, in Mt. 7:11, Jesus seems to indicate (according to most English translations) that even though parents are evil they know how to give good (proper) gifts to their children. When translated literally, it reads: "If then, you (plural) *who are evil ones*, you know how to give good things to your children, how much more shall your Father who is in heaven give good things to those who ask Him?" But the intended meaning in Aramaic is, "And if, then, *you who make mistakes* know how, etc." See also Mt. 6:13, footnote 18.

44. Yet I am saying to you: Love[41] your enemies and bless anyone who is cursing you,[42] and do good to them who are hating you; and pray for those who are oppressing you and are persecuting you.

45. So that you may be the children of your Father who is in heaven, He who lets His sun shine upon the good and upon the bad, and who lets His rain fall upon the just and the unjust.[43]

46. If, then, you are loving only those who love you, what payment do you have? Behold, are not they, the tax collectors, also doing the same?

47. And if you are greeting your brothers only, what more are you doing? Are not they, the tax collectors, also doing the same?

48. Therefore, be all-inclusive[44] even as your Father who is in heaven is all-inclusive.

---

41 "Love," ܚܘܒܐ, חובא, Ḥooba, (in this verse "love" is in the imperative form, ܐܚܒܘ, אחבו, Aḥiw.) comes from the root ܚܒ, חב, Ḥav which means *to warm, kindle, set on fire*. In Hebrew the word is Aheb. In the Semitic languages of Aramaic and Hebrew, this word has many shades of meaning. The word "love" as it is translated in this verse refers to being warm towards, kindly, amicable, that is, "to be well-disposed toward." Here, it does not imply sentimentality or ardent affection. "If thine enemy be hungry, give him bread to eat; and if he be thirsty, give him water to drink." Prov. 25:21, KJV. Anyone, then, actualizing this kind of attitude and disposition toward an "enemy" has no "enemy." Jesus constantly stressed the highest ideals in man so that humankind may practice peace and reconciliation. Hatred and vengeance only breed more hatred and vengeance, but love nourishes and encourages the finest in human beings.

42 "Cursing," here, means to pronounce curses, that is, invoke evils, misfortunes, to proclaim calamities upon someone. Easterners feel that their personal enemies are God's enemies and that as such they deserve ruin and utter destruction. An Easterner may hurl at his enemy such cursing as: *May God burn the bones of your fathers; May God exterminate your seed (offspring) from the earth; May God cut off your supply of bread; May your children be orphaned and your wife widowed.* See Ps. 109:5-20. Jesus exhorted his disciples to bless those who were cursing them.

43 The ancient belief held that only the righteous prosper and the wicked do not, that God blesses the just but the unjust receive no blessings. See Job 20:4, 5-7, 12, 14; 27:13-14, 16-18. The Master taught that his Father blesses the good and the bad, the just and the unjust. Central to Jesus' teaching is his stance that God desires mercy and compassion above all religious ordinances and sacrifices because the LORD Himself is compassionate. See Mt. 9:13 and Hos. 6:6. God is detached from man's formal arguments over moral world order and is associated with the goodness, power, and mystery of the natural order. The laws of God call upon humanity to act and behave justly, with compassion, true judgment and discernment.

44 ܓܡܝܪܐ, נמירא, Gmeera, - *complete, whole, mature, perfect, thorough, all-inclusive, rounded out*. It also refers to a *mature individual* and *one who is thorough*. Jesus encouraged his disciples to accept and treat everyone in the same manner as God blesses the good and the bad, the just and the unjust.

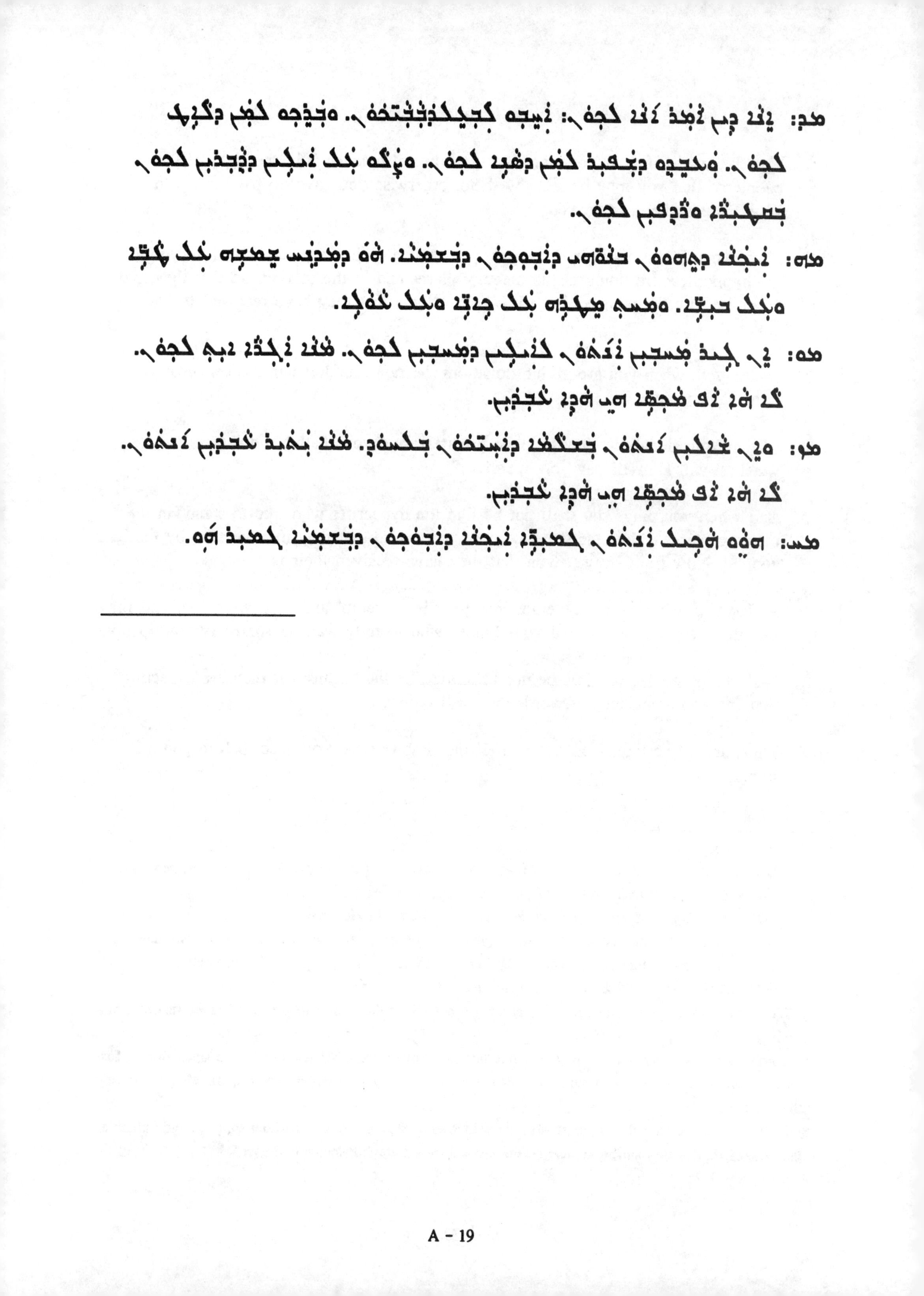

Chapter 6

1. Now be aware of your donation[1] that you do not practice it in the sight of the people so that you may be seen by them; otherwise you have no payment with your Father who is in heaven.

2. Thus, when you are giving donations, you shall not blow a trumpet[2] before you as the hypocrites[3] are doing in the meeting places and in the markets so that they may be praised by the people. But truly I say to you that they have received their payment.

3. As for you, when you are giving donations, let not your left hand know what your right hand is doing.

4. So that your donations may be done privately; and your Father who secretly watches, will Himself pay you openly.

5. And when you pray, you shall not be like the hypocrites who like to stand[4] in the meeting places and at the street corners[5] to pray so that they may be seen by the people. Now truly I say to you that they have received their pay.

6. As for you, when you pray, enter into your inner room[6] and lock your door and pray privately to your Father; and your Father who secretly watches shall pay you openly.

7. And when you are praying, be not babbling like the pagans; for they are expecting that through abundance of words they will be heard.[7]

8. Thus, do not be like them; for your Father knows what you need, before you ask him.

---

1 ܙܕܩܬܐ, זדקתא, Zedhqatha, *a right, law, rule; a just or righteous act, a right or proper thing to do*. This Aramaic word means an act of goodness which involves the giving of money.

2 ܩܪܢܐ, קרנא, Qarna, *horn, a horn of an animal, trumpet*. In Hebrew the word for "horn," "trumpet" is Shofar. Some rabbinic textual experts suggest that the original Aramaic or Hebrew may have read "You shall not pass the horn before you." The horn, or shofar, was used as an offering plate.

3 ܢܣܒܝ ܒܐܦܐ, נסבי באפא, Nasbay bapeh, *taker of faces;* hence, "an actor."

4 "To stand and pray" was a required position when reciting the "Amidah," i.e., the prayer recited while standing.

5 Communal prayer was done in the synagogues. Prayers were recited out in the open during fast days. However, when the set time of prayer came, people prayed, whether at work, traveling, or in any other circumstance.

6 ܬܘܢܐ, תונא, Tawanaah – a room without windows, a closet, a room in which supplies and valuables may be stored. "Inner room" may also be understood as a metaphor meaning "heart."

7 See 1 Ki. 18:26-29.

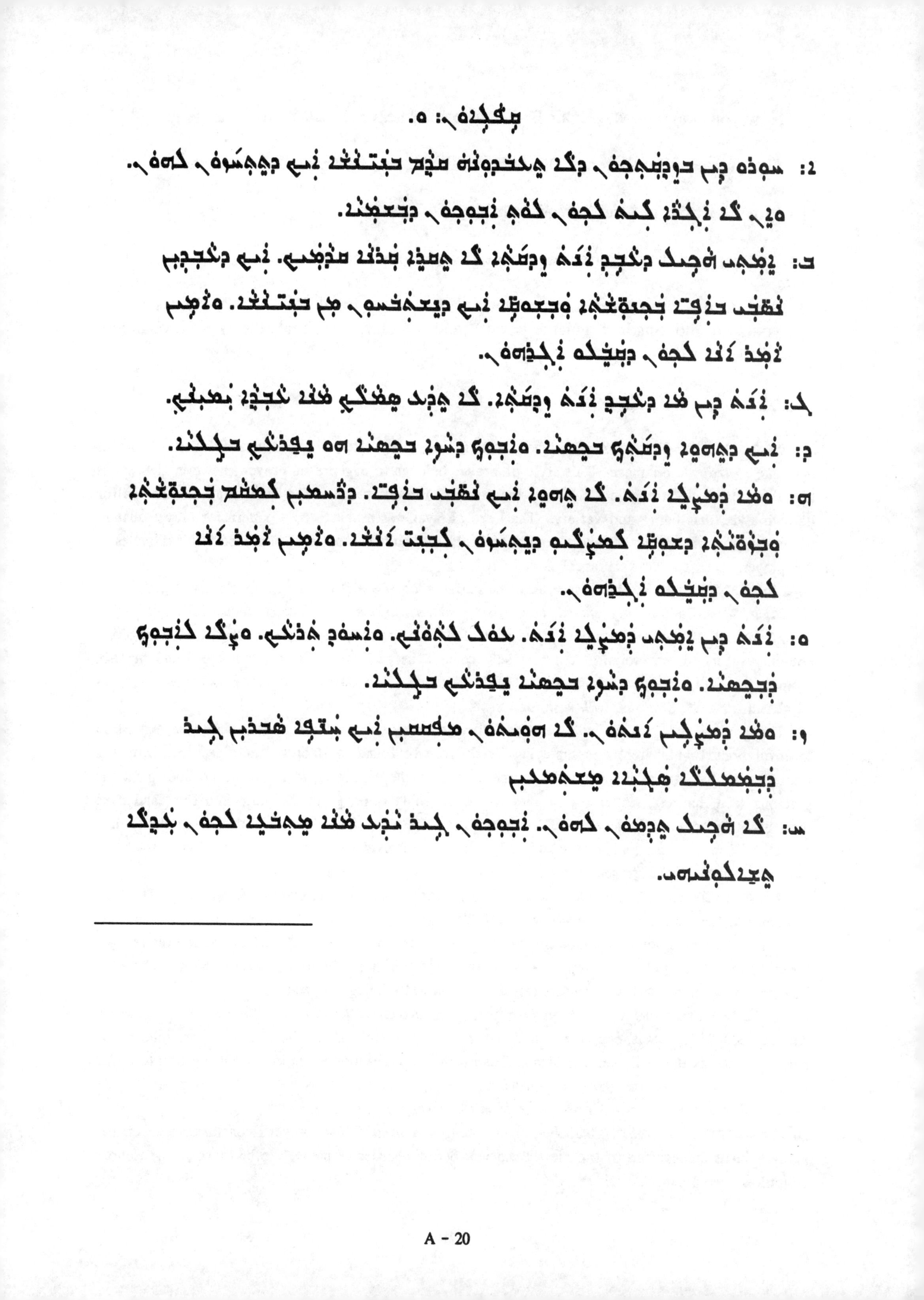

9. Now you pray this way.[8] Our Father who is in heaven.[9] Let Your name be holy.[10]

10. Let Your kingdom[11] come. Let Your will[12] be, as in heaven also on earth.

11. Provide us our needful[13] bread from day to day.

12. And forgive[14] us our offenses[15] as we have forgiven our offenders.

13. And do not let us enter into temptation,[16] but set us free[17] from evil.[18] Because yours are the kingdom and the power[19] and the glory[20] from all the ages, throughout all the ages.

---

8 ܨܠܘܬܐ, צלותא, Ṣlotha, *prayer*, comes from the root ܨܠܐ, צלא, Ṣla, and means *to incline, to turn towards, to trap, lay a snare*. This style of prayer belongs to a genre of prayer known in Hebrew as the "short prayer." It does not belong to the liturgical form of prayer. The "short prayer" is known for its own style, originality and variety. The Lord's Prayer was meant to be a pattern for prayer, that is, when one prays it should be "short" and contain the same ideas that Jesus presented to his disciples in this prayer. See "The Lord's Prayer," p. A - 21.

9 ܫܡܝܐ, שמיא, Shmaya, *sky, heaven, heavens, universe, cosmos* and by implication "everywhere."

10 ܩܕܫ, קדש, Qadash, *holy, sacred; that is, set apart, set to one side, distinct, dedicated*.

11 ܡܠܟܘܬܐ, מלכותא, Malkootha. The root of the word means "to counsel." Thus, God's "kingdom" not only refers to "sovereignty" but to God's "counsel" as well. See Mt. 3:2, footnote 4 and Mt. 5:3, footnote 5.

12 ܨܒܝܢܐ, צבינא, Ṣewyana, *will, wish, desire*.

13 The phrases - "Let Your will be" and "Provide us our needful bread" (especially the expression "needful bread" which refers to supplying "needs") can be found in Hebrew "short prayers." Bread is treated with the utmost respect by Easterners because they literally, in the name of God, plant the precious seed, harvest, scatter the sheaves on the threshing floor, grind the grain into flour and bake their daily bread in a "God-centered" consciousness. The prayer for "needful bread from day to day" reflects a deep inner gratitude and acknowledgment of the Provider of all "good and perfect gifts."

14 ܫܒܩ, שבק, Shwak, *forgive, set free, let go, release*.

15 ܚܘܒܝܢ, חובין, Ḥowbain, from ܚܘܒܐ, חובא, Ḥowba, *debt, offense, obligation, sin, guilt*. The term "sins" in Lk. 11:4 means "mistakes, wrongs, errors."

16 "Do not let us enter into temptation" is a common saying among many such Aramaic expressions - "keep us out of temptation," "keep us from sin (making a mistake,)" "don't let us be in want." The word "temptation" ܢܣܝܘܢܐ, נסיונא, Nisyona, refers also to worldly living; i.e., materialism.

17 ܦܨܢ, פצן, Paṣan, *deliver, save, set free, part or separate*.

18 ܒܝܫܐ, בישא, Beesha, *bad, error, mistake, difficulty, trouble, a bad inclination*. Some interpreters believe it means the "evil one;" i.e., satan. Satan is an externalization of an internal inclination toward a wrong; i.e., "beesha" - *evil, error, deep trouble*.

19 ܚܝܠܐ, חילא, Ḥila, *power*, in the sense of *might, energy, force and strength*.

20 ܬܫܒܘܚܬܐ, תשבוחתא, Tishboḥta, *glory, song and praise*. The Prayer's conclusion is missing in many ancient manuscripts of the New Testament but this particular phrase can be found in the Hebrew Scriptures. See 1 Chron. 29:11; Ps. 45:6.

THE LORD'S PRAYER

This simple and direct prayer composed by Jesus contains the essence of his entire teaching. It is a capsule summary of the message he preached for three and one-half years and the essential kernel of the Hebrew Bible. The prayer is a brief summary of Jesus' beliefs about God, humankind and the world. It is a synopsis of his understanding of the relationship between the material realm of the seen and the spiritual realm of the unseen. His method of prayer is succinct, earnest and devotional. We are told by experts of first century Judaism that there are many parallels and similarities between the "language" of the Lord's Prayer and that of both the Hebrew Scripture and rabbinic prayer. According to these scholars, a few of the sources would be various prayers that are recited on Mondays and Thursdays before returning the Torah scrolls to the ark, the *kaddish*, the "short prayer" of the early *Tanna*, the *Shemoneh-Esreh* (Eighteen Benedictions) and in certain Talmudic prayers. But when the Lord's prayer is taken in its entirety, it is original and singular. The prayer reflects Jesus' own religious genius, creativity and spiritual understanding.

Jesus' instruction about prayer may be summed up in two words - Be sincere. The time, place or number of words are not essential but an open, trusting and receptive heart and mind are indeed necessary for communing with God. Through Jesus' inspiring and beautiful prayer, there comes specific but simple realizations, such as: 1) That God is a loving parent who is forever at hand and concerned about the welfare of His entire human family. 2) That we are all children of a gracious Father who has provided for us in all ways. 3) That God's Kingdom (counsel) and Will are to be expressed on earth. 4) That we understand the value of forgiveness, both for ourselves and for others, even as our loving Father forgives all who ask of Him. 5) That God, as a good parent, helps us not to enter into temptation but delivers us from error. 6) That He has the kingdom, power and glory to accomplish all that is needed. 7) That He is the same throughout all the ages.

14. For if you forgive people their offenses,[21] your Father who is in heaven shall also forgive yours.

15. If, then, you do not forgive people, neither does your Father forgive you your offenses.

16. Now when you are fasting, be not sad like the hypocrites; for they disfigure their faces[22] so that they may be seen by the people that they are fasting. Truly I say to you that they have received their pay.

17. As for you, when you fast, wash your face and anoint your head;

18. So that it may not be seen by the people that you are fasting but privately by your Father. Then your Father who watches secretly will pay you.

19. Do not put aside for yourselves treasures buried in the ground[23] a place where moth and rust destroy; and where thieves break through and steal.

20. But put aside for yourselves treasures in heaven[24] where neither moth nor rust destroy; and where thieves do not break through and steal.

21. For where your treasure is, there also is your heart.[25]

22. The lamp of the body is the eye; if, then, your eye is simple,[26] your entire body is also lighted.

23. But, if your eye is bad,[27] your entire body will be dark. If, then, the light which is

---

21 ܣܟܠܘܬܐ, סכלותא, Sakhlwatha, *folly, offence, mistake, evil doing*. See Mt. 18:23-35.
22 Saffron was used on the faces so that those who fasted would appear with a yellowish and sickly look.
23 In Biblical days, Easterners buried their valuables and coins of gold and silver in the ground. Expensive clothes, priceless scrolls and other goods were also hidden in specially constructed places in the walls of the homes. All these things were in danger of being eaten by moths, destroyed by rust or stolen by thieves or treasure hunters.
24 "Treasures in heaven" are good deeds which never perish.
25 People who buried their valuables and money would always be worried that someone might find the hidden treasure. Thus, these individuals' hearts (minds) were buried with their treasures. But those who put aside treasures in heaven were free from the worry of material things.
26 ܦܫܝܛܐ, פשיטא, Psheeta, *simple, pure, normal*. "A simple eye" is a person who has no evil intention or ulterior motive. In modern Aramaic, a person who is devious and crafty is said to have "salty eyes." The expression "salty eyes" is comparable to the American idiom "shifty eyes."
27 "A bad eye" is the same as "salty eyes." See the above footnote 26.

ܝܕ: ܐܢ ܓܝܪ ܬܫܒܩܘܢ ܠܒܢܝ̈ܢܫܐ ܣܟܠܘܬܗܘܢ. ܢܫܒܘܩ ܐܦ ܠܟܘܢ ܐܒܘܟܘܢ
ܕܒܫܡܝܐ.
ܝܗ: ܐܢ ܕܝܢ ܠܐ ܬܫܒܩܘܢ ܠܒܢܝ̈ ܐܢܫܐ. ܐܦܠܐ ܐܒܘܟܘܢ ܫܒܩ ܠܟܘܢ ܣܟܠܘܬܟܘܢ.
ܝܘ: ܐܡܬܝ ܕܝܢ ܕܨܝܡܝܢ ܐܢܬܘܢ. ܠܐ ܬܗܘܘܢ ܟܡܝܪ̈ܐ ܐܝܟ ܢܣܒ̈ܝ ܒܐܦ̈ܐ. ܡܚܒܠܝܢ
ܓܝܪ ܐܦ̈ܝܗܘܢ ܐܝܟ ܕܢܬܚܙܘܢ ܠܒܢܝ̈ܢܫܐ ܕܨܝܡܝܢ. ܘܐܡܝܢ ܐܡܪ ܐܢܐ
ܠܟܘܢ ܕܢܣܒܘ ܐܓܪܗܘܢ.
ܝܙ: ܐܢܬ ܕܝܢ ܡܐ ܕܨܐܡ ܐܢܬ. ܐܫܝܓ ܐܦ̈ܝܟ. ܘܡܫܘܚ ܪܫܟ.
ܝܚ: ܐܝܟ ܕܠܐ ܢܬܚܙܐ ܠܒܢܝ̈ܢܫܐ ܕܨܐܡ ܐܢܬ. ܐܠܐ ܠܐܒܘܟ ܕܒܟܣܝܐ. ܘܐܒܘܟ ܕܚܙܐ
ܒܟܣܝܐ ܗܘ ܢܦܪܥܟ.
ܝܛ: ܠܐ ܬܣܝܡܘܢ ܠܟܘܢ ܣܝ̈ܡܬܐ ܒܐܪܥܐ. ܐܝܟܐ ܕܣܐܣܐ ܘܐܟܠܐ ܡܚܒܠܝܢ.
ܘܐܝܟܐ ܕܓܢܒ̈ܐ ܦܠܫܝܢ ܘܓܢܒܝܢ.
ܟ: ܐܠܐ ܣܝܡܘ ܠܟܘܢ ܣܝ̈ܡܬܐ ܒܫܡܝܐ. ܐܝܟܐ ܕܠܐ ܣܐܣܐ ܘܠܐ ܐܟܠܐ ܡܚܒܠܝܢ.
ܘܐܝܟܐ ܕܓܢܒ̈ܐ ܠܐ ܦܠܫܝܢ ܘܠܐ ܓܢܒܝܢ.
ܟܐ: ܐܝܟܐ ܓܝܪ ܕܐܝܬܝܗ ܣܝܡܬܟܘܢ. ܬܡܢ ܗܘ ܐܦ ܠܒܟܘܢ.
ܟܒ: ܫܪܓܐ ܕܦܓܪܐ ܐܝܬܝܗ ܥܝܢܐ. ܐܢ ܥܝܢܟ ܗܟܝܠ ܬܗܘܐ ܦܫܝܛܐ. ܐܦ ܟܠܗ
ܦܓܪܟ ܢܗܝܪ ܗܘ.
ܟܓ: ܐܢ ܕܝܢ ܥܝܢܟ ܬܗܘܐ ܒܝܫܐ ܟܠܗ ܦܓܪܟ ܚܫܘܟܐ ܢܗܘܐ. ܐܢ ܗܟܝܠ ܢܘܗܪܐ
ܕܒܟ ܚܫܘܟܐ ܗܘ. ܚܫܘܟܟ ܟܡܐ ܢܗܘܐ.

The last half of the English translation of the Aramaic scriptural verse 23 (ܟܓ): ܕܒܟ ܚܫܘܟܐ ܗܘ. ܚܫܘܟܟ ܟܡܐ ܢܗܘܐ. is continued on the next page (p. 23).

in you is dark, how much more will be your darkness![28]

24. No one can work for two masters because he will either dislike the one and like the other; or he will honor the one and neglect the other. You cannot work for God and for money.

25. For this reason I say to you: Do not be concerned about yourselves, what you will eat, and what you will drink, nor for your body what you will wear. Behold is not the entire being[29] more important than food and the body than clothes?[30]

26. Observe the birds of the sky, they do not sow; neither do they harvest, nor gather into barns; yet your Father who is in heaven feeds them. Behold, are you not more important than they?

27. Now who is it among you while being determined can increase his stature one cubit?[31]

28. And about clothes, why are you concerned? Examine how the lilies of the field grow. They are not wearing themselves out; and they are not weaving.

29. But I say to you that not even Solomon in all his magnificence was clothed like one of them.

30. If, then, God so clothes the grass of the field, which exists today and tomorrow falls into the oven, will He not abundantly do so for you, you of little faith?

31. Now then, do not be concerned or say: What will we eat, or what will we drink, or with what will we be clothed?

32. Because the people of the world are looking for all these things. Yet your Father who is in heaven knows that you also are in need of all these things.

33. But first you look for the kingdom of God and His justice and all these things shall abundantly be given to you.

34. Now do not worry about tomorrow because tomorrow will take care of itself. Enough for the day is its own trouble.[32]

---

28 Expression of speech: If a shifty, cunning person calls the crooked things he does "good," how much worse are the things he calls "bad?"
29 ܢܦܫܐ, נפשא, Nowsha, *being, life, self, soul.*
30 Jesus emphasizes the proper priority of values for his disciples.
31 A cubit is a measure, 18 inches, originally from the elbow to the end of the middle finger.
32 Prov. 27:1.

ܟܕ: ܐܢ ܐܢܬ ܡܥܡܠܬ ܓܘܪܒܐ ܚܕܬܐ ܠܥܒܕܬ. ܐܘ ܓܘ ܠܒܫ ܡܫܚܝܐ ܘܓܐܚܪܢܐ
ܡܙܒܢ. ܐܘ ܠܒܫ ܒܢܒܐ ܘܓܐܚܪܢܐ ܒܣܘܩ. ܐܢ ܡܥܡܠܬ ܐܢܬܘܢ
ܠܓܠܬܐ ܠܥܒܕܬ ܘܠܚܡܦܐ.

ܟܗ: ܡܫܟܠ ܗܘܐ ܐܡܪܐ ܐܢܐ ܠܟܘܢ: ܐܢ ܦܪܨܘܦܘܢ ܠܒܘܫܟܘܢ ܗܘܐ ܦܪܟܠܘܢ ܘܗܘܐ
ܦܫܟܘܢ. ܘܐܢ ܠܦܓܪܟܘܢ ܗܘܐ ܦܠܚܢ. ܐܢ ܗܘܐ ܒܘܫܐ ܒܫܒܬܐ ܡܢ ܟܣܬܐ.
ܘܦܓܪܐ ܡܢ ܠܒܘܫܐ.

ܟܘ: ܚܘܪܘ ܒܦܪܚܬܐ ܕܫܡܝܐ ܕܐܢ ܙܪܥܝ ܘܐܢ ܚܨܕܝ ܘܐܢ ܟܢܫܝ ܒܐܘܨܪܐ.
ܘܐܒܘܟܘܢ ܕܒܫܡܝܐ ܡܬܪܣܐ ܠܗܘܢ. ܐܢ ܗܘܐ ܐܝܬܘܢ ܡܝܬܪܝܢ ܐܢܬܘܢ ܡܢܗܘܢ.

ܟܙ: ܡܢܘ ܡܢ ܡܢܟܘܢ ܟܕ ܝܨܦ. ܡܫܟܚ ܠܡܘܣܦܘ ܥܠ ܩܘܡܬܗ ܐܡܬܐ ܚܕܐ.

ܟܚ: ܘܥܠ ܠܒܘܫܐ ܗܘܐ ܝܨܦܝܢ ܐܢܬܘܢ. ܬܒܩܘ ܒܫܘܫܢܐ ܕܕܒܪܐ ܐܝܟܢܐ ܪܒܝܢ.
ܕܐܢ ܠܐܝܬ ܘܐܢ ܙܩܠܝܢ.

ܟܛ: ܐܡܪܐ ܐܢܐ ܠܟܘܢ ܕܡܢ ܕܐܦܠܐ ܫܠܝܡܘܢ ܒܫܘܒܚܗ ܫܘܒܚܗ ܬܦܫܬ ܚܕܐ ܡܢ
ܡܢܗܘܢ:

ܠ: ܐܢ ܕܡܢ ܓܠܡܒܪܐ ܕܚܩܠܐ ܕܝܘܡܢܐ ܐܝܬܘܗܝ. ܘܡܚܪ ܒܐܫܠܐ ܒܬܢܘܪܐ ܐܠܗܐ
ܗܟܢܐ ܡܠܒܫ. ܐܢ ܗܘܐ ܒܫܒܐ ܠܟܘܢ ܙܥܘܪܝ ܗܝܡܢܘܬܐ.

ܠܐ: ܐܢ ܗܟܢܐ ܦܪܨܘܦܘܢ ܐܘ ܦܪܡܪܘܢ: ܗܘܐ ܝܨܦܠ. ܐܘ ܗܘܐ ܡܫܬܐ. ܐܘ ܗܘܐ
ܡܠܒܫ.

ܠܒ: ܟܠܗܘܢ ܓܘ ܗܠܝܢ ܒܥܡܡܐ ܗܘ ܕܒܥܠܡܐ ܒܥܝܢ ܠܗܘܢ. ܐܒܘܟܘܢ ܕܡܢ ܕܒܫܡܝܐ
ܝܕܥ ܕܐܦ ܠܟܘܢ ܡܣܬܢܩܝܢ ܗܠܝܢ ܟܠܗܘܢ.

ܠܓ: ܒܥܘ ܕܡܢ ܠܘܩܕܡ ܡܠܟܘܬܗ ܕܐܠܗܐ ܘܙܕܝܩܘܬܗ. ܘܟܠܗܘܢ ܗܠܝܢ ܡܬܬܘܣܦܢ
ܠܟܘܢ.

ܠܕ: ܐܢ ܗܟܢܐ ܦܪܨܘܦܘܢ ܕܡܚܪ ܗܘ ܓܘ ܡܚܪ ܐܝܟ ܕܝܘܡܗ. ܣܦܩ ܠܗ ܠܝܘܡܐ
ܒܒܝܫܘܬܗ.

Chapter 7

1. Do not criticize otherwise you will be judged, because with the same criticism you are judging, you shall be judged[1]

2. And with the same measure you are measuring, it shall be measured to you.[2]

3. Why, then, do you notice the straw in your brother's eye, but the plank which is in your own eye you do not see?

4. Or, how can you say to your brother: Let me take the straw out of your eye; and behold! a beam is in your own eye?

5. Hypocrite! First take the beam out of your own eye; and then you can see how to take the straw out of your brother's eye.

6. Do not give a holy thing to dogs and do not throw your pearls before hogs;[3] otherwise, they trample them with their feet, then turn and mangle you.[4]

7. Ask,[5] and it shall be given to you; search, and you shall find;[6] knock, and it shall be opened to you.

---

1 Judged by God, that is, you will receive your just deserts.
2 "Give and it will be given to you; good measure shaken down and running over they will pour into your robe. For the measure that you measure, it will be measured to you." Lk. 6:38. The Eastern custom is that every measure must "run over." The seller of grain becomes known by his generous (running over) measurement. When individuals purchase or borrow, they expect to receive the same measure given to them that they gave to their neighbors when they sold or loaned. Those who cheat were, in turn, cheated. Those who give liberally were, in turn, treated generously. See "The Bountiful Measure," p. A - 24.
3 "Do not give ... holy ... to dogs and do not throw ... pearls before hogs" is typical Semitic poetry called parallelism. "Give" means "present," "holy thing" refers to the "holy teachings," "pearls" means the "precious wisdom or teaching," "dogs" and "hogs" refer to ignorant people who do not want to understand nor have any respect for the holy or precious. Dogs were not domesticated in the Near East and were usually wild and considered unclean animals. Hence the saying means, "do not teach what is holy and precious to those who do not want to understand nor respect the scriptural, spiritual wisdom - the holy teaching." There is also a play on words with the Aramaic word "throw" ܬܪܡܘܢ, תרמון, Tarmon. It is similar to the Aramaic word ܬܪܐ, תרא, Traa which means to instruct, guide and teach.
4 Those who do not want to understand might ridicule the teaching and create physical disputes or other unwanted and unnecessary difficulties.
5 "Ask" is another term for prayer. In Hebrew "ask," Sha'al, is an expression for prayer.
6 See Prov. 8:17; Isa. 55:6.

ܡܟܝܠܬܐ ܛܒܬܐ

THE BOUNTIFUL MEASURE

In the marketplace one of the most intriguing transactions to watch is that of the measurer. It is he who gives the "good measure, pressed down, shaken together, running over." The motto is: Friendship must forever mingle itself with business. Even liquid, such as milk and oil, must run over at least a little into the buyer's vessel because it is understood that "for with the measure you measure, it will be measured to you." An easterner carries grain in the skirt of his garments much as a woman sometimes carries things in the folds of her apron. The grain is sold in this manner: once the price is agreed upon, the seller spreads an ample cloak on the ground and pours the golden grain on it in a heap. Then the seller kneels by his little mound of wheat. While calling upon the name of God, he thrusts the square wooden measure (box) into the heap of wheat. Grain is considered sacred; thus, the selling of it must be accompanied by pious language. When the measurer tosses the first scoop into the skirt of the buyer's cloak, he intones, "Blessing." That means "measure number one." Then he says, "From God," which means "two." He counts out the remaining scoops—"three," "four," and so on. When the measurer first thrusts the measuring box into the wheat, he will whirl the wheat around, lift it slightly and let it drop several times. Then with the palms of his hands he will pack it firmly down. Again he will whirl it, press it, and shake it up, until the wheat overflows the rim of the container. Through referring to this simple custom, Jesus emphasized the abundant joy of generous giving from the fullness of a spiritual life. *"There is no void which the divine life cannot fill, no need which it cannot meet, and no hunger which it cannot satisfy."* Abraham M. Rihbany, THE SYRIAN CHRIST, p. 268.

8. Positively everyone who asks, receives; and anyone who searches, finds; and to the one who knocks, it will be opened to him.

9. Or, who is the man among you, of whom his son may ask bread, is he going to hand him a stone?

10. And if he may ask for a fish, is he going to hand him a snake?[7]

11. And if, then, you who make mistakes[8] know how to give proper gifts to your children, how much more shall your Father who is in heaven give beneficial things to those who ask Him?[9]

12. Whatever you want that people may do for you, then you also do for them. Because this is the law and the prophets.

13. Enter through the narrow door because wide is the door and spacious is the road which leads to destruction; and many are those who are traveling on it.

14. How narrow the door! And how narrow the road which leads to life! And few are those who find it![10]

15. Watch out for lying prophets who come to you in sheep's clothing, but inside they are ravenous wolves.

16. By their fruits[11] then, you will recognize them! Do they gather grapes from thorn bushes, or figs from thistles?[12]

---

[7] Verses 9 and 10 refer to the custom of a parent who is very careful in handing food to the children. At night when children cry, parents tend to quiet them with bread, fish or whatever food may be available. Sometimes a snake may crawl into a basket with fish. Then again, Easterners who live in tents keep their bread in a pile of thin, flat, round stones which resemble eastern bread. The stones are used as a bread box. Thus it would be easy to pick up a stone or a small serpent at night; nonetheless they are very careful only to give good things to their children.

[8] ܒܒܝܫܐ, בִּישָׁא, Beesheh - *those who are capable of making errors*. In this usage the word "Beesheh" which is normally translated as "evil" or "bad" does not refer to any kind of intrinsic or inherent evil. It connotes the human tendency for errors or mistakes. See "Beesha-Evil and Its Many Subtle Shades of Meaning," p. A - 18.

[9] Since parents, who err; i.e., make mistakes, know how to give proper gifts to their children, then God even more so knows how and when to bestow the beneficial things for which one asks.

[10] Verses 13 and 14 present a choice between two ways: life or destruction. See Deut. 11:26-28, 30:15; the list of blessings and misfortunes Deut. 28.

[11] A typical Semitic saying "by the fruit of their deeds." See James 3:13.

[12] Grapes and figs are the two major and famous fruit products of Israel.

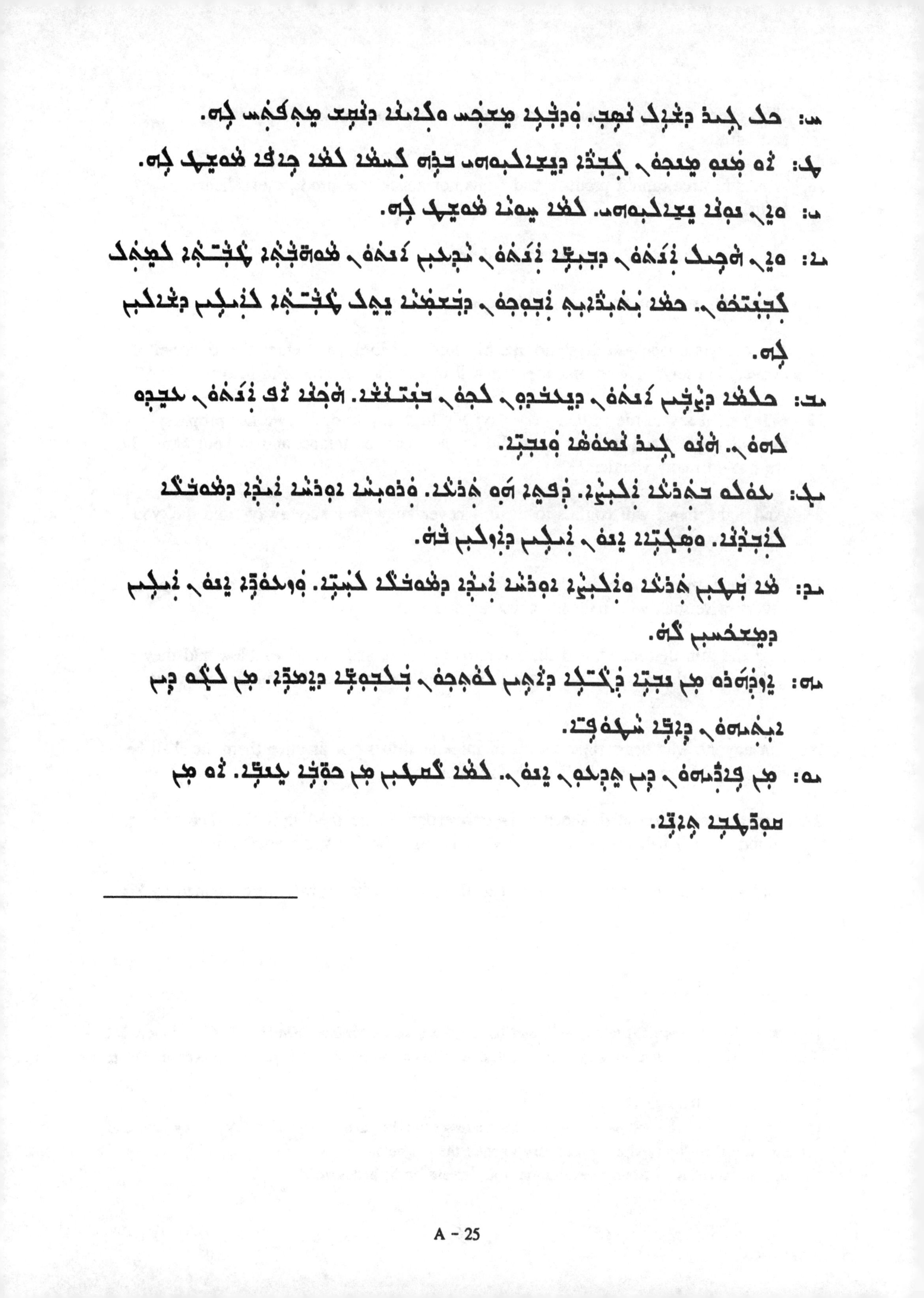

17. Thus every healthy tree produces excellent fruits but a sick tree produces bad[13] fruits.

18. A healthy tree cannot produce bad fruits nor a sick tree produce excellent fruits.

19. Every tree that does not produce good fruits is cut down and falls into the fire.[14]

20. Now then, by their fruits you will recognize them.

21. Not everyone who just says[15] to me: My lord, my lord, shall enter the kingdom of heaven, but anyone who practices the will of my Father who is in heaven.

22. Many shall say to me in that very day: My lord, my lord, did we not prophesy in your name,[16] and in your name did we not heal the insane, and in your name did we not do many wonders?

23. And right then I will confess to them: I never knew you; stay away from me, you wicked workers.

24. Everyone, then, who hears these words of mine and practices them, he shall be like a very wise man who built his house upon a rock.

25. And the rain descended, and the rivers overflowed, and the winds blew and they pounded on that very house, but it did not collapse because its foundations were laid upon a rock.

26. But anyone who hears these words of mine and does not practice them, he shall be like a foolish man who built his house upon sand.

27. And the rain descended, and the rivers overflowed and the winds blew and they pounded on that house, and it collapsed and its downfall was tremendous!

28. And so it was that when Jesus finished these words the crowds were stunned by his teaching.

---

13 ܒܝܫܐ, בִּישָׁא, Beesha, literally *evil, bad* but it means *unripe, rotten, inedible*. The Aramaic word "Beesha," "evil" has dozens of meanings. Context usually determines the best translation needed. See p. A - 18.

14 See Mt. 3:10, footnote 12.

15 "Not everyone who just says, ... ". Jesus stresses "works," that is, acts of justice, mercy, love and not just "words" or "lip service" as necessary to enter the kingdom.

16 "In your name" is an Aramaic expression which means "to be authorized."

ܝܙ: ܗܟܢܐ ܟܠ ܐܝܠܢܐ ܛܒܐ ܦܐܪ̈ܐ ܫܦܝܪ̈ܐ ܥܒܕ. ܐܝܠܢܐ ܕܝܢ ܒܝܫܐ ܦܐܪ̈ܐ ܒܝ̈ܫܐ ܥܒܕ.

ܝܚ: ܠܐ ܡܫܟܚ ܐܝܠܢܐ ܛܒܐ ܦܐܪ̈ܐ ܒܝ̈ܫܐ ܠܡܥܒܕ. ܘܠܐ ܐܝܠܢܐ ܒܝܫܐ ܦܐܪ̈ܐ ܫܦܝܪ̈ܐ ܠܡܥܒܕ.

ܝܛ: ܟܠ ܐܝܠܢܐ ܕܠܐ ܥܒܕ ܦܐܪ̈ܐ ܫܦܝܪ̈ܐ. ܡܬܦܣܩ ܘܒܢܘܪܐ ܢܦܠ.

ܟ: ܡܟܝܠ ܡܢ ܦܐܪ̈ܝܗܘܢ ܬܕܥܘܢ ܐܢܘܢ.

ܟܐ: ܠܐ ܗܘܐ ܟܠ ܕܐܡܪ ܠܝ ܡܪܝ ܡܪܝ ܥܐܠ ܠܡܠܟܘܬܐ ܕܫܡܝܐ. ܐܠܐ ܡܢ ܕܥܒܕ ܨܒܝܢܗ ܕܐܒܝ ܕܒܫܡܝܐ.

ܟܒ: ܣܓܝܐܐ ܢܐܡܪܘܢ ܠܝ ܒܗܘ ܝܘܡܐ: ܡܪܝ ܡܪܝ ܠܐ ܒܫܡܟ ܐܬܢܒܝܢ. ܘܒܫܡܟ ܫܐܕ̈ܐ ܐܦܩܢ. ܘܒܫܡܟ ܚܝ̈ܠܐ ܣܓܝ̈ܐܐ ܥܒܕܢ.

ܟܓ: ܘܗܝܕܝܢ ܐܘܕܐ ܠܗܘܢ: ܕܡܢ ܡܬܘܡ ܠܐ ܝܕܥܬܟܘܢ. ܐܙܠܘ ܠܟܘܢ ܡܢܝ ܦܠܚܝ ܥܘܠܐ.

ܟܕ: ܟܠ ܗܟܝܠ ܕܫܡܥ ܡܠܝ̈ ܗܠܝܢ ܘܥܒܕ ܠܗܝܢ. ܢܬܕܡܐ ܠܓܒܪܐ ܚܟܝܡܐ. ܗܘ ܕܒܢܐ ܒܝܬܗ ܥܠ ܫܘܥܐ.

ܟܗ: ܘܢܚܬ ܡܛܪܐ. ܘܐܬܘ ܢܗܪ̈ܘܬܐ. ܘܢܫܒ ܪ̈ܘܚܐ. ܘܐܬܛܪܝܘ ܒܗ ܒܒܝܬܐ ܗܘ. ܘܠܐ ܢܦܠ ܫܬܐܣܘ̈ܗܝ ܓܝܪ ܥܠ ܫܘܥܐ ܣܝܡܢ ܗܘ̈ܝ.

ܟܘ: ܘܟܠ ܡܢ ܕܫܡܥ ܡܠܝ̈ ܗܠܝܢ ܘܠܐ ܥܒܕ ܠܗܝܢ. ܢܬܕܡܐ ܠܓܒܪܐ ܣܟܠܐ. ܕܒܢܐ ܒܝܬܗ ܥܠ ܚܠܐ.

ܟܙ: ܘܢܚܬ ܡܛܪܐ. ܘܐܬܘ ܢܗܪ̈ܘܬܐ. ܘܢܫܒ ܪ̈ܘܚܐ. ܘܐܬܛܪܝܘ ܒܒܝܬܐ ܗܘ. ܘܢܦܠ. ܘܗܘܬ ܡܦܘܠܬܗ ܪܒܬܐ.

ܟܚ: ܘܗܘܐ ܕܟܕ ܫܠܡ ܝܫܘܥ ܡܠܝ̈ ܗܠܝܢ. ܬܡܝܗܝܢ ܗܘܘ ܟܢܫ̈ܐ ܥܠ ܡܠܦܢܘܬܗ.

29. Because he was teaching them as one having authority and not like their scribes and Pharisees.[17]

---

17 See Mt. 11:27, 28:18. Jesus spoke and taught from a direct inner knowledge of Scripture. He did not teach like the Scribes and Pharisees who followed the traditional manner of speaking by quoting the authorities from whom the traditions were being transmitted. His style of presentation was indeed rare and stunned the listeners. See Mt. 3:7, footnote 7 and p. A - 8, "The Pharisees." We may reasonably suppose that the teachings in Matt. 5-7 are the direct and spiritual ethics of Jesus himself, and not just those of the primitive church. It is also believed by some New Testament experts that these sayings (Matt 5-7) are not "a collection of unrelated sayings of diverse origins." These scholars also suggest that the utterances of Christ as a tradition were faithfully memorized, repeated and passed on among the churches. It is typical of Semitic peoples to memorize complete teachings and pass them on from one generation to another. Jesus taught in a deliberate poetic style so that his sayings could be remembered easily. See Mt. 8:20, footnote 11; also JESUS AND THE JUDAISM OF HIS TIME, Irving M. Zeitlin, Ch. 8, Jesus' Originality and Creative Genius, pp 99-100.

܂܂: ܡܟܝܟ ܐܢܐ ܕܥܘܗܝ ܠܗܕ ܢܚ ܡܝܠܟܐ. ܘܠܐ ܢܚ ܗܕܝܢܘܗܝ ܦܩܕܝܢ܂
_____

CHAPTER 8

JESUS HEALS A LEPER, THE CENTURION'S BOY AND SIMON'S MOTHER-IN-LAW

1. Now when he came down from the mountain, large crowds followed him.

2. And behold a leper came, prostrated himself before him, and said: My lord,[1] if you are willing, you can make me clean.

3. And Jesus reached out his hand, touched him and said: I do will it, be clean! And immediately his leprosy[2] was cleansed.

4. Then Jesus said to him: Look, you should not be telling everyone,[3] but go, show yourself to the priests and present an offering as Moses had commanded for a testimony to them.[4]

5. Now when Jesus entered Capernaum, a centurion approached him, and he was imploring him,

6. And saying: My lord, my boy lies at home, paralyzed and suffering terribly.

7. Jesus said to him: I am coming and will heal him.

8. And this centurion answered and said: My lord, I do not deserve that you should enter under my roof;[5] but only say a word and my boy shall be healed.

9. Because I also am a man under authority and there are soldiers under my hand and I say to this one, Go, and he goes; and to another, Come, and he comes; and to my servant, Do this, and he does it.

10. Then when Jesus heard it, he was surprised and he said to those who were following him: Truly, I say to you that not even in Israel have I found faith like this!

---

1 ܡܪܐ, מרא, Mara, *sir, lord, master*. Used when addressing a superior. See p. A - 28, "The Aramaic Term - "Lord"; also Mt. 22:44-45, footnote 16.
2 The term "leprosy" in biblical days refers to a variety of skin disorders or afflictions. See Lev. 13:1-59.
3 Jesus avoided as much notoriety as possible. He also wanted the cleansed leper to comply with the Mosaic law, "but go, show yourself to the priests, etc." See Lev. 14:1-3.
4 Lev. 14:4-32.
5 The centurion, a Gentile, knew the Jewish tradition that any Jew entering a Gentile's house would be declared unclean. Thus, the centurion very politely asks Jesus to speak the word rather than enter his home. See Jn. 18:28 and Acts 10:28.

THE ARAMAIC TERM – "LORD"

The term "lord" was employed by the Eastern people of the first century C.E. in a very ordinary way. For example, a wife may call her husband "my lord"; a son also could call his father "my lord." It was used not only to address a superior or ruler but also to address an outstanding rabbi, teacher, holy man and a worker of miracles. . . . . (Continued on p. A-29)

A - 28

11. Now I say to you that many will come from the east and from the west and shall recline with Abraham, Isaac and Jacob in the kingdom of heaven.[6]

12. But the children of the kingdom shall go out into outer darkness; there will be crying and gnashing of teeth.[7]

13. Then Jesus said to the centurion: Go, it will be as you have believed! And his boy was healed in that very hour.

14. And Jesus came to Simon's home and saw his mother-in-law lying down and stricken by a fever.

15. Then he took hold of her hand and the fever left her and she stood up and was serving them.

16. Now when evening came, they brought before him many insane people and he freed them by the word; and all those who were terribly afflicted, he healed them.

17. So that what was spoken by the prophet Isaiah might be fulfilled who said: He will take away our pains and carry off our illnesses.[8]

18. Then when Jesus saw the large crowds surrounding him, he commanded that they should go to the crossing place.[9]

TESTING DISCIPLES

19. And a scribe[10] approached him and said to him: Teacher, I will follow you wherever you go.

---

6 This entire verse (11) points to a universal celebration. A "feast" or "celebration" prophetically represents the blessings of the Messiah's reign. Jesus refers to the Messianic banquet of the just which was to be extended to the entire Gentile world. According to Isaiah, the Messiah was to be a light to the Gentiles even to the ends of the earth. See Isa. 49:6.

7 Idiom: Disappointment, overwhelming regret, despair and rage.

8 Isa. 53:4.

9 ܥܒܪܐ, עברא, Aiwra, *shore, crossing place, land beyond the lake.* The eastern bank of the Lake of Tiberias (Sea of Galilee) which is located on the Syrian side.

10 ܣܦܪܐ, ספרא, Sapra, *scribe* - expert, versed in the law; a learned member of the Pharisees. Scribes made the systematic study of the law and its exposition their professional occupation.

ܝܐ: ܐܡܪ ܐܢܐ ܠܟܘܢ ܕܝܢ: ܕܣܓܝܐܐ ܢܐܬܘܢ ܡܢ ܡܕܢܚܐ ܘܡܢ ܡܥܪܒܐ. ܘܢܣܬܡܟܘܢ
ܥܡ ܐܒܪܗܡ ܘܐܝܣܚܩ ܘܝܥܩܘܒ ܒܡܠܟܘܬܐ ܕܫܡܝܐ.

ܝܒ: ܒܢܝܗ ܕܝܢ ܕܡܠܟܘܬܐ ܢܦܩܘܢ ܠܚܫܘܟܐ ܒܪܝܐ. ܬܡܢ ܢܗܘܐ ܒܟܝܐ ܘܚܘܪܩ ܫܢܐ.

ܝܓ: ܘܐܡܪ ܝܫܘܥ ܠܩܢܛܪܘܢܐ ܗܘ: ܙܠ. ܐܝܟܢܐ ܕܗܝܡܢܬ ܢܗܘܐ ܠܟ. ܘܐܬܐܣܝ
ܛܠܝܗ ܒܗ ܒܫܥܬܐ.

ܝܕ: ܘܐܬܐ ܝܫܘܥ ܠܒܝܬܗ ܕܫܡܥܘܢ. ܘܚܙܐ ܠܚܡܬܗ ܕܪܡܝܐ ܘܐܚܝܕܐ ܠܗ ܐܫܬܐ.

ܝܗ: ܘܩܪܒ ܠܐܝܕܗ ܘܫܒܩܬܗ ܐܫܬܐ. ܘܩܡܬ ܘܡܫܡܫܐ ܗܘܬ ܠܗܘܢ.

ܝܘ: ܟܕ ܗܘܐ ܕܝܢ ܪܡܫܐ. ܩܪܒܘ ܩܕܡܘܗܝ ܕܝܘܐ ܣܓܝܐܐ. ܘܐܦܩ ܕܝܘܝܗܘܢ ܒܡܠܬܐ.
ܘܠܟܠܗܘܢ ܐܝܠܝܢ ܕܒܝܫܐܝܬ ܥܒܝܕܝܢ ܗܘܘ ܐܣܝ ܗܘܐ.

ܝܙ: ܐܝܟ ܕܢܬܡܠܐ ܡܕܡ ܕܐܬܐܡܪ ܒܝܕ ܐܫܥܝܐ ܢܒܝܐ ܕܐܡܪ: ܕܗܘ ܢܣܒ ܟܘܪܗܢܝܢ
ܘܟܐܒܝܢ ܛܥܢ.

ܝܚ: ܟܕ ܚܙܐ ܕܝܢ ܝܫܘܥ ܟܢܫܐ ܣܓܝܐܐ ܕܚܕܪܝܢ ܠܗ. ܦܩܕ ܕܢܐܙܠܘܢ ܠܥܒܪܐ.

ܝܛ: ܘܩܪܒ ܣܦܪܐ ܚܕ ܘܐܡܪ ܠܗ: ܪܒܝ. ܐܬܐ ܐܢܐ ܒܬܪܟ ܠܐܝܟܐ ܕܐܙܠ ܐܢܬ.

(Continued from p. A - 28)

Jesus' disciples when speaking to their master used the term "lord." Matthew records this Aramaic form of address to include the teaching and religious aspects of Jesus' ministry and personality. Jewish historians consider Matthew's use of "lord" as more authentic and faithful to the original Aramaic genre of story-telling. The term "lord" was widely employed in the first century C.E. and is well attested by extra biblical evidence. See JESUS THE JEW, Geza Vermes, pp 103-128, "Jesus the lord."

20. Jesus said to him: Foxes have holes and the birds of the sky a shelter;[11] but this Human Being[12] has no place even to lay his head.[13]

21. Then another of his disciples said to him: My lord, first allow me to leave and bury my father.[14]

22. But Jesus said to him: Follow me and let the dead bury their dead.[15]

JESUS CALMS THE STORM

23. And when Jesus went up into the boat, his disciples went up with him.

---

11 Semitic style of poetry known as parallelism. See Mt. 7:6, footnote 2. According to New Testament experts there are five forms of parallelism: Synonymous as in Mt. 7:7-8; Antithetical - Mt. 7:17-18; Synthetic - Mt. 23:5-10; Climatic - Mt. 5:17; Chiasmic - Mt. 23:12. Eastern poetry is based on rhythm and not rhyme.

12 ܒܪܗ ܕܐܢܫܐ, ברה דאנשא, Breh dnasha, literally - *son of man*, but more accurately translated as *human being*. This term is used by Aramaic-speaking people in reference: 1) to mankind in general, 2) to an individual male, 3) to one whose identity is unknown, 4) to distinguish human beings from the animal creation. See Mt. 4:4, footnote 6. The demonstrative adjective "this" is used for clarification in the above verse (20). It is not present in the Aramaic text. Thus the translation of the term ܒܪܗ ܕܐܢܫܐ, Breh dnasha, "this Human Being" will be employed throughout the gospel of Matthew instead of "the son of man." Jesus most frequently referred to himself as Breh dnasha, "son of man." It is an indirect Aramaic style of speech when humbling oneself. In this manner, the Eastern speaker shows modesty and humility. Many New Testament scholars believe this expression "the son of man" to be a Messianic title, but this is debated among biblical experts. In any case, Jesus would not use a verbal Messianic title such as "son of man." It would have been dangerous for him to do so. He often forbid people to refer to him as the Messiah for this reason. It is interesting to note that the Hebrew term בן אדם, *Ben Adam* - "*son of man*" which is used in the book of Ezekiel refers to the prophet as "an ordinary human being." This expression in Hebrew emphasizes the mortal nature of man even when he has the privilege of beholding the glory of God. It also indicates that whatever spiritual height a human being may reach, he remains just "an ordinary man." Jesus, like Ezekiel, was expressing his humility. *Ben Adam* is often used as a poetic synonym for "man." "What is a man that You remember him, or a human being (Ben Adam or Bar-nasha) that You see after him." (Ps. 8:4, Aramaic text, Errico translation.) In Dan. 7:13, where it is a Chaldee (Aramaic) phrase, it signifies "a man."

13 Homeless.

14 Idiom: My father is very old and I must take care of him until he dies.

15 A troublesome verse to interpret. Among the Assyrian-Chaldean people there is an idiom still in use: *SHWOQ MEETHEH DQRY MEETHAY*. It is the same expression as Mt. 8:22, "... let the dead bury the dead," but the meaning today is *Don't become involved in other people's problems. Let them take care of their own difficulties*. Usually this advice is given to those people who do not mind their own business. Jesus could be saying, "Let others take care of their own problems. You follow me." There are many suggested interpretations of this difficult verse but one particular interpretation I have found helpful is "Let the community take care of your father." See GOSPEL LIGHT, Lamsa, pp 62-63.

ܟ: ܐܡܪ ܠܗ ܝܫܘܥ ܠܬܥܠܐ ܢܩܥܐ ܐܝܬ ܠܗܘܢ. ܘܠܦܪܚܬܐ ܕܫܡܝܐ ܡܛܠܠܐ.
ܠܒܪܗ ܕܝܢ ܕܐܢܫܐ ܠܝܬ ܠܗ ܐܝܟܐ ܕܢܣܡܘܟ ܪܫܗ.

ܟܐ: ܐܚܪܢܐ ܕܝܢ ܡܢ ܬܠܡܝܕܘܗܝ ܐܡܪ ܠܗ: ܡܪܝ ܐܦܣ ܠܝ ܠܘܩܕܡ. ܐܙܠ ܐܩܒܘܪ
ܐܒܝ.

ܟܒ: ܝܫܘܥ ܕܝܢ ܐܡܪ ܠܗ: ܬܐ ܒܬܪܝ. ܘܫܒܘܩ ܠܡܝܬܐ ܕܩܒܪܝܢ ܡܝܬܝܗܘܢ.

ܟܓ: ܘܟܕ ܣܠܩ ܝܫܘܥ ܠܣܦܝܢܬܐ. ܣܠܩܘ ܥܡܗ ܬܠܡܝܕܘܗܝ.

24. And behold, a violent motion occurred in the sea,[16] so much so that the boat was covered by the waves; but Jesus was napping.[17]

25. And his disciples touched him, awakening him and saying: Our lord, save us, we are perishing!

26. Jesus said to them: Why are you fearful, you of little faith! Then he stood up and rebuked the wind and the sea; and there was a great calm.

27. Now the men were amazed saying: Who is this man that the winds and the sea obey him?

THE MANIACS OF GADARA

28. And when Jesus came to the other side, to the country of the Gadarenes,[18] he was met by two maniacs coming out of the cemetery[19] and they were so dangerous that no one was able to pass by that road.

---

16 The Lake of Galilee lying deep among precipitous mountains is exposed, like all mountain lakes, to sudden gusts of wind from all sides, which sweep down the valleys and violently agitate the waters.

17 Take note of the contrasts and the subtle humor: the "violent" wind storm, the "fearful" and "perishing" disciples and the "napping" Jesus. In the book of Jonah, we have almost the same description: "The LORD (Yahweh) sent out a *violent wind* into the sea, and there was a *terrible tempest* in the sea, so that the ship was in danger of being broken. Then the mariners were afraid and cried every man to his god, ... But Jonah had gone down into the inner hold of the ship and was lying down *snoring*." Jonah 1:4-5, Peshitta Text, Errico translation. In the Hebrew text of the prophet Jonah, the telling of the story in the humorous form is clearer: "But as for YHWH (the LORD), He *hurled* a powerful wind to the sea and a raging tempest was in the sea; but as for the ship, it planned to break itself up. And the sailors were afraid and each man cried out to his god and they *hurled* the cargo which was on the ship into the sea. But as for Jonah, he went down to the hold of the ship and he laid down and he snored. Then the captain approached him and said to him: What is the matter with you; Oh snoring one? Get up! Cry out to your God! Perhaps, the God may turn to take notice of us so that we shall not perish." Jonah 1:4-6, Biblia Hebraica, Stuttgartensia, Errico translation.

18 Gadara, a city in Syria. Also one of the cities of the Decapolis (the ten cities - see Mt. 4:25, footnote 23), about 6 miles southeast of the Lake of Galilee.

19 Institutions for the mentally ill were unknown in the East and in many areas are still unknown. The insane roam about the towns and live in cemeteries or in uninhabited places such as old ruins.

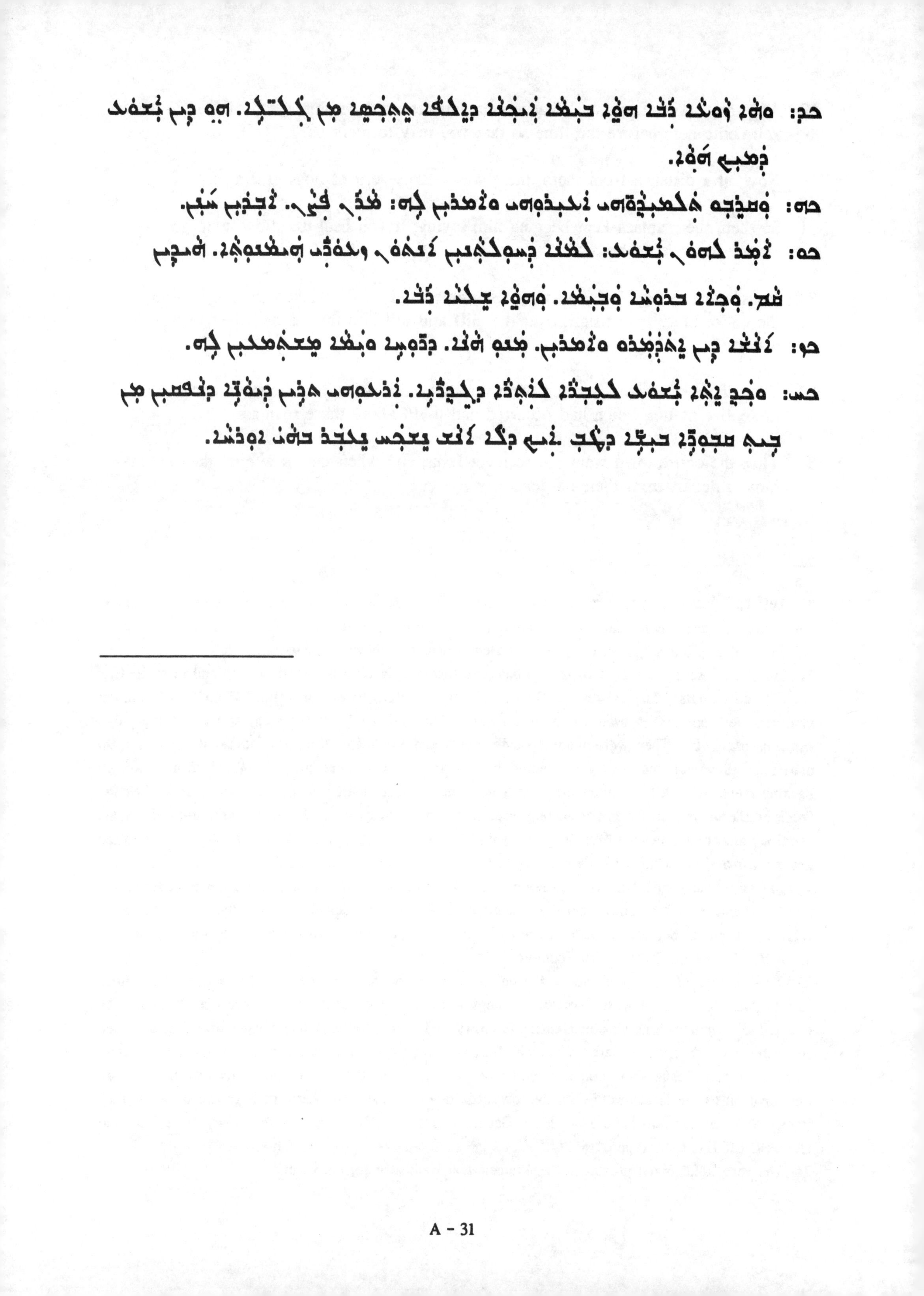

حز: .

29. And they shouted saying: What is your business with us, Jesus, son of God?[20] Have you come here before the time so that you may torment us?[21]

30. Now, at a distance from them, there was a large herd of hogs grazing.

31. So then, the maniacs kept begging him saying: If you heal us, allow us to go among the herd of hogs.

32. Jesus said to them: Go! And they left immediately and attacked the hogs. And the entire herd[22] went right over the cliff and fell into the sea and died in the waters.[23]

33. Then those who were herding them ran away and went into the town and related the entire matter which had occurred and told[24] about those maniacs.

34. Thus the entire town went out to meet Jesus; and when they saw him, they urged him to depart from their borders.

---

20 ܒܪ ܕܐܠܗܐ, Bar dalaha, *son of God* has various meanings in Aramaic which are not just theological. The meaning depends on context. In verse 29, the term "son of God" is indicative of a gifted holy one, i.e., a man of God, a healer. See Mt. 3:17, footnote 18.

21 Since the insane were free to roam about the towns, they were constantly teased and tormented by certain individuals. The expression "before the time" refers to evening time, when these roaming madmen were sometimes used for entertainment at special meals of the rich, noble and even high ranking officials. They were made to sing, curse and say many things to amuse the guests. On occasions, they were physically tormented by young men who were present. When men or women became mentally sick, they were taken to a holy man, priest, healer or a sacred shrine for their cure. Some of the ancient methods for healing were crude and in many cases the insane were tortured. Some religious men recommended branding them with a hot iron and the extremely violent were buried in the ground for a short while with an opening left so that they could breathe. Therefore, the mentally ill were afraid of holy men, healers or religious men. Jesus never resorted to such torturous treatments.

22 The expression "the entire herd" is an amplification; i.e., an embellishment which is typical when relating an event. See Mk. 1:33, "And *the entire city* was gathered at the door." Also Mt. 2:3, footnote 5; Mt. 13:34, footnote 7; Mt. 21:10, footnote 7.

23 This section of the narrative is difficult to understand and has become the subject of various interpretations. According to Mosaic law, hogs were considered unclean and were not allowed to be touched or eaten. Jesus was in Gentile territory and evidently in a hog raising town. It has been suggested by a biblical expert on ancient Eastern customs that the insane men destroyed the pigs to demonstrate to Jesus their sincerity and true conversion to the Jewish faith since swine were an abomination to the Israelites. When the townsfolk saw that "the entire herd" of hogs had drowned, they immediately decided to have Jesus leave Gadara (verse 34). See "Entering the Hogs," p. A - 32 and GOSPEL LIGHT, Lamsa, pp 64-66.

24 The verb "told" is not present in the Aramaic text I added it for clarification.

ܟܛ: ܘܩܥܘ ܘܐܡܪܝܢ: ܡܐ ܠܢ ܘܠܟ ܝܫܘܥ ܒܪܗ ܕܐܠܗܐ. ܐܬܝܬ ܠܟܐ ܩܕܡ ܙܒܢܐ
ܕܬܫܢܩܢ.

ܠ: ܐܝܬ ܗܘܐ ܕܝܢ ܠܘܬ ܛܘܪܐ ܒܩܪܐ ܕܚܙܝܪܐ ܣܓܝܐܐ ܕܪܥܝܐ.

ܠܐ: ܗܢܘܢ ܕܝܢ ܫܐܕܐ ܒܥܝܢ ܗܘܘ ܡܢܗ ܘܐܡܪܝܢ: ܐܢ ܡܦܩ ܐܢܬ ܠܢ ܐܦܣ ܠܢ ܕܢܐܙܠ
ܠܒܩܪܐ ܕܚܙܝܪܐ.

ܠܒ: ܐܡܪ ܠܗܘܢ ܝܫܘܥ ܙܠܘ ܘܡܚܕܐ ܢܦܩܘ ܘܥܠܘ ܒܚܙܝܪܐ. ܘܟܠܗ ܒܩܪܐ ܗܝ
ܪܗܛܬ ܠܫܩܝܦܐ. ܘܢܦܠܘ ܒܝܡܐ ܘܡܝܬܘ ܒܡܝܐ.

ܠܓ: ܗܢܘܢ ܕܝܢ ܕܪܥܝܢ ܗܘܘ ܥܪܩܘ. ܘܐܙܠܘ ܠܡܕܝܢܬܐ. ܘܚܘܝܘ ܟܠ ܡܕܡ ܕܗܘܐ
ܘܕܗܢܘܢ ܕܫܐܕܐ.

ܠܕ: ܘܢܦܩܬ ܟܠܗ ܡܕܝܢܬܐ ܠܐܘܪܥܗ ܕܝܫܘܥ. ܘܟܕ ܚܙܝܘܗܝ ܒܥܘ ܡܢܗ. ܕܢܫܢܐ
ܡܢ ܬܚܘܡܗܘܢ.

ENTERING THE HOGS

"It is interesting to know that Eastern people still believe that every sickness is caused and controlled by demons. This crude belief is no doubt due to the fact that the actual causes of diseases were not known. Such beliefs in demonology are found not only among Semites but among all people living even today under primitive conditions in Asia . . . We are, however, grateful to science and truth for demonstrating that diseases are due to physical and nervous disorders, delusions and fears, and have nothing to do with demons and evil spirits. There are other instances which cause confusion when (Aramaic words or expressions) are taken literally. The Aramaic AL (ܥܠ) means "enter into," "attack," "chase"; but it has been exclusively translated "enter into," so as to imply, as in Matthew 8:31, that the demons entered into the swine. According to the context and the style of Aramaic speech, the word here means that, not the demons but the lunatics attacked the swine. These lunatics were Syrians or Gadarenes, whose people kept swine, which was an abomination to the Jews. Jesus was a Jewish prophet. As a mark of appreciation of what Jesus was doing for them and as a proof of their conversion, these lunatics were willing to destroy the herd of swine which belonged to their people. This was doubtless one reason why the owners of the swine got into a panic and "urged" Jesus to leave their land, lest their business be completely destroyed by more conversions to the Jewish faith. On the other hand, the demons did not need Jesus' permission to enter into the swine any more than they needed any permission to enter into the lunatics." INTRODUCTION TO THE GOSPELS FROM ARAMAIC, George M. Lamsa, pp 13-14, 1933.

CHAPTER 9

JESUS HEALS A PARALYTIC

1. Then he went up into the boat and crossed over and came to his own town.[1]

2. They brought to him a paralytic lying on a bedroll.[2] And Jesus saw their faith and said to the paralytic: Be consoled, my son, your sins are forgiven[3] you.

3. Then some of the scribes said among themselves: This person blasphemes![4]

4. But Jesus knew their thoughts and he said to them: Why are you thinking evil in your hearts?

5. Because which is simpler to say, your sins are forgiven you or to say, stand up and walk?

6. But that you may know that this Human Being[5] has authority on earth to forgive sins; then he said to the paralytic: Stand up, pick up your bedroll and go to your home.

7. And he stood up and went to his home.

8. Then when the crowds saw it, they were in awe and praised God[6] because He gave such authority as this to human beings.[7]

---

1 See Mt. 4:13. Jesus had left Nazareth to live in Capernaum. Today there is no trace of Capernaum except some ruins on the northwest bank of the Lake of Galilee. Capernaum was called Jesus' hometown because scholars think he lived there for eighteen months, half of his ministerial life. Geographically, it was very important because the city served as a bridge into the Jewish world. Gentiles came from Asia Minor and mingled with the Jews of Palestine and this created an atmosphere of open-mindedness to the new teaching.

2 Generally composed of a quilt and one or two small rugs. The bedroll was also used for reclining while eating or conversing.

3 In Judaism at that time, it was believed that sickness was a consequence of sin. Hence a prayer for forgiveness must precede a prayer for healing. But Jesus deviated from the usual form by directly forgiving the paralytic's wrongs (sins).

4 An individual could forgive any sin or wrong committed against himself but not for others.

5 See Mt. 4:4, footnote 5 and particularly Mt. 8:20, footnote 12; also for the Galilean Aramaic usage of "son of man" I recommend JESUS THE JEW, pp 160-191, "Jesus the son of man" and JESUS AND THE WORLD OF JUDAISM, pp 89-99, "The Present State of the Son of Man Debate," by Geza Vermes.

6 On such a momentous occasion people would shout praises to God and recite a blessing.

7 The Aramaic word ܒܢܝܢܫܐ, בנינשא, Bnaynasha is the plural form of ܒܪܢܫܐ, בר נשא, Bar-nasha, and means *human beings, mortals, humankind.* See the above footnote 5, "Son of Man."

ܡܬܝ: ܛ.

ܐ: ܘܣܠܩ ܠܣܦܝܢܬܐ. ܘܥܒܪ ܠܡܕܝܢܬܗ.

ܒ: ܘܩܪܒܘ ܠܗ ܡܫܪܝܐ ܟܕ ܪܡܐ ܒܥܪܣܐ. ܘܚܙܐ ܝܫܘܥ ܗܝܡܢܘܬܗܘܢ. ܘܐܡܪ ܠܗܘ ܡܫܪܝܐ: ܐܬܠܒܒ ܒܪܝ. ܡܫܬܒܩܝܢ ܠܟ ܚܛܗܝܟ.

ܓ: ܐܢܫܐ ܕܝܢ ܡܢ ܣܦܪܐ ܐܡܪܘ ܒܢܦܫܗܘܢ: ܗܢܐ ܡܓܕܦ.

ܕ: ܝܫܘܥ ܕܝܢ ܝܕܥ ܡܚܫܒܬܗܘܢ. ܘܐܡܪ ܠܗܘܢ: ܠܡܢܐ ܡܬܚܫܒܝܢ ܐܢܬܘܢ ܒܝܫܬܐ ܒܠܒܟܘܢ.

ܗ: ܐܝܕܐ ܓܝܪ ܦܫܝܩܐ ܠܡܐܡܪ. ܕܡܫܬܒܩܝܢ ܠܟ ܚܛܗܝܟ. ܐܘ ܠܡܐܡܪ. ܩܘܡ ܗܠܟ.

ܘ: ܕܬܕܥܘܢ ܕܝܢ ܕܫܘܠܛܢܐ ܐܝܬ ܠܒܪܗ ܕܐܢܫܐ ܒܐܪܥܐ ܠܡܫܒܩ ܚܛܗܐ. ܐܡܪ ܠܗܘ ܡܫܪܝܐ. ܩܘܡ ܫܩܘܠ ܥܪܣܟ. ܘܙܠ ܠܒܝܬܟ.

ܙ: ܘܩܡ ܐܙܠ ܠܒܝܬܗ.

ܚ: ܟܕ ܚܙܘ ܕܝܢ ܟܢܫܐ ܕܚܠܘ. ܘܫܒܚܘ ܠܐܠܗܐ ܕܝܗܒ ܫܘܠܛܢܐ ܐܝܟ ܗܢܐ ܠܒܢܝܢܫܐ.

MATTHEW BECOMES A DISCIPLE

9. And when Jesus passed from there, he saw a man sitting at the tax office whose name was Matthew,[8] and he said to him: Follow me! Then he stood up and went after him.

10. And while reclining[9] at home,[10] many tax collectors and sinners[11] came and were reclining with Jesus and with his disciples.

11. But when the Pharisees saw it, they were saying to his disciples: Why is your teacher eating with tax collectors and sinners?[12]

12. Now when Jesus heard it, he said to them: The healthy do not need a doctor[13] but those who are very sick.

13. Go, learn[14] what this means: Compassion do I desire and not animal sacrifices;[15] because I have not come to invite the just but sinners.

---

8 According to Mk. 2:14 and Lk. 5:27-29, Matthew has another name, Levi. The name ܡܬܝ, מתי, Mattay is Aramaic and it means *the gift of Yahweh (God)*. It is suggested by some biblical scholars that the Apostle Matthew, being literate, was the writer and collector of the sayings and miracles of Jesus. But he was not the author of the final (edition) manuscript of the gospel of Matthew which appears in the New Testament. See "Authorship and Date," p. A - 1; THE NEW JEROME BIBLICAL COMMENTARY, 1990, p. 649; GOSPEL LIGHT, Lamsa, pp 1-4.

9 I.e., reclining and eating.

10 According to Lk. 5:29 it was Matthew's home.

11 Tax collectors were rejected and despised because of their oppressive and cruel ways. They collected tax on salt, property, livestock and certain export and import goods. The common people were at the mercy of the dishonest tax collectors who accepted bribes, took undue taxes and used excessive force and violence in their extraction of payment. At times they made public examples of people who could not pay. Property was confiscated and the men in the family were stripped and severely beaten. This made it easier to collect taxes from others. In the East tax collectors' bread was known as the "bread of blood." During this period the religious body and the general populace connected them with sinners and harlots.

12 It was difficult for the Pharisees to eat with tax collectors and sinners because of their strict observance of the laws of purification. These tax collectors and sinners were not versed in those laws nor did they care to practice them. See Mt. 3:7, footnote 8 and "The Pharisees," p. A - 8.

13 ܐܣܝܐ, אסיא, Asya, - *healer, physician*. The term "doctor" does not mean a medical doctor as we understand the meaning today. The ancient Eastern "doctor" comforted the ill, discussed their difficulty, inquired as to their moral and physical state, encouraged them with prayer and suggested fasts. There was another class of "doctors" who mended broken bones and used herbs on wounds. Many people preferred to consult with priests, holy men and seers for their afflictions.

14 A Semitic expression used particularly in language of debate or in challenge.

15 Hosea 6:6.

ܛ: ܘܟܕ ܥܒܪ ܝܫܘܥ ܡܢ ܬܡܢ. ܚܙܐ ܓܒܪܐ ܕܝܬܒ ܒܝܬ ܡܟܣܐ ܕܫܡܗ ܡܬܝ. ܘܐܡܪ ܠܗ: ܬܐ ܒܬܪܝ. ܘܩܡ ܐܙܠ ܒܬܪܗ.

ܝ: ܘܟܕ ܣܡܝܟܝܢ ܒܒܝܬܐ. ܣܓܝܐܐ ܡܟܣܐ ܘܚܛܝܐ ܐܬܘ ܣܡܟܘ ܥܡ ܝܫܘܥ ܘܥܡ ܬܠܡܝܕܘܗܝ.

ܝܐ: ܘܟܕ ܚܙܘ ܦܪܝܫܐ. ܐܡܪܝܢ ܠܬܠܡܝܕܘܗܝ: ܠܡܢܐ ܥܡ ܡܟܣܐ ܘܚܛܝܐ ܐܟܠ ܪܒܟܘܢ.

ܝܒ: ܝܫܘܥ ܕܝܢ ܟܕ ܫܡܥ ܐܡܪ ܠܗܘܢ: ܠܐ ܣܢܝܩܝܢ ܚܠܝܡܐ ܠܐܣܝܐ. ܐܠܐ ܐܝܠܝܢ ܕܒܝܫܐܝܬ ܥܒܝܕܝܢ.

ܝܓ: ܙܠܘ ܝܠܦܘ ܡܢܘ: ܚܢܢܐ ܨܒܐ ܐܢܐ ܘܠܐ ܕܒܚܬܐ. ܠܐ ܓܝܪ ܐܬܝܬ ܕܐܩܪܐ ܠܙܕܝܩܐ. ܐܠܐ ܠܚܛܝܐ.

14. Then the disciples of John approached him, asking: Why do we and the Pharisees fast much and your disciples do not fast?

15. Jesus said to them: Can the guests of the wedding feast fast as long as the groom is with them? But the days are coming when the groom will be taken from them and they shall fast.

16. No one sews a new patch on an old garment because the new patch will pull away from that garment and make the hole larger.[16]

17. And they do not pour new wine into worn out skins,[17] otherwise the skins will burst and the wine run out and the skins are ruined. But they pour new wine into new skins and both are preserved.

JESUS RAISES JARIUS' DAUGHTER
AND HEALS
A WOMAN WITH A HEMORRHAGING MALADY

18. Then while he was discussing these things with them, there came a certain leader[18] who drew near, bowed before him and said: My daughter has just died, but come, place your hand on her, and she will live.

19. And Jesus got up and his disciples followed him.

20. Then behold, a woman who had been hemorrhaging twelve years[19] came from behind him and touched the hem[20] of his outer garment.

21. Because she was telling herself, If I can only touch his garment, I will be healed.

---

16 Jesus' teaching of the Law and Prophets contradicted the traditions and teachings of the Elders. A new "garment" (understanding) was needed because one cannot patch old traditions with new teachings.
17 "Skins" mean goat hide which is still used today in the East as a bottle or container. The insides of the goat are removed, the legs are tied together and an opening is made in the neck. The Assyrian people in Northern Iraq still carry water, wine, milk and other liquids in goat skins. Bedouins churn milk in the goat skins to make butter.
18 According to Mk. 5:21-23 and Lk. 8:40-42 the man's name was Jarius, the head of an assembly, the synagogue or perhaps the Sanhedrin. (The Sanhedrin was an assembly of 71 ordained scholars who functioned both as Supreme Court and as legislature.)
19 A woman who had suffered from hemorrhages during a twelve year period.
20 See also Mt. 14:36, footnote 15. Easterners believed that the blue fringe on the garment of a holy man possessed healing powers. The color blue and the knotting of the fringes were prescribed by Moses. See Num. 15:38-40.

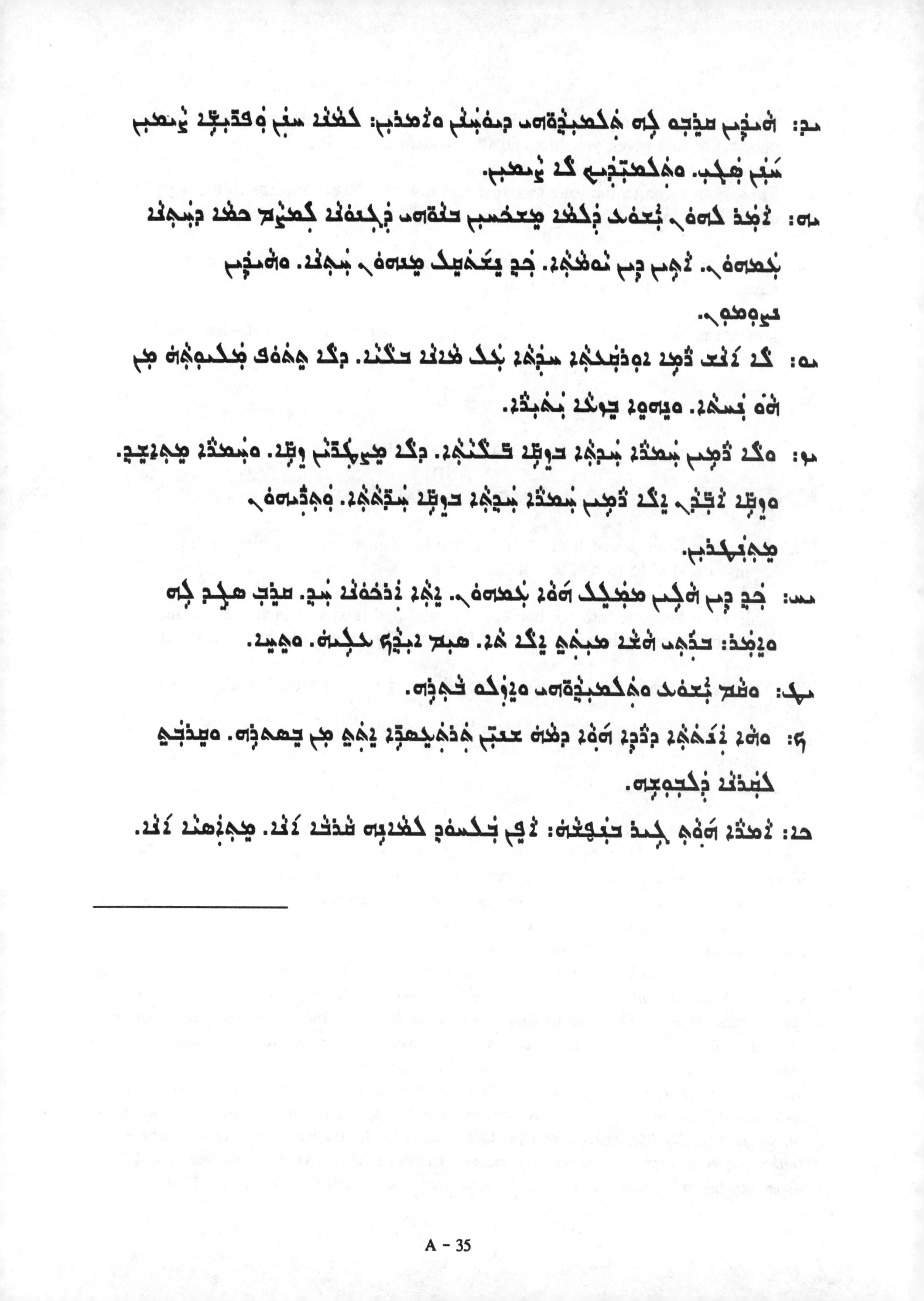

مج: .

22. Then Jesus turned around, looked at her and said to her: Be brave, my daughter, your faith[21] has given you life; and that woman was healed instantly.

23. Then Jesus came to the leader's home and saw the singers and the disorderly crowds[22]

24. And he said to them: Go away; because the little girl has not died, but she is sleeping. Then they ridiculed him.

25. And when he sent the crowds away, he entered and held her by the hand and the little girl stood up.

26. And this news spread all over that area.

JESUS HEALS TWO BLIND MEN
AND
A DEMENTED DEAF-MUTE

27. And when Jesus passed through there, two blind men followed him, crying out and saying: Be kind to us, Oh son of David![23]

28. And when he came into the house, the same blind men approached him. Jesus said to them: Do you believe[24] that I can do this? They replied to him: Yes, our lord.

29. Then he touched their eyes and said: According to your faith it shall be to you!

---

21 ܗܝܡܢܘܬܐ, הימנותא, Haymanootha. In Hebrew Scripture, the word means *firmness, truth, faithfulness*. In its usage in the New Testament, the word also means *faith, religion, creed, belief*. It comes from the Aramaic root word ܐܡܢ, אמן, Amen, meaning *to make firm*.

22 At the time of death, Eastern people expressed their overwhelming grief with very moving and emotional songs of lamentation. Sometimes the wailing would be so great and the lamenting so deep that hysteria and disorder would result.

23 Usually the term "son of David" refers to the Messiah. See Mt. 1:1, footnote 3. But in this passage and in many others just like it, "son of David" does not necessarily mean that the supplicants were calling Jesus the actual blood son of King David or the Messiah. The term was sometimes used as an expression of admiration and deep respect which was paid to healers of great reputation and men of renown. Easterners often call valiant men the sons of famous kings and noble men of the past. This was a great honor to be called "son of David." The blind men who wanted to be healed were asking for mercy and compassion from the Teacher-Healer whose fame had spread everywhere. See Mt. 20:30.

24 ܡܗܝܡܢܝܢ, מהימנין, Mhaymneen from ܡܗܝܡܢܐ, מהימנא, Mhaymnah and means *to believe, have faith, have confidence in, to be faithful, trusted*. It comes from the Aramaic root word ܐܡܢ, אמן, Amen meaning *to make firm, to be constant, persevere, persist, steadfast*. See footnote 21.

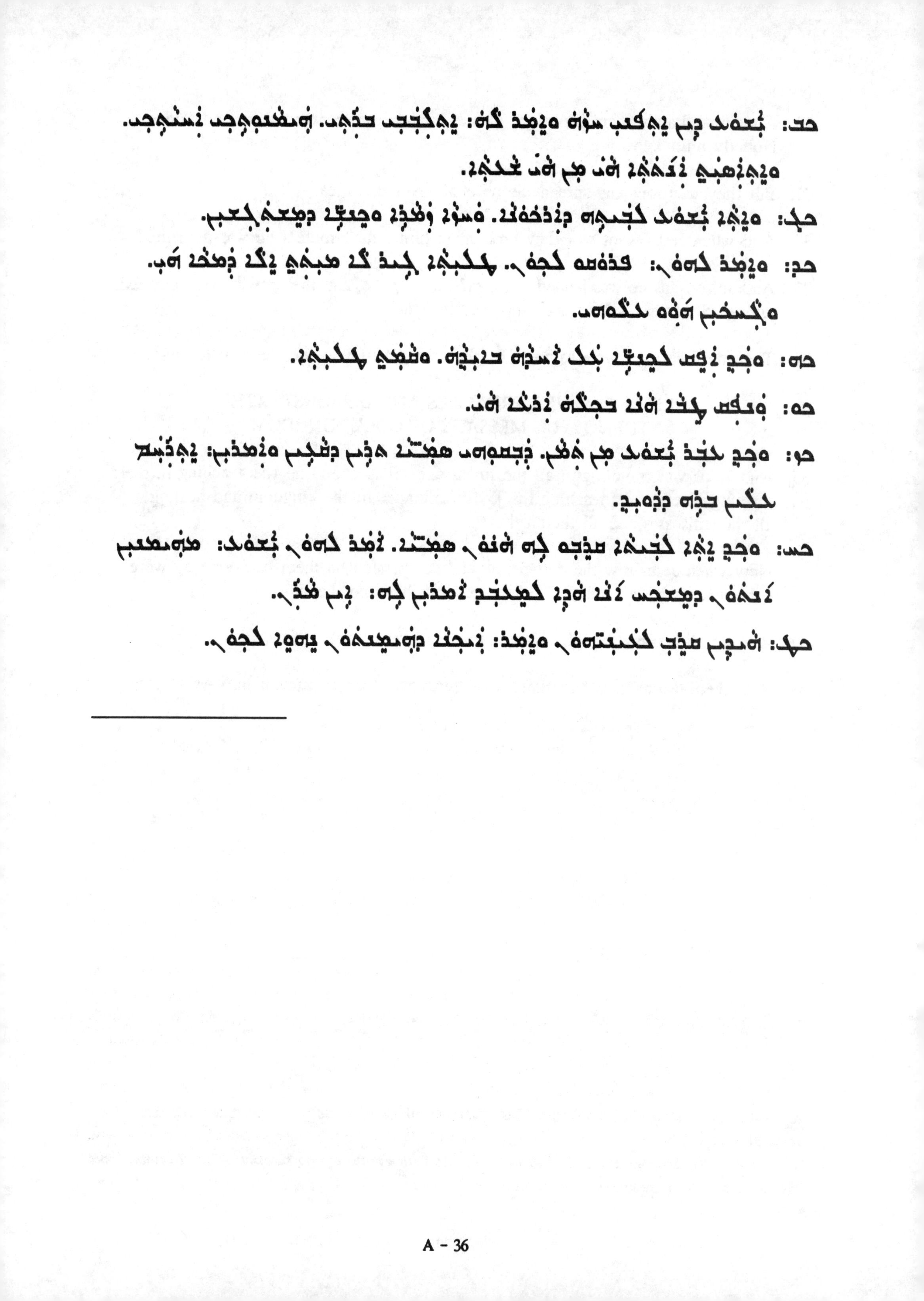

ܟܒ: ܝܫܘܥ ܕܝܢ ܐܬܦܢܝ ܚܙܗ̇ ܘܐܡܪ ܠܗ̇: ܐܬܠܒܒܝ ܒܪܬܝ. ܗܝܡܢܘܬܟܝ ܐܚܝܬܟܝ.
ܘܐܬܚܠܡܬ ܐܢܬܬܐ ܗܝ ܡܢ ܗܝ ܫܥܬܐ.

ܟܓ: ܘܐܬܐ ܝܫܘܥ ܠܒܝܬܗ ܕܪܒܟܢܘܫܬܐ. ܘܚܙܐ ܙܡܪܐ ܘܟܢܫܐ ܕܡܬܥܓܠܝܢ.

ܟܕ: ܘܐܡܪ ܠܗܘܢ: ܦܪܘܩܘ ܠܟܘܢ. ܛܠܝܬܐ ܓܝܪ ܠܐ ܡܝܬܬ ܐܠܐ ܕܡܟܐ ܗܝ.
ܘܓܚܟܝܢ ܗܘܘ ܥܠܘܗܝ.

ܟܗ: ܘܟܕ ܐܦܩ ܠܟܢܫܐ ܥܠ ܐܚܕܗ̇ ܒܐܝܕܗ̇. ܘܩܡܬ ܛܠܝܬܐ.

ܟܘ: ܘܢܦܩ ܛܒܐ ܗܢܐ ܒܟܠܗ̇ ܐܪܥܐ ܗܝ.

ܟܙ: ܘܟܕ ܥܒܪ ܝܫܘܥ ܡܢ ܬܡܢ. ܢܩܦܘܗܝ ܣܡܝܐ ܬܪܝܢ ܕܩܥܝܢ ܘܐܡܪܝܢ: ܐܬܪܚܡ
ܥܠܝܢ ܒܪܗ ܕܕܘܝܕ.

ܟܚ: ܘܟܕ ܐܬܐ ܠܒܝܬܐ ܩܪܒܘ ܠܗ ܗܢܘܢ ܣܡܝܐ. ܐܡܪ ܠܗܘܢ ܝܫܘܥ: ܡܗܝܡܢܝܢ
ܐܢܬܘܢ ܕܡܫܟܚ ܐܢܐ ܗܕܐ ܠܡܥܒܕ ܐܡܪܝܢ ܠܗ: ܐܝܢ ܡܪܢ.

ܟܛ: ܗܝܕܝܢ ܩܪܒ ܠܥܝܢܝܗܘܢ ܘܐܡܪ: ܐܝܟܢܐ ܕܗܝܡܢܘܬܟܘܢ ܢܗܘܐ ܠܟܘܢ.

30. And immediately their eyes were opened. And Jesus charged them and said: Nobody must know.[25]

31. But they went out and spread the news all over that area.

32. And when Jesus went out, they brought to him a deaf-mute who was demented.

33. And as soon as he was healed, the deaf-mute spoke, and the crowds were amazed, saying: Never has it been seen this way in Israel!

34. Then the Pharisees were saying: By the prince of devils does he heal the insane.

JESUS TEACHES, PREACHES AND DEMONSTRATES THE JOYFUL MESSAGE OF GOD'S KINGDOM

35. And Jesus was traveling in all the towns and villages; and he was teaching in their meeting places and preaching the joyful assurance of the kingdom and healing all their diseases and all their pains.

36. Now when Jesus saw the crowds, he had compassion on them because they were exhausted and near collapse[26] like sheep that have no shepherd.

37. And he said to his disciples: The harvest is great, workers few;

38. Ask, then, the owner of the harvest to send out workers into his harvest.

---

25 Authentic healers shun publicity. But a miracle like this would be difficult to keep secret. See verse 31.

26 ܐܒܕ, שרין, Shren, – *to scatter, to be overcome with exhaustion, to succumb*. This Aramaic word has more than thirty meanings.

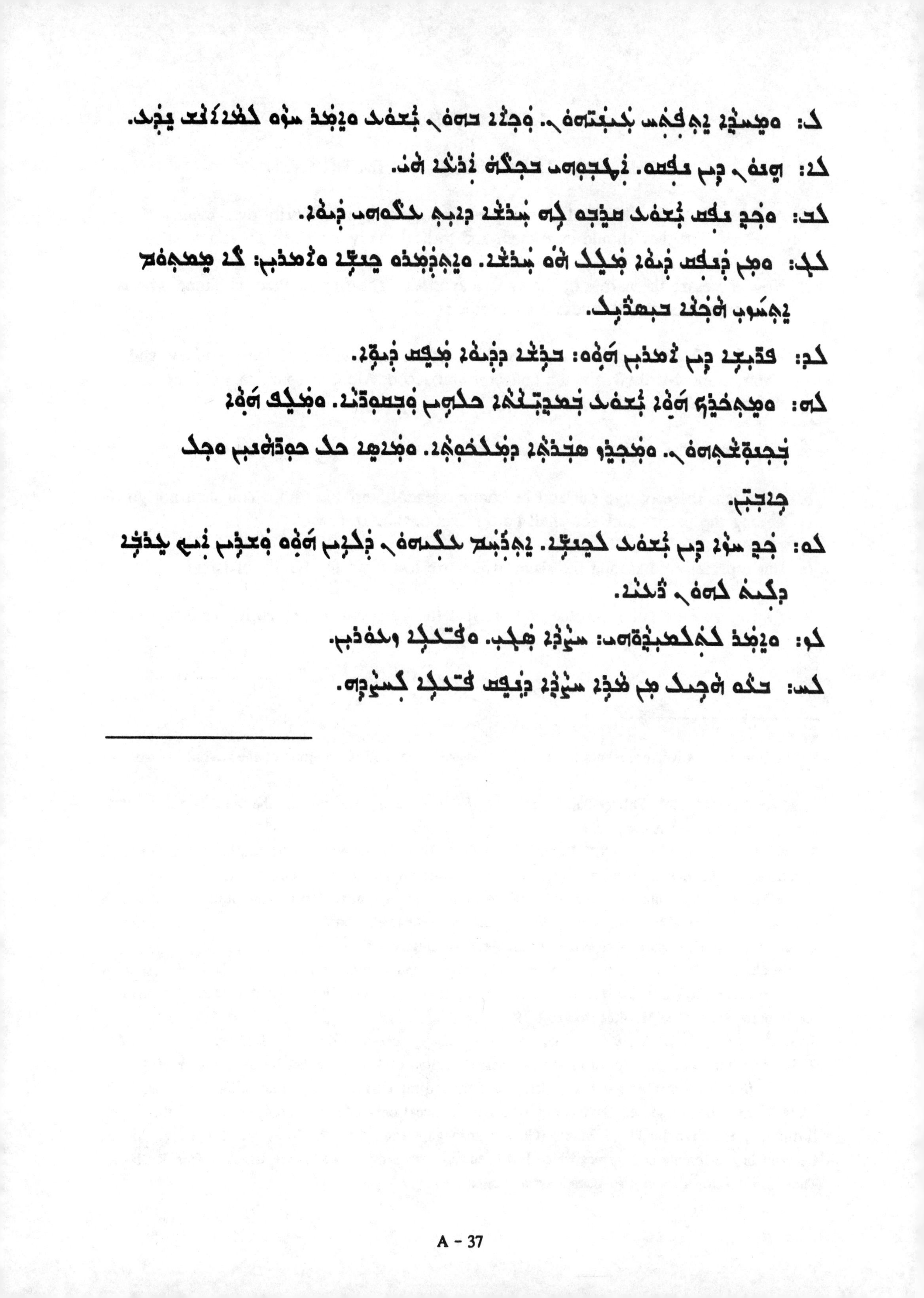

ܠ: ܘܐܬܦܬܚ ܥܝܢܝܗܘܢ. ܘܟܐܐ ܒܗܘܢ ܝܫܘܥ ܘܐܡܪ ܚܙܘ ܠܐ ܐܢܫ ܢܕܥ.

ܠܐ: ܗܢܘܢ ܕܝܢ ܢܦܩܘ. ܐܟܪܙܘܗܝ ܒܟܠܗ ܐܪܥܐ ܗܝ.

ܠܒ: ܘܟܕ ܢܦܩܘ ܗܢܘܢ ܩܪܒܘ ܠܗ ܚܪܫܐ ܕܐܝܬ ܒܗ ܫܐܕܐ.

ܠܓ: ܘܟܕ ܢܦܩ ܫܐܕܐ ܡܠܠ ܗܘ ܚܪܫܐ. ܘܐܬܕܡܪܘ ܟܢܫܐ ܘܐܡܪܝܢ: ܠܐ ܡܡܬܘܡ
ܐܬܚܙܝܬ ܗܟܢܐ ܒܐܝܣܪܝܠ.

ܠܕ: ܦܪܝܫܐ ܕܝܢ ܐܡܪܝܢ ܗܘܘ: ܕܒܪܫܐ ܕܫܐܕܐ ܡܦܩ ܫܐܕܐ.

ܠܗ: ܘܡܚܕܪ ܗܘܐ ܝܫܘܥ ܒܡܕܝܢܬܐ ܟܠܗܝܢ ܘܒܩܘܪܝܐ. ܘܡܠܦ ܗܘܐ
ܒܟܢܘܫܬܗܘܢ. ܘܡܟܪܙ ܣܒܪܬܐ ܕܡܠܟܘܬܐ. ܘܡܐܣܐ ܟܠ ܟܘܪܗܢ ܘܟܠ
ܟܐܒ.

ܠܘ: ܟܕ ܚܙܐ ܕܝܢ ܝܫܘܥ ܠܟܢܫܐ. ܐܬܪܚܡ ܥܠܝܗܘܢ. ܕܠܐܝܢ ܗܘܘ ܘܫܪܝܢ ܐܝܟ ܥܢܐ
ܕܠܝܬ ܠܗܘܢ ܪܥܝܐ.

ܠܙ: ܘܐܡܪ ܠܬܠܡܝܕܘܗܝ: ܚܨܕܐ ܣܓܝ. ܘܦܥܠܐ ܙܥܘܪܝܢ.

ܠܚ: ܒܥܘ ܗܟܝܠ ܡܢ ܡܪܐ ܚܨܕܐ ܕܢܦܩ ܦܥܠܐ ܠܚܨܕܗ.

CHAPTER 10

THE APOSTLES CHOSEN AND INSTRUCTED

1. And he summoned his twelve[1] disciples[2] and gave them authority over mental illnesses[3] that they should cure them and to heal every kind of pain and sickness.

2. Now these are the names of the twelve apostles: The first of them is Simon who is nicknamed Peter[4] and Andrew his brother;

3. And Jacob,[5] Zebedee's son and John his brother; and Philip and Bartholomew[6] and Thomas and Matthew, the tax collector and Jacob, Alpheus' son; and Lebbeus nicknamed Thaddeus.

4. And Simon the zealous and Judas of Iscariot, the same who betrayed him.

5. Jesus sent these twelve out and he commissioned them and said: You shall not go among the pagans and you shall not enter a Samaritan town.[7]

6. But especially go among the sheep which are lost from the family of Israel.

7. And as you are going, preach and say that the kingdom of heaven has arrived.

---

1 The number twelve represents the twelve tribes of Israel and is symbolic of the restoration work of the Messiah for all Israel.

2 ܬܠܡܝܕܐ, תלמידא, Talmeedha, - *student, disciple, pupil*. The root of the word is ܠܡܕ, למד, Lmad, - *to put together, compile, learn*.

3 ܪܘܚܐ ܛܢܦܬܐ, רוחא טנפתא, Rooḥeh Tanpatha, - literally *unclean spirits*; i.e., those who have evil intentions, inclinations, those with mental disorders, the unruly and insane. See Lk. 9:1.

4 See Mt. 4:18, footnote 17. Also Jn. 1:42, "And he brought him to Jesus. And Jesus looked at him and said: You are Simon, the son of Jonah, you are nicknamed Peter (Kepa - stone)." Aramaic text, Errico translation. Kepa is a nickname in the Aramaic language.

5 ܝܥܩܘܒ, יעקוב, Yaqob, *Jacob*. The name "James" found in most translations of the New Testament was a mistake. It was unknown in biblical languages. It was correctly translated as "Jacob" throughout the Hebrew Bible. See Mt. 4:21, footnote 19.

6 ܒܪ ܬܘܠܡܝ, בר תולמי, Bar Toolmay, *Son of Ptolemy - one who resembles Ptolemy*.

7 Samaria had been the capitol of the northern kingdom of Israel. In 721 B.C.E. the King of Assyria carried off the ten northern tribes of Israel and settled mixed races of people in Samaria. See 2 Ki. 17:24. These newly settled Samaritans (the mixed races) only adopted certain aspects of the Jewish faith; i.e., the five books of Moses (Genesis through Deuteronomy). They worshipped on Mount Gerizim in the temple and shrines which had been established by the dethroned Israelite King Jeroboam. They also developed their own priesthood and rituals.

ܦܪܩܐ: ܝ.

ܐ: ܘܩܪܐ ܠܬܪܥܣܪ ܬܠܡܝܕܘܗܝ. ܘܝܗܒ ܠܗܘܢ ܫܘܠܛܢܐ ܥܠ ܪܘ̈ܚܐ ܛܢ̈ܦܬܐ.
ܕܢܦܩܘܢ. ܘܠܡܐܣܝܘ ܟܠ ܟܘܪܗܢ ܘܟܘܪܗܢ.

ܒ: ܕܬܪܥܣܪ ܕܝܢ ܫܠܝܚ̈ܐ ܐܝܬܝܗܘܢ ܫܡܗ̈ܝܗܘܢ ܗܠܝܢ: ܩܕܡܝܐ ܫܡܥܘܢ
ܕܡܬܩܪܐ ܟܐܦܐ ܘܐܢܕܪܐܘܣ ܐܚܘܗܝ.

ܓ: ܘܝܥܩܘܒ ܒܪ ܙܒܕܝ ܘܝܘܚܢܢ ܐܚܘܗܝ. ܘܦܝܠܝܦܘܣ ܘܒܪ ܬܘܠܡܝ ܘܬܐܘܡܐ
ܘܡܬܝ ܡܟܣܐ. ܘܝܥܩܘܒ ܒܪ ܚܠܦܝ ܘܠܒܝ ܕܐܬܟܢܝ ܬܕܝ.

ܕ: ܘܫܡܥܘܢ ܩܢܢܝܐ ܘܝܗܘܕܐ ܣܟܪܝܘܛܐ ܗܘ ܕܐܫܠܡܗ.

ܗ: ܠܗܠܝܢ ܬܪܥܣܪ ܫܕܪ ܝܫܘܥ. ܘܦܩܕ ܐܢܘܢ ܘܐܡܪ: ܒܐܘܪܚܐ ܕܚܢ̈ܦܐ ܠܐ
ܬܐܙܠܘܢ. ܘܠܡܕܝܢܬܐ ܕܫܡܪ̈ܝܐ ܠܐ ܬܥܠܘܢ.

ܘ: ܐܙܠܘ ܕܝܢ ܝܬܝܪܐܝܬ ܠܘܬ ܥܢ̈ܐ ܕܐܒ̈ܝܕܝ ܡܢ ܒܝܬ ܐܝܣܪܝܠ

ܙ: ܘܟܕ ܐܙܠܝܢ ܐܢܬܘܢ ܐܟܪܙܘ ܘܐܡܪܘ: ܕܩܪܒܬ ܡܠܟܘܬܐ ܕܫܡܝܐ.

8. Heal the sick, cleanse the leper, cure the insane, freely you have received, freely give.[8]

9. Do not keep gold nor silver nor brass in your bags.[9]

10. Nor a carrying case[10] nor two coats, nor shoes,[11] nor a staff;[12] because a worker deserves his food.

11. So then, into whatever town or village you enter, ask who in it is reliable[13] and stay there until you leave.

12. And when you enter the home, greet the family with peace.

13. And if the family is reliable, your peace shall come upon it, and if, then, it is not reliable, your greeting shall return to you.

14. Now anyone who does not welcome you nor listens to your words when you leave the home or the village shake the dust from your feet.[14]

15. Truly I say to you that it will be more restful for the land of Sodom and Amorah[15] in the judgment day than for that city.

---

8 I.e., do not use your gifts for your own private advantage.

9 "Do not keep gold nor silver etc." signifies more than "don't carry money with you." It means do not go after or hoard any money. Accumulating money while the Apostles were traveling would have been dangerous for them because they would have become ready prey for thieves and road bandits. Hoarding money might have also created problems among the Apostles.

10 ܬܪܡܠܐ, תרמלא, Tarmala - a woven woolen bag, approximately 12" x 18" in size.

11 Once again Jesus has the safety of the Apostles in mind. The fewer material things they possessed, the fewer difficulties they would encounter.

12 ܫܒܛܐ, שׁבטא, Shawta, - staff. According to the gospel of Mark, Jesus permitted his Apostles to carry a staff which would be more in keeping with Eastern custom. (Mk. 6:8.) The Eastern proverb states, "The staff is a companion on the road." The staff was helpful for a traveler in climbing steep hills and crossing streams of water. It also served as a protection against snakes, vicious dogs and bandits.

13 That is, deserving of your confidence; devout and well-disposed.

14 The sign of an unfriendly home. Normally the dust would have been washed from their feet had they been welcomed into the home.

15 ܥܡܘܪܐ, עמורא, Amorah and not Gomorrah. The first letter of the word in Hebrew as well as Aramaic, is ע, ܥ, "a," Ayin, Ai, and not ג, ܓ, "g," Gimmel, Gamal.

س: .

د: .

16. Behold I am sending you like lambs among wolves; so be wise like snakes[16] and innocent like doves.[17]

17. Now be aware of people because they will hand you over to the courts[18] and will beat you in their meeting places.

18. And they will bring you before governors and kings because of me for a testimony to them and to the Gentiles.

19. But when they arrest you, do not be concerned about how or what you shall answer; because it will be given to you immediately what you are to speak.

20. Because it is not you who speaks but the spirit of your Father speaking through you.

21. Now a brother shall put his brother to death; and a father his son; and children shall betray their parents and have them put to death.

22. And everyone will be hating you because of my name, but he who endures to the end, shall live.

23. And when they persecute you in this city, flee to another; for truly I say to you, You shall not finish teaching in all the towns of Israel until this Human Being shall return.

24. There is no disciple more important than his teacher, and no servant than his owner.

25. It is enough for a disciple to be like his teacher and a servant like his owner. If then they have called the owner of the house, Beelzebub,[19] how much more the children of his household.

26. Do not, then, be afraid of them; because there is nothing covered that will not be revealed nor hidden that will not be known.

---

16 In simple language, "Be shrewd." When a snake is in danger, it coils and keeps its head in the center of its coil so that its head may be protected. "Be as wise as serpents" means be shrewd, guard your faith which protects you; don't be afraid of your enemy.

17 Doves are gentle and bring joy to people around them. The expression "innocent like doves" also means - Be kind, unassuming.

18 A religious court. See Mt. 5:21.

19 ܒܥܠܙܒܘܒ, בעליזבוב, Belzwow. Beelzebub was one of the Canaanite gods. The name "Beelzebub" became equal to satan. Also known as Baal-zebub, the "lord of the fly," or "lord of the high place," the god of Ekron, 2 Ki. 1:2. See Mt. 12:24, footnote 13.

ܝܘ: ܗܐ ܐܢܐ ܡܫܕܪ ܐܢܐ ܠܟܘܢ ܐܝܟ ܐܡܪܐ ܒܝܬ ܕܐܒܐ. ܗܘܘ ܗܟܝܠ ܚܟܝܡܐ ܐܝܟ
ܚܘܘܬܐ ܘܬܡܝܡܐ ܐܝܟ ܝܘܢܐ.

ܝܙ: ܐܙܕܗܪܘ ܕܝܢ ܡܢ ܒܢܝܢܫܐ. ܡܫܠܡܝܢ ܠܟܘܢ ܓܝܪ ܠܒܝܬ ܕܝܢܐ.
ܘܒܟܢܘܫܬܗܘܢ ܢܢܓܕܘܢܟܘܢ.

ܝܚ: ܘܩܕܡ ܗܓܡܘܢܐ ܘܡܠܟܐ ܡܩܪܒܝܢ ܠܟܘܢ ܡܛܠܬܝ ܠܣܗܕܘܬܐ ܕܝܠܗܘܢ
ܘܕܥܡܡܐ.

ܝܛ: ܡܐ ܕܝܢ ܕܡܫܠܡܝܢ ܠܟܘܢ. ܠܐ ܬܬܝܨܦܘܢ ܐܝܟܢܐ ܐܘ ܡܢܐ ܬܡܠܠܘܢ. ܡܬܝܗܒ
ܠܟܘܢ ܓܝܪ ܒܗ̇ ܒܫܥܬܐ ܡܢܐ ܕܬܡܠܠܘܢ.

ܟ: ܠܐ ܗܘܐ ܓܝܪ ܐܢܬܘܢ ܡܡܠܠܝܢ ܐܠܐ ܪܘܚܐ ܕܐܒܘܟܘܢ ܡܡܠܠܐ ܒܟܘܢ.

ܟܐ: ܢܫܠܡ ܕܝܢ ܐܚܐ ܠܐܚܘܗܝ ܠܡܘܬܐ ܘܐܒܐ ܠܒܪܗ. ܘܢܩܘܡܘܢ ܒܢܝܐ ܥܠ
ܐܒܗܝܗܘܢ. ܘܢܡܝܬܘܢ ܐܢܘܢ.

ܟܒ: ܘܬܗܘܘܢ ܣܢܝܢ ܡܢ ܟܠ ܐܢܫ ܡܛܠ ܫܡܝ. ܡܢ ܕܝܢ ܕܢܣܝܒܪ ܥܕܡܐ
ܠܫܘܠܡܐ ܗܘ ܢܚܐ.

ܟܓ: ܡܐ ܕܪܕܦܝܢ ܠܟܘܢ ܕܝܢ ܒܡܕܝܢܬܐ ܗܕܐ. ܥܪܘܩܘ ܠܟܘܢ ܠܐܚܪܬܐ. ܐܡܝܢ ܓܝܪ
ܐܡܪ ܐܢܐ ܠܟܘܢ: ܕܠܐ ܬܫܠܡܘܢ ܟܠܗܝܢ ܡܕܝܢܬܐ ܕܒܝܬ ܐܝܣܪܝܠ
ܥܕܡܐ ܕܢܐܬܐ ܒܪܗ ܕܐܢܫܐ.

ܟܕ: ܠܝܬ ܬܠܡܝܕܐ ܕܪܒ ܡܢ ܪܒܗ ܘܐܦܠܐ ܥܒܕܐ ܡܢ ܡܪܗ.

ܟܗ: ܣܦܩ ܠܗ ܠܬܠܡܝܕܐ ܕܢܗܘܐ ܐܝܟ ܪܒܗ. ܘܠܥܒܕܐ ܐܝܟ ܡܪܗ. ܐܢ ܠܡܪܗ
ܕܒܝܬܐ ܩܪܘ ܒܥܠܙܒܘܒ. ܟܡܐ ܠܒܢܝ ܒܝܬܗ.

ܟܘ: ܠܐ ܗܟܝܠ ܬܕܚܠܘܢ ܡܢܗܘܢ. ܠܝܬ ܓܝܪ ܡܕܡ ܕܟܣܐ ܕܠܐ ܢܬܓܠܐ.
ܘܕܡܛܫܝ ܕܠܐ ܢܬܝܕܥ.

27. Anything I tell you in the dark, you tell it in the light;[20] and the thing you hear in your ears, you preach it on the housetops.[21]

28. And do not be afraid of those who kill the body for they cannot kill the soul; but be especially afraid of the one who can destroy the body and soul in the fire of Gehenna.[22]

29. Are not two sparrows sold for a penny? And yet not one of them falls to the ground without the knowledge of your Father.

30. But as for you, even the hairs of your head are all counted.

31. Now then, do not be afraid, you are more important than many sparrows.

32. Everyone, then, who confesses me before people I shall confess him also before my Father who is in heaven.

33. But anyone who denies me before people I shall deny him also before my Father who is in heaven.

34. Do not imagine that I have come to bring peace on the earth; I have not come to bring peace but war.[23]

35. Because I have come to divide a man against his father and a daughter against her her mother and a daughter-in-law against her mother-in-law.

36. And a man's enemies are among his family.

37. Anyone who cares for a father or a mother more than me does not deserve me. And anyone who cares for a son or a daughter more than me does not deserve me.

---

20 Dark – nighttime; light – daytime.

21 Eastern custom: *"From the housetop the muleteer merchant shouts his wares; from the housetop men call one another for various purposes; from the housetop men appointed by the municipality to watch the vineyards proclaim the names of trespassers; and from that elevation the special orders of the governor of the district are proclaimed to the populace. By night or by day, whenever we heard a voice calling from a housetop, we instinctively listened . . . "* THE SYRIAN CHRIST, Abraham Rihbany, "The Housetop," p. 269.

22 Jesus' statement, "But be especially afraid of the one who can destroy the body and soul in the fire of Gehenna" means be acutely respectful of God who really has the power of life and death; don't be afraid of human beings who can only destroy the physical form. The "fire of Gehenna" is a metaphor referring to destruction. See Mt. 5:22, footnote 26.

23 ܚܪܒܐ, חרבא, Ḥarba, – *sword* as well as *war*. In either case, the word is used as a metaphor connoting "division."

ܟܙ: ܡܕܡ ܕܐܡܪ ܐܢܐ ܠܟܘܢ ܒܚܫܘܟܐ. ܐܡܪܘܗܝ ܐܢܬܘܢ ܒܢܘܗܪܐ. ܘܡܕܡ ܕܒܐܕܢܝ̈ܟܘܢ ܫܡܥܝܢ ܐܢܬܘܢ. ܐܟܪܙܘ ܥܠ ܐܓܪ̈ܐ.

ܟܚ: ܘܠܐ ܬܕܚܠܘܢ ܡܢ ܐܝܠܝܢ ܕܩܛܠܝܢ ܦܓܪܐ. ܢܦܫܐ ܕܝܢ ܠܐ ܡܫܟܚܝܢ ܠܡܩܛܠ. ܕܚܠܘ ܕܝܢ ܝܬܝܪ ܡܢ ܗܘ ܕܡܫܟܚ ܕܠܢܦܫܐ ܘܠܦܓܪܐ ܢܘܒܕ ܒܓܗܢܐ.

ܟܛ: ܠܐ ܬܪ̈ܝܢ ܨܦܪ̈ܝܢ ܡܙܕܒܢܢ ܒܐܣܪ. ܘܚܕ ܡܢܗܘܢ ܒܠܥܕ ܡܢ ܐܒܘܟܘܢ، ܠܐ ܢܦܠ ܥܠ ܐܪܥܐ.

ܠ: ܕܝܠܟܘܢ ܕܝܢ ܐܦ ܡܙ̈ܐ ܕܪܫܟܘܢ، ܟܠܗܘܢ ܡܢܝܢ ܐܢܘܢ.

ܠܐ: ܠܐ ܗܟܝܠ ܬܕܚܠܘܢ، ܡܢ ܨܦܪ̈ܐ ܣܓܝܐܬܐ ܡܝܬܪܝܢ ܐܢܬܘܢ.

ܠܒ: ܟܠ ܐܢܫ ܗܟܝܠ ܕܢܘܕܐ ܒܝ ܩܕܡ ܒܢܝ̈ ܐܢܫܐ. ܐܘܕܐ ܒܗ ܐܦ ܐܢܐ ܩܕܡ ܐܒܝ ܕܒܫܡܝܐ.

ܠܓ: ܡܢ ܕܝܢ ܕܢܟܦܘܪ ܒܝ ܩܕܡ ܒܢܝ̈ ܐܢܫܐ ܐܟܦܘܪ ܒܗ ܐܦ ܐܢܐ ܩܕܡ ܐܒܝ ܕܒܫܡܝܐ.

ܠܕ: ܠܐ ܬܣܒܪܘܢ ܕܐܬܝܬ ܕܐܪܡܐ ܫܝܢܐ ܒܐܪܥܐ. ܠܐ ܐܬܝܬ ܕܐܪܡܐ ܫܝܢܐ. ܐܠܐ ܚܪܒܐ.

ܠܗ: ܐܬܝܬ ܓܝܪ ܕܐܦܠܓ ܓܒܪܐ ܥܠ ܐܒܘܗܝ. ܘܒܪܬܐ ܥܠ ܐܡܗ. ܘܟܠܬܐ ܥܠ ܚܡܬܗ.

ܠܘ: ܘܒܥܠܕܒܒ̈ܘܗܝ ܕܓܒܪܐ ܒܢܝ̈ ܒܝܬܗ.

ܠܙ: ܡܢ ܕܪܚܡ ܐܒܐ ܐܘ ܐܡܐ ܝܬܝܪ ܡܢܝ. ܠܐ ܫܘܐ ܠܝ ܘܡܢ ܕܪܚܡ ܒܪܐ ܐܘ ܒܪܬܐ ܝܬܝܪ ܡܢܝ. ܠܐ ܫܘܐ ܠܝ.

---

38. And anyone who does not carry his cross[24] and follows me does not deserve me.

39. Anyone who is looking out for his life, shall lose it; and anyone who loses his life because of me shall find it.[25]

40. Anyone who welcomes you, welcomes me; and anyone who welcomes me, welcomes Him who sent me.

41. Anyone who welcomes a prophet in the name of a prophet, receives a prophet's reward; and anyone who welcomes a righteous man in the name of a righteous man, receives a righteous man's reward.

42. And anyone who gives a drink to one of these little ones,[26] if only a cup of cool water, in the name of a disciple, truly I say to you, that one shall never lose his reward.

---

24 Idiom: Be willing to endure suffering, hardships and even death if necessary.
25 The entire phrase is a play on words in Aramaic. Literally translated, it reads "Anyone who is finding his (self, life, being, soul) shall lose it; but anyone who loses his (self, life, being, soul) because of me shall find it." The word ܢܰܦܫܳܐ, נפשא, Nawsha means *being, self, life, soul*.
26 The expression "little ones" refers to Jesus' Apostles and disciples. See Mk. 9:41.

ܠܚ: ܘܟܠ ܕܠܐ ܫܩܠ ܙܩܝܦܗ ܘܐܬܐ ܒܬܪܝ. ܠܐ ܫܘܐ ܠܝ.

ܠܛ: ܡܢ ܕܐܫܟܚ ܢܦܫܗ. ܢܘܒܕܝܗ. ܘܡܢ ܕܢܘܒܕ ܢܦܫܗ ܡܛܠܬܝ. ܢܫܟܚܝܗ.

ܡ: ܡܢ ܕܡܩܒܠ ܠܟܘܢ. ܠܝ ܡܩܒܠ. ܘܡܢ ܕܠܝ ܡܩܒܠ. ܠܡܢ ܕܫܕܪܢܝ ܡܩܒܠ.

ܡܐ: ܡܢ ܕܡܩܒܠ ܢܒܝܐ ܒܫܡ ܢܒܝܐ. ܐܓܪܐ ܕܢܒܝܐ ܢܣܒ. ܘܡܢ ܕܡܩܒܠ ܙܕܝܩܐ ܒܫܡ ܙܕܝܩܐ. ܐܓܪܐ ܕܙܕܝܩܐ ܢܣܒ.

ܡܒ: ܘܟܠ ܕܢܫܩܐ ܠܚܕ ܡܢ ܗܠܝܢ ܙܥܘܪܐ ܟܣܐ ܕܩܪܝܪܐ ܒܠܚܘܕ ܒܫܡܐ ܕܬܠܡܝܕܐ. ܐܡܝܢ ܐܡܪ ܐܢܐ ܠܟܘܢ ܕܠܐ ܢܐܒܕ ܐܓܪܗ.

CHAPTER 11

1. And so it was that when Jesus had finished commanding his twelve disciples, he departed from there to teach and to preach in their towns.

JOHN THE BAPTIZER QUESTIONS JESUS

2. Now when John heard in prison[1] of the works of the Messiah, he sent word by his disciples,

3. And asked him: Are you he who is coming[2] or are we to expect another?

4. Jesus answered and said to them: Go and tell John these things which you are hearing and seeing.

5. The blind see and the lame walk; the lepers are cleansed and the deaf hear; the dead are raised[3] and the poor are given assurance.[4]

6. And delighted is he who does not stumble because of me.

7. Now when they went away, Jesus began to tell the crowds about John: What did you go out in the deserted region to see? A reed shaken by the wind?[5]

8. And if not, what did you go out to see? A man dressed in fine clothes? Behold those who wear fine clothes are in the homes of kings.[6]

9. And if not, what did you go out to see? A prophet? Yes, I tell you and much more than a prophet![7]

10. Because this is he of whom it is written: Behold, I am sending my messenger before you that he shall prepare the way before you.[8]

---

1 The fortress of Machaerus on the east side of the Dead Sea.
2 I.e., Are you the Messiah?
3 Healing was one of the signs of the appearance of the Messiah. See Isa. 35:5-6; 61:1.
4 The Aramaic word ܡܣܬܒܪܝܢ מסתברין, Misthabreen, means *to be given hope, assurance, the joyful message.* "The poor" refers to the devout – See Mt. 5:3, footnote 4, Judaism and the term "poor."
5 In the Arabah by the banks of the Jordan the long cane grass (reed) was abundant.
6 Cotton and linen clothes were very expensive and only worn by rulers and the very wealthy. The common people usually wore woolen garments. John wore a garment made of camel's hair which was also worn by the Nomads or semi-Nomads in the Arabian desert. This style of apparel was very ancient and indigenous to Israel. See Mt. 3:4.
7 An usher of the Messiah.
8 Isa. 40:3.

THE MARKETPLACE

See Mt. 11:16-17. In The Near East the marketplace or the square is more than just a place to sell goods. It is a gathering spot where business can be conducted as well as the social "business" of gossip and friendly conversation. To an Easterner there can be no sort of transaction without a demonstration of hospitality. When one enters a place of business—be it under a tent, in a booth, or in a store—one must be prepared for a friendly visit with the proprietor. The marketplace is also the place where many parables are told and retold and local proverbs exchanged. This kind of social exchange is referred to in Jesus' warning to his disciples, ... (Continued on p. A - 44)

11. Truly, I say to you that among those born of women[9] no one has appeared as great as John the Baptizer. Yet the least one in the kingdom of heaven is greater than he![10]

12. But from the days of John the Baptizer until now, the kingdom of heaven has been governed by force and the forceful have usurped it.

13. Because all the prophets and the Torah[11] prophesied until John.

14. And if you wish,[12] accept this, that he is Elijah who is about to come.[13]

15. Anyone who has ears to hear, let him hear.[14]

16. But to what shall I compare this generation?[15] It is like little boys sitting in the marketplace and calling to their friends,

17. And saying, We sang to you[16] but you did not dance; we wailed to you but you did not mourn.

18. Now John came not eating and drinking, yet you are saying, He is a madman!

19. This Human Being has come eating and drinking[17] and you are saying, Behold, a man who eats and drinks wine, a friend of tax collectors and sinners. Yet wisdom is justified by its works.[18]

JESUS REBUKES THE CITIES THAT DID NOT TURN TO GOD.

20. Then Jesus began rebuking the towns in which his many wonders were done but they did not turn to God, and he was exclaiming:

---

9 Idiom: mortal, a human being
10 John the Baptizer, although great, the son of a priest and educated, would not come to know the secret of the kingdom as did the least of the disciples of Jesus who were mostly fishermen.
11 ܐܘܪܝܬܐ, אוֹרַיְתָא, Aoraita - *The five books of Moses, Genesis to Deuteronomy.*
12 A typical Semitic idiom comparable to "may I suggest."
13 See Mal. 4:5-6.
14 Idiom: *Listen and understand* what I am telling you.
15 A common rabbinic style which introduces a parable.
16 Idiom: "We've told you" or "we've informed you." Jesus likened the fickle and peevish men of his time to children playing in the squares and marketplaces. See "The Marketplace," p. A - 43.
17 Common form of speech among Eastern Semites even today. It means "to be well taken care of" or "to live comfortably." It is comparable to our idiom "to have three square meals a day." John came "not eating and drinking," (fasting) but Jesus was welcomed into homes for meals and was cared for.
18 Wisdom is proven true by its results.

ܝܐ: ܫܪܝܪ ܐܡܪ ܐܢܐ ܠܘܟܼܘܢ: ܕܠܐ ܩܡ ܒܝܠܝܕ̈ܝ ܢܫ̈ܐ ܪܒܐ ܡܢ ܝܘܚܢܢ ܡܥܡܕܢܐ.
ܘܙܥܘܪܐ ܕܝܢ ܒܡܠܟܘܬܐ ܕܫܡܝܐ. ܪܒܐ ܝܠܗ ܡܢܗ.

ܝܒ: ܡܢ ܝܘܡ̈ܢܐ ܕܝܘܚܢܢ ܡܥܡܕܢܐ ܘܗܠ ܗܫܐ ܡܠܟܘܬܐ ܕܫܡܝܐ ܒܩܛܝܪܐ
ܡܬܕܒܪܐ. ܘܩܛܝܪ̈ܢܐ ܡܚܛܦܝ ܠܗ.

ܝܓ: ܟܠܗܘܢ ܢܒܝ̈ܐ ܘܐܘܪܝܬܐ ܗܕܡܐ ܠܝܘܚܢܢ ܢܒܝܘܗ

ܝܕ: ܘܐܢ ܨܒܝܬܘܢ ܕܩܒܠܝܬܘܢ ܗܘ ܝܠܗ ܐܠܝܐ ܕܥܬܝܕ ܠܡܬܝܐ.

ܝܗ: ܐܢܝ ܕܐܝܬ ܠܗ ܢܬ̈ܐ ܕܫܡܥܐ ܫܡܥܐ.

ܝܘ: ܠܡܢ ܕܝܢ ܕܡܝܢܢ ܠܫܪܒܬܐ ܗܕܐ ܕܡܝܐ ܠܛܠܝ̈ܐ ܕܝܬܒܝܢ ܒܫܘܩܐ. ܘܩܪܝܢ
ܠܚܒܪ̈ܘܗܝ.

ܝܙ: ܘܐܡܪܝ: ܙܡܪܢ ܠܘܟܼܘܢ ܘܠܐ ܪܩܕܠܘܟܼܘܢ. ܘܐܠܝܢ ܠܘܟܼܘܢ ܘܠܐ ܐܪܩܕܠܘܟܼܘܢ.

ܝܚ: ܐܬܐ ܝܘܚܢܢ ܕܠܐ ܐܟܠ ܘܠܐ ܫܬܐ. ܘܐܡܪܝ: ܫܐܕܐ ܐܝܬ ܒܗ.

ܝܛ: ܐܬܐ ܒܪܗ ܕܐܢܫܐ ܐܟܠ ܘܫܬܐ. ܘܐܡܪܝ: ܗܐ ܓܒܪܐ ܐܟܘܠܐ ܘܫܬܝܐ ܚܡܪܐ.
ܘܪܚܡܐ ܕܡܟܣ̈ܐ ܘܕܚܛܝ̈ܐ. ܘܐܙܕܕܩܬ ܚܟܡܬܐ ܡܢ ܒܢ̈ܝܗ.

ܟ: ܗܝܕܝܢ ܫܪܝ ܝܫܘܥ ܠܡܚܣܕܘ ܡܕܝܢ̈ܬܐ ܐܝܟܢ ܕܗܘܘ ܒܓܘܝ ܚܝܠܘ̈ܬܗ ܣܓܝ̈ܐܬܐ
ܘܠܐ ܬܒܘ. ܘܐܡܪ ܗܟܢܐ.

(Continued from p. A - 43)

"Beware of the scribes which like to go about in long robes and love to be greeted in the marketplace." Mk. 12:38. The scribes were frequent visitors to the market, where people of all classes would extend them recognition for their special social position. It was also a favorite place for children to gather. Here they could play their pranks and watch the busy activities of their elders. Jesus told the men that they were like little boys playing in the marketplace but did not respond to the singing and crying of other children. The Eastern saying, "We sang to you, we wailed to and you did not dance nor mourn" means "we have done everything we can to inform you and you did not respond." Jesus used this saying because the men did not respond to him nor did they listen to John the Baptizer when he called them to return to God. See footnote 16, p. 44.

21. Woe to you, Oh Chorazin! Woe to you, Oh Bethsaida! Because if the wonders done in you, had been done in Tyre and Sidon, doubtless, they would have long ago, turned to God in sackcloth and ashes.[19]

22. But I say to you that it shall be more restful for Tyre and Sidon on the judgment day than for you.

23. And you, Oh Capernaum, which has been exalted to heaven, to Sheol shall you be brought down;[20] because if the wonders which were done in you, had been done in Sodom, it would be standing to this very day.

24. But I say to you that it shall be more restful for the land of Sodom on the judgment day than for you.

JESUS' PRAYER AND CALL

25. At that time, Jesus answered and said: I thank you, my Father, Lord of heaven and earth, because You have hidden these things from the wise and the knowledgeable and revealed them to babies.[21]

26. Yes, my Father, for so it was pleasing before You.

27. Everything has been given to me by my Father and no one knows the son except the Father; also no one knows the Father except the son and he to whom the son is willing to reveal (the Father).

28. Come to me all you who are worn out and carry burdens and I will rest you.[22]

29. Take my yoke upon you and learn from me that I am restful and I am humble in my heart and you shall find rest for yourselves.[23]

30. Because my yoke is delightful and my burden is little.

---

19 "... sackcloth and ashes" are signs of mourning.
20 ܐܫܝܘܠ, שׁיול, Sheol is used metaphorically to indicate total ruin, destruction. This saying is similar to Isa. 14:13-15.
21 Semitic term meaning "the simple and inexperienced"; also "little ones."
22 During the messianic era, "rest" was promised to the weary pious.
23 This entire phrase is a play on the word ܢܝܚܐ, נייחא, Nyaḥa, *rest*, in Aramaic. It may also be translated: "Come to me all of you who are worn out and carry burdens and I will *refresh* you. Take my yoke upon you and learn from me because I am *refreshing* and I am humble in my heart and you *shall refresh* yourselves." A modern paraphrasing may be rendered: "Come to me all of you who are worn out and carry burdens and I *will cheer* you. Take my yoke upon you and learn from me that I am *cheerful* and I am humble in my heart and you shall find *cheer* for yourselves."

THE SECRETS BETWEEN THE FATHER AND THE SON

See Mt. 11: 27. Jesus had utter faith and trust in his unique relationship he knew he had with his "*Abba*" - Father. According to Eastern custom, special family trade secrets of various arts and handicrafts are handed down from one generation to another from father to son. A father will teach and reveal everything to his son. A son who is to receive the secrets from his early age is brought up under the watchful eye of his father. The son will eat, work and share his life with his father constantly. The father knows his son and the son knows his father. The son can do nothing of himself, only what the father has taught him. If one wishes to know the father, he must come to the son. The father and the son work in harmony with each other. They are of one accord. See Jn. 5:19-20; 10:30; 14:6-11; also "The Father-Son Relationship," p. A - 10.

A - 45

CHAPTER 12

JESUS TEACHES MAN IS LORD OF THE SABBATH

1. At that time Jesus was walking through the fields of grain on Saturday;[1] and his disciples were hungry and began to cut and rub the ears of wheat[2] and eat.

2. Then when the Pharisees saw them, they said to him: Behold your disciples are doing things that are not lawful to do on Saturday.[3]

3. But he said to them: Have you not read what David did when he was hungry and those who were with him?[4]

4. How he entered the house of God[5] and ate the bread of the LORD'S table, that which was not lawful for him to eat, nor for those who were with him, but only for the priests?[6]

5. Or have you not read in the Torah that the priests in the sanctuary disregard Saturday and are blameless?

6. But I say to you that someone greater than the sanctuary is here!

7. But if you had known what this means, I desire compassion and not sacrifice; you would not have condemned those who are blameless.[7]

8. Because a human being is lord of Saturday.[8]

JESUS PRACTICES HEALING ON THE SABBATH

9. Then Jesus departed from there and came to their meeting place.

10. And a man was there whose hand had atrophied. And they were questioning him, saying: Is it lawful to heal on Saturday?[9] This was so they might accuse him.

---

1 ܫܒܬܐ, שבתא, Shabtha – Sabbath, *Saturday*. See "The Sabbath," p. A – 46.
2 "To cut and rub ears of wheat" was comparable to "reaping" which was prohibited on the Sabbath.
3 See Ex. 34:21.
4 See 1 Sam. 21:1–6.
5 "The tent of meeting" which housed the ark of the covenant.
6 See Lev. 24:5–9.
7 I.e., the disciples.
8 The Sabbath was made for man and not man for the Sabbath.
9 Rabbinic interpretation permitted healing on the Sabbath providing the life was in danger or there was an emergency which needed immediate treatment.

THE SABBATH

Moses instituted the Sabbath as a day of rest from everyday labors. Israel had been commanded to observe the Sabbath so that as a people they would always remember their slavery in and deliverance from Egypt. The Hebrews, their servants, slaves, strangers and even their cattle must rest. Sabbath (the seventh day of the week - Saturday) was a Jewish holy day. See Ex. 20:8-11. In the law of the sabbatical year the land is to rest and lie fallow. See Ex. 23:10. The law was the same for everyone including the land.

11. But he said to them: Who is the man among you who has one sheep,[10] and if it falls into a pit on Saturday, does he not take hold of it and lift it out?

12. Now, how much more important is a human being than a sheep? What then, is it lawful to do good on Saturday?

13. Then he said to the man: Stretch out your hand. And he stretched out his hand and it was made whole exactly like the other.

14. And the Pharisees went out and they took counsel against him so they might do away with him.

15. But Jesus surmised it and departed from there; and many large crowds followed him and he healed all of them.

16. And he warned them not to reveal where he was.

17. So that it might be fulfilled what was spoken by the prophet Isaiah when he said:

18. Behold my servant, I am delighted with him! My beloved one, my being has longed for him;[11] I shall put my spirit upon him and he will preach justice to the nations.

19. He will not quarrel, nor shall he raise his voice and no one shall hear his voice in the streets.

20. He shall not break a bruised reed and he will not put out a flickering lamp until he brings justice to victory.

21. And in his name shall nations hope.

22. Then they brought to him a man who was insane, dumb and blind; and he healed him so that the dumb and blind one could speak and see.

23. And all the crowds were amazed saying: Maybe this is the son of David?[12]

---

10 Common Semitic style of writing and speaking: ". . . one . . ." is not making a comparison with other numbers but Jesus is simply saying, "Who is the man among you who has a sheep, . . ."
11 Verse 18 may also be translated as "My beloved one, my soul has rejoiced in him." However, based on the prime meaning of the Aramaic word ܨܒܝܬ, this reading would be second in choice. "My servant" refers to the Messiah as a servant of God. Eastern emissaries and high ranking government officials were known as "servants of the King." The Messiah acts as God's spokesman. Matthew in verses 18-21 quotes the prophet Isaiah (42:1-4) who used Semitic figures of speech to describe some of the characteristics of God's ideal servant - the Messiah. See "Semitic Figures of Speech," p. A - 47.
12 I.e., the Messiah. See Mt. 1:1, footnote 3, son of David.

ܝܒ: ܗܘ ܕܝܢ ܝܗܒ ܠܗܘܢ܂ ܦܢܐ ܡܢܟܘܢ ܓܒܪܐ ܕܐܝܬ ܠܗ ܥܪܒܐ ܚܕ܂ ܘܐܢ ܢܦܠ
ܒܫܒܬܐ ܒܚܦܪܐ ܕܒܐܪܥܐ܂ ܠܐ ܐܚܕ ܘܡܩܝܡ ܠܗ܂

ܝܓ: ܟܡܐ ܕܝܢ ܝܬܝܪ ܒܪܢܫܐ ܡܢ ܥܪܒܐ ܗܟܢ ܫܠܝܛ ܗܘ ܒܫܒܬܐ ܠܡܥܒܕ ܕܛܒܬܐ܂

ܝܕ: ܐܡܪ ܕܝܢ ܝܗܒ ܠܗܘ ܓܒܪܐ܂ ܦܫܘܛ ܐܝܕܟ܂ ܘܦܫܛ ܐܝܕܗ܂ ܘܬܩܢܬ ܐܝܟ ܚܒܪܬܗ܂

ܝܗ: ܘܦܪܫܘ ܦܪܝܫܐ܂ ܘܡܠܟܐ ܢܣܒܘ ܥܠܘܗܝ ܐܝܟ ܕܢܘܒܕܘܢܝܗܝ܂

ܝܘ: ܝܫܘܥ ܕܝܢ ܝܕܥ܂ ܘܫܢܝ ܠܗ ܡܢ ܬܡܢ܂ ܘܐܙܠܘ ܒܬܪܗ ܟܢܫܐ ܣܓܝܐܐ܂ ܘܐܣܝ
ܠܟܠܗܘܢ܂

ܝܙ: ܘܟܐܐ ܒܗܘܢ ܕܠܐ ܢܓܠܘܢܝܗܝ܂

ܝܚ: ܕܢܬܡܠܐ ܡܕܡ ܕܐܬܐܡܪ ܒܝܕ ܐܫܥܝܐ ܢܒܝܐ ܕܐܡܪ܂

ܝܛ: ܗܐ ܥܒܕܝ ܕܐܨܛܒܝܬ ܒܗ܂ ܚܒܝܒܝ ܕܣܘܚܬ ܒܗ ܢܦܫܝ܂ ܪܘܚܝ ܐܣܝܡ ܥܠܘܗܝ܂
ܘܕܝܢܐ ܠܥܡܡܐ ܢܟܪܙ܂

ܝܟ: ܠܐ ܢܬܚܪܐ ܘܠܐ ܢܩܥܐ܂ ܘܠܐ ܐܢܫ ܢܫܡܥ ܩܠܗ ܒܫܘܩܐ܂

ܟ: ܩܢܝܐ ܪܥܝܥܐ ܠܐ ܢܬܒܪ܂ ܘܫܪܓܐ ܕܡܛܦܛܦ ܠܐ ܢܕܥܟ܂ ܥܕܡܐ ܕܢܦܩ
ܠܙܟܘܬܐ ܕܝܢܐ܂

ܟܐ: ܘܒܫܡܗ ܥܡܡܐ ܢܣܒܪܘܢ܂

ܟܒ: ܗܝܕܝܢ ܩܪܒܘ ܠܗ ܕܝܘܢܐ ܚܕ ܕܫܬܝܩ ܗܘܐ ܘܥܘܝܪ܂ ܘܐܣܝܗ ܐܝܟܢܐ ܕܚܪܫܐ ܘܥܘܝܪܐ
ܢܡܠܠ ܘܢܚܙܐ܂

ܟܓ: ܘܡܬܕܡܪܝܢ ܗܘܘ ܟܠܗܘܢ ܟܢܫܐ܂ ܘܐܡܪܝܢ܂ ܕܠܡܐ ܗܢܘ ܒܪܗ ܕܕܘܝܕ܂

SEMITIC FIGURES OF SPEECH

In Mt. 12:19-20 we find several Aramaic figures of speech: "He will not quarrel, raise his voice and no one shall hear his voice in the streets" mean God's servant would not campaign, cry out in the streets, marshal an army nor lead a revolt. Everything would be done in an undemonstrative manner. "He shall not break a bruised reed and put out a flickering lamp" denotes the Messiah's meekness and gentleness. . . . . (Continued on page A - 48.)

24. But when the Pharisees heard it they said: This one does not heal the insane except by Beelzebub,[13] the prince of devils.

JESUS IS ACCUSED OF HEALING BY THE POWER OF SATAN, HIS DEFENSE AND THE UNFORGIVABLE ERROR.

25. But Jesus knew their thoughts and he said to them: Every kingdom which is divided against itself will be destroyed; and every house and town which is divided against itself will not stand.

26. And if satan heals satan, he is divided against himself; how then will his kingdom stand?

27. And if I, by Beelzebub, heal the insane, by what do your sons[14] heal? For this reason they will be your judges.

28. And if by the spirit of God I am healing the insane, then the kingdom of God has come to you.

29. Or how can one enter the home of a strong man and plunder his goods, unless he first tie the strong man? And then he may plunder his household.

30. Anyone who is not with me is against me: and anyone who does not gather with me, scatters.

31. For this reason I say to you that all sins and blasphemies will be forgiven people, but blasphemy against the Spirit shall not be forgiven people.

32. And anyone who says a word against this Human Being will be forgiven; but anyone who speaks against the Holy Spirit shall not be forgiven,[15] neither in this world nor in the world to come.

---

13 Beelzebub – "lord of the fly." Some New Testament experts translate Beelzebub as "lord of the high place." The Jews had contemptuously altered the name from *zebub* to *zebul*, from Hebrew *zebel*, "dung." In the ancient days, Beelzebub was a popular Canaanite deity. During New Testament times, he was known as "prince of the house of devils." The epithet came to be attached to satan. See Mt. 10:25, footnote 19.

14 That is, "your disciples."

15 An individual or group of individuals who holds a particular state of mind or attitude which attributes evil to the power of the Holy Spirit, that is, the healing power, is unforgivable so long as that attitude exists. The best way to describe this state of mind is that it stubbornly persists in calling goodness, evil and light, darkness. Such was the case among those who were resisting the healing spirit through Jesus' ministry. Thus, this deliberate and stubborn attitude itself creates the unforgivable state. When this kind of attitude ceases, forgiveness is present.

ܟܕ: ܦܪܝܫܐ ܕܝܢ ܟܕ ܫܡܥܘ ܐܡܪܝܢ: ܗܢܐ ܠܐ ܡܦܩ ܫܐܕܐ ܐܠܐ ܒܒܥܠܙܒܘܒ ܪܫܐ
ܕܫܐܕܐ.
ܟܗ: ܝܫܘܥ ܕܝܢ ܝܕܥ ܡܚܫܒܬܗܘܢ. ܘܐܡܪ ܠܗܘܢ: ܟܠ ܡܠܟܘ ܕܬܬܦܠܓ ܥܠ
ܢܦܫܗ ܬܚܪܒ. ܘܟܠ ܒܝܬ ܘܡܕܝܢܐ ܕܬܬܦܠܓ ܥܠ ܢܦܫܗ ܠܐ ܬܩܘܡ.
ܟܘ: ܘܐܢ ܣܛܢܐ ܠܣܛܢܐ ܡܦܩ. ܥܠ ܢܦܫܗ ܐܬܦܠܓ. ܐܝܟܢܐ ܗܟܝܠ ܩܝܡܐ
ܡܠܟܘܬܗ.
ܟܙ: ܘܐܢ ܐܢܐ ܒܒܥܠܙܒܘܒ ܡܦܩ ܐܢܐ ܫܐܕܐ. ܒܢܝܟܘܢ ܒܡܢܐ ܡܦܩܝܢ ܠܗܘܢ.
ܡܛܠ ܗܢܐ ܗܢܘܢ ܢܗܘܘܢ ܠܟܘܢ ܕܝܢܐ.
ܟܚ: ܘܐܢ ܒܪܘܚܐ ܕܐܠܗܐ ܐܢܐ ܡܦܩ ܐܢܐ ܫܐܕܐ. ܩܪܒܬ ܠܗ ܥܠܝܟܘܢ ܡܠܟܘܬܐ
ܕܐܠܗܐ.
ܟܛ: ܐܘ ܐܝܟܢܐ ܐܢܫ ܡܫܟܚ ܕܢܥܘܠ ܠܒܝܬܗ ܕܚܣܝܢܐ ܘܡܐܢܘܗܝ ܢܒܘܙ. ܐܠܐ ܐܢ
ܠܘܩܕܡ ܢܐܣܘܪܝܘܗܝ ܠܚܣܝܢܐ. ܘܗܝܕܝܢ ܒܝܬܗ ܢܒܘܙ.
ܠ: ܡܢ ܕܠܐ ܗܘܐ ܥܡܝ. ܠܘܩܒܠܝ ܗܘ. ܘܡܢ ܕܠܐ ܟܢܫ ܥܡܝ. ܡܒܕܪܘ ܡܒܕܪ.
ܠܐ: ܡܛܠ ܗܢܐ ܐܡܪ ܐܢܐ ܠܟܘܢ: ܕܟܠ ܚܛܗܝܢ ܘܓܘܕܦܝܢ ܢܫܬܒܩܘܢ ܠܒܢܝ
ܐܢܫܐ. ܓܘܕܦܐ ܕܝܢ ܕܥܠ ܪܘܚܐ ܠܐ ܢܫܬܒܩ ܠܒܢܝ ܐܢܫܐ.
ܠܒ: ܘܟܠ ܡܢ ܕܢܐܡܪ ܡܠܬܐ ܥܠ ܒܪܗ ܕܐܢܫܐ. ܢܫܬܒܩ ܠܗ. ܟܠ ܕܝܢ ܕܥܠ ܪܘܚܐ
ܕܩܘܕܫܐ ܢܐܡܪ ܠܐ ܢܫܬܒܩ ܠܗ. ܠܐ ܒܥܠܡܐ ܗܢܐ ܘܠܐ ܒܥܠܡܐ ܕܥܬܝܕ.

(Continued from page A - 47)

The Messiah (God's servant) would not hurt even the weakest but, at the same time, insists on justice being done. The servant of God, quietly and unobtrusively, would spread his spiritual influence to all nations of the earth. (Jewish interpretation is divided as to whom Isaiah (Isa. 42:1) referred when he said, "my servant." Rabbinic commentators suggest that Isaiah may have meant himself, Israel, or the Messiah. But others think the allusion is to Cyrus, the Persian King. According to the gospel of Matthew, "my servant" refers to the Messiah and in particular to Jesus' fulfillment of this prophecy. See Mt. 12:16-17.)

33. Either produce like a healthy tree, good fruits; or produce like a sick tree, bad fruits; for a tree is known by its fruits.

34. O brood of poisonous snakes, how can you speak good things when you are bad? Because from the fullness of the heart the mouth speaks.

35. A good man out of good treasures brings good things, and a bad man out of bad treasures brings bad things.

36. For I say to you that every untruth which people speak, they shall give an account of it on the judgment day.[16]

37. Because by your words you shall be justified and by your words shall you be condemned.

THE SIGN OF THE PROPHET JONAH

38. Then some of the scribes and Pharisees answered saying to him: Teacher, we wish to see a sign from you.

39. Then he answered and said to them: A wicked and adulterous generation looks for a sign; and no sign will be given to it, except the sign of the prophet Jonah.

40. For as Jonah was in the stomach of the fish three days and three nights, so this Human Being will be in the heart of the earth three days and three nights.

41. The people of Nineveh shall rise in the judgment with this generation and will condemn it; because they turned to God through the preaching of Jonah, and behold a greater one than Jonah is here!

42. The queen of the south[17] shall rise in the judgment with this generation and will condemn it; because she came from the ends of the earth so that she might hear the wisdom of Solomon, and behold a greater one than Solomon is here!

43. Now when an unclean spirit goes out of a person,[18] it travels in places where there is no water; and it looks for rest and does not find it.

44. Then it says, I will return to my home from where I left; so it goes back and finds it vacant, warm and well furnished.

---

16 Each individual will be held responsible for lies and defamatory remarks made against another.
17 I.e., the Queen of Sheba.
18 A Semitic saying which means "when a person is healed."

ܠܓ: ܐܘ ܥܒܕܘ ܐܝܠܢܐ ܛܒܐ ܘܦܐܪ̈ܘܗܝ ܛܒ̈ܐ. ܐܘ ܥܒܕܘ ܐܝܠܢܐ ܒܝܫܐ
ܘܦܐܪ̈ܘܗܝ ܒܝܫ̈ܐ. ܡܢ ܦܐܪ̈ܘܗܝ ܗܘ ܓܝܪ ܡܬܝܕܥ ܐܝܠܢܐ.
ܠܕ: ܝܠܕ̈ܐ ܕܐܟܕ̈ܢܐ. ܐܝܟܢܐ ܡܫܟܚܝܢ ܐܢܬܘܢ ܛܒ̈ܬܐ ܠܡܡܠܠܘ ܕܒܝܫ̈ܐ ܐܢܬܘܢ.
ܡܢ ܬܘܬܪ̈ܝ ܠܒܐ ܓܝܪ ܡܡܠܠ ܦܘܡܐ.
ܠܗ: ܓܒܪܐ ܛܒܐ ܡܢ ܣܝܡܬܐ ܛܒܬܐ ܡܦܩ ܛܒ̈ܬܐ. ܘܓܒܪܐ ܒܝܫܐ ܡܢ ܣܝܡܬܐ
ܒܝܫܬܐ ܡܦܩ ܒܝܫ̈ܬܐ.
ܠܘ: ܐܡܪ ܐܢܐ ܠܟܘܢ ܓܝܪ: ܕܟܠ ܡܠܐ ܒܛܝܠܐ ܕܢܐܡܪܘܢ ܒܢܝ̈ܢܫܐ. ܢܬܠܘܢ
ܦܬܓܡܗ ܒܝܘܡܐ ܕܕܝܢܐ.
ܠܙ: ܡܢ ܡܠܝܟ ܓܝܪ ܬܙܕܕܩ. ܘܡܢ ܡܠܝܟ ܬܬܚܝܒ.
ܠܚ: ܗܝܕܝܢ ܥܢܘ ܐܢܫܐ ܡܢ ܣܦܪ̈ܐ ܘܡܢ ܦܪ̈ܝܫܐ ܘܐܡܪܝܢ ܠܗ: ܡܠܦܢܐ ܨܒܝܢ ܚܢܢ
ܕܢܚܙܐ ܡܢܟ ܐܬܐ.
ܠܛ: ܗܘ ܕܝܢ ܥܢܐ ܘܐܡܪ ܠܗܘܢ: ܫܪܒܬܐ ܒܝܫܬܐ ܘܓܝܪܬܐ ܐܬܐ ܒܥܝܐ. ܘܐܬܐ ܠܐ
ܡܬܝܗܒ ܠܗ. ܐܠܐ ܐܬܗ ܕܝܘܢܢ ܢܒܝܐ.
ܡ: ܐܝܟܢܐ ܓܝܪ ܕܗܘܐ ܝܘܢܢ ܒܟܪܣܗ ܕܢܘܢܐ ܬܠܬܐ ܐܝܡܡܝ̈ܢ ܘܬܠܬܐ ܠܠܘ̈ܢ.
ܗܟܢܐ ܢܗܘܐ ܒܪܗ ܕܐܢܫܐ ܒܠܒܗ ܕܐܪܥܐ ܬܠܬܐ ܐܝܡܡܝ̈ܢ ܘܬܠܬܐ ܠܠܘ̈ܢ.
ܡܐ: ܓܒܪ̈ܐ ܢܝܢܘܝ̈ܐ ܢܩܘܡܘܢ ܒܕܝܢܐ ܥܡ ܫܪܒܬܐ ܗܕܐ ܘܢܚܝܒܘܢܗ. ܕܗܢܘܢ ܬܒܘ
ܒܟܪܘܙܘܬܗ ܕܝܘܢܢ. ܘܗܐ ܕܝܬܝܪ ܡܢ ܝܘܢܢ ܗܪܟܐ.
ܡܒ: ܡܠܟܬܐ ܕܬܝܡܢܐ ܬܩܘܡ ܒܕܝܢܐ ܥܡ ܫܪܒܬܐ ܗܕܐ ܘܬܚܝܒܝܗ. ܕܐܬܬ ܡܢ
ܥܒܪ̈ܝ ܐܪܥܐ ܕܬܫܡܥ ܚܟܡܬܗ ܕܫܠܝܡܘܢ. ܘܗܐ ܕܝܬܝܪ ܡܢ ܫܠܝܡܘܢ ܗܪܟܐ.
ܡܓ: ܐܡܬܝ ܕܝܢ ܕܪܘܚܐ ܛܢܦܬܐ ܬܦܘܩ ܡܢ ܒܪܢܫܐ. ܡܬܟܪܟܐ ܒܕܘܟ̈ܝܬܐ ܕܠܝܬ
ܒܗܝܢ ܡܝ̈ܐ. ܘܒܥܝܐ ܢܝܚܐ. ܘܠܐ ܡܫܟܚܐ.
ܡܕ: ܗܝܕܝܢ ܐܡܪܐ: ܐܗܦܘܟ ܠܒܝܬܝ ܡܢ ܟܪܐ ܕܢܦܩܬ. ܘܐܬܝܐ ܡܫܟܚܐ ܠܗ ܕܣܪܝܩ
ܘܡܟܢܫ ܘܡܨܒܬ.

45. Then it goes away and brings with it seven other spirits worse than itself and they enter and live in it; and the end of that person becomes worse than at first.[19] Such will happen to this wicked generation.

JESUS' FAMILY

46. While he was speaking to the crowds, his mother and his brothers[20] came and were standing outside and they desired to speak with him.

47. Then someone said to him: Behold, your mother and your brothers are standing outside and desire to speak with you.

48. But he answered and said to him who had spoken to him: Who is my mother and who are my brothers?

49. And he stretched out his hand toward his disciples and said: Behold my mother and behold my brothers!

50. Anyone, then, who practices the will of my Father who is in heaven, he is my brother and my sister and my mother.

---

19 Verses 43-45 are based on Hebrew folklore. Jesus is saying that it is impossible for one to remain neutral. Being clean but empty is insufficient because a person will return to the old destructive habits and become worse than before.

20 The word "brother" in Aramaic and Hebrew is also used to indicate close relatives. See Gen. 13:8, 14:16. In Mt. 13:55 - "Is he not the carpenter's son? Is not his mother named Mary, and his brothers, Jacob, and Joseph, and Simon, and Judah?" In Mt. 27:56 - "One of them was Mary of Magdala; and others were Mary, the mother of Jacob and Joses, and the mother of the sons of Zebedee." We see from Mt. 27:56 that the two brothers Jacob and Joses were the sons of Mary who may have been a relative of Jesus' mother. See Jn. 19:25. (In some manuscripts, Jn. 19:25, states that Mary of Cleopas is the sister; i.e., a relative, of Jesus' mother.) Therefore, the terms "brothers and sisters" does not necessarily mean blood brothers and sisters. In this verse "brothers" may refer to the relatives of Jesus. But it may also mean Jesus' actual brothers. To this day among Aramaic-speaking people, "brothers and sisters" are synonymous with "close relatives."

A - 50

CHAPTER 13

THE SEVEN PARABLES OF THE KINGDOM

1. Then in that same day, Jesus went out of the house and sat by the seaside.[1]

2. And many people crowded around him so that he had to board and sit in the boat and the entire crowd was standing along the bank.

1. THE PARABLE OF THE SEED (SOWER)

3. And he was speaking many things to them in parables[2] and said: Behold a sower went out to sow.

4. And as he sowed, some seed fell by the roadside; then a bird came and ate it.

5. And other seed fell upon a rock where it did not have much soil; and immediately it sprang up because the ground was not deep enough.

6. But when the sun shone, it was scorched and because it had no root, it dried out.

7. And other seed fell among thorns and the thorns sprang up and choked it.

8. And other seed fell on good soil and it produced fruits, some one hundredfold, some sixty and some thirty.

---

1 The term "seaside" refers to the Lake of Galilee and not the Mediterranean Sea.

2 ܦܠܐܬܐ, פלאתא, Pilatha - *Parables*. The Aramaic word Pilatha means *metaphors, similes, parables, proverbs, allegories, and illustrations*. Teaching and carrying on a conversation in parables, proverbs and illustrations is characteristic of Eastern people. Wisemen, wazirs, court officials, rabbis, prophets, teachers and politicians always make use of parables in their debates and lectures. Businessmen and their customers while bargaining often mention a few parables. Eastern poets and musicians sing parables, proverbs and riddles as they play their musical instruments. "I will incline my ear to parables. I will sing my proverbs upon the harp." Ps. 49:4, Aramaic text, Errico translation. A parable is verbal imagery which portrays and illustrates an event or a teaching. The main purpose of a parable is to make an impression and not to construct definitions or establish dogmas. In Mt. 13 Jesus' discourse on the kingdom is expressed through seven parables: 1) The Parable of the Seed (Sower). Jesus explains the success and failure in establishing his kingdom. 2) and 3) The Parables of the Wheat and Tares and the Net. These parables encourage his disciples and followers to be patient for in the fullness of his kingdom evildoers will be removed. 4) and 5) The Parables of the Mustard Seed and the Leaven. The kingdom begins as something small but will grow and come into its own power and glory in its consummation. 6) and 7) The Parables of the Hidden Treasure and the Pearl of Great Price. These parables encourage people to sell everything, that is, to make sacrifices for the sake of the kingdom. Membership in the kingdom will bring great joy and is well worth everything that has been surrendered.

ܨܚܚܐ: ܝܓ.

ܐ: ܒܗܘ ܕܝܢ ܝܘܡܐ ܢܦܩ ܝܫܘܥ ܡܢ ܒܝܬܐ. ܘܝܬܒ ܥܠ ܝܕ ܝܡܐ.

ܒ: ܘܐܬܟܢܫܘ ܠܘܬܗ ܟܢܫܐ ܣܓܝܐܐ. ܐܝܟ ܕܢܣܩ ܢܬܒ ܠܗ ܒܐܠܦܐ ܘܟܠܗ ܟܢܫܐ ܩܐܡ ܗܘܐ ܥܠ ܣܦܪ ܝܡܐ.

ܓ: ܘܣܓܝܐܬܐ ܡܡܠܠ ܗܘܐ ܥܡܗܘܢ ܒܡܬܠܐ ܘܐܡܪ: ܗܐ ܢܦܩ ܙܪܘܥܐ ܠܡܙܪܥ.

ܕ: ܘܟܕ ܙܪܥ. ܐܝܬ ܕܢܦܠ ܥܠ ܝܕ ܐܘܪܚܐ ܘܐܬܬ ܦܪܚܬܐ ܘܐܟܠܬܗ.

ܗ: ܘܐܚܪܢܐ ܢܦܠ ܥܠ ܫܘܥܐ. ܐܝܟܐ ܕܠܝܬ ܗܘܐ ܡܪܒܐ ܣܓܝܐܐ. ܘܡܚܕܐ ܐܦܪܥ ܡܛܠ ܕܠܝܬ ܗܘܐ ܥܘܡܩܐ ܕܐܪܥܐ.

ܘ: ܟܕ ܕܢܚ ܕܝܢ ܫܡܫܐ. ܚܡ ܘܡܛܠ ܕܠܝܬ ܗܘܐ ܠܗ ܥܩܪܐ. ܝܒܫ.

ܙ: ܘܐܚܪܢܐ ܢܦܠ ܒܝܬ ܟܘܒܐ. ܘܣܠܩܘ ܟܘܒܐ ܘܚܢܩܘܗܝ.

ܚ: ܘܐܚܪܢܐ ܢܦܠ ܒܐܪܥܐ ܛܒܬܐ. ܘܝܗܒ ܦܐܪܐ ܐܝܬ ܕܡܐܐ ܘܐܝܬ ܕܫܬܝܢ. ܘܐܝܬ ܕܬܠܬܝܢ.

---

9. Anyone who has ears, let him hear.

10. Now his disciples approached him, asking him: Why do you talk to them in parables?

11. Then he answered and said to them: Because to you it is given to know the mystery of the kingdom of heaven but to them it is not given.[3]

12. Now to anyone who has, it shall be given and it shall increase for him; but to anyone who has not, even what he has shall be taken from him.

13. For this reason I speak to them in parables because they look but do not see, and they listen but do not hear and do not understand.[4]

14. Because in them is fulfilled the prophecy of Isaiah who said: Listening you will hear but you will not understand, and looking you will see but you will not know.

15. Because the heart of this people has become hard and with their ears they hear as if deaf, and their eyes they have closed as if blind, that they should not see with their eyes and hear with their ears and understand with their hearts, and return to me so that I might heal them.

16. But delighted are your eyes for they see and your ears for they hear.

17. For truly I say to you that many prophets and righteous people have longed to see what you are seeing but did not see and to hear what you are hearing but did not hear.

18. Now you listen to the parable of the seed.

19. Everyone who hears the word of the kingdom and does not understand it, the evil one comes and steals the word which has been sown in the heart. This is that which was sown along the roadside.

20. Then that which was sown upon a rock is he who hears the word and immediately receives it with joy;

---

[3] Jesus spoke in parables to the multitudes so they might have an easier grasp of the mystery of the kingdom of heaven. The disciples were always with Jesus and had constant, daily access to his teaching, knowledge and understanding of the kingdom.

[4] Jesus spoke in parables to the Pharisees who saw his miracles but did not believe. See Mt. 11:16–19. Jesus' desire was to communicate with them and his only means was through parables.

ܛ: ܡܢ ܕܐܝܬ ܠܗ ܐܕܢܐ ܕܢܫܡܥ. ܢܫܡܥ.

ܝ: ܘܩܪܒܘ ܬܠܡܝܕܘܗܝ. ܘܐܡܪܝܢ ܠܗ: ܠܡܢܐ ܒܡܬܠܐ ܡܡܠܠ ܐܢܬ ܥܡܗܘܢ.

ܝܐ: ܗܘ ܕܝܢ ܥܢܐ ܘܐܡܪ ܠܗܘܢ: ܕܠܟܘܢ ܗܘ ܝܗܝܒ ܠܡܕܥ ܐܪܙܐ ܕܡܠܟܘܬܐ
ܕܫܡܝܐ. ܠܗܢܘܢ ܕܝܢ ܠܐ ܝܗܝܒ.

ܝܒ: ܠܡܢ ܓܝܪ ܕܐܝܬ ܠܗ. ܢܬܝܗܒ ܠܗ ܘܢܬܝܬܪ ܠܗ. ܘܠܡܢ ܕܠܝܬ ܠܗ. ܘܐܦ ܗܘ
ܕܐܝܬ ܠܗ ܢܫܬܩܠ ܡܢܗ.

ܝܓ: ܡܛܠ ܗܢܐ ܒܡܬܠܐ ܡܡܠܠ ܐܢܐ ܥܡܗܘܢ. ܡܛܠ ܕܚܙܝܢ ܘܠܐ ܚܙܝܢ.
ܘܫܡܥܝܢ ܘܠܐ ܫܡܥܝܢ ܘܠܐ ܡܣܬܟܠܝܢ.

ܝܕ: ܘܫܠܡܐ ܒܗܘܢ ܢܒܝܘܬܗ ܕܐܫܥܝܐ ܕܐܡܪ: ܕܫܡܥܐ ܬܫܡܥܘܢ ܘܠܐ ܬܣܬܟܠܘܢ.
ܘܡܚܙܐ ܬܚܙܘܢ ܘܠܐ ܬܕܥܘܢ.

ܝܗ: ܐܬܥܒܝ ܠܗ ܓܝܪ ܠܒܗ ܕܥܡܐ ܗܢܐ. ܘܒܐܕܢܝܗܘܢ ܝܩܝܪܐܝܬ ܫܡܥܘ.
ܘܥܝܢܝܗܘܢ ܥܡܨܘ. ܕܠܐ ܢܚܙܘܢ ܒܥܝܢܝܗܘܢ. ܘܢܫܡܥܘܢ ܒܐܕܢܝܗܘܢ.
ܘܢܣܬܟܠܘܢ ܒܠܒܗܘܢ. ܘܢܬܦܢܘܢ ܘܐܐܣܐ ܐܢܘܢ.

ܝܘ: ܕܝܠܟܘܢ ܕܝܢ ܛܘܒܝܗܝܢ ܠܥܝܢܝܟܘܢ ܕܚܙܝܢ. ܘܠܐܕܢܝܟܘܢ ܕܫܡܥܢ.

ܝܙ: ܐܡܝܢ ܓܝܪ ܐܡܪ ܐܢܐ ܠܟܘܢ: ܕܣܓܝܐܐ ܢܒܝܐ ܘܙܕܝܩܐ ܐܬܪܓܪܓܘ ܕܢܚܙܘܢ ܡܕܡ
ܕܚܙܝܢ ܐܢܬܘܢ ܘܠܐ ܚܙܘ. ܘܠܡܫܡܥ ܡܕܡ ܕܫܡܥܝܢ ܐܢܬܘܢ ܘܠܐ ܫܡܥܘ.

ܝܚ: ܐܢܬܘܢ ܕܝܢ ܫܡܥܘ ܡܬܠܐ ܕܙܪܘܥܐ.

ܝܛ: ܟܠ ܕܫܡܥ ܡܠܬܐ ܕܡܠܟܘܬܐ ܘܠܐ ܡܣܬܟܠ ܒܗ ܐܬܐ ܒܝܫܐ ܘܚܛܦ ܡܠܬܐ
ܕܙܪܝܥܐ ܒܠܒܗ. ܗܢܘ ܗܘ ܕܥܠ ܝܕ ܐܘܪܚܐ ܐܙܕܪܥ.

ܟ: ܗܘ ܕܝܢ ܕܥܠ ܫܘܥܐ ܐܙܕܪܥ. ܗܢܘ ܗܘ. ܕܫܡܥ ܡܠܬܐ. ܘܡܚܕܐ ܒܚܕܘܬܐ
ܡܩܒܠ ܠܗ.

21. Yet it has no root in him except for a short time and when there is trouble or persecution on account of the word, he quickly stumbles.

22. Now that which was sown among thorns is he who hears the word, but the concerns of this world and the deceptiveness of riches choke the word and it becomes fruitless.

23. Now that which was sown in good soil is he who hears my word and understands and produces some one hundred, some sixty and some thirty.

2. THE PARABLE OF THE TARES AND WHEAT

24. Then he related another parable to them and said: The kingdom of heaven is like a man who sowed good seed in his field,

25. And while the people slept, his enemy came and sowed tares[5] among the wheat and left.

26. Now when the grass sprang up and produced fruits then the tares also appeared.

27. And the servants of the lord of the house approached and said to him, Our lord, did you not sow good seed in your field? How did the tares get in it?

28. Then he said to them, Some man, an enemy, has done this; his servants replied to him, Do you want us to go and gather them out?

29. Then he said to them, Perhaps while you are gathering out the tares, you might also uproot the wheat.

30. Let them both grow together until the harvest; and at the time of the harvest, I will say to the reapers, gather up the tares first and bind them into bundles that they may be burned, but gather the wheat into my barns.

3. THE PARABLE OF MUSTARD SEED

31. He related another parable to them and said: The kingdom of heaven is like a grain of mustard seed which a man took and sowed in his field.

---

5 ܙܝܙܢܐ, זיזנא, Zeezana. A noxious weed; the annual bearded darnel or rye grass that flourishes in wheat fields. It is difficult to tell it from wheat or rye until it heads. Sometimes when tares are ground inadvertently with the wheat and eaten, extreme dizziness and nausea occur similar to seasickness. In an agricultural country, enemies often take revenge by damaging the other person's crop.

ܟܐ: ܠܝܬ ܠܗ ܕܝܢ ܥܩܪܐ ܒܗ. ܐܠܐ ܕܙܒܢܐ ܗܘ. ܘܡܐ ܕܗܘܝܐ ܐܘܠܨܢܐ ܐܘ ܪܕܘܦܝܐ
ܡܛܠ ܡܠܬܐ. ܥܓܠ ܡܬܟܫܠ.

ܟܒ: ܗܘ ܕܝܢ ܕܒܝܬ ܟܘܒܐ ܐܙܕܪܥ. ܗܘ ܗܘ. ܕܫܡܥ ܡܠܬܐ. ܘܪܢܝܐ ܕܥܠܡܐ ܗܢܐ
ܘܛܘܥܝܝ ܕܥܘܬܪܐ ܚܢܩܝܢ ܠܗ ܠܡܠܬܐ. ܘܕܠܐ ܦܐܪܐ ܗܘܝܐ.

ܟܓ: ܗܘ ܕܝܢ ܕܒܐܪܥܐ ܛܒܬܐ ܐܙܕܪܥ. ܗܘ ܗܘ. ܕܫܡܥ ܡܠܬܝ ܘܡܣܬܟܠ
ܘܝܗܒ ܦܐܪܐ. ܘܥܒܕ ܐܝܬ ܕܡܐܐ ܘܐܝܬ ܕܫܬܝܢ ܘܐܝܬ ܕܬܠܬܝܢ.

ܟܕ: ܐܚܪܢܐ ܡܬܠܐ ܐܡܬܠ ܠܗܘܢ ܘܐܡܪ: ܕܡܝܐ ܡܠܟܘܬܐ ܕܫܡܝܐ ܠܓܒܪܐ ܕܙܪܥ
ܙܪܥܐ ܛܒܐ ܒܩܪܝܬܗ.

ܟܗ: ܘܟܕ ܕܡܟܘ ܒܢܝܢܫܐ. ܐܬܐ ܒܥܠܕܒܒܗ. ܘܙܪܥ ܙܝܙܢܐ ܒܝܬ ܚܛܐ ܘܐܙܠ.

ܟܘ: ܟܕ ܕܝܢ ܝܥܐ ܥܣܒܐ ܘܥܒܕ ܦܐܪܐ. ܗܝܕܝܢ ܐܬܚܙܝܘ ܐܦ ܙܝܙܢܐ.

ܟܙ: ܘܩܪܒܘ ܥܒܕܘܗܝ ܕܡܪܐ ܒܝܬܐ. ܘܐܡܪܘ ܠܗ ܡܪܢ. ܠܐ ܗܐ ܙܪܥܐ ܛܒܐ ܙܪܥܬ
ܒܩܪܝܬܟ. ܡܢ ܐܝܟܐ ܐܝܬ ܒܗ ܙܝܙܢܐ.

ܟܚ: ܗܘ ܕܝܢ ܐܡܪ ܠܗܘܢ: ܓܒܪܐ ܒܥܠܕܒܒܐ ܥܒܕ ܗܕܐ. ܐܡܪܝܢ ܠܗ ܥܒܕܘܗܝ:
ܨܒܐ ܐܢܬ ܢܐܙܠ ܢܓܒܝܘܗܝ.

ܟܛ: ܗܘ ܕܝܢ ܐܡܪ ܠܗܘܢ: ܕܠܡܐ ܟܕ ܡܓܒܝܢ ܐܢܬܘܢ ܙܝܙܢܐ. ܬܥܩܪܘܢ ܥܡܗܘܢ
ܐܦ ܚܛܐ.

ܠ: ܫܒܘܩܘ ܬܪܝܗܘܢ ܢܪܒܘܢ ܐܟܚܕܐ ܥܕܡܐ ܠܚܨܕܐ. ܘܒܙܒܢܐ ܕܚܨܕܐ ܐܡܪ ܐܢܐ
ܠܚܨܘܕܐ: ܓܒܘ ܠܘܩܕܡ ܙܝܙܢܐ ܘܐܣܘܪܘ ܐܢܘܢ ܡܩܛܘܢܝܬܐ ܕܢܐܩܕܘܢ.
ܚܛܬܐ ܕܝܢ ܟܢܫܘ ܠܐܘܨܪܝ.

ܠܐ: ܐܚܪܢܐ ܡܬܠܐ ܐܡܬܠ ܠܗܘܢ ܘܐܡܪ: ܕܡܝܐ ܡܠܟܘܬܐ ܕܫܡܝܐ ܠܦܪܕܬܐ
ܕܚܪܕܠܐ ܕܢܣܒ ܓܒܪܐ ܙܪܥ ܒܚܩܠܗ.

32. And it is the smallest of all the seeds but when it is grown, it is larger than all the herbs, and it becomes a tree so that the birds of the sky may come and nest in its branches.

4. THE PARABLE OF THE LEAVEN (YEAST)

33. He told them another parable: The kingdom of heaven is like yeast which a woman took and buried in three measures of flour[6] until all of it had risen.

34. Jesus spoke all these things to the crowds in parables and without parables he did not speak to them.[7]

35. So that it might be fulfilled what was spoken through the prophet who said: I will open my mouth in parables, and I will bring to light secrets from before the foundation of the world.[8]

36. Now Jesus left the crowds and went into the house; and his disciples approached him saying: Explain to us that parable about the tares and the field.

37. Then he answered and said to them: He who sows good seed is this Human Being.

38. The field is the world; now the good seed are the children of the kingdom, but the tares are the children of the evil one.

39. Now the enemy that sowed them is satan; the harvest is the end of the world and the reapers are the messengers.

---

6 Kneading is usually done in this manner: After the flour is packed in the shape of a crescent on one side of a large earthen kneading basin, about thirty inches in diameter, the individual (usually one of the females of the family, the mother, grandmother or oldest daughter) dissolves some salt in warm water, which is then poured in the basin by an embankment of flour. The woman blesses in the name of God as she takes out the leaven, usually a lump of dough saved from the former baking, which she had "buried" in flour to keep it from overfermentation. This leaven is carefully dissolved in the salt water, and by slowly mixing the flour with this fluid, the woman buries the leaven in the meal. The kneading done, the lump is blessed again and then covered so that it may rise. Everything is done with a godly and grateful attitude. The same thankful attitude prevails when the risen dough is shaped into loaves, baked and served. Leaven (yeast) is held in high and reverential esteem by Easterners. It is a symbol of growth and fruitfulness.

7 This all encompassing generalization is typical of Eastern expression when one wishes to impress. It is an amplified assertion to make an impression. Jesus, at times, did speak to the crowds "without" using parables. The idea is that Jesus spoke in parables quite often which was common, Mt. 13:3, footnote 2. Also Mt. 8:32, footnote 22 - "amplification."

8 Ps. 78:2.

كد: .

لد: .

لد: ،.

لה: .

له: .

لو: .

لس: .

لח: .

_____

ܠܒ: ܘܗܝ ܙܥܘܪܬܐ ܗ̄ܝ ܡܢ ܟܠܗܘܢ ܙܪܥܘܢܐ. ܗ̄ܝ ܕܝܢ ܕܪܒܝܬ܆ ܪܒܐ ܗ̄ܝ ܡܢ ܟܠܗܘܢ
ܝܪ̈ܩܘܢܐ. ܘܗܘܝܐ ܐܝܠܢܐ ܐܝܟ ܕܦܪ̈ܚܬܐ ܕܫܡܝܐ ܐܬܝܢ ܡܓܢܢ ܒܣܘ̈ܟܘܗ̇.

ܠܓ: ܐܚܪܢܐ ܡܬܠܐ ܡܡܠܠ ܠܗܘܢ܆ ܕܡܝܐ ܡܠܟܘܬܐ ܕܫܡܝܐ ܠܚܡܝܪܐ ܗܘ ܕܫܩܠܬ
ܐܢܬܬܐ. ܛܡܪܬܗ ܒܬܠܬ ܣܐ̈ܝܢ ܕܩܡܚܐ. ܥܕܡܐ ܕܚܡܥ ܟܠܗ.

ܠܕ: ܗܠܝܢ ܟܠܗܝܢ ܡܠܠ ܝܫܘܥ ܒܡܬ̈ܠܐ ܠܟܢ̈ܫܐ. ܘܕܠܐ ܡܬ̈ܠܐ ܠܐ ܡܡܠܠ
ܗܘܐ ܥܡܗܘܢ.

ܠܗ: ܐܝܟ ܕܢܬܡܠܐ ܡܕܡ ܕܐܬܐܡܪ ܒܝܕ ܢܒܝܐ ܕܐܡܪ܆ ܐܦܬܚ ܦܘܡܝ ܒܡܬ̈ܠܐ.
ܘܐܒܥ ܟ̈ܣܝܬܐ ܕܡܢ ܩܕܡ ܬܪܡܝܬܗ ܕܥܠܡܐ.

ܠܘ: ܗܝܕܝܢ ܫܒܩ ܝܫܘܥ ܠܟܢ̈ܫܐ. ܘܐܬܐ ܠܒܝܬܐ. ܘܩܪܒܘ ܠܘܬܗ ܬܠܡܝ̈ܕܘܗܝ
ܘܐܡܪܝܢ ܠܗ܆ ܦܫܘܩ ܠܢ ܡܬܠܐ ܗܘ ܕܙܝ̈ܙܢܐ ܘܕܚܩܠܐ.

ܠܙ: ܗܘ ܕܝܢ ܥܢܐ ܘܐܡܪ ܠܗܘܢ܆ ܗܘ ܕܙܪܥ ܙܪܥܐ ܛܒܐ ܐܝܬܘܗܝ ܒܪܗ ܕܐܢܫܐ.

ܠܚ: ܚܩܠܐ ܐܝܬܘܗܝ ܥܠܡܐ. ܙܪܥܐ ܕܝܢ ܛܒܐ ܒܢܝܗ̇ ܐܢܘܢ ܕܡܠܟܘܬܐ. ܙܝ̈ܙܢܐ ܕܝܢ
ܐܝܬܝܗܘܢ ܒܢܘ̈ܗܝ ܕܒܝܫܐ.

ܠܛ: ܒܥܠܕܒܒܐ ܕܝܢ ܕܙܪܥ ܐܢܘܢ ܐܝܬܘܗܝ ܣܛܢܐ. ܚܨܕܐ ܕܝܢ ܐܝܬܘܗܝ ܫܘܠܡܗ
ܕܥܠܡܐ. ܚܨܘ̈ܕܐ ܕܝܢ ܡܠܐ̈ܟܐ.

40. So as the tares are gathered out and burned in the fire, so shall it be at the end of this world.

41. This Human Being shall send his messengers and they shall gather out of his kingdom all those that cause stumbling and all wicked doers.

42. And they will throw them into the furnace of fire; there shall be crying and gnashing of teeth.[9]

43. Then the righteous shall shine as the sun in the kingdom of their Father; anyone who has ears that hear, let him hear.

5. THE PARABLE OF THE HIDDEN TREASURE

44. Again, the kingdom of heaven is like a treasure that is hidden in a field[10] which a man found and hid and because of his joy, he went and sold everything he had and purchased the field.

6. THE PARABLE OF THE COSTLY PEARL

45. Again, the kingdom of heaven is like a merchant who is searching for precious pearls.

46. Then when he found an expensive pearl, he went and sold all that he had and purchased it.

7. THE PARABLE OF THE NET

47. Again, the kingdom of heaven is like a net which is thrown into the sea and it collected fish of every kind.

48. And when it was full, they pulled it to the seashore and sat down and sorted them, and the good ones they put in bags and the bad ones[11] were thrown away.

---

9 Metaphorical language: Torment, despair and rage.

10 ܩܪܝܬܐ, קריתא, Qritha means a *village*. The word for field in Aramaic is ܚܩܠܐ, חקלא, Ḥaqla and means *a small piece of land*. The words Qritha and Ḥaqla are used interchangeably in the Aramaic language. However in this case, the word "qritha" refers to a village-field. See Acts 1:19. A qritha, "village," may be composed of 10 to 50 homes or more which is surrounded by many fields owned by the villagers. A hidden treasure is usually understood as a treasure of gold or silver which had been buried in a field owned by the villagers. In the East it is believed that hidden treasures may be found anywhere in the land, especially among ancient ruins. The purpose of the parable was to impress the hearers with the matchless value of the kingdom of heaven which the Messiah came to reveal to the world.

11 "Bad ones" refer to fish which were inedible according to the dietary laws of Moses. See Lev. 11:9-12.

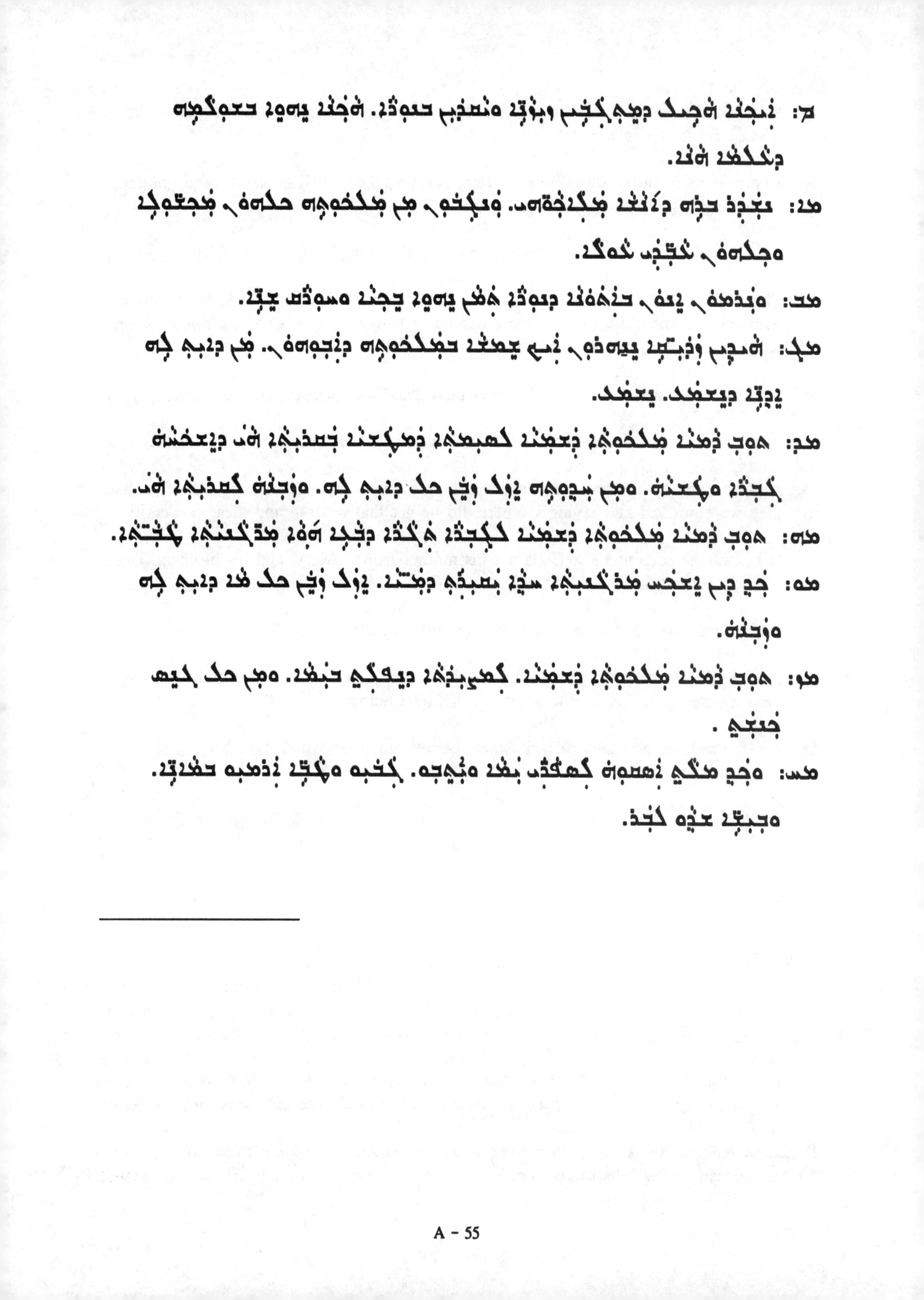

49. So will it be in the end of the world; the messengers shall go out and separate the wicked from among the righteous.

50. And they shall throw them into the fiery furnace; there shall be crying and gnashing of teeth.

51. Jesus asked them: Have you understood all these things?

52. They answered him: Yes, our lord. He said to them: For this reason every scribe who has become a disciple for the kingdom of heaven is like a man, a householder, who brings out of his treasure things new and old.

53. And so it was that when Jesus finished these parables, he departed from there.

JESUS REJECTED AT NAZARETH

54. And he came to his town[12] and was speaking to them in their meeting places so that they were amazed and saying: Where did he get this wisdom and these powers?[13]

55. Is he not the carpenter's son? Is not his mother named Mary, and his brothers, Jacob and Joseph and Simon and Judah?

56. And behold are not all his sisters with us? Where did he get all these things?

57. And they were doubtful about him; but Jesus said: There is no prophet who is despised except in his own town and in his own home.

58. And he did not do many miracles there because of their disbelief.

---

12 Most of the time Jesus' hometown was Nazareth. Mt. 2:23; Lk. 1:26-28, 2:39-40 and 51; Jn 1:45-46. But in other passages of the New Testament, Capernaum is referred to as Jesus' hometown. See Mt. 9:1, footnote 1.

13 ܚܝܠܐ, חילא, Hila – *power, force, energy, strength, a miracle, a wonder.* "These" is not present in the Aramaic text, I added it for clarification.

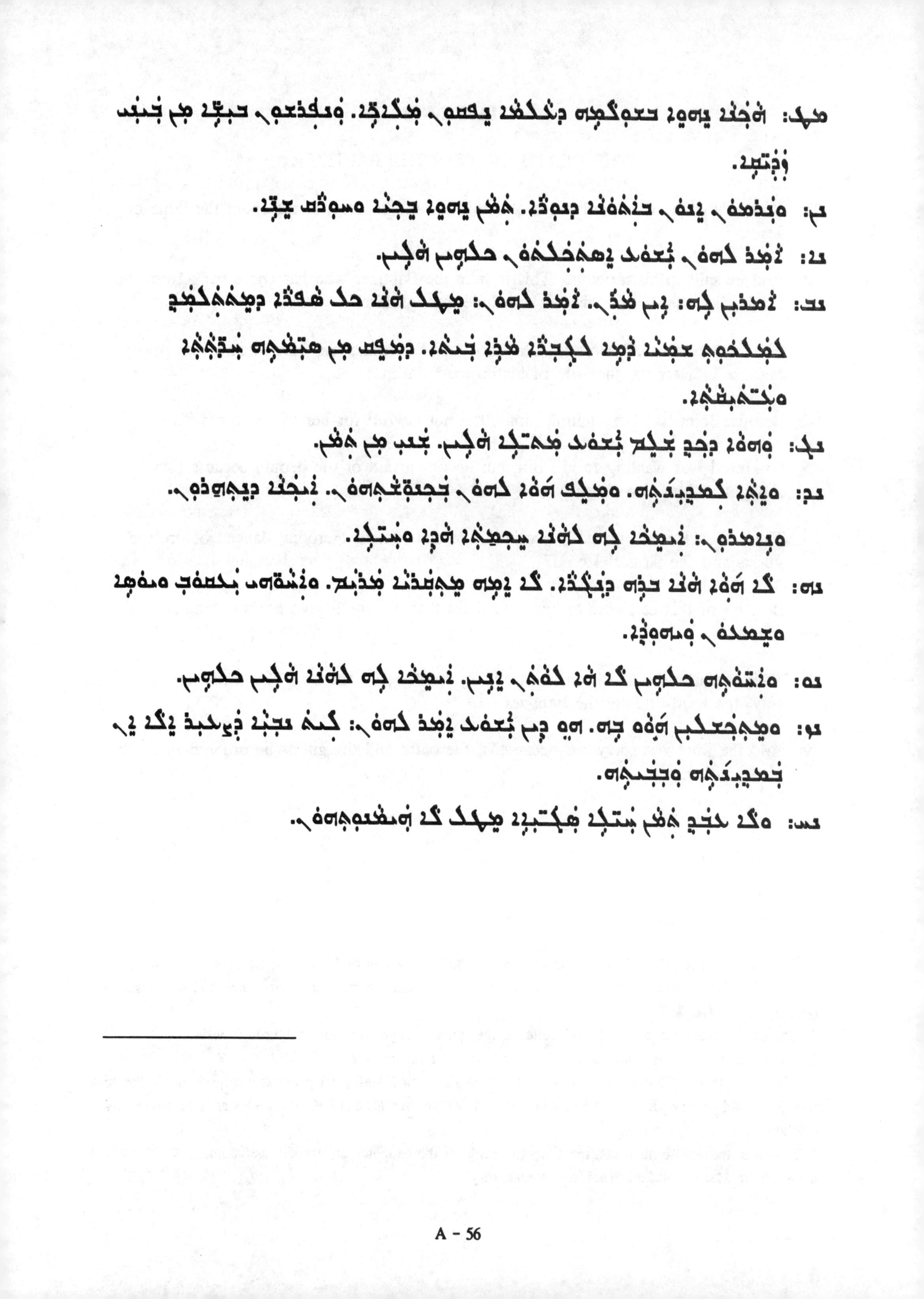

مه: .

CHAPTER 14

THE DEATH OF JOHN THE BAPTIZER

1. Now at that time, Herod,[1] ruler of a third of the country, heard about the fame of Jesus.

2. And he said to his servants: This is John the Baptizer who has come back from the tomb;[2] because of this miracles are done through him.

3. Now this Herod had arrested John and bound him and had him thrown into prison because of Herodia, the wife of his brother[3] Philip.

4. Because John had been telling him: It is not lawful[4] for her to be your wife.

5. So Herod was wanting to kill him but he was afraid of the people because they thought of him as a prophet.

6. Then when Herod's birthday occurred, the daughter of Herodia[5] danced before the guests and she pleased Herod.

7. Because of this he swore to her with oaths that he would give her anything she might ask.

8. Then, because she had been instructed by her mother, she said: Give me here on a tray[6] the head of John the Baptizer.

9. And the king was sorry but because of the oaths and the guests he ordered that it be given to her.

---

1 This is Herod Antipas, younger brother of Archelaus, the son of Herod the Great who had the little boys of Bethlehem killed. See Mt. 2:16. He is also the same Herod to whom Pilate had sent Jesus to be judged. See Lk. 23:7.
2 The implication here is that Herod believed the spirit of John was working through Jesus.
3 The term "brother" here means half-brother from his mother's side.
4 See Lev. 18:16. In reality Antipas had been married to a Nabatean princess but he divorced her so that he could marry Herodia. Herodia had left her former husband Herod who was a commoner so that she could marry Antipas.
5 Josephus, the Jewish historian, mentions the name of the daughter of Herodia as Salome.
6 Aramaic: ܦܝܢܟܐ, פינכא, Peenkha – *a reed tray*.

A – 57

10. So he sent messengers to the prison and had John beheaded.[7]

11. And his head was brought on a tray;[8] and it was given to the girl and she took it to her mother.

12. Then his disciples came and carried away his body and buried it; and they came and informed Jesus.

THE FEEDING OF THE FIVE THOUSAND

13. Now Jesus, when he heard it, departed from there by boat alone to a deserted place[9] and when the crowds heard about it, they went after him by land from the towns.

14. And Jesus went out and saw the large crowds and he had compassion on them and he healed their sick.

15. Now when it was evening, his disciples approached him and said to him: This is a deserted place and it is getting late, dismiss the crowds so that the people may go to the villages and buy food for themselves.

16. Then he said to them: They do not have to go; you give them something to eat.

17. But they said to him: We have nothing here except five loaves of bread and two fish.

18. Jesus replied to them: Bring them here to me.

19. And he ordered the crowds to sit on the ground; and he took the five loaves and the two fish and he looked towards the sky and he blessed and broke and gave[10] them to his disciples; and the disciples placed them before the crowds.

---

[7] Jewish law sanctioned beheading as a capital punishment but only after a trial and conviction. Antipas committed a second illegal act by beheading John the Baptizer. (The first illegal act was his marriage to Herodia.)

[8] See footnote 6.

[9] Jesus needed solitude for rest, to make decisions and prepare himself for greater opposition.

[10] "Blessed, broke and gave." This is the daily Jewish procedure at meals which begins by a spoken blessing over the bread, "Blessed art Thou, O LORD our God, King of the universe, who brings forth bread from the earth." After this, the bread is broken and distributed among those who are at the meal. See also Jn. 6:11.

ܝ: ܘܫܕܪ ܦܣܩ ܪܫܗ ܕܝܘܚܢܢ ܒܒܝܬ ܐܣܝܪܐ.

ܝܐ: ܘܐܝܬܝܘܗܝ ܪܫܗ ܒܦܝܢܟܐ. ܘܐܬܝܗܒ ܠܛܠܝܬܐ. ܘܐܝܬܝܬܗ ܠܐܡܗ.

ܝܒ: ܘܩܪܒܘ ܬܠܡܝܕܘܗܝ. ܫܩܠܘ ܫܠܕܗ ܩܒܪܘ. ܘܐܬܘ ܚܘܝܘ ܠܝܫܘܥ.

ܝܓ: ܝܫܘܥ ܕܝܢ ܟܕ ܫܡܥ ܫܢܝ ܡܢ ܬܡܢ ܒܐܠܦܐ ܠܐܬܪܐ ܚܘܪܒܐ ܒܠܚܘܕܘܗܝ. ܘܟܕ
ܫܡܥܘ ܟܢܫܐ. ܢܦܩܘ ܒܬܪܗ ܒܪܓܠܝܗܘܢ ܡܢ ܡܕܝܢܬܐ.

ܝܕ: ܘܢܦܩ ܝܫܘܥ. ܚܙܐ ܟܢܫܐ ܣܓܝܐܐ. ܘܐܬܪܚܡ ܥܠܝܗܘܢ ܘܐܣܝ ܟܪܝܗܝܗܘܢ.

ܝܗ: ܟܕ ܗܘܐ ܕܝܢ ܪܡܫܐ. ܩܪܒܘ ܠܘܬܗ ܬܠܡܝܕܘܗܝ ܘܐܡܪܘ ܠܗ: ܐܬܪܐ ܚܘܪܒܐ ܗܘ.
ܘܥܕܢܐ ܥܒܪ ܠܗ. ܫܪܝ ܟܢܫܐ ܕܢܐܙܠܘܢ. ܠܩܘܪܝܐ ܘܢܙܒܢܘܢ ܠܗܘܢ
ܡܐܟܘܠܬܐ.

ܝܘ: ܗܘ ܕܝܢ ܐܡܪ ܠܗܘܢ: ܠܐ ܣܢܝܩܝܢ ܠܗܘܢ ܠܡܐܙܠ. ܗܒܘ ܠܗܘܢ ܐܢܬܘܢ
ܠܡܐܟܠ.

ܝܙ: ܗܢܘܢ ܕܝܢ ܐܡܪܘ ܠܗ: ܠܝܬ ܠܢ ܗܪܟܐ ܐܠܐ ܚܡܫ ܠܚܡܝܢ ܘܬܪܝܢ ܢܘܢܝܢ.

ܝܚ: ܐܡܪ ܠܗܘܢ ܝܫܘܥ: ܐܝܬܘ ܐܢܘܢ ܠܝ ܠܗܪܟܐ.

ܝܛ: ܘܦܩܕ ܠܟܢܫܐ ܠܡܣܬܡܟܘ ܥܠ ܥܣܒܐ. ܘܢܣܒ ܗܢܘܢ ܚܡܫܐ ܠܚܡܝܢ ܘܬܪܝܢ
ܢܘܢܝܢ ܘܚܪ ܒܫܡܝܐ. ܘܒܪܟ ܘܩܨܐ. ܘܝܗܒ ܠܬܠܡܝܕܘܗܝ ܘܗܢܘܢ ܬܠܡܝܕܐ
ܣܡܘ ܠܟܢܫܐ.

20. And they all ate and were full; and they took up the fragments which were left over, twelve full baskets.[11]

21. Now the men who ate were five thousand, aside from the women and children.

WALKING ON THE WATER AND PETER'S FALTERING FAITH

22. And immediately he urged his disciples to board the boat and to go ahead of him to the crossing place while he dismissed the crowds.

23. And when he had dismissed the crowds, he went up the mountain alone to pray; and when it became dark, he was there alone.

24. But the boat was already many miles from land, tossed by the waves for the wind was against it.

25. Now in the fourth part of the night,[12] Jesus came to them walking on the water.[13]

26. And his disciples saw him walking on the water and they became frightened and were saying: It is a false vision and they cried out in fear.

27. Now Jesus spoke to them right away and said: Be brave! I, it is I, do not be afraid!

28. Then Peter answered and said to him: My lord, if it is you, command me to come to you on the water.

---

11 Prophets and holy men often increased the food supply to meet the needs of the people. See 1 Ki. 17:9-16; 2 Ki. 4:1-7, 38-44. The twelve baskets represent the twelve tribes of Israel and the twelve Apostles. Some scholars refer to the multiplication of the loaves and fish as a "nature miracle" or "moral miracle," that is, Jesus touched the hearts of the people so that they began to share their bread which was carried and hidden in their robes as an emergency supply of food. And since the baskets also increased from two to twelve, we can see that other supplies of bread came from unexpected sources.

12 Night was divided into four parts, that is, from sunset to sunrise: First part - 6:00 to 9:00 p.m.; Second part - 9:00 to 12:00 p.m.; Third part - 12:00 to 3:00 a.m.; Fourth part - 3:00 to 6:00 a.m. This division of the night was introduced by the Romans. The ancient Hebrews divided the night into three watches, Ex. 14:24, Jud. 7:19 and Lam. 2:19. After using the Roman division (four parts), night was divided into six parts or watches.

13 It is interesting to note that the Aramaic preposition ܥܠ, עַל, Al, has many meanings such as - *on, by, upon, toward, alongside*. In Aramaic the phrase ܡܗܠܟ ܥܠ ܡܝܐ, מהלך על מיא, Mhalekh al maya, "to walk on the water" can also mean "to walk by the sea," "to walk along the shore," and "to wade into the water."

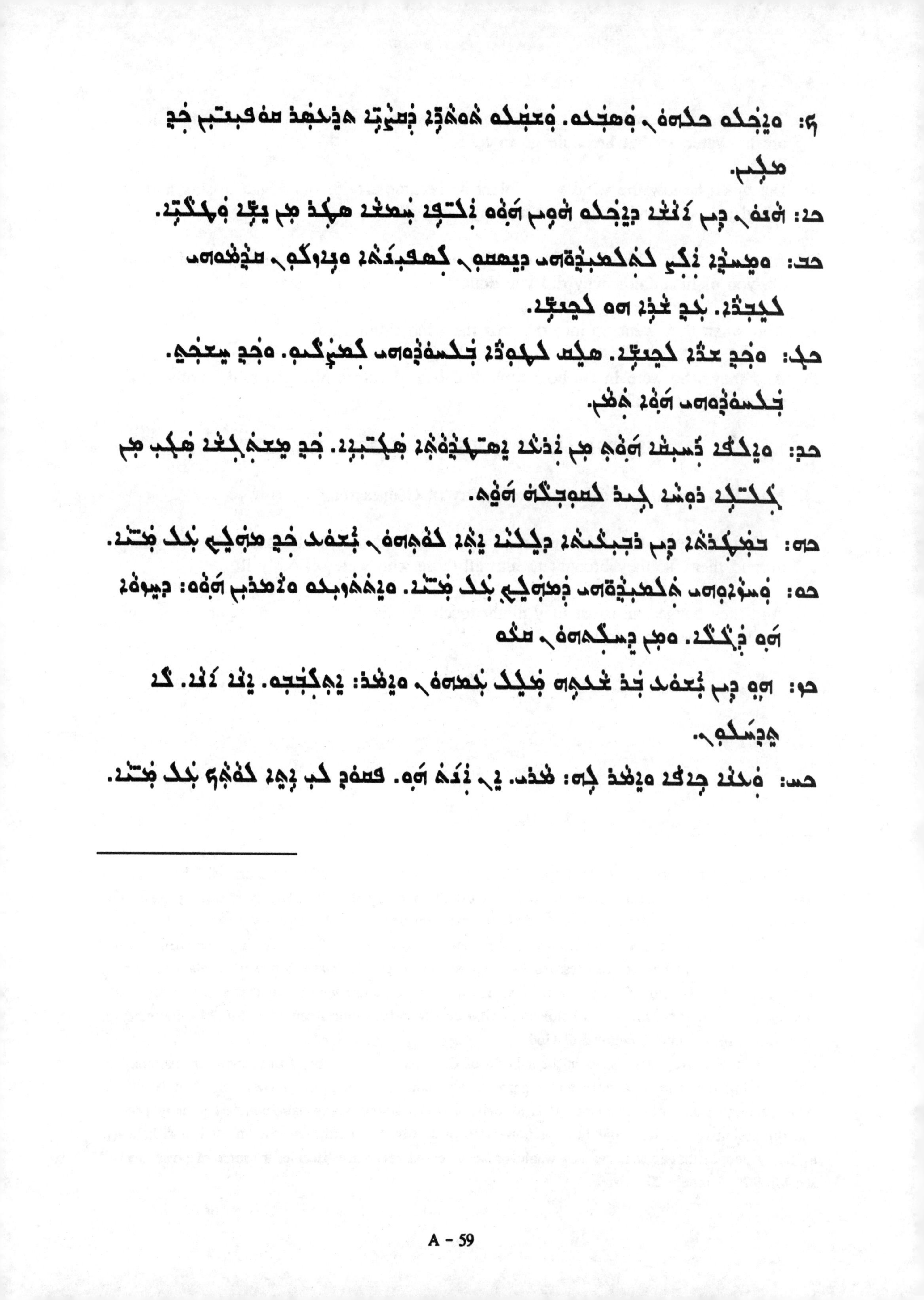

29. Then Jesus answered him: Come! So Peter went down from the boat and walked on the water, so that he could go to Jesus.

30. But when he saw the wind was violent he became afraid, and began to sink and he raised his voice and said: Save me, my lord!

31. And immediately, our lord stretched out his hand and grabbed him and said to him: Oh you of little faith, why did you doubt?

32. And when they went up into the boat the wind calmed down.

33. And they who were in the boat came and bowed before him and said: Truly, you are the son of God![14]

JESUS' HEALING MINISTRY IN GENNESARET

34. Now they rowed and came to the country of Gennesaret.[15]

35. And the people of that country recognized him and they sent word to all the villages around them; so they brought to him all those who were seriously ill.

36. And they begged him that they might touch just the hem of his robe, and those who touched it were healed.[16]

---

14 Among Easterners, when an impossible deed or task is accomplished, there will be a sudden outburst of deep and sincere gratitude which is usually accompanied by a highly exalting phrase. For example, an individual having solved a difficult problem or performing a nearly impossible feat might be called a man of God or the son of a famous person. The Apostle Simon, feeling overwhelmed with joy and gratitude at having been rescued by Jesus, acknowledged his master's powerful relationship with God. Jesus had no fear. God was with him. He was in one accord with the Father and was constantly abiding in that union. Jesus was beloved of God and therefore God's son. See Mt. 3:17, footnote 18. Also Mt. 16:16, foonote 7, Beloved of God.

15 Gennesaret, a very small town in the suburbs of Capernaum. No trace of this town remains today.

16 Touching the hem of a holy man's garment was considered a great privilege and had become a means for spiritual reinforcement. It is a common belief among many nationalities that holy persons and things impart spiritual and healing powers to those who reverently touch them. It is also believed by many people that "whomever and whatever we love and reverence becomes a source of power to us." See Mt. 9:20, footnote 20.

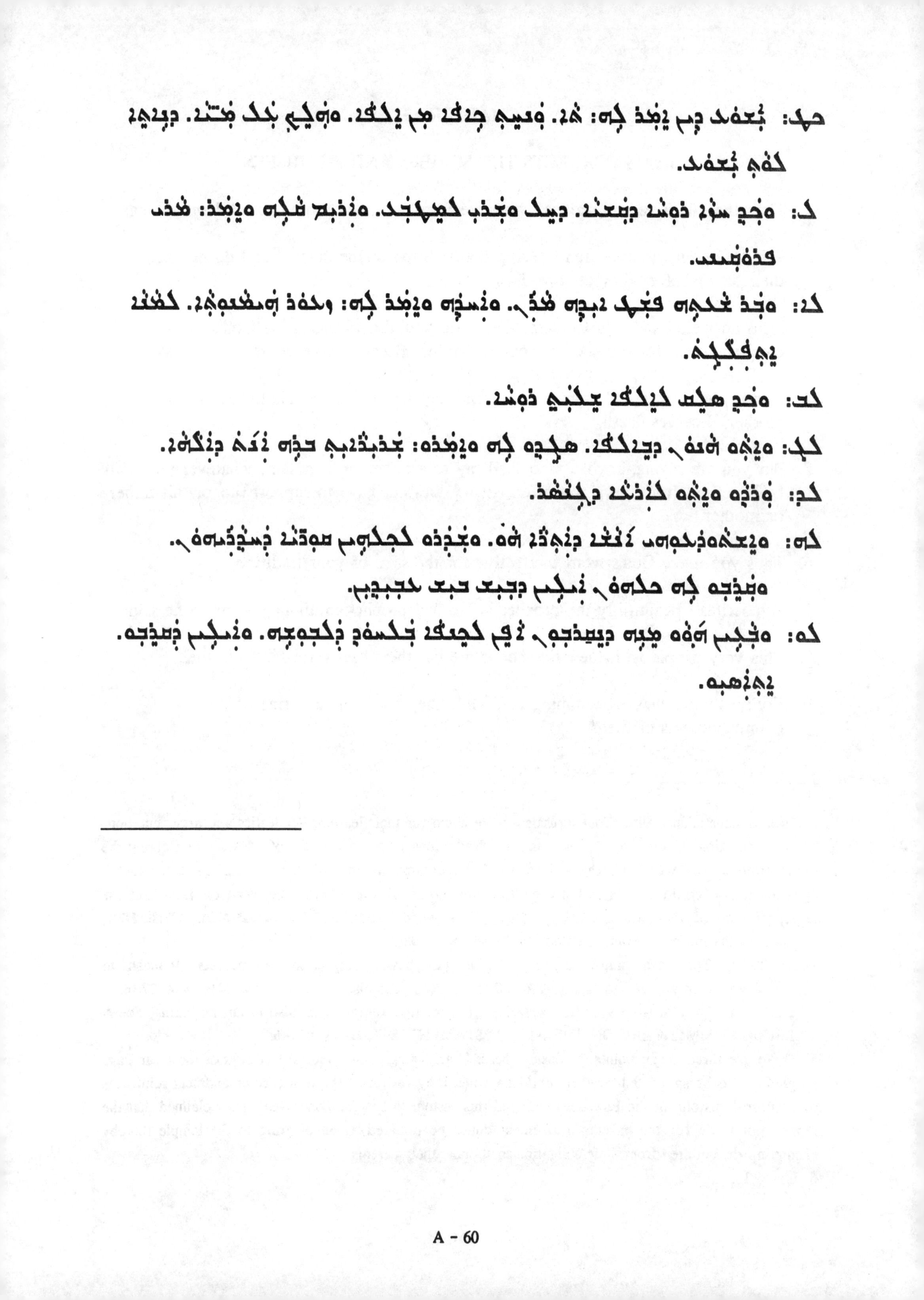

ܟܛ: ܝܫܘܥ ܕܝܢ ܐܡܪ ܠܗ: ܬܐ. ܘܢܚܬ ܟܐܦܐ ܡܢ ܣܦܝܢܬܐ. ܘܗܠܟ ܥܠ ܡܝ̈ܐ. ܕܢܐܬܐ
ܠܘܬ ܝܫܘܥ.

ܠ: ܘܟܕ ܚܙܐ ܪܘܚܐ ܕܩܫܝܐ. ܕܚܠ ܘܫܪܝ ܠܡܛܒܥ. ܘܩܥܐ ܒܩܠܗ ܘܐܡܪ: ܡܪܝ
ܦܪܘܩܝܢܝ.

ܠܐ: ܘܒܪ ܫܥܬܗ ܦܫܛ ܐܝܕܗ ܝܫܘܥ. ܘܐܚܕܗ ܘܐܡܪ ܠܗ: ܙܥܘܪ ܗܝܡܢܘܬܐ. ܠܡܢܐ
ܐܬܦܠܓܬ.

ܠܒ: ܘܟܕ ܣܠܩܘ ܠܣܦܝܢܬܐ ܫܠܝܬ ܪܘܚܐ.

ܠܓ: ܘܐܬܘ ܗܢܘܢ ܕܒܣܦܝܢܬܐ. ܣܓܕܘ ܠܗ ܘܐܡܪܘ: ܫܪܝܪܐܝܬ ܒܪܗ ܐܢܬ ܕܐܠܗܐ.

ܠܕ: ܘܥܒܪܘ ܘܐܬܘ ܠܐܪܥܐ ܕܓܢܣܪ.

ܠܗ: ܘܐܫܬܘܕܥܘܗܝ ܐܢܫܐ ܕܐܬܪܐ ܗܘ. ܘܫܕܪܘ ܠܟܠܗܘܢ ܩܘܪ̈ܝܐ ܕܚܕܪܝܗܘܢ.
ܘܩܪܒܘ ܠܗ ܟܠܗܘܢ ܐܝܠܝܢ ܕܒܝܫ ܒܝܫ ܥܒܝܕܝܢ.

ܠܘ: ܘܒܥܝܢ ܗܘܘ ܡܢܗ ܕܢܬܩܪܒܘܢ ܐܦܢ ܠܟܢܦܐ ܕܢܚܬܗ. ܘܐܝܠܝܢ ܕܩܪܒܘ
ܐܬܐܣܝܘ.

CHAPTER 15

JESUS CORRECTS THE SCRIBES AND PHARISEES

1. Then the Pharisees and scribes who were from Jerusalem[1] approached Jesus asking:

2. Why are your disciples transgressing the tradition of the elders,[2] and do not wash their hands before they eat bread?

3. Jesus answered and said to them: Why are you also transgressing God's commandment for the sake of your tradition? Because God has said:

4. Honor your father and your mother,[3] and anyone who curses his father and his mother, deserves death.

5. But you are saying, anyone who shall say to a father or a mother, whatever you shall be benefited from me is my offering;[4] he does not have to support (honor) his father or mother.[5]

6. Thus you make God's word ineffective for the sake of your tradition.

7. Hypocrites! Beautifully the prophet Isaiah had prophesied about you when he said:

8. This very people with their lips honor me but their hearts are far from me.

9. Fruitlessly are they worshipping me, while they teach the doctrine of the commandments of men.[6]

---

1 These academic specialists from Jerusalem were noted for their learning, dialectics and argumentation.
2 "The tradition of the elders" was a group of additions made to the law of Moses. In Hebrew the expression is "the words of the elders" or " the commandments of the elders," in order that a differentiation could be made between the commands of the Torah, the Written Law and the interpretation of the elders, the Oral Law. The word "tradition," ܡܫܠܡܢܘܬܐ, משלמנותא, Mashlmanootha means *to hand down, to hand over, surrender*.
3 Ex. 20:12. The word "honor" means more than just showing respect to your parents. It means to support them financially and to take care of all their needs. See also Ex. 21:17; Lev. 20:9; Deut. 27:16.
4 ܩܘܪܒܢ, קורבן, Qorban - *sacrifice, offering*. In tannaitic literature, it also means an "oath." See A RABBINIC COMMENTARY ON THE NEW TESTAMENT, S. T. Lachs, p. 246.
5 There are three major points to consider here: 1) according to the cultural tradition of the Near East, parents are to be supported by their children when they retire; 2) the fourth commandment reinforces this cultural custom; 3) the Pharisees changed this custom to benefit themselves. They claimed that the money put aside for the parents' retirement could be donated as an offering to the temple thereby exempting the children from their obligation to support their parents.
6 Isa. 29:13.

ܡܬܝܘܣ: ܝܗ.

ܐ: ܗܝܕܝܢ ܐܬܘ ܠܘܬ ܝܫܘܥ ܣܦܪܐ ܘܦܪܝܫܐ ܕܡܢ ܐܘܪܫܠܡ ܘܐܡܪܝܢ:

ܒ: ܠܡܢܐ ܬܠܡܝܕܝܟ ܥܒܪܝܢ ܥܠ ܡܫܠܡܢܘܬܐ ܕܩܫܝܫܐ. ܘܠܐ ܡܫܝܓܝܢ
ܐܝܕܝܗܘܢ ܡܐ ܕܠܚܡܐ ܐܟܠܝܢ.

ܓ: ܗܘ ܕܝܢ ܥܢܐ ܘܐܡܪ ܠܗܘܢ: ܠܡܢܐ ܐܦ ܐܢܬܘܢ ܥܒܪܝܢ ܐܢܬܘܢ ܥܠ ܦܘܩܕܢܐ
ܕܐܠܗܐ ܡܛܠ ܡܫܠܡܢܘܬܟܘܢ. ܐܠܗܐ ܓܝܪ ܐܡܪ:

ܕ: ܝܩܪ ܠܐܒܘܟ ܘܠܐܡܟ. ܘܡܢ ܕܡܨܚܐ ܠܐܒܘܗܝ ܘܠܐܡܗ. ܡܡܬ ܢܡܘܬ.

ܗ: ܐܢܬܘܢ ܕܝܢ ܐܡܪܝܢ ܐܢܬܘܢ ܟܠ ܡܢ ܕܢܐܡܪ ܠܐܒܐ ܐܘ ܠܐܡܐ: ܩܘܪܒܢܝ ܡܕܡ
ܕܬܬܗܢܐ ܡܢܝ. ܘܠܐ ܢܝܩܪ ܠܐܒܘܗܝ ܐܘ ܠܐܡܗ.

ܘ: ܘܒܛܠܬܘܢ ܡܠܬܗ ܕܐܠܗܐ ܡܛܠ ܡܫܠܡܢܘܬܟܘܢ.

ܙ: ܢܣܒܝ ܒܐܦܐ. ܫܦܝܪ ܐܬܢܒܝ ܥܠܝܟܘܢ ܐܫܥܝܐ ܢܒܝܐ ܘܐܡܪ:

ܚ: ܥܡܐ ܗܢܐ ܒܣܦܘܬܗ ܗܘ ܡܝܩܪ ܠܝ. ܠܒܗܘܢ ܕܝܢ ܣܓܝ ܪܚܝܩ ܡܢܝ.

ܛ: ܘܣܪܝܩܐܝܬ ܕܚܠܝܢ ܠܝ. ܟܕ ܡܠܦܝܢ ܝܘܠܦܢܐ ܕܦܘܩܕܢܐ ܕܒܢܝ ܐܢܫܐ.

---

10. Then he summoned the crowds and said to them: Listen and understand!

11. It is not what enters the mouth which makes a person unclean, but what comes out of the mouth, that is what makes a person unclean.

12. Now his disciples approached him saying to him: Do you know that the Pharisees who heard this saying were offended?

13. Then he answered and said to them: Every plant which my Father who is in heaven has not planted shall be uprooted.

14. Leave them alone; they are blind leaders of the blind. Now if the blind lead the blind they will both fall into a ditch.

15. Simon Peter answered and said to him: My lord, explain this saying to us.

16. Then he answered and said to them: Even now, you still do not understand?

17. Do you not know that what enters the mouth goes to the stomach and from there it is expelled from the intestines?

18. But what comes out of the mouth comes out of the heart, and that is what makes a person unclean.

19. Because from the very heart comes evil thoughts, adultery, murder, prostitution, theft, false witness, blasphemy.

20. These are the things that make a person unclean; but if someone eats while his hands are unwashed, he is not unclean.

21. And Jesus departed from there and came to the area of Tyre and Sidon.

JESUS HEALS A CANAANITE WOMAN'S DAUGHTER

22. And behold, a Canaanite woman[7] came out from that area, calling and saying: Have compassion on me, my lord, oh, son of David! My daughter is seriously oppressed with insanity.

23. But he did not reply to her. Then his disciples approached begging him saying: Dismiss her, she keeps calling after us.

---

7 A Canaanite woman refers to a Gentile woman; therefore, Jesus did not immediately respond to her request.

ܝ: ܘܩܪܐ ܠܟܢܫܐ ܘܐܡܪ ܠܗܘܢ: ܫܡܥܘ ܘܐܣܬܟܠܘ.
ܝܐ: ܠܐ ܗܘܐ ܡܕܡ ܕܥܐܠ ܠܦܘܡܐ. ܡܛܢܦ ܠܒܪܢܫܐ. ܐܠܐ ܡܕܡ ܕܢܦܩ ܡܢ ܦܘܡܐ.
ܗܘ ܗܘ ܡܛܢܦ ܠܒܪܢܫܐ.
ܝܒ: ܗܝܕܝܢ ܩܪܒܘ ܬܠܡܝܕܘܗܝ ܘܐܡܪܝܢ ܠܗ: ܝܕܥ ܐܢܬ ܕܦܪ̈ܝܫܐ ܕܫܡܥܘ ܡܠܬܐ
ܗܕܐ ܐܬܟܫܠܘ.
ܝܓ: ܗܘ ܕܝܢ ܥܢܐ ܘܐܡܪ ܠܗܘܢ: ܟܠ ܢܨܒܬܐ ܐܝܕܐ ܕܠܐ ܢܨܒܗ ܐܒܝ ܕܒܫܡܝܐ.
ܬܬܥܩܪ.
ܝܕ: ܫܒܘܩܘ ܠܗܘܢ. ܣܡ̈ܝܐ ܐܢܘܢ ܡܕܒܪ̈ܢܐ ܕܣܡ̈ܝܐ. ܣܡܝܐ ܕܝܢ ܠܣܡܝܐ ܐܢ ܡܕܒܪ
ܬܪ̈ܝܗܘܢ ܒܓܘܡܬܐ ܢܦܠܝܢ.
ܝܗ: ܘܥܢܐ ܫܡܥܘܢ ܟܐܦܐ ܘܐܡܪ ܠܗ: ܡܪܝ ܦܫܘܩ ܠܢ ܡܬܠܐ ܗܢܐ.
ܝܘ: ܗܘ ܕܝܢ ܐܡܪ ܠܗܘܢ: ܥܕܡܐ ܠܗܫܐ ܐܦ ܐܢܬܘܢ ܠܐ ܡܣܬܟܠܝܢ ܐܢܬܘܢ.
ܝܙ: ܠܐ ܡܣܬܟܠܝܢ ܐܢܬܘܢ ܕܡܕܡ ܕܥܐܠ ܠܦܘܡܐ. ܠܟܪܣܐ ܗܘ ܐܙܠ ܘܡܢ ܬܡܢ
ܒܬܕܪܝܬܐ ܡܫܬܕܐ ܠܒܪ.
ܝܚ: ܡܕܡ ܕܝܢ ܕܡܢ ܦܘܡܐ ܢܦܩ. ܡܢ ܠܒܐ ܢܦܩ. ܘܗܘܝܘ ܡܛܢܦ ܠܗ ܠܒܪܢܫܐ.
ܝܛ: ܡܢ ܠܒܐ ܗܘ ܓܝܪ ܢܦܩܢ ܡܚܫܒ̈ܬܐ ܒܝ̈ܫܬܐ. ܩܛܠܐ. ܓܘܪܐ. ܙܢܝܘܬܐ.
ܓܢܒܘܬܐ. ܣܗܕܘܬ ܫܘܩܪܐ. ܓܘܕܦܐ
ܟ: ܗܠܝܢ ܐܢܝܢ ܕܡܛܢܦܢ ܠܒܪܢܫܐ. ܐܢ ܐܟܠ ܕܝܢ ܐܢܫ ܟܕ ܠܐ ܫܝܓܢ ܐܝ̈ܕܘܗܝ.
ܠܐ ܡܛܢܦ.
ܟܐ: ܘܢܦܩ ܡܢ ܬܡܢ ܝܫܘܥ. ܘܐܬܐ ܠܬܚܘܡܐ ܕܨܘܪ ܘܕܨܝܕܢ.
ܟܒ: ܘܗܐ ܐܢܬܬܐ ܟܢܥܢܝܬܐ ܡܢ ܬܚܘܡܐ ܗܢܘܢ ܢܦܩܬ. ܩܥܝܐ ܗܘܬ ܘܐܡܪܐ: ܐܬܪܚܡ
ܥܠܝ ܡܪܝ ܒܪܗ ܕܕܘܝܕ. ܒܪܬܝ ܒܝܫܐܝܬ ܡܫܬܢܩܐ ܡܢ ܫܐܕܐ.
ܟܓ: ܗܘ ܕܝܢ ܠܐ ܦܢܝ ܦܬܓܡܐ. ܘܩܪܒܘ ܬܠܡܝܕܘܗܝ ܒܥܘ ܡܢܗ ܘܐܡܪܝܢ: ܫܪܝܗ
ܕܩܥܝܐ ܒܬܪܢ.

24. Then he answered and said to them: I have not been sent except to the sheep which have strayed from the family of Israel.

25. But she came and bowed before him and said: Help me, my lord!

26. Jesus said to her: It is not proper to take the children's bread and throw it to the dogs.[8]

27. Then she said: Yes, my lord, but even dogs eat the crumbs that fall from the large trays of their owners and they live.

28. Then Jesus said to her: Oh woman,[9] and great is your faith! Let it be to you as you wish; and her daughter was healed immediately.[10]

THE LARGE CROWDS HEALED AND FED

29. Now Jesus departed from there and came to the seaside of Galilee, and he went up the mountain and sat down there.

30. And large crowds approached him; and with them were the crippled, the blind, the dumb, the paralyzed and many others; and they laid them out before the feet of Jesus and he healed them.

31. So that the crowds were amazed when seeing the dumb speak, and the paralyzed made whole, and the crippled walk, and the blind see; and they praised the God of Israel.

32. Then Jesus summoned his disciples and said to them: I care about these people. Behold these three days they have stayed with me and they have nothing to eat, and I am unwilling to send them away fasting; perhaps they might faint on the road.

---

8 Gentiles, pagans.

9 ܐܳܢܬܬܳܐ ܐܳܘ, או אנתתא, O, Attha - "oh, woman." The term "woman" is the polite form of addressing a female in Aramaic. Jesus addressed his mother as "woman," Jn. 2:4; 19:26 and another woman whom he healed of rheumatism, "Jesus saw her and called to her and said, *Woman, you are cured of your sickness!*" Lk. 13:12. See also Jn. 4:21.

10 Jesus at first appears to confirm religious prejudice. But by granting the woman's request, he gave us two good lessons: 1) He taught his disciples that such religious prejudice should not exist in his kingdom. His kingdom was ready to receive anyone at any time and place. See Mt. 28:18-20. 2) By healing the Canaanite woman's daughter, Jesus gave assurance to her and all Gentiles that they would receive the blessings of his kingdom.

ܟܕ: ܗܘ ܕܝܢ ܥܢܐ ܘܐܡܪ ܠܗܘܢ: ܠܐ ܐܫܬܕܪܬ ܐܠܐ ܠܘܬ ܥܪܒܐ ܕܐܒܕܘ ܡܢ ܒܝܬ ܐܝܣܪܝܠ.

ܟܗ: ܗܝ ܕܝܢ ܐܬܬ ܣܓܕܬ ܠܗ: ܡܪܝ ܥܕܪܝܢܝ.

ܟܘ: ܐܡܪ ܠܗ ܝܫܘܥ: ܠܐ ܫܦܝܪ ܠܡܣܒ ܠܚܡܐ ܕܒܢܝܐ ܘܠܡܪܡܝܘ ܠܟܠܒܐ.

ܟܙ: ܗܝ ܕܝܢ ܐܡܪܬ: ܐܝܢ ܡܪܝ. ܐܦ ܟܠܒܐ ܐܟܠܝܢ ܡܢ ܦܬܘܬܐ ܕܢܦܠܝܢ ܡܢ ܦܬܘܪܐ ܕܡܪܝܗܘܢ ܘܚܝܝܢ.

ܟܚ: ܗܝܕܝܢ ܐܡܪ ܠܗ ܝܫܘܥ: ܐܘ ܐܢܬܬܐ. ܪܒܐ ܗܝ ܗܝܡܢܘܬܟܝ. ܢܗܘܐ ܠܟܝ ܐܝܟ ܕܨܒܝܐ ܐܢܬܝ. ܘܐܬܐܣܝܬ ܒܪܬܗ ܡܢ ܗܝ ܫܥܬܐ.

ܟܛ: ܘܫܢܝ ܡܢ ܬܡܢ ܝܫܘܥ. ܘܐܬܐ ܥܠ ܓܢܒ ܝܡܐ ܕܓܠܝܠܐ. ܘܣܠܩ ܠܛܘܪܐ ܘܝܬܒ ܬܡܢ.

ܠ: ܘܩܪܒܘ ܠܘܬܗ ܟܢܫܐ ܣܓܝܐܐ. ܕܐܝܬ ܗܘܐ ܥܡܗܘܢ ܚܓܝܪܐ ܘܣܡܝܐ ܘܚܪܫܐ ܘܟܦܝܦܐ ܘܐܚܪܢܐ ܣܓܝܐܐ. ܘܐܪܡܝܘ ܐܢܘܢ ܠܘܬ ܪܓܠܘܗܝ ܕܝܫܘܥ ܘܐܣܝ ܐܢܘܢ.

ܠܐ: ܐܝܟ ܕܢܬܕܡܪܘܢ ܟܢܫܐ ܟܠܗܘܢ. ܕܚܙܘ ܚܪܫܐ ܕܡܡܠܠܝܢ. ܘܟܦܝܦܐ ܕܡܬܚܠܡܝܢ. ܘܚܓܝܪܐ ܕܡܗܠܟܝܢ. ܘܣܡܝܐ ܕܚܙܝܢ. ܘܫܒܚܘ ܠܐܠܗܐ ܕܐܝܣܪܝܠ.

ܠܒ: ܗܘ ܕܝܢ ܝܫܘܥ ܩܪܐ ܠܬܠܡܝܕܘܗܝ. ܘܐܡܪ ܠܗܘܢ: ܡܬܪܚܡ ܐܢܐ ܥܠ ܟܢܫܐ ܗܢܐ. ܕܗܐ ܬܠܬܐ ܝܘܡܝܢ ܩܘܝܢ ܠܘܬܝ. ܘܠܝܬ ܠܗܘܢ ܡܕܡ ܕܢܐܟܠܘܢ. ܘܕܐܫܪܐ ܐܢܘܢ ܟܕ ܨܝܡܝܢ ܠܐ ܨܒܐ ܐܢܐ. ܕܠܡܐ ܢܬܡܚܘܢ ܒܐܘܪܚܐ.

33. His disciples replied to him: Where can we get bread in this deserted place to satisfy all these people?

34. Jesus asked them: How many loaves do you have? They answered him: Seven and a few small fish.

35. Then he ordered the crowds to sit on the ground.

36. And he took those seven loaves and the fish, gave thanks, broke them and gave them to his disciples; the disciples gave them to the crowds.

37. And they all ate and were full and they took up the fragments which were left over, seven full baskets.[11]

38. And all of those who ate were four thousand men besides women and children.

39. And when he dismissed the crowds, he boarded the boat and arrived at the border of Magadan.

---

11 See Mt. 14:19–20, footnote 11.

ܠܓ: ܐܡܪܝܢ ܠܗ ܬܠܡܝܕܘܗܝ: ܐܝܟܐ ܠܢ ܒܚܘܪܒܐ ܠܚܡܐ ܕܢܣܒܥ ܟܢܫܐ ܗܢܐ
ܟܠܗ.

ܠܕ: ܐܡܪ ܠܗܘܢ ܝܫܘܥ: ܟܡܐ ܠܚܡܐ ܐܝܬ ܠܟܘܢ. ܐܡܪܝܢ ܠܗ: ܫܒܥܐ ܘܩܠܝܠ
ܢܘܢܐ ܙܥܘܪܐ.

ܠܗ: ܘܦܩܕ ܠܟܢܫܐ ܕܢܣܬܡܟܘܢ ܥܠ ܐܪܥܐ.

ܠܘ: ܘܢܣܒ ܠܗܢܘܢ ܫܒܥܐ ܠܚܡܝܢ ܘܠܢܘܢܐ. ܘܒܪܟ ܘܩܨܐ. ܘܝܗܒ ܠܬܠܡܝܕܘܗܝ.
ܘܬܠܡܝܕܐ ܝܗܒܘ ܠܟܢܫܐ.

ܠܙ: ܘܐܟܠܘ ܟܠܗܘܢ ܘܣܒܥܘ. ܘܫܩܠܘ ܬܘܬܪܐ ܕܩܨܝܐ ܡܠܝܐ ܫܒܥܐ ܐܣܦܝܕܝܢ.

ܠܚ: ܗܢܘܢ ܕܝܢ ܕܐܟܠܘ ܗܘܘ ܐܪܒܥܐ ܐܠܦܝܢ ܓܒܪܐ ܣܛܪ ܡܢ ܢܫܐ ܘܛܠܝܐ.

ܠܛ: ܘܟܕ ܫܪܐ ܠܟܢܫܐ ܣܠܩ ܠܣܦܝܢܬܐ ܘܐܬܐ ܠܬܚܘܡܐ ܕܡܓܕܘ

CHAPTER 16

A SIGN FROM HEAVEN

1. Now the Pharisees and Sadducees approached, testing him and asking him that he might show them a sign from heaven.[1]

2. Then he answered and said to them: When it is evening, you say, it is clear for the sky has become red.

3. And in the morning you say, it is a wintry day because the sky has become red with dark cloudiness.

4. Hypocrites! You know how to discern the appearance of the sky, but the signs of this time you do not know how to distinguish;[2] a wicked and adulterous generation looks for a sign; and no sign will be given to it except the sign of the prophet Jonah.[3] Then he left them and went away.

THE YEAST OF THE PHARISEES

5. Now when his disciples came to the crossing place they had forgotten to take bread with them.

6. Then he said to them: Be careful and aware of the yeast[4] of the Pharisees and Sadducees.[5]

7. Then they were thinking among themselves and saying: It was because they had taken no bread.

8. But Jesus knew it and said to them: What are you thinking among yourselves, you of little faith, is it because you have brought no bread?

9. Up till now have you not understood? Do you not remember those five loaves of bread of the five thousand, and how many baskets you took up?

---

1 "Heaven," a euphemism for "God." See Mt. 3:2, footnote 4.
2 What we have here is a play on words (verses 1-4). The Pharisees and Sadducees wanted a sign from Jesus which was from heaven (God). Jesus, however, tells them they are able to read the signs of heaven (the appearance of the sky) but they cannot discern the signs of what is now happening, that is, the will of heaven (God).
3 See Mt. 12:38-40. See "The Sign of the Prophet Jonah," p. A - 65.
4 The term "yeast" is used as a metaphor. It means "a teaching"; also "corruption."
5 The yeast of the Pharisees and Sadducees refers to their bad policies and teachings which could corrupt Jesus' disciples and followers. See Mt. 15:14; 16:11; 23:2-3,13-33.

ܩܦܠܐܘܢ: ܝܘ.

[Syriac text - verses 1-9]

THE SIGN OF THE PROPHET JONAH

" . . . a wicked and adulterous generation looks for a sign; and no sign will be given to it except the sign of the prophet Jonah." (16:4) See also Mt. 12:38-40. Jesus informs the Pharisees and Sadducees that it is useless to ask for or seek a spectacular sign. The sign of Jonah refers to several points: 1) Jonah being thrown into the sea represents Jesus' crucifixion and death. 2) Being swallowed by an appointed fish and held in its stomach for three days and nights refers to Jesus' burial and entombment. 3) Being expelled by the fish symbolizes Jesus' resurrection and his triumph over Sheol and death. The Resurrection was the greatest of all signs. 4) Jonah's message to a Gentile nation was his preaching of repentance (turning to God) and the doing of good works. This also was the sign to which Jesus referred. His teaching of the joyful message of the kingdom of God was to be shared with the Gentile world.

10. Nor those seven loaves of the four thousand and how many baskets you took up?

11. How come you do not understand that it was not about bread that I spoke to you; but that you should be aware of the yeast of the Pharisees and Sadducees.

12. Now they understood that he did not mean that they should be aware of the bread yeast but of the teaching of the Pharisees and Sadducees.

SIMON PETER'S REVELATION

13. Then when Jesus came to the country of Caesarea of Philippi,[6] he was asking his disciples and saying: What are the people saying about me, that I am an ordinary person?

14. Now they said: Some are saying that you are John the Baptizer, then others Elijah, and still others Jeremiah or one of the prophets.

15. He said to them: Now who do you say that I am?

16. Simon Peter answered and said: You are the Messiah, the son of the living God![7]

17. Jesus answered and said to him: Fortunate are you, Simon, son of Jonah, because flesh and blood[8] did not reveal it to you but my Father who is in heaven.

18. I am also saying to you that you are a rock and upon this rock I shall build my church[9] and the doors of Sheol shall not conquer it.[10]

19. I give you the keys[11] of the kingdom of heaven, and anything you bind on earth will be bound in heaven, and anything you loose on earth will be loosed in heaven.[12]

---

6 Today it is called Banias, 40 kilometers (approximately 25 miles) north of Tiberias.

7 "Son of the living God" is a Messianic title. "Son" means the "Beloved" See Mt. 3:17, footnotes 18 and 19.

8 "Flesh and blood" - Aramaic idiom. A mortal, human being.

9 The word "church," ܥܕܬܐ, עדתא, Adatha, in this passage refers to the followers of Jesus forming a universal assembly.

10 ܬܪܥܐ ܕܫܝܘܠ, תרעא דשיול, Tareh dasheol, - *doors of Sheol*. See Isa. 38:10. Doors are symbolic of strength. Even death cannot prevent the Church (the disciples and followers of Jesus) from expanding. See also "Peter - Rock," p. A - 66.

11 ܩܠܝܕܐ, קלידא, Qleedeh, - *keys*. See Isa. 22:22. The term "keys" refers to the right or authority; i.e., power.

12 "Bind and loose" is an idiom. Jesus gave authority to his disciples to oversee the moral and doctrinal issues among his followers. They were assured that God (heaven) would back them.

―――――――――

KEPA (PETER) ROCK

See Mt. 16:18, p. 66, a play on words with the Apostle Simon's nickname *"Kepa"* and the Aramaic word rock-*kepa*. Among Easterners when an individual is given a nickname, it is done because of a certain characteristic which the individual so named displays. The Apostle's true name ܫܡܥܘܢ, Shimon comes from the root ܫܡܥ, shma, "to hear" and as a proper name it means "He who hears," "One who is keen, sharp and perceptive." Shimon is a popular, common name among Semitic peoples and has religious significance. Presumably, Simon's friends or townspeople had nicknamed him "Kepa" because instead of being quick-witted and alert which the name Simon implies, he was slow in his comprehension of matters and situations. . . . . (Continued on p. A - 67)

20. Then he commanded his disciples not to tell anyone that he is the Messiah.[13]

JESUS PREDICTS HIS DEATH AND RESURRECTION

21. From that time Jesus began to show to his disciples that he would very soon go to Jerusalem and suffer a great deal from the elders and from the high priests and scribes and would be killed but on the third day[14] he would rise up.

22. So Peter took him aside and began to reprimand him and he said: Far be it from you, my lord, that this should happen to you!

23. But he turned and said to Peter: Get behind me satan;[15] you are an offense to me because you are not thinking the things of God but things of people.

24. Then Jesus said to his disciples: If anyone wants to come after me,[16] let him deny himself and carry his cross and follow me.[17]

25. For, anyone who wills to keep himself alive, shall lose his life; and anyone who loses his life because of me shall find it.

26. For what does it profit an individual if he gain the whole world but shall lose himself? Or what will an individual give in exchange for himself?

27. Because this Human Being is ready to come in the splendor of his Father with His holy messengers; and then he will pay to each individual according to his deeds.

28. Truly I say to you, there are some people who are here now that shall not taste death till they see this Human Being coming in his kingdom.

---

13 See Jn. 6:15 where Jesus refused to be made a political or militant Messiah. He did not want the people to consider him in such an official capacity.

14 Jesus begins his disclosure as the suffering servant (See Isa. 53) to further de-emphasize any hopes of him becoming a political or militant ruler. But this revelation was not readily accepted by his own Apostles or followers, as they and most of Israel were eagerly hoping for political deliverance from their Roman conquerors.

15 The term "satan" ܣܛܢܐ, סטנא, Satana, is a common Aramaic and Arabic expression and it should not be understood literally. In this passage "satan" refers to anyone who misleads. Jesus called Peter "satan" because Peter's statement was misleading. He believed the way the people were thinking; that is, the people expected a powerful, worldly-wise, militant, Messiah-King, who would live forever and save them from Roman domination and oppression. All the Apostles believed in a political Messiah and kingdom (Mt. 20:20-21) even after the Resurrection (Acts 1:6).

16 I.e., become my disciple.

17 Meet the challenge, be willing to suffer and even to die for the sake of his teachings.

ܟܐ: ܘܗܝܕܝܢ ܦܩܝܕ ܠܬܠܡܝܕܘ̈ܗܝ ܕܠܐܢܫ ܠܐ ܢܐܡܪܘܢ ܕܗܘܝܘ ܡܫܝܚܐ.

ܟܒ: ܘܡܢ ܗܝܕܝܢ ܫܪܝ ܝܫܘܥ ܠܡܚܘܝܘ ܠܬܠܡܝܕܘ̈ܗܝ ܕܥܬܝܕ ܗܘ ܕܢܐܙܠ ܠܐܘܪܫܠܡ. ܘܣܓܝ ܢܚܫ ܡܢ ܩܫܝ̈ܫܐ ܘܡܢ ܪ̈ܒܝ ܟܗ̈ܢܐ ܘܣܦܪ̈ܐ ܘܢܬܩܛܠ. ܘܠܝܘܡܐ ܕܬܠܬܐ ܢܩܘܡ.

ܟܓ: ܘܕܒܪܗ ܟܐܦܐ ܘܫܪܝ ܠܡܟܐܐ ܒܗ ܘܐܡܪ: ܚܣ ܠܟ ܡܪܝ. ܕܬܗܘܐ ܠܟ ܗܕܐ.

ܟܕ: ܗܘ ܕܝܢ ܐܬܦܢܝ ܘܐܡܪ ܠܟܐܦܐ: ܙܠ ܠܟ ܠܒܣܬܪܝ ܣܛܢܐ. ܬܘܩܠܬܐ ܐܢܬ ܠܝ. ܕܠܐ ܡܬܪܥܐ ܐܢܬ ܕܐܠܗܐ. ܐܠܐ ܕܒܢܝ̈ܢܫܐ.

ܟܗ: ܗܝܕܝܢ ܐܡܪ ܝܫܘܥ ܠܬܠܡܝܕܘ̈ܗܝ: ܡܢ ܕܨܒܐ ܕܢܐܬܐ ܒܬܪܝ. ܢܟܦܘܪ ܒܢܦܫܗ. ܘܢܫܩܘܠ ܙܩܝܦܗ ܘܢܐܬܐ ܒܬܪܝ.

ܟܘ: ܡܢ ܕܨܒܐ ܓܝܪ ܕܢܚܐ ܢܦܫܗ ܢܘܒܕܝܗ. ܘܡܢ ܕܢܘܒܕ ܢܦܫܗ ܡܛܠܬܝ. ܢܫܟܚܝܗ.

ܟܙ: ܡܢܐ ܓܝܪ ܢܬܗܢܐ ܒܪܢܫܐ ܐܢ ܟܠܗ ܥܠܡܐ ܢܐܬܪ ܘܢܦܫܗ ܢܚܣܪ. ܐܘ ܡܢܐ ܢܬܠ ܒܪܢܫܐ ܚܠܦܐ ܕܢܦܫܗ.

ܟܚ: ܥܬܝܕ ܗܘ ܓܝܪ ܒܪܗ ܕܐܢܫܐ ܕܢܐܬܐ ܒܬܫܒܘܚܬܐ ܕܐܒܘܗܝ ܥܡ ܡܠܐܟܘ̈ܗܝ ܩܕܝ̈ܫܐ. ܘܗܝܕܝܢ ܢܦܪܘܥ ܠܐܢܫ ܐܢܫ ܐܝܟ ܥܒܕܘ̈ܗܝ.

ܟܛ: ܐܡܝܢ ܐܡܪ ܐܢܐ ܠܟܘܢ: ܕܐܝܬ ܐܢܫܐ ܕܩܝܡܝܢ ܬܢܢ ܕܠܐ ܢܛܥܡܘܢ ܡܘܬܐ ܥܕܡܐ ܕܢܚܙܘܢ ܠܒܪܗ ܕܐܢܫܐ ܕܐܬܐ ܒܡܠܟܘܬܗ.

(Continued from p. A - 66)

Jesus, by making a positive play on the nickname, "kepa" which had negative connotations, encouraged Simon. "Kepa," rock metaphorically also means *protection, shelter, support, truth*. The psalmist declared, "God is my rock," i.e., "God is my support, shelter and protection." The Apostle Simon had just stated a powerful truth, "You are the Messiah, the son of the living God!" He had received a revelation from God and confessed it without hesitation. Simon's confession and quickness in seeing the truth about his master was heartening to Jesus, so he told him — "You are a rock (a support) and upon this rock (truth - Peter's statement) I will build my church." Simon would be a "rock" to the followers of Jesus, he would strengthen the brethren and help build the church on the messianic truth of Jesus.

CHAPTER 17

THE TRANSFIGURATION OF JESUS

1. Now after six days,[1] Jesus took Peter and Jacob and John his brother and brought them up into a high mountain[2] alone.

2. And Jesus was transformed in front of them; and his face shone like the sun[3] and his clothes turned white like light.[4]

3. Then Moses and Elijah were seen by them,[5] speaking with him.

4. Now Peter responded and said to Jesus: My lord, it is wonderful for us to be here and if you wish let us make three huts[6] here, one for you, one for Moses and one for Elijah.

5. And while he was speaking, behold a bright cloud overshadowed them;[7] and there was a voice from the cloud,[8] saying: This is my son, the beloved, in whom I take delight. Listen to him!

6. And when the disciples heard it, they bowed their faces to the ground and were exceedingly afraid.

7. Then Jesus approached them and touched them and said: Stand up, do not be afraid!

---

1 "After six days" refers to the time when the Apostle Simon confessed Jesus as the Messiah, the son of the living God. See Mt. 16:15-16. The "six days" may also refer to Exod. 24:13-16 to parallel the appearance of God on Mt Sinai.

2 Some biblical authorities believe "the high mountain" to be Mt. Tabor which today is called Jabal Alshaikh and means *the mountain of the Chief*. The mountain could also be Carmel or Hermon. Be that as it may, "a high mountain" is the proper and appropriate place for a Theophany; i.e., an appearance of God.

3 A comparison with Moses' radiant face, see Ex. 34:30.

4 Eastern mysticism from rabbinic and esoteric sources: The faces of the just are to beam with light and the splendor of God; likewise the brilliant garments are the markings of the chosen.

5 Matthew's purpose for introducing Moses and Elijah at this point in Jesus' ministry was to show that they were the last witnesses under the old Covenant to see the fulfillment of the promised Messiah. Moses represented the law and Elijah, the prophets. The Messiah was to take pre-eminence over Moses and Elijah because of Moses' own prediction. See Deut. 18:15.

6 Simon wanted to build three booths as in the Feast of Booths or Tabernacles. See Deut. 16:13-15, the Feast of Tabernacles.

7 The Shekinah - *the Divine Presence*.

8 In the Bible "clouds" are symbolic of God's presence and glory. See Ex. 24:15, 33:9, 40:34. As God spoke to Moses from the cloud, He now speaks to His son from the cloud.

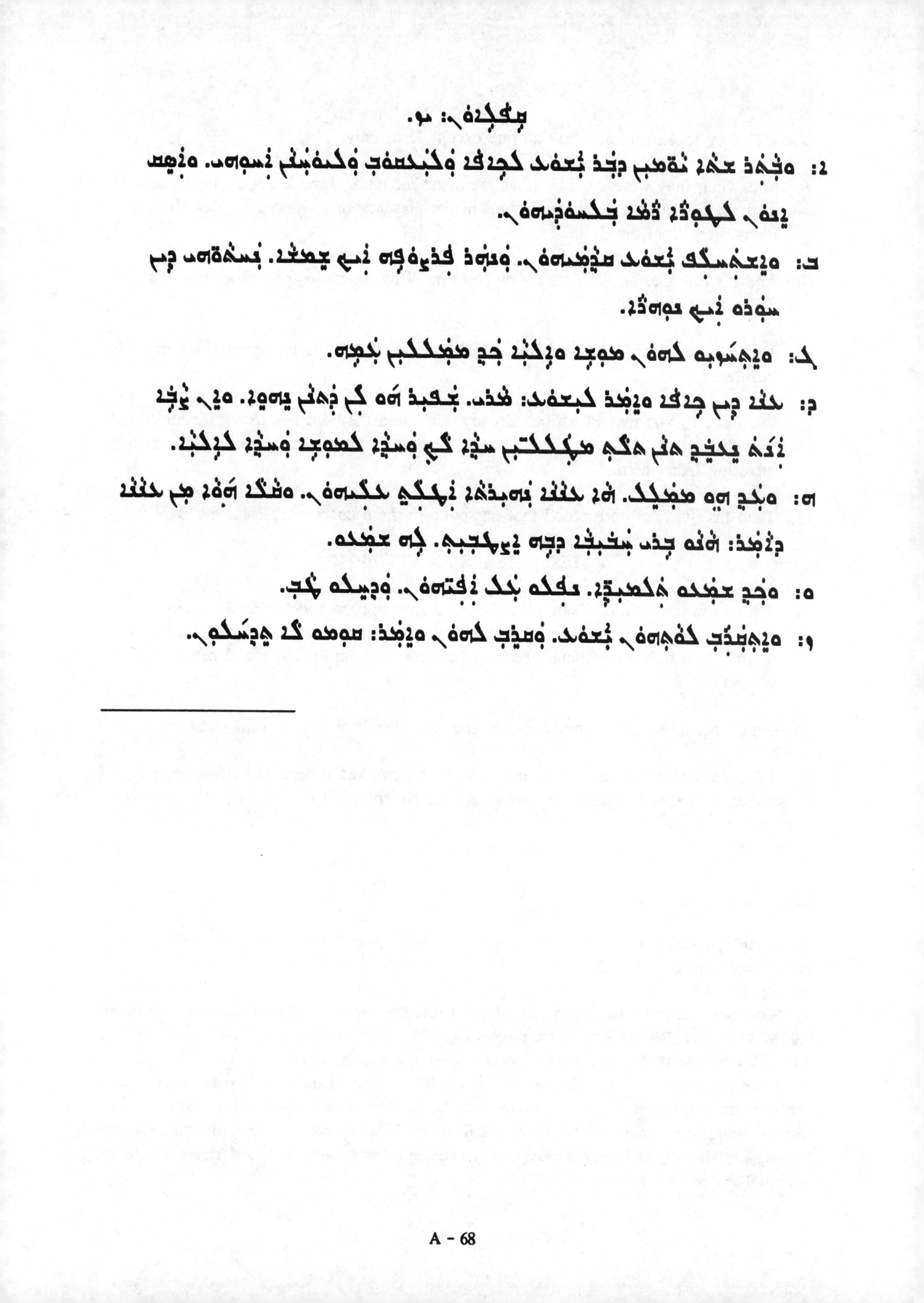

8. And they looked up and saw no one except Jesus only.

9. And when they were coming down from the mountain Jesus charged them and said to them: Do not speak of this vision[9] in the presence of anyone until this Human Being rises from the dead.

10. And his disciples asked him, saying to him: Why, then, do the scribes say that Elijah must come first?

11. Jesus answered and said to them: Elijah does come first so that everything may be fulfilled.[10]

12. But I say to you that Elijah has already come and they did not recognize him[11] and they did to him whatever they wanted. Thus this Human Being, also, is about to be suffering from them.

13. Then his disciples understood that he spoke to them concerning John the Baptizer.

JESUS HEALS AN EPILEPTIC

14. And when they came towards the crowd, a man approached him and bowed himself on his knees and said to him: My lord have compassion on me, my son is subject to fits[12] and is badly afflicted; because he often falls into the fire and often into the water.

15. And I brought him to your disciples and they were not able to heal him.

16. Jesus answered and said: Oh, unbelieving and crooked generation! How long shall I remain with you? And how long shall I be patient with you? Bring him here to me!

---

9 An inner spiritual event. Most scholars accord the Apostle Simon Peter as the recipient of the mystical realization.

10 See Mal. 4:5-6.

11 Some believed Jesus was Elijah, see Mt.16:14, Lk. 9:8, but more believed John the Baptizer was Elijah. In Jn. 1:21, John denies he is the prophet Elijah.

12 ܒܪ ܐܓܪܐ, בר אגרא, Bar Agarey means *lunatic, one who is subject to uncontrollable fits*. This word is a compound noun ܒܪ, בר, bar-son, ܐܓܪܐ, אגרא, Agara-terrace, *son-terrace*. When joined, the meaning is different. See Mt. 4:24, footnote 22. In those days it was believed that a full moon caused traumatic physiological and psychological changes in certain people. The usual symptoms which accompanied the disorder were burning fever, extreme coldness with chills and rigors, erratic and uncontrollable physical movment.

ܚ: ܘܐܪܝܡܘ ܥܝܢܝܗܘܢ. ܘܠܐܢܫ ܠܐ ܚܙܘ ܐܠܐ ܐܢ ܠܝܫܘܥ ܒܠܚܘܕܘܗܝ.

ܛ: ܘܟܕ ܢܚܬܝܢ ܡܢ ܛܘܪܐ ܦܩܕ ܐܢܘܢ ܝܫܘܥ ܘܐܡܪ ܠܗܘܢ: ܠܐܢܫ ܠܐ
ܬܐܡܪܘܢ ܚܙܘܐ ܗܢܐ. ܥܕܡܐ ܕܢܩܘܡ ܒܪܗ ܕܐܢܫܐ ܡܢ ܡܝܬܐ.

ܝ: ܘܫܐܠܘܗܝ ܬܠܡܝܕܘܗܝ ܘܐܡܪܝܢ ܠܗ: ܡܢܐ ܗܟܝܠ ܣܦܪܐ ܐܡܪܝܢ ܕܐܠܝܐ ܘܠܐ
ܕܢܐܬܐ ܠܘܩܕܡ.

ܝܐ: ܥܢܐ ܝܫܘܥ ܘܐܡܪ: ܐܠܝܐ ܐܬܐ ܠܘܩܕܡ. ܕܟܠ ܡܕܡ ܢܫܠܡ.

ܝܒ: ܐܡܪ ܐܢܐ ܠܟܘܢ ܕܝܢ: ܕܗܐ ܐܠܝܐ ܐܬܐ ܘܠܐ ܝܕܥܘܗܝ. ܘܥܒܕܘ ܒܗ ܟܠ ܡܐ
ܕܨܒܘ. ܗܟܢܐ ܐܦ ܒܪܗ ܕܐܢܫܐ ܥܬܝܕ ܕܢܚܫ ܡܢܗܘܢ.

ܝܓ: ܗܝܕܝܢ ܐܣܬܟܠܘ ܬܠܡܝܕܐ ܕܥܠ ܝܘܚܢܢ ܡܥܡܕܢܐ ܐܡܪ ܠܗܘܢ.

ܝܕ: ܘܟܕ ܐܬܘ ܠܘܬ ܟܢܫܐ. ܩܪܒ ܠܗ ܓܒܪܐ ܘܒܪܟ ܥܠ ܒܘܪܟܘܗܝ ܘܐܡܪ ܠܗ:
ܡܪܝ. ܐܬܪܚܡ ܥܠ ܒܪܝ ܕܐܝܬ ܠܗ ܒܪ ܐܓܪܐ. ܘܒܝܫܐܝܬ ܡܬܕܒܪ. ܙܒܢܝܢ ܓܝܪ
ܣܓܝܐܢ. ܒܢܘܪܐ ܢܦܠ ܘܙܒܢܝܢ ܣܓܝܐܢ ܒܡܝܐ.

ܝܗ: ܘܩܪܒܬܗ ܠܬܠܡܝܕܝܟ. ܘܠܐ ܐܫܟܚܘ ܠܡܐܣܝܘܬܗ.

ܝܘ: ܥܢܐ ܝܫܘܥ ܘܐܡܪ: ܐܘ ܫܪܒܬܐ ܕܠܐ ܗܝܡܢܘܬܐ ܘܡܥܩܡܬܐ. ܥܕܡܐ ܐܡܬܝ
ܐܗܘܐ ܥܡܟܘܢ. ܘܥܕܡܐ ܐܡܬܝ ܐܣܝܒܪܟܘܢ. ܐܝܬܐܘܗܝ ܠܝ ܠܟܐ.

17. And Jesus rebuked him and the malady[13] left him; and the boy was healed immediately.

18. Then the disciples approached Jesus privately and said to him: Why were we not able to heal him?

19. Jesus said to them: Because of your unbelief. For truly I say to you that if there be in you faith as tiny as a mustard seed, you may say to this mountain, move from here to there,[14] and it shall move away and nothing shall prevail against you.

20. But this kind[15] does not leave except through fasting and through prayer.

21. Now while they were returning through Galilee, Jesus said to them: This Human Being is about to be turned over to the hands of men.

22. And they shall kill him, but on the third day he will arise. And they grieved exceedingly.

JESUS PAYS TAXES

23. Then when they came to Capernaum, those who collect two coins of silver[16] as head tax approached Peter and said to him: Does not your teacher pay his two coins?

24. He said to them: Yes. And when Peter entered the house, Jesus expected him and said to him: What do you think, Simon? From whom do the kings of the land collect custom duties and head tax, from their children or from strangers?

25. Simon said to him: From strangers. Jesus replied to him: Then the children are free.

26. But so as not to offend them, go to the sea, throw out a hook and the first fish which comes up, open its mouth and you will find a coin,[17] take it and give it for me and for you.

---

13 צבנא, שאדא, Sheda. In Aramaic the noun Sheda *lunatic, demon* is used to describe an unhealthy physical or psychological mood, state or condition. It refers to anyone who is *frantic, raving, frenzied, insane, one who is in a senseless rage, confusion of mind, ill tempered.* In the case of this man's son, (see verse 14, above) Jesus healed the physical condition which had been symptomized in fitful and frenzied behavior.

14 Idiom: The ability to conquer any obstacle or difficulty.

15 This particular kind of illness.

16 Two coins of silver were levied on the male population over twenty years of age to maintain the expenses of the temple. This tax was collected six weeks before Passover. See Ex. 30:13, 38:26.

17 An Aramaic figure of speech. The fish was worth the amount owing for the head tax.

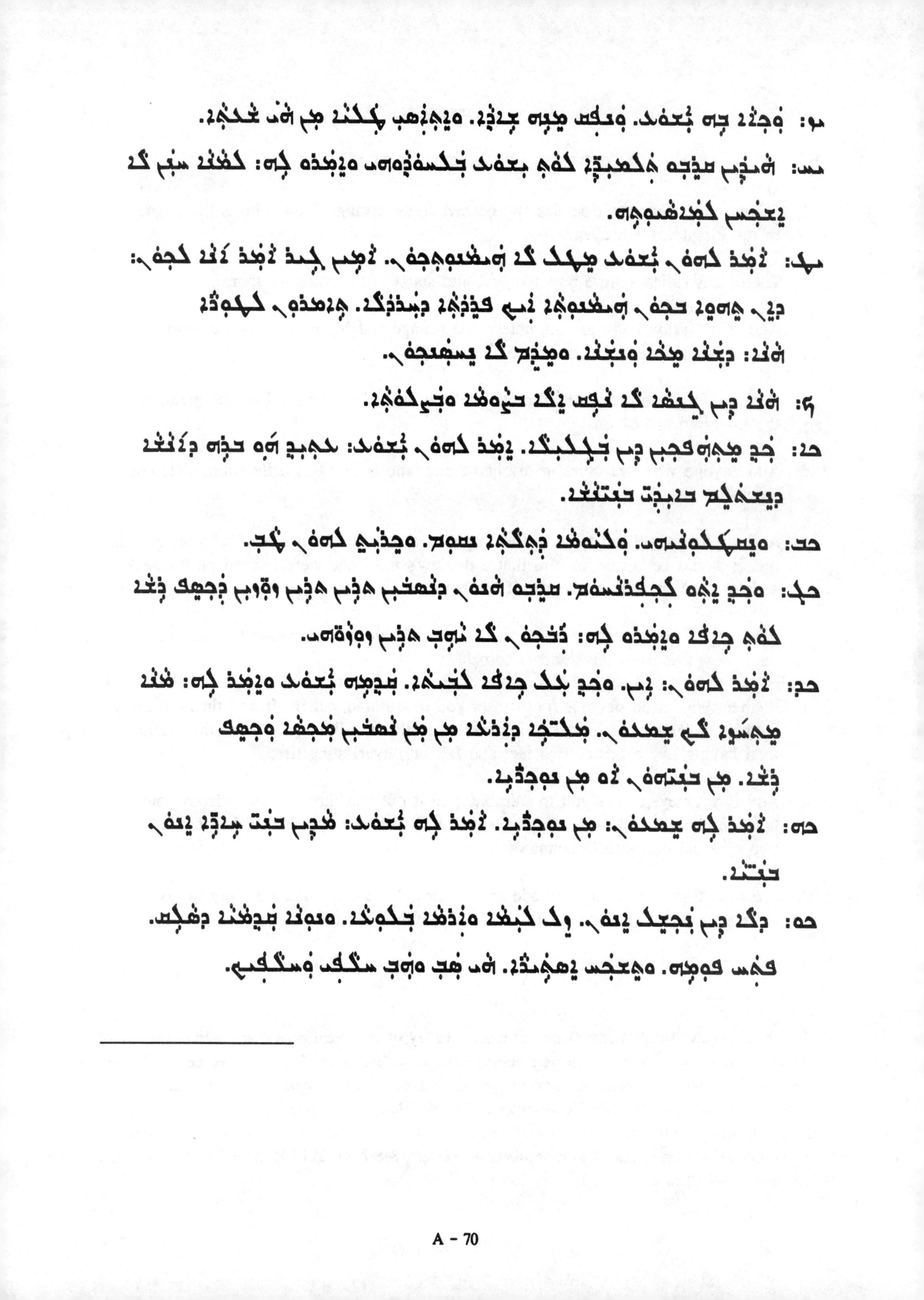

A - 70

ܝܚ: ܘܟܐܐ ܒܗ ܝܫܘܥ. ܘܢܦܩ ܡܢܗ ܫܐܕܐ. ܘܐܬܐܣܝ ܛܠܝܐ ܡܢ ܗܝ ܫܥܬܐ.
ܝܛ: ܗܝܕܝܢ ܩܪܒܘ ܬܠܡܝܕܐ ܠܘܬ ܝܫܘܥ ܒܠܚܘܕܝܗܘܢ ܘܐܡܪܝܢ ܠܗ: ܠܡܢܐ ܚܢܢ ܠܐ
ܐܫܟܚܢ ܠܡܐܣܝܘܬܗ.
ܟ: ܐܡܪ ܠܗܘܢ ܝܫܘܥ ܡܛܠ ܠܐ ܗܝܡܢܘܬܟܘܢ. ܐܡܝܢ ܓܝܪ ܐܡܪ ܐܢܐ ܠܟܘܢ:
ܕܐܢ ܬܗܘܐ ܠܟܘܢ ܗܝܡܢܘܬܐ ܐܝܟ ܦܪܕܬܐ ܕܚܪܕܠܐ. ܬܐܡܪܘܢ ܠܛܘܪܐ
ܗܢܐ: ܕܫܢܝ ܡܟܐ ܘܢܫܢܐ. ܘܡܕܡ ܠܐ ܢܙܟܝܟܘܢ.
ܟܐ: ܗܢܐ ܕܝܢ ܓܢܣܐ ܠܐ ܢܦܩ ܐܠܐ ܒܨܘܡܐ ܘܒܨܠܘܬܐ.
ܟܒ: ܟܕ ܡܬܗܦܟܝܢ ܕܝܢ ܒܓܠܝܠܐ. ܐܡܪ ܠܗܘܢ ܝܫܘܥ: ܥܬܝܕ ܗܘ ܒܪܗ ܕܐܢܫܐ
ܕܢܫܬܠܡ ܒܐܝܕܝ ܒܢܝܢܫܐ.
ܟܓ: ܘܢܩܛܠܘܢܗ. ܘܠܝܘܡܐ ܕܬܠܬܐ ܢܩܘܡ. ܘܟܪܝܬ ܠܗܘܢ ܛܒ.
ܟܕ: ܘܟܕ ܐܬܘ ܠܟܦܪܢܚܘܡ. ܩܪܒܘ ܗܢܘܢ ܕܢܣܒܝܢ ܗܘܘ ܬܪܬܝ ܕܪܟܡܘܢܝܢ
ܠܘܬ ܟܐܦܐ ܘܐܡܪܝܢ ܠܗ: ܪܒܟܘܢ ܠܐ ܝܗܒ ܬܪܬܝ ܕܪܟܡܘܢܝܢ.
ܟܗ: ܐܡܪ ܠܗܘܢ: ܐܝܢ. ܘܟܕ ܥܠ ܟܐܦܐ ܠܒܝܬܐ. ܩܕܡܗ ܝܫܘܥ ܘܐܡܪ ܠܗ: ܡܢܐ
ܡܬܚܙܐ ܠܟ ܫܡܥܘܢ. ܡܠܟܐ ܕܐܪܥܐ ܡܢ ܡܢ ܢܣܒܝܢ ܡܟܣܐ ܘܟܣܦ
ܪܫܐ. ܡܢ ܒܢܝܗܘܢ. ܐܘ ܡܢ ܢܘܟܪܝܐ.
ܟܘ: ܐܡܪ ܠܗ ܫܡܥܘܢ: ܡܢ ܢܘܟܪܝܐ. ܐܡܪ ܠܗ ܝܫܘܥ: ܡܕܝܢ ܚܐܪܝܢ ܐܢܘܢ
ܒܢܝܐ.
ܟܙ: ܕܠܐ ܕܝܢ ܢܟܫܠ ܐܢܘܢ. ܙܠ ܠܝܡܐ ܘܐܪܡܐ ܚܟܬܐ. ܘܢܘܢܐ ܕܣܠܩ ܩܕܡܝܐ
ܦܬܚ ܦܘܡܗ. ܘܬܫܟܚ ܐܣܬܪܐ. ܣܒ ܗܘ ܘܗܒ ܚܠܦܝ ܘܚܠܦܝܟ.

CHAPTER 18

JESUS TEACHES TRUE GREATNESS

1. At that very hour the disciples approached Jesus, asking: Now who is the greatest in the kingdom of heaven?

2. Then Jesus called a little boy and had him stand in the midst of them,

3. And said: Truly I say to you, unless you change and become like little children, you shall not enter the kingdom of heaven.

4. Anyone, then, who humbles himself like this little child, he shall be the greatest in the kingdom of heaven.

5. And anyone who welcomes in my name one who is like this little child, welcomes me.

6. And anyone who becomes a bad example to one of these little ones who believes in me, it would be better for him that a donkey's millstone were hanged on his neck and he were sunk in the depths of the sea.

7. Woe to the world because of scandals! Scandals are sure to come; but woe to the man by whose hand the scandals come!

8. If, then, your hand or your foot causes you to stumble, cut it off and throw it away from you; for it is much better for you to go through life lame or maimed rather than having two hands or two feet and fall into everlasting fire.

9. And if your eye causes you to stumble, pull it out and throw it away from you; because it is better for you to go through life with one eye, rather than having two eyes and fall into Gehenna of fire.[1]

10. See to it that you do not degrade one of these little ones; because I say to you that their guardians in heaven[2] at all times are seeing the face[3] of my Father who is in heaven.

---

[1] ܓܗܢܐ ܕܢܘܪܐ, נהנא דנורא, Gehenna dnoora, valley of Ben Hinnom, a place outside the city of Jerusalem where waste and rubbish were burned. The terms "everlasting fire" and "Gehenna of fire" are used idiomatically and refer to torment, regret and destruction. Verses 8 and 9 should not be understood literally, see Mt. 5:29-30, footnotes 27-29; also "Hell Fire," p. A - 17.

[2] Guardian angels.

[3] Semitic expression meaning "to have direct access to." See 2 Ki. 25:19 Hebrew text, ". . . of them that saw the king's face."

ܡܬܝ: ܝܚ.

ܐ: ܒܗܘ ܥܕܢܐ ܩܪܒܘ ܬܠܡܝܕܐ ܠܘܬ ܝܫܘܥ ܘܐܡܪܝܢ: ܡܢܘ ܟܝ ܪܒ ܒܡܠܟܘܬܐ
ܕܫܡܝܐ.

ܒ: ܘܩܪܐ ܝܫܘܥ ܛܠܝܐ. ܘܐܩܝܡܗ ܒܡܨܥܬܗܘܢ.

ܓ: ܘܐܡܪ ܐܡܝܢ ܐܡܪ ܐܢܐ ܠܟܘܢ: ܕܐܢ ܠܐ ܬܬܗܦܟܘܢ ܘܬܗܘܘܢ ܐܝܟ ܛܠܝܐ. ܠܐ
ܬܥܠܘܢ ܠܡܠܟܘܬܐ ܕܫܡܝܐ.

ܕ: ܡܢ ܗܟܝܠ ܕܡܟܝܟ ܢܦܫܗ ܐܝܟ ܗܢܐ ܛܠܝܐ. ܗܘ ܢܗܘܐ ܪܒ ܒܡܠܟܘܬܐ ܕܫܡܝܐ.

ܗ: ܘܡܢ ܕܢܩܒܠ ܐܝܟ ܛܠܝܐ ܗܢܐ ܒܫܡܝ. ܠܝ ܗܘ ܡܩܒܠ.

ܘ: ܘܟܠ ܕܢܟܫܠ ܠܚܕ ܡܢ ܗܠܝܢ ܙܥܘܪܐ ܕܡܗܝܡܢܝܢ ܒܝ. ܦܩܚ ܗܘܐ ܠܗ ܕܬܬܬܠܐ
ܪܚܝܐ ܕܚܡܪܐ ܒܨܘܪܗ. ܘܢܬܛܒܥ ܒܥܘܡܩܘܗܝ ܕܝܡܐ.

ܙ: ܘܝ ܠܥܠܡܐ ܡܢ ܡܟܫܘܠܐ. ܐܢܢܩܐ ܓܝܪ ܕܢܐܬܘܢ ܡܟܫܘܠܐ. ܘܝ ܕܝܢ ܠܓܒܪܐ
ܕܒܐܝܕܗ ܢܐܬܘܢ ܡܟܫܘܠܐ.

ܚ: ܐܢ ܕܝܢ ܐܝܕܟ ܐܘ ܪܓܠܟ ܡܟܫܠܐ ܠܟ. ܦܣܘܩܝܗ ܘܫܕܝܗ ܡܢܟ. ܛܒ ܗܘ ܠܟ
ܓܝܪ ܕܬܥܘܠ ܠܚܝܐ ܟܕ ܚܓܝܣ ܐܘ ܟܕ ܦܫܝܓ. ܘܠܐ ܟܕ ܐܝܬ ܠܟ
ܬܪܬܝܢ ܐܝܕܝܢ ܐܘ ܬܪܬܝܢ ܪܓܠܝܢ ܬܦܠ ܒܢܘܪܐ ܕܠܥܠܡ.

ܛ: ܘܐܢ ܗܘ ܕܥܝܢܟ ܡܟܫܠܐ ܠܟ. ܚܨܝܗ ܘܫܕܝܗ ܡܢܟ. ܛܒ ܗܘ ܠܟ ܕܒܚܕܐ
ܥܝܢܐ ܬܥܘܠ ܠܚܝܐ. ܘܠܐ ܟܕ ܐܝܬ ܠܟ ܬܪܬܝܢ ܥܝܢܝܢ ܬܦܠ ܒܓܗܢܐ ܕܢܘܪܐ.

ܝ: ܚܙܘ ܠܐ ܬܒܣܘܢ ܥܠ ܚܕ ܡܢ ܗܠܝܢ ܙܥܘܪܐ. ܐܡܪ ܐܢܐ ܠܟܘܢ ܓܝܪ:
ܕܡܠܐܟܝܗܘܢ ܒܫܡܝܐ ܒܟܠܙܒܢ ܚܙܝܢ ܐܦܘܗܝ ܕܐܒܝ ܕܒܫܡܝܐ.

THE LOST SHEEP

11. Because this Human Being has come to give life to anyone who is lost.

12. How does it seem to you? If someone should have one hundred sheep, and one of them should stray, will he not leave the ninety-nine in the mountains, and go and look for the one that strayed?

13. And if he find it, truly I say to you, he rejoices over it more than the ninety-nine that did not stray.

14. Even so, it is not the will of your Father who is in heaven that one of these little ones[4] should perish.

THE ADMONITION CONCERNING A BROTHER AT FAULT

15. Now then if your brother is at fault with you, go and reprimand him[5] just between you and him. If he listens to you, then you have won your brother.

16. But if he does not listen to you, take one or two with you, because from the mouth of two or three witnesses every word shall stand.[6]

17. Now if he will also not listen to them, tell the congregation; then if he will also not listen to the congregation, then regard him as a tax collector and as a pagan.

18. And truly I say to you, whatever you bind on earth will be bound in heaven and whatever you release on earth will be released in heaven.[7]

19. Again I say to you, that if two of you are deserving[8] on earth concerning anything you wish and ask for, it shall be granted to them from my Father who is in heaven.

20. Because wherever two or three gather in my name,[9] I am there among them.

---

4 I.e., "humble believers," or minor community members.
5 Lev. 19:17.
6 Num. 35:30; Deut 17:6, 19:15.
7 "Bind and release" means "forbid and permit." See Mt. 16:19, footnote 12.
8 The term "deserving" in this instance refers to those who have the ability to be responsible for the thing they are requesting. (Example: A father would not give his child a donkey if he did not know how to ride it or care for it.)
9 By my authority and for my service and honor.

ܡܒ: ܐܬܐ ܓܝܪ ܒܪܗ ܕܐܢܫܐ ܕܢܚܐ ܡܕܡ ܕܐܒܝܕ ܗܘܐ.

ܡܓ: ܡܢܐ ܡܬܚܙܐ ܠܟܘܢ. ܐܢ ܢܗܘܘܢ ܠܓܒܪ ܡܐܐ ܥܪܒܝܢ. ܘܢܛܥܐ ܚܕ ܡܢܗܘܢ.
ܠܐ ܫܒܩ ܬܫܥܝܢ ܘܬܫܥܐ ܒܛܘܪܐ. ܘܐܙܠ ܒܥܐ ܠܗܝ ܕܛܥܝܐ.

ܡܕ: ܘܐܢ ܢܫܟܚܝܗ ܐܡܝܢ ܐܡܪ ܐܢܐ ܠܟܘܢ: ܕܚܕܐ ܒܗ ܝܬܝܪ ܡܢ ܬܫܥܝܢ ܘܬܫܥܐ
ܕܠܐ ܛܥܘ.

ܡܗ: ܗܟܢܐ ܠܝܬ ܨܒܝܢܐ ܩܕܡ ܐܒܘܟܘܢ ܕܒܫܡܝܐ ܕܢܐܒܕ ܚܕ ܡܢ ܗܠܝܢ ܙܥܘܪܐ.

ܡܘ: ܐܢ ܕܝܢ ܢܣܟܠ ܒܟ ܐܚܘܟ. ܙܠ ܟܘܢܝܗܝ ܒܝܢܝܟ ܘܠܗ ܒܠܚܘܕ. ܐܢ ܫܡܥܟ.
ܝܬܪܬ ܐܚܘܟ.

ܡܙ: ܘܐܢ ܠܐ ܫܡܥܟ. ܕܒܪ ܥܡܟ ܚܕ ܐܘ ܬܪܝܢ. ܕܥܠ ܦܘܡ ܬܪܝܢ ܐܘ ܬܠܬܐ ܣܗܕܝܢ
ܬܩܘܡ ܟܠ ܡܠܐ.

ܡܚ: ܐܢ ܕܝܢ ܐܦ ܠܗܘܢ ܠܐ ܢܫܡܥ. ܐܡܪ ܠܥܕܬܐ. ܐܢ ܕܝܢ ܐܦ ܠܥܕܬܐ ܠܐ ܢܫܡܥ.
ܢܗܘܐ ܠܟ ܐܝܟ ܡܟܣܐ ܘܐܝܟ ܚܢܦܐ.

ܡܛ: ܘܐܡܝܢ ܐܡܪ ܐܢܐ ܠܟܘܢ: ܕܟܠ ܡܐ ܕܬܐܣܪܘܢ ܒܐܪܥܐ ܢܗܘܐ ܐܣܝܪ
ܒܫܡܝܐ. ܘܡܕܡ ܕܬܫܪܘܢ ܒܐܪܥܐ. ܢܗܘܐ ܫܪܐ ܒܫܡܝܐ.

ܢ: ܬܘܒ ܐܡܪ ܐܢܐ ܠܟܘܢ: ܕܐܢ ܬܪܝܢ ܡܢܟܘܢ ܢܫܬܘܘܢ ܒܐܪܥܐ ܥܠ ܟܠ ܨܒܘ
ܕܢܫܐܠܘܢ. ܢܗܘܐ ܠܗܘܢ ܡܢ ܠܘܬ ܐܒܝ ܕܒܫܡܝܐ.

ܢܐ: ܐܝܟܐ ܓܝܪ ܕܐܝܬܝܗܘܢ ܬܪܝܢ ܐܘ ܬܠܬܐ ܟܢܝܫܝܢ ܒܫܡܝ. ܬܡܢ ܐܢܐ ܒܡܨܥܬܗܘܢ.

THE PRINCIPLE OF FORGIVENESS

21. Then Peter approached him and said to him: My lord, if my brother does a wrong to me, how many times should I forgive him? Up to seven times?[10]

22. Jesus said to him: I do not say to you up to seven times but up to seventy times seven, seven times.[11]

23. Therefore the kingdom of heaven is likened to some king who wished to take an accounting from his servants.

24. And when he began to take the accounting, they brought to him one who owed a million talents.[12]

25. And when he could not pay, his lord ordered that he should be sold, he and his wife and his children and everything he had so he could pay.

26. And that servant fell down and bowed before him and said: My lord, be patient with me and I will pay you everything.

27. Now the lord of that servant had compassion, and released him and cancelled his debt.

28. Then that servant left and found one of his fellow servants, who owed him one hundred dinareh and he grabbed him and was choking him and said to him: Give me everything you owe me.

29. And that fellow servant fell on his knees and begged him and said: Be patient with me and I will pay you.

30. But he was not willing; so he sent and threw him in jail until he might pay him whatever he owed him.

31. Now when their fellow servants saw what was happening they were exceedingly sad, so they came and made known to their lord everything that had occurred.

---

10 The Apostle Simon Peter suggested the sacred number "seven" as a very generous and broad-minded measure of forgiveness.
11 Eastern saying which means *indefiniteness*. See Gen. 4:23.
12 "talent" A weighed amount of money, a weight. In today's money market (1990) a talent would be about $200.00.

ܟܐ: ܗܝܕܝܟ ܩܪܒ ܠܗܘܢ ܟܐܦܐ ܘܐܡܪܐ: ܡܪܝ. ܟܡܐ ܓܗ̈ܐ ܝܢ ܒܚܛܐ ܡܢ ܐܚܐ.

ܝܫܒܘܩ ܠܗ. ܚܕܟܡܐ ܠܫܒܥܐ ܓܗ̈ܝܢ.

ܟܒ: ܐܡܪܐ ܠܗ ܝܫܘܥ: ܠܐ ܐܡܪܐ ܐܢܐ ܠܟ. ܚܕܟܡܐ ܠܫܒܥܐ ܝܠܐ ܚܕܟܡܐ ܠܫܒܥܝܢ

ܓܗ̈ܝܢ ܫܒܥܐ.

ܟܓ: ܡܛܠ ܗܢܐ ܝܗܕܡܝܐ ܡܠܟܘܬܐ ܕܫܡܝܐ ܠܚܕ ܡܠܟܐ ܕܒܥܐ ܕܫܩܠ ܚܘܫܒܢܐ

ܡܢ ܥܒܕ̈ܘܗܝ.

ܟܕ: ܘܟܕ ܫܪܝ ܠܡܫܩܠ ܩܪܒܘ ܠܗ ܚܕ. ܕܚܝܒ ܪܒܘ ܟܟܪ̈ܝܢ.

ܟܗ: ܘܟܕ ܠܝܬ ܗܘܐ ܠܗ ܠܡܦܪܥ. ܦܩܕ ܡܪܗ ܕܙܒܢܝ ܗܘ ܘܐܢܬܬܗ ܘܒܢ̈ܘܗܝ

ܘܟܠ ܡܕܡ ܕܐܝܬ ܠܗ ܘܢܬܦܪܥ.

ܟܘ: ܘܢܦܠ ܗ̇ܘ ܥܒܕܐ ܣܓܕ ܠܗ ܘܐܡܪܐ: ܡܪܝ ܢܓܪ ܪܘܚܟ ܥܡܝ. ܘܟܠ ܡܕܡ ܦܪܥ

ܐܢܐ ܠܟ.

ܟܙ: ܘܐܬܪܚܡ ܡܪܗ ܕܥܒܕܐ ܗ̇ܘ. ܘܫܪܝܠܗ. ܘܫܒܩܠܗ ܚܘܒܐ ܠܗ.

ܟܚ: ܢܦܩ ܕܝܢ ܥܒܕܐ ܗ̇ܘ. ܘܐܫܟܚ ܠܚܕ ܡܢ ܟܢܘ̈ܬܗ. ܕܚܝܒ ܗܘܐ ܠܗ ܕܝܢܪ̈ܐ ܡܐܐ.

ܘܐܚܕܗ ܘܚܢܩ ܗܘܐ ܠܗ ܘܐܡܪܐ ܠܗ: ܗܒ ܠܝ ܡܕܡ ܕܚܝܒ ܐܢܬ ܠܝ.

ܟܛ: ܘܢܦܠ ܗ̇ܘ ܟܢܘܬܗ ܥܠ ܪ̈ܓܠܘܗܝ. ܒܥܐ ܡܢܗ ܘܐܡܪܐ: ܢܓܪ ܪܘܚܟ ܥܡܝ

ܘܦܪܥ ܐܢܐ ܠܟ.

ܠ: ܗܘ ܕܝܢ ܠܐ ܨܒܐ. ܐܠܐ ܐܙܠ ܐܪܡܝܗ ܒܒܝܬ ܐܣܝܪ̈ܐ. ܚܕܟܡܐ ܕܦܪܥ ܠܗ ܗ̇ܘ ܕܚܝܒ

ܠܗ.

ܠܐ: ܟܕ ܚܙܘ ܕܝܢ ܟܢܘ̈ܬܗ ܡܕܡ ܕܗܘܐ. ܟܪܝ ܠܗܘܢ ܛܒ. ܘܐܬܘ ܐܘܕܥܘ

ܠܡܪܗܘܢ ܟܠ ܗ̇ܘ ܕܗܘܐ.

32. Then his lord summoned him and said to him: Wicked servant! Behold, I cancelled that entire debt of yours because you begged me.

33. Should you not have had compassion on your fellow servant, even as I had compassion on you?

34. So his lord was angry and turned him over to the torturers until he should pay him everything he owed him.

35. Thus will my Father who is in heaven do to you if each of you do not forgive his (your) brother his mistakes from your hearts.[13]

---

[13] Jesus reinforces the meaning of the "wicked servant" parable with this last statement. The objective of the parable and this last statement is to contrast the spirit of kindness with that of cruelty. In this typical Eastern manner of speaking he encourages his students and followers to practice forgiveness – releasement. See Mt. 6:15.

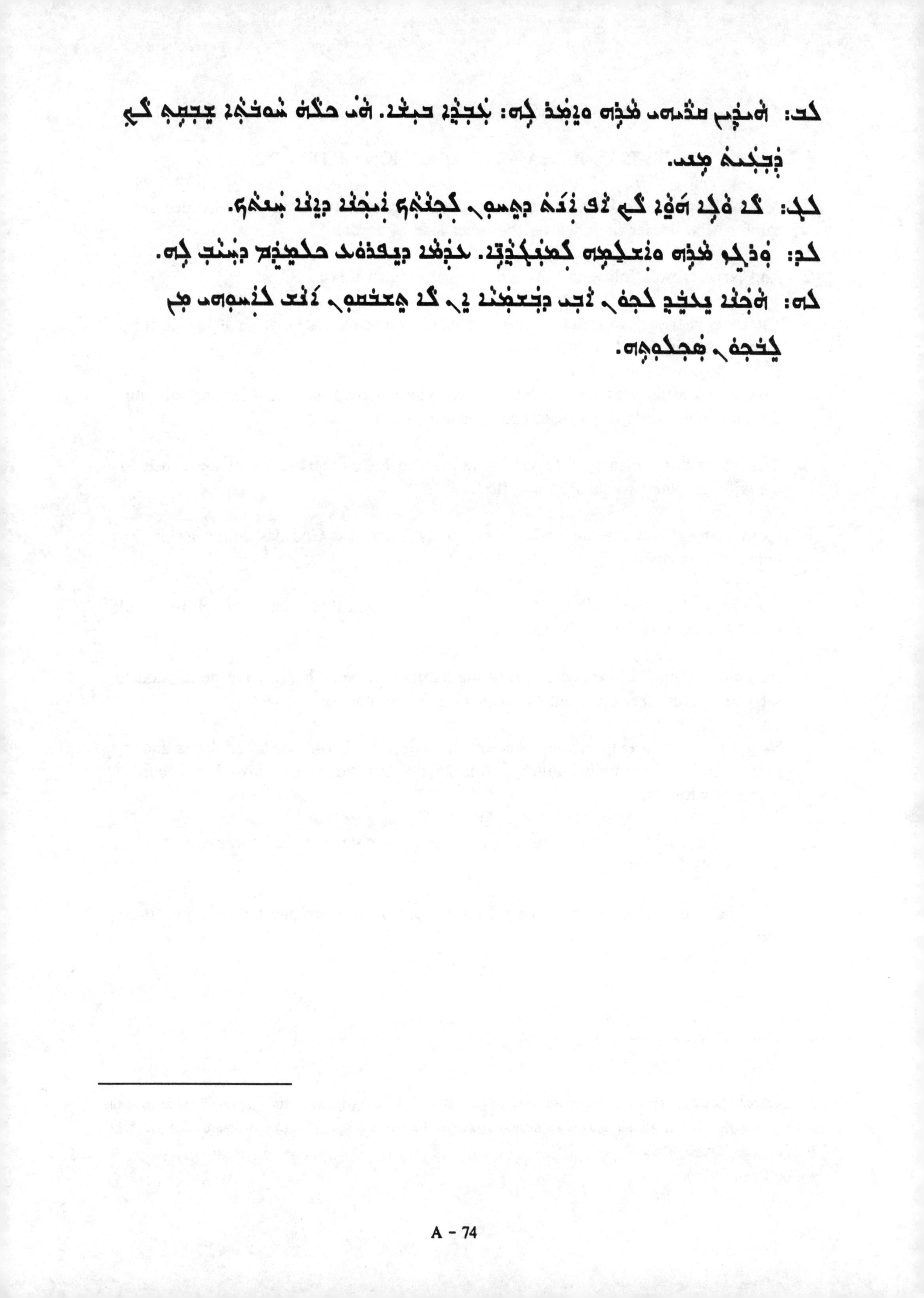

CHAPTER 19

JESUS IN JUDEA – THE QUESTION OF DIVORCE

1. And so it was when Jesus had finished these words, he departed from Galilee and came to the border of Judea on the other side of Jordan.

2. And large crowds followed him and he healed them there.

3. Then the Pharisees approached him and were testing him, saying: Is it lawful for a man to set his wife free for any cause?

4. Now he answered and said to them: Have you not read that He who created from the beginning made them male and female?[1] Then he said:

5. Because of this a man shall leave[2] his father and his mother[3] and shall be joined to his wife and the two shall be one flesh.

6. From then on they are not two, but one body; thus what God has united let no human being divide.

7. They replied to him: Why, then, did Moses command that a letter of release should be given and then let her be set free?[4]

8. He said to them: Moses, considering the hardness of your heart, gave permission to set your wives free, but from the beginning it was not so.

9. Now I say to you that anyone who sets his wife free that is not an adultress and marries another, commits adultery. And anyone who marries an abandoned woman commits adultery.

10. His disciples said to him: If such is the case between a man and a woman, it is not worthwhile to marry.

11. Then he said to them: This saying does not pertain to everyone but to whom it is given.

---

1 Gen. 1:27.
2 ܢܫܒܘܩ, נשׁבוֹק, Nishboq, from the root ܫܒܩ, שׁבק, meaning *to separate, leave*. This is also the same word used for a woman who is separated from her husband; also a divorced woman. See Mt. 5:32.
3 See Gen. 2:24.
4 See Deut. 24:1–4.

_____
A - 75

12. Because there are some eunuchs born so from their mother's womb; there are some eunuchs who were made eunuchs by men; and there are some eunuchs who have made themselves faithful ones[5] because of the kingdom of heaven. To anyone who can take it, let him accept it.

JESUS BLESSES THE CHILDREN – THE RICH YOUNG MAN

13. Now they brought little children to him so that he might place his hand on them[6] and pray; yet his disciples rebuked them.

14. Then Jesus said to them: Allow the little children to come to me and do not stop them; because the kingdom of heaven is for such as these.[7]

15. And he placed his hand on them, then he went from there.

16. And one came, approached, and said to him: Oh, wonderful[8] teacher! What good thing shall I do so that eternal life will be mine?

17. Then he said to him: Why do you call me wonderful? There is no one wonderful except the one God.[9] But if you wish to enter into life, obey the commandments.

18. He replied to him: Which ones? And Jesus said to him: You shall not murder;[10] you shall not commit adultery;[11] you shall not steal;[12] you shall not bear false witness;[13]

---

5 ܡܗܝܡܢܐ, מהימנא, Mheymna has many meanings in Aramaic. Its primary meaning is *faithful, someone who is sincere, a servant, a steward, and trustworthy*. Its final meaning is *eunuch*. Those who made themselves eunuchs for the kingdom's sake refers to people who became faithful servants of the kingdom by voluntarily giving up their right to marry; i.e., by becoming celibates.

6 Semitic custom when giving a blessing. See Gen. 48:14.

7 For disciples who are like children.

8 ܛܒܐ, מבא, Tawa, *good, wonderful, well, righteous*. In this context the word Tawa means a wonderfully skilled teacher. It refers to quality of work such as a wonderful carpenter, shepherd and so on.

9 God is the only wonderful teacher. What Jesus taught was not his own teaching, but it was given to him by the one who sent him, his heavenly Father. "Jesus answered saying: My teaching is not mine, but his who sent me." Jn. 7:16.

10 Ex. 20:13, Deut. 5:17.

11 Ex. 20:14, Deut. 5:18.

12 Ex. 20:15, Deut. 5:19.

13 Ex. 20:16, Deut. 5:20.

مد: .

مح: .

مو: .

مح: .

مه: .

مو: .

مح: .

───────────

19. And honor your father and your mother[14] and you shall love your neighbor as yourself.[15]

20. That young man said to him: All these things have I kept from my childhood, what do I lack?

21. Jesus said to him: If you wish to be complete,[16] go, sell your possessions and give to the poor[17] and you will have a treasure in heaven; then follow me.

22. But when the young man heard that word, he went away sad, because he had many possessions.

23. Then Jesus said to his disciples: Truly I say to you, it is difficult for a rich man to enter the kingdom of heaven.

24. Now again I say to you, it is easier for a rope[18] to enter the eye of a needle than for a rich man to enter the kingdom of God.

25. Then when the disciples heard it, they were exceedingly surprised, saying: Who then can have eternal life?

26. Jesus looked at them and said to them: According to human dealings this is impossible but according to God's way everything is possible.

THE BLESSINGS IN THE MESSIANIC AGE

27. Then Peter answered and said to him: Behold we have left everything and have followed you, what will we have?

28. Jesus replied to them: Truly, I say to you that as for you who have followed me in the new world[19] when this Human Being sits upon the throne of his glory, you also will sit on twelve chairs and judge the twelve tribes of Israel.

---

14 Ex. 20:12, Deut. 5:16.
15 Lev. 19:18.
16 ܓܡܝܪܐ, גמירא, Gmeera, *complete, thorough;* i.e., one who observes all of the law. See Mt. 5:48, footnote 44.
17 The young man would have to divest himself of his possessions so he would not become burdened with the care of those things while becoming a disciple. Wealth, at that time, largely consisted of cattle and sheep.
18 ܓܡܠܐ, גמלא, Gamla in this verse is traditionally translated as "camel." The Aramaic term "Gamla" has several meanings. One is *rope;* another is *camel.* But in this context, it refers to a "rope."
19 In the Messianic era.

ܝܛ: ܘܝܩܪ ܠܐܒܘܟ ܘܠܐܡܟ. ܘܐܚܒ ܠܩܪܝܒܟ ܐܝܟ ܢܦܫܟ.

ܟ: ܐܡܪ ܠܗ: ܗܘ ܥܠܝܡܐ: ܗܠܝܢ ܟܠܗܝܢ ܢܛܪܬ ܐܢܝܢ ܡܢ ܛܠܝܘܬܝ. ܡܢܐ ܚܣܝܪ ܐܢܐ.

ܟܐ: ܐܡܪ ܠܗ ܝܫܘܥ: ܐܢ ܨܒܐ ܐܢܬ ܕܬܗܘܐ ܓܡܝܪܐ. ܙܠ ܙܒܢ ܩܢܝܢܟ. ܘܗܒ ܠܡܣܟܢܐ ܘܬܗܘܐ ܠܟ ܣܝܡܬܐ ܒܫܡܝܐ. ܘܬܐ ܒܬܪܝ.

ܟܒ: ܫܡܥ ܕܝܢ ܗܘ ܥܠܝܡܐ ܡܠܬܐ ܗܕܐ. ܘܐܙܠ ܟܕ ܟܪܝܐ ܠܗ. ܐܝܬ ܗܘܐ ܠܗ ܓܝܪ ܢܟܣܐ ܣܓܝܐܐ.

ܟܓ: ܝܫܘܥ ܕܝܢ ܐܡܪ ܠܬܠܡܝܕܘܗܝ: ܐܡܝܢ ܐܡܪ ܐܢܐ ܠܟܘܢ. ܕܥܛܠܐ ܠܥܬܝܪܐ ܠܡܥܠ ܠܡܠܟܘܬ ܫܡܝܐ.

ܟܕ: ܘܬܘܒ ܕܝܢ ܐܡܪ ܐܢܐ ܠܟܘܢ. ܕܦܫܝܩ ܗܘ ܠܓܡܠܐ ܠܡܥܠ ܒܚܪܘܪܐ ܕܡܚܛܐ ܐܘ ܥܬܝܪܐ ܠܡܥܠ ܠܡܠܟܘܬܐ ܕܐܠܗܐ.

ܟܗ: ܬܠܡܝܕܐ ܕܝܢ ܟܕ ܫܡܥܘ. ܬܡܗܘ ܛܒ ܘܐܡܪܝܢ: ܡܢܘ ܟܝ ܡܫܟܚ ܠܡܚܐ.

ܟܘ: ܚܪ ܒܗܘܢ ܝܫܘܥ. ܘܐܡܪ ܠܗܘܢ: ܠܘܬ ܒܢܝܢܫܐ ܗܕܐ ܠܐ ܡܫܟܚܐ. ܠܘܬ ܐܠܗܐ ܕܝܢ ܟܠܡܕܡ ܡܫܟܚܐ.

ܟܙ: ܗܝܕܝܢ ܥܢܐ ܟܐܦܐ ܘܐܡܪ ܠܗ: ܗܐ ܚܢܢ ܫܒܩܢ ܟܠܡܕܡ ܘܐܬܝܢ ܒܬܪܟ. ܡܢܐ ܟܝ ܢܗܘܐ ܠܢ.

ܟܚ: ܐܡܪ ܠܗܘܢ ܝܫܘܥ: ܐܡܝܢ ܐܡܪ ܐܢܐ ܠܟܘܢ. ܕܐܢܬܘܢ ܕܐܬܝܬܘܢ ܒܬܪܝ ܒܥܠܡܐ ܚܕܬܐ. ܡܐ ܕܝܬܒ ܒܪܗ ܕܐܢܫܐ ܥܠ ܟܘܪܣܝܐ ܕܫܘܒܚܗ. ܬܬܒܘܢ ܐܦ ܐܢܬܘܢ ܥܠ ܬܪܥܣܪ ܟܘܪܣܘܢ. ܘܬܕܘܢܘܢ ܬܪܥܣܪ ܫܒܛܝܢ ܕܐܝܣܪܝܠ.

29. And anyone who gives up houses, or brothers or sisters or a father or a mother or a wife or children or small villages because of my name, will receive a hundred fold and inherit eternal life.

30. But many who are first will be last and the last, first.

ܟܛ: ܘܟܠ ܐܢܫ ܕܫܒܩ ܒ̈ܬܐ. ܐܘ ܐܚ̈ܐ. ܐܘ ܐܚ̈ܘܬܐ. ܐܘ ܐܒܐ. ܐܘ ܐܡܐ. ܐܘ ܐܢܬܬܐ.
ܐܘ ܒܢ̈ܝܐ. ܐܘ ܩܘܪ̈ܝܐ ܡܛܠ ܫܡܝ. ܚܕ ܒܡܐܐ ܢܣܒ. ܘܚܝ̈ܐ ܕܠܥܠܡ ܢܐܪܬ.
ܠ: ܣܓܝ̈ܐܐ ܕܝܢ ܩܕܡ̈ܝܐ ܕܢܗܘܘܢ ܐܚܪ̈ܝܐ. ܘܐܚܪ̈ܝܐ ܩܕܡ̈ܝܐ.

CHAPTER 20

THE PARABLE OF THE WORKERS IN THE VINEYARD

1. Now the kingdom of heaven is like a man, a householder who left early in the morning so he might hire workers for his vineyard.

2. Then he contracted with the workers for a dinara a day[1] and he sent them to his vineyard.

3. And he went out at the third hour[2] and saw others standing idle in the marketplace.

4. And he said to them: You also go to the vineyard, and whatever is right I will give it to you.

5. Then they went, and again he went out at the sixth hour[3] and the ninth hour[4] and did the same thing.

6. And around the eleventh hour,[5] he went out and found others standing idle, and he said to them: Why are you standing idle all day?

7. They replied to him: No one has hired us. He said to them: You also go to the vineyard and you will receive what you deserve.

8. And when it was evening, the owner of the vineyard said to his steward: Summon the workers and give them their earnings and start with the last until the first.

9. Then came the eleventh hour ones and they each received a dinara.

10. And when the first ones arrived, they were expecting to receive extra, but they also each received a dinara.

11. And when they received it, they complained to the householder,

12. Saying: These last ones worked only one hour and you have made them equal with us who have carried the burden of the day and its heat.

---

1 The standard minimum wage for a day's work.
2 Nine o'clock.
3 Noon.
4 Three o'clock.
5 Five o'clock.

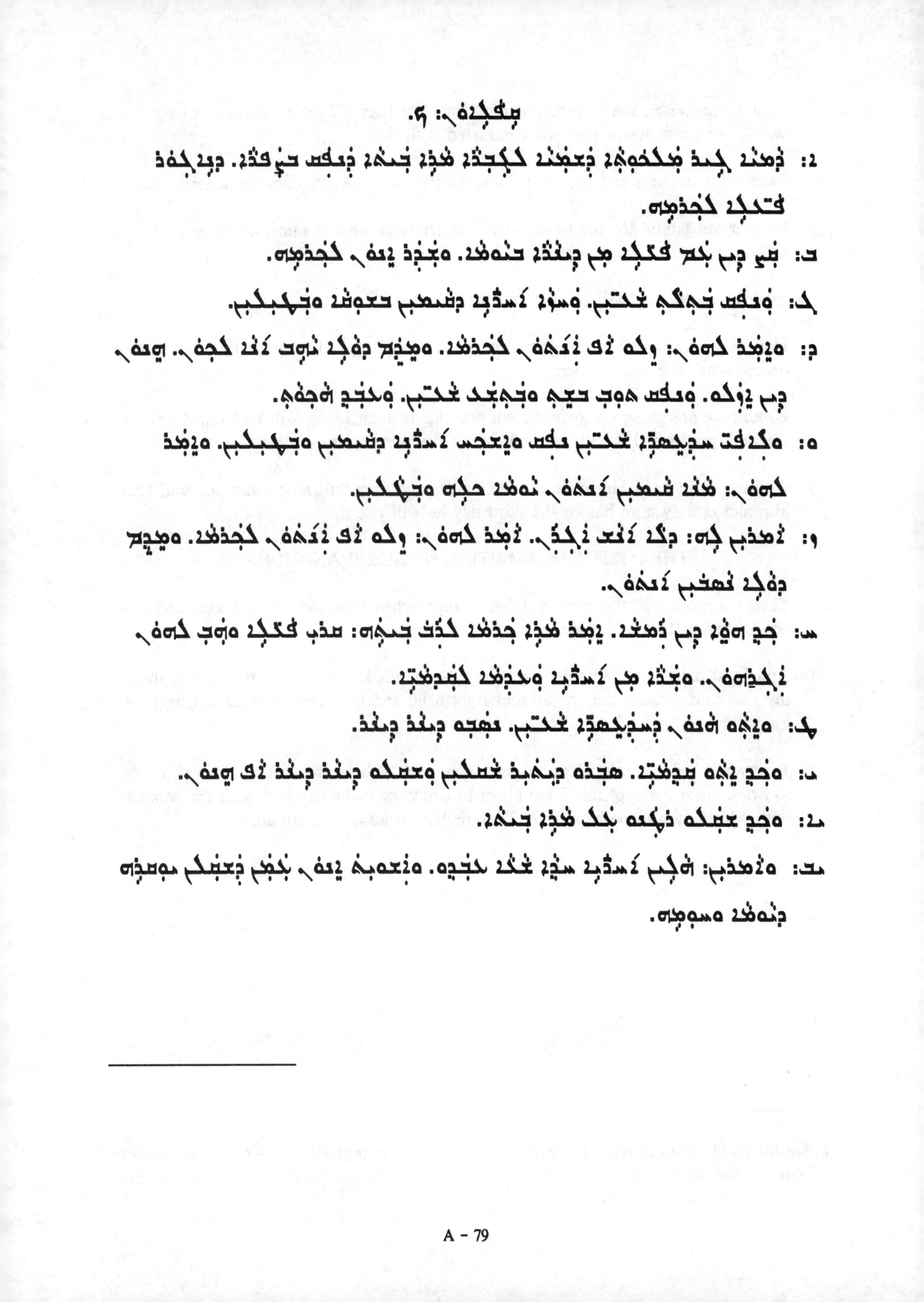

A - 79

13. Now he answered and said to one of them: My friend, I do no injustice to you, was it not for a dinara that you contracted with me?

14. Take what is yours and go, for I desire to give to these last ones the same as you.

15. Or is it not lawful for me to do what I desire with what is mine, or are you envious because I am generous?

16. In this way the last will be first and the first, last.

17. Now Jesus was about to go up to Jerusalem and he took the twelve disciples aside on the road, and said to them:

18. Behold we are going up to Jerusalem and this Human Being will be handed over to the high priests and the scribes and they will sentence him to death.

19. And they will hand him over to the Gentiles and they will mock him and will beat him and crucify him; but on the third day he will rise up.

THE POLITICAL AMBITION OF JACOB AND JOHN

20. Then the mother of the sons of Zebedee approached him, she and her sons; and she bowed before him, and asked something of him.

21. And he said to her: What do you wish? She replied to him: Command that these my two sons will sit, the one at your right hand and the other on your left, in your kingdom.

22. Jesus answered and said: You do not know what you are requesting. Are you able to drink from the cup[6] that I am about to drink, or to be baptized with the baptism with which I am to be baptized? They replied to him: We are able!

---

6 See Mt. 26:39. The cup refers to the cup of death. Jesus, through the symbol of the cup, points to his suffering and death.

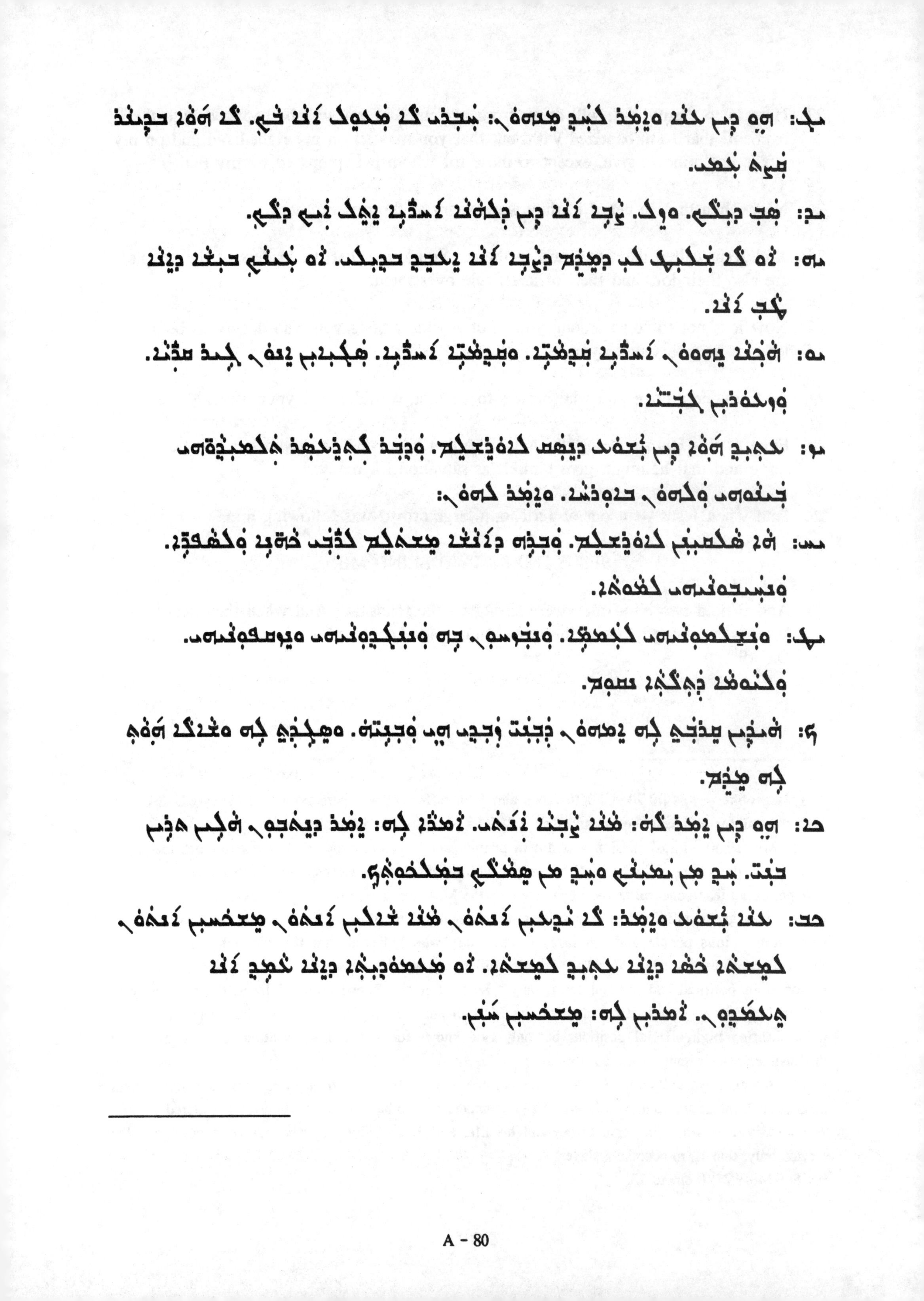

23. He said to them: You will drink from my cup and you will be baptized with the baptism[7] that I am baptized with, but that you may sit on my right hand and on my left is not mine to give, except to those for whom it is prepared by my Father.[8]

24. Now when the ten heard it, they were angry at the two brothers.

25. And Jesus called them and said to them: You know that the leaders of the people are also their lord and their officials rule over them.

26. Now it is not to be so among you. But anyone among you who desires to be great, let him be a servant to you.

27. And anyone among you who desires to be first, consider him your server.[9]

28. Even as this Human Being did not come that he should be served but that he might serve and that he might give himself as salvation for many.

29. And when Jesus went out of Jericho, a large crowd was following him.

JESUS HEALS TWO BLIND MEN

30. And behold two blind men were sitting by the roadside. And when they heard Jesus was passing by, they shouted saying: Have compassion on us, my lord, son of David![10]

---

7 This prophecy was fulfilled. Both Jacob and John suffered, were persecuted and martyred. See Acts 12:2, the murder of Jacob (James) and Rev. 1:9, John exiled on the island of Patmos.

8 See Mk. 10:40. Jesus' mission was not to promote one apostle over another but to teach the joyful message of the kingdom and to seal his gospel with his death and resurrection. At that time there were two popular ideas concerning the appearance of the Messiah: 1) the majority believed that the Messiah was to be a great military leader who was to subjugate all nations to Israel. See Dan. 7:14; 2) there were some pious people and scholars of Jesus' day who believed that the Messiah was to be the suffering servant. See Isa. 53. The Apostles did not grasp the message of the suffering Messiah but reasoned in political and militant terms only. Even after the Resurrection of Jesus, their minds were still influenced by the political ideal of the Messiah and his kingdom, see Acts 1:6. Jacob and John were wanting high official positions but only God knows for whom those positions are prepared. In this manner Jesus dismissed the entire matter.

9 The Aramaic word ܥܒܕܐ, עַבְדָא, Awda is derived from the verb *to do* or *to serve* and has several meanings: 1) an individual who is under the command of another and does whatever is ordered of him, 2) an individual who will serve throughout his life, and 3) an individual who has been purchased for service only, that is, to become a slave.

10 See Mt. 9:27, footnote 23.

ܟܓ: ܐܡܪ ܠܗܘܢ: ܟܣܝ ܬܫܬܘܢ. ܘܡܥܡܘܕܝܬܐ ܕܐܢܐ ܥܡܕ ܐܢܐ ܬܥܡܕܘܢ.
ܕܬܬܒܘܢ ܕܝܢ ܡܢ ܝܡܝܢܝ ܘܡܢ ܣܡܠܝ. ܠܐ ܗܘܬ ܕܝܠܝ ܠܡܬܠ. ܐܠܐ
ܠܐܝܠܝܢ ܕܡܛܝܒܐ ܡܢ ܐܒܝ.

ܟܕ: ܟܕ ܕܝܢ ܫܡܥܘ ܥܣܪܐ. ܐܬܚܡܬܘ ܥܠ ܬܪܝܗܘܢ ܐܚܐ.

ܟܗ: ܘܩܪܐ ܐܢܘܢ ܝܫܘܥ ܘܐܡܪ ܠܗܘܢ: ܝܕܥܝܢ ܐܢܬܘܢ ܕܪ̈ܫܢܐ ܕܥܡ̈ܡܐ
ܡܪ̈ܝܗܘܢ ܐܢܘܢ. ܘܪܘܪ̈ܒܢܝܗܘܢ ܫܠܝܛܝܢ ܥܠܝܗܘܢ.

ܟܘ: ܠܐ ܕܝܢ ܗܟܢܐ ܢܗܘܐ ܒܟܘܢ. ܐܠܐ ܡܢ ܕܨܒܐ ܒܟܘܢ ܕܢܗܘܐ ܪܒܐ. ܢܗܘܐ
ܠܟܘܢ ܡܫܡܫܢܐ.

ܟܙ: ܘܡܢ ܕܨܒܐ ܒܟܘܢ ܕܢܗܘܐ ܩܕܡܝܐ. ܢܗܘܐ ܠܟܘܢ ܥܒܕܐ.

ܟܚ: ܐܝܟܢܐ ܕܒܪܗ ܕܐܢܫܐ ܠܐ ܐܬܐ ܕܢܫܬܡܫ. ܐܠܐ ܕܢܫܡܫ. ܘܕܢܬܠ ܢܦܫܗ
ܦܘܪܩܢܐ ܚܠܦ ܣܓܝܐܐ.

ܟܛ: ܘܟܕ ܢܦܩ ܝܫܘܥ ܡܢ ܐܝܪܝܚܘ. ܐܬܐ ܒܬܪܗ ܟܢܫܐ ܣܓܝܐܐ.

ܠ: ܘܗܐ ܣܡܝܐ ܬܪܝܢ ܝܬܒܝܢ ܗܘܘ ܥܠ ܝܕ ܐܘܪܚܐ. ܘܟܕ ܫܡܥܘ ܕܝܫܘܥ ܥܒܪ.
ܩܥܘ ܠܡܐܡܪ: ܐܬܪܚܡ ܥܠܝܢ ܡܪܢ ܒܪܗ ܕܕܘܝܕ.

31. Now the crowd reprimanded them that they might be quiet. But they raised their voice more, saying: Our lord, have compassion on us, son of David![11]

32. And Jesus stopped and called them and said: What do you wish that I should do for you?

33. They replied to him: Our lord, oh, that our eyes may be opened!

34. And Jesus had compassion on them and he touched their eyes and immediately their eyes were opened and they followed him.

---

11 See Mt. 9:27, footnote 23.

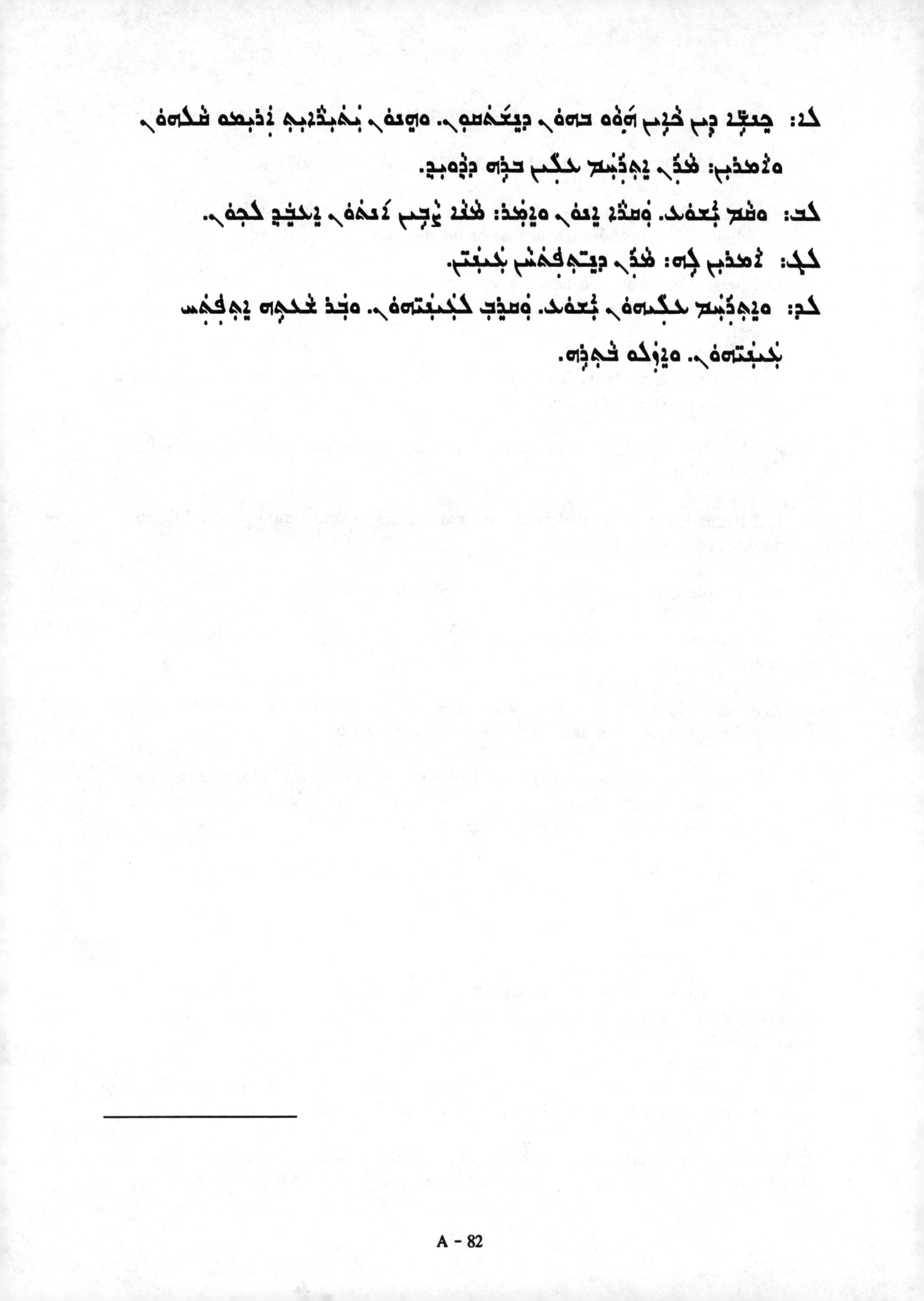

CHAPTER 21

JESUS ENTERS JERUSALEM ON A DONKEY - A SPIRITUAL TRIUMPH

1. Now when they approached Jerusalem and they came to Bethphage[1] on the side of the Mount of Olives,[2] Jesus sent two of his disciples,

2. And he said to them: Go into this village which is in front of you, and right away you will find a donkey tied and a colt with her. Untie them and lead them to me.

3. And if someone says anything to you, tell him that they are needed by our lord; and he will immediately send them here.

4. All this, then, happened so that what was spoken by the prophet might be fulfilled when he said:

5. Tell the daughter of Zion, Behold your king comes to you, humble and riding on a donkey, and on a colt the foal of a donkey.[3]

6. And the disciples went and did as Jesus had ordered them.

7. And they led the donkey and the colt and they put their garments on the colt, then Jesus rode on it.

8. And tremendous crowds spread their clothes on the road;[4] then others were cutting branches from the trees and spreading them on the road.

9. And the crowds who were going ahead of him and coming behind him were shouting and saying: Oshana[5] to the son of David! Blessed is he who comes in the name of the LORD![6] Oshana in the highest!

10. And when he entered Jerusalem, the entire city was shaken[7] and they were asking: Who is this?

---

1 Literal meaning, *house of unripe figs*. A small village near Jerusalem and Bethany.
2 Part of the range of mountains which runs north and south through central and southern Israel.
3 See Zech 9:9.
4 See 2 Ki. 9:13.
5 ܐܘܿܫܲܥܢܵܐ, אוֹשַׁעְנָא, Oshana. In Hebrew "Hosanna." Literally it means *save now*. This is an idiomatic phrase of praise, joy and celebration. It also means "God save," or "God bring the victory."
6 See Ps. 118:25-26.
7 "Shaken" as if by an earthquake. "The entire city was shaken" is an Eastern amplification. See Mt. 2:3, footnote 5, Mt. 8:32, footnote 22 and Mt. 13:34, footnote 7.

ܡܬܝ: ܟܐ.

ܐ: ܘܟܕ ܩܪܒ ܠܐܘܪܫܠܡ. ܘܐܬܐ ܠܒܝܬ ܦܐܓܐ ܥܠ ܓܢܒ ܛܘܪܐ ܕܙܝܬܐ. ܫܕܪ
ܝܫܘܥ ܬܪܝܢ ܡܢ ܬܠܡܝܕܘܗܝ.

ܒ: ܘܐܡܪ ܠܗܘܢ: ܙܠܘ ܠܩܪܝܬܐ ܗܕܐ ܕܠܘܩܒܠܟܘܢ. ܘܡܚܕܐ ܡܫܟܚܝܢ ܐܢܬܘܢ
ܚܡܪܐ ܕܐܣܝܪܐ ܘܥܝܠܐ ܥܡܗ. ܫܪܘ ܐܝܬܘ ܠܝ.

ܓ: ܘܐܢ ܐܢܫ ܢܐܡܪ ܠܟܘܢ ܡܕܡ. ܐܡܪܘ ܠܗ: ܕܠܡܪܢ ܡܬܒܥܝܢ. ܘܡܚܕܐ ܡܫܕܪ
ܠܗܘܢ ܠܟܐ.

ܕ: ܗܕܐ ܕܝܢ ܕܗܘܬ ܕܢܬܡܠܐ ܡܕܡ ܕܐܬܐܡܪ ܒܝܕ ܢܒܝܐ ܕܐܡܪ:

ܗ: ܐܡܪܘ ܠܒܪܬ ܨܗܝܘܢ. ܗܐ ܡܠܟܟܝ ܐܬܐ ܠܟܝ ܡܟܝܟ ܘܪܟܝܒ ܥܠ ܚܡܪܐ ܘܥܠ
ܥܝܠܐ ܒܪ ܐܬܢܐ.

ܘ: ܘܐܙܠܘ ܬܠܡܝܕܐ. ܘܥܒܕܘ ܐܝܟܢܐ ܕܦܩܕ ܠܗܘܢ ܝܫܘܥ.

ܙ: ܘܐܝܬܝܘ ܠܚܡܪܐ ܘܠܥܝܠܐ. ܘܣܡܘ ܥܠ ܥܝܠܐ ܢܚܬܝܗܘܢ. ܘܪܟܒ ܥܠܘܗܝ
ܝܫܘܥ.

ܚ: ܘܣܘܓܐܐ ܕܟܢܫܐ ܡܫܘܝܢ ܗܘܘ ܢܚܬܝܗܘܢ ܒܐܘܪܚܐ. ܐܚܪܢܐ ܕܝܢ ܦܣܩܝܢ ܗܘܘ
ܣܘܟܐ ܡܢ ܐܝܠܢܐ. ܘܪܡܝܢ ܒܐܘܪܚܐ.

ܛ: ܟܢܫܐ ܕܝܢ ܕܐܙܠܝܢ ܗܘܘ ܩܕܡܘܗܝ ܘܐܬܝܢ ܒܬܪܗ. ܩܥܝܢ ܗܘܘ ܘܐܡܪܝܢ:
ܐܘܫܥܢܐ ܠܒܪܗ ܕܕܘܝܕ. ܒܪܝܟ ܗܘ ܕܐܬܐ ܒܫܡܗ ܕܡܪܝܐ. ܐܘܫܥܢܐ
ܒܡܪܘܡܐ.

ܝ: ܘܟܕ ܥܠ ܠܐܘܪܫܠܡ. ܐܬܬܙܝܥܬ ܟܠܗ ܡܕܝܢܬܐ ܘܐܡܪܝܢ ܗܘܘ: ܡܢܘ ܗܢܐ.

11. And the crowds were answering: This is Jesus the prophet who is from Nazareth of Galilee!

THE PROVOCATION IN THE TEMPLE

12. So Jesus entered the temple of God and he put out all those who were buying and selling in the temple; and he overturned the trays of the money changers[8] and the stands of those who sold doves.[9]

13. And he said to them: It is written that my house shall be called a house of prayer but you have made it a cave of bandits.[10]

14. And in the temple they brought to him the blind and the lame and he healed them.

15. But when the high priests and the Pharisees saw the wonders he did and the children shouting in the temple and saying Oshana to the son of David,[11] they were displeased,

16. And were saying to him: Do you hear what these (children) are saying? Jesus said to them: Yes. Have you never read, Out of the mouths of children and little ones, You have prepared a chant?[12]

THE BARREN FIG TREE AND A LESSON IN FAITH

17. And he left them and went outside the city to Bethany and he lodged there.

18. Then early morning when he returned to the city, he became hungry.

19. And he saw a fig tree by the road and he came to it and found nothing on it except leaves only, then he said to it: There shall never be any fruit on you again, forever![13] And right away the fig tree dried up.

---

8 Foreign coins were not allowed in the temple because they bore the inscription of their foreign kings, and in particular, the Emperor Caesar. See Mt. 22:19-21. The money changers exchanged the foreign coins for the temple coins.
9 Doves were the offering of the poor people.
10 Some of the vendors were abusing their privileges and were profiteering. See Isa. 56:5-7 and Jer. 7:11.
11 In this verse "son of David" refers to the Messiah.
12 Ps. 8:2.
13 This is an Eastern saying which expresses great disappointment. Jesus was hungry and expressed his disappointment when he discovered there were no figs on the tree. Sometimes, Easterners put a curse on the "thing" which disappoints them. A curse spoken by a holy man has power.

مد: ܚܕܝܪ ܕܝܢ ܐܡܪܝܢ ܐܢܘܢ: ܐܦܠܐ ܐܢܥܢܐ ܝܕܥܝܢ ܕܡܢ ܐܝܟܐ ܗܘ ܒܝܟܒܝܢܐ.

מה: ܘܐܡܪ ܠܗܘܢ ܝܫܘܥ ܐܦܠܐ ܐܢܐ ܐܡܪ ܐܢܐ ܠܟܘܢ. ܒܐܝܢܐ ܫܘܠܛܢܐ ܗܠܝܢ ܥܒܕ ܐܢܐ. ܘܫܪܝ ܠܡܐܡܪ ܡܬܠܐ ܗܢܐ ܠܘܬ ܥܡܐ ܓܒܪܐ ܚܕ ܢܨܒ ܟܪܡܐ.

מי: ܘܐܘܚܕܗ ܠܦܠܚܐ ܘܪܚܩ ܠܗ ܙܒܢܐ ܣܓܝܐܐ. ܘܒܙܒܢܐ ܫܕܪ ܠܘܬ ܦܠܚܐ ܥܒܕܗ ܕܢܬܠܘܢ ܠܗ ܡܢ ܦܐܪܐ ܕܟܪܡܐ.

מז: ܦܠܚܐ ܕܝܢ ܡܚܐܘܗܝ ܘܫܕܪܘܗܝ ܣܪܝܩܐܝܬ. ܘܐܘܣܦ ܬܘܒ.

מח: ܠܡܫܕܪ ܥܒܕܐ ܐܚܪܢܐ ܗܢܘܢ ܕܝܢ ܐܦ ܠܗܘ ܡܚܐܘܗܝ ܘܨܥܪܘܗܝ ܘܫܕܪܘܗܝ ܣܪܝܩܐܝܬ.

מט: ܘܐܘܣܦ ܬܘܒ ܠܡܫܕܪ ܐܚܪܢܐ ܐܦ ܠܗܢܐ ܨܠܦܘܗܝ ܘܫܕܪܘܗܝ. ܐܡܪ ܕܝܢ ܡܪܐ ܟܪܡܐ ܡܢܐ ܐܥܒܕ ܐܫܕܪ ܒܪܝ ܚܒܝܒܐ ܟܒܪ ܢܚܙܘܢܝܗܝ ܘܢܬܟܚܕܘܢ.

נ: ܟܕ ܚܙܐܘܗܝ ܕܝܢ ܦܠܚܐ ܐܡܪܝܢ ܒܢܦܫܗܘܢ. ܗܢܘ ܝܪܬܐ ܬܘ ܢܩܛܠܝܘܗܝ ܘܬܗܘܐ ܝܪܬܘܬܐ ܕܝܠܢ.

נא: ܘܐܦܩܘܗܝ ܠܒܪ ܡܢ ܟܪܡܐ ܘܩܛܠܘܗܝ ܡܢܐ ܗܟܝܠ ܢܥܒܕ ܠܗܘܢ ܡܪܐ ܟܪܡܐ.

נב: ܢܐܬܐ ܘܢܘܒܕ ܠܦܠܚܐ ܗܢܘܢ ܘܢܬܠ ܟܪܡܐ ܠܐܚܪܢܐ ܟܕ ܫܡܥܘ ܐܡܪܘ ܚܣ.

נג: ܗܘ ܕܝܢ ܚܪ ܒܗܘܢ ܘܐܡܪ ܘܡܢܘ ܗܢܐ ܕܟܬܝܒ ܟܐܦܐ ܕܐܣܠܝܘ ܒܢܝܐ ܗܝ ܗܘܬ ܠܪܫ ܙܘܝܬܐ. ܘܟܠ ܕܢܦܠ ܥܠ ܟܐܦܐ ܗܝ ܢܬܪܥܥ ܘܟܠ ܕܗܝ ܬܦܠ ܥܠܘܗܝ ܬܕܪܝܘܗܝ.

─────────

A - 84

20. When the disciples saw it, they were surprised and were saying: How quickly the fig tree has dried up!

21. Jesus answered and said to them: Truly I say to you that if there is faith in you, and you do not doubt, you may not only do this same thing with the fig tree but also if you will tell this mountain, Be uprooted and fall into the sea,[14] it will be!

22. And anything you ask in prayer and believe, you will receive!

JESUS' AUTHORITY QUESTIONED

23. Then when Jesus came to the temple the high priests and elders of the people approached him as he was teaching and said to him: By what authority are you doing these things?[15] And who gave you this right?

24. Jesus answered and said to them: I will also ask you a question and if you answer me I will also answer you by what authority I do these things.

25. The baptism of John, from where is it? Is it from heaven or from the people? Then they reasoned among themselves saying, now if we say from heaven, he will say to us, Why did you not believe him?

26. And if we should say, From the people, we are afraid of the crowd because they all regard John as a prophet.

27. And they answered saying to him: We do not know. Jesus said to them: Neither will I answer you by what authority I do these things.

THE PARABLE OF THE TWO SONS

28. Now how does it seem to you? A certain man had two sons, and he approached the first one and said to him, My son, go and work in the vineyard today.

29. Then that one answered and said, I do not want to! But afterwards he changed his mind and went.

30. And he approached the other one and said the same thing to him. And he answered and said, Here am I, my lord. But he did not go.

---

14 See Mt. 17:19, footnote 13.

15 The elders and high priests wanted to know who gave Jesus the authority to overturn the trays of the money changers, release the doves, and heal the blind.

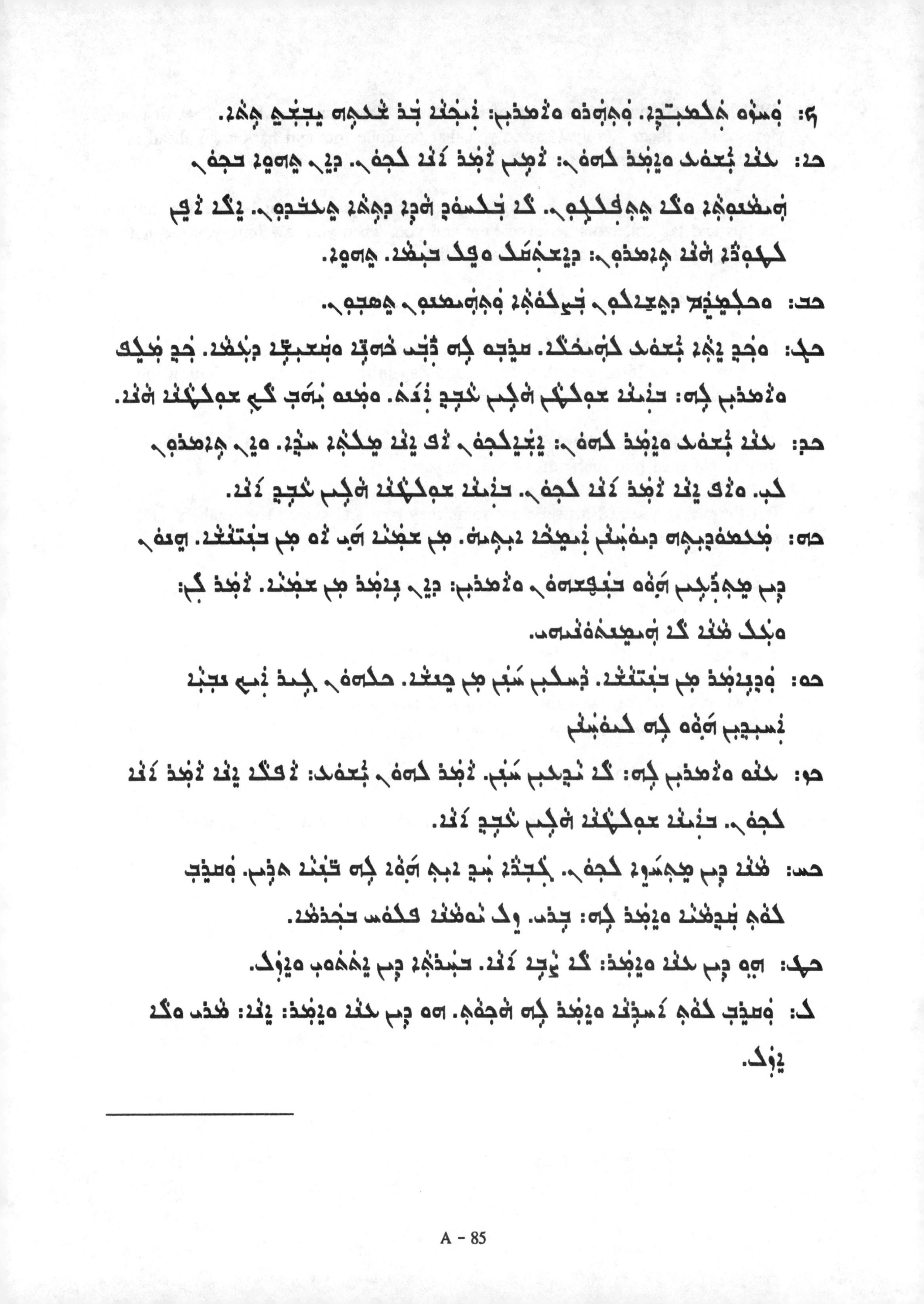

31. Which of these two did the wish of his father? They answered him: That first one. Jesus said to them: Truly I say to you that tax collectors and harlots go ahead of you into the kingdom of God.

32. Now John came to you in the way of goodness and you did not believe him but the harlots and tax collectors believed him; and you, when you saw him, you did not even then turn to God that you might believe in him.

ALLEGORY OF THE WICKED VINEYARD WORKERS

33. Listen to another parable: A certain man, the owner of the house, planted a vineyard and enclosed it with a hedge, and dug in it a winepress and built a tower and then leased it to workers and went traveling.

34. Then when the season for the fruits arrived, he sent his servants to the workers that they might send him the fruits of the vineyard.

35. But the workers seized his servants; some they beat and stoned some others and some they killed.

36. And again he sent other servants more numerous than the first; but they treated them the same way.

37. Then finally he sent his son to them, saying: Maybe they will respect my son.

38. But when the workers saw the son they said among themselves, This is the heir; come, let us kill him and keep his inheritance.

39. And they seized him and took him out of the vineyard and killed him.

40. Now when the owner of the vineyard comes what will he do to those workers?

41. They said to him: He shall completely destroy them and lease his vineyard to other workers who will give him fruits in their season.

ܠܐ: ܡܢܘ ܡܢ ܬܪܝܗܘܢ ܥܒܕ ܨܒܝܢܐ ܕܐܒܘܗܝ. ܐܡܪܝܢ ܠܗ: ܗܘ ܩܕܡܝܐ. ܐܡܪ
ܠܗܘܢ ܝܫܘܥ: ܐܡܝܢ ܐܡܪ ܐܢܐ ܠܟܘܢ. ܕܡܟܣܐ ܘܙܢܝܬܐ ܩܕܡܝܢ ܠܟܘܢ
ܠܡܠܟܘܬܐ ܕܐܠܗܐ.

ܠܒ: ܐܬܐ ܓܝܪ ܠܘܬܟܘܢ ܝܘܚܢܢ ܒܐܘܪܚܐ ܕܟܐܢܘܬܐ. ܘܠܐ ܗܝܡܢܬܘܢܝܗܝ. ܡܟܣܐ
ܕܝܢ ܘܙܢܝܬܐ ܗܝܡܢܘܗܝ. ܐܢܬܘܢ ܕܝܢ ܐܦܠܐ ܒܬܪ ܕܚܙܝܬܘܢ. ܬܘܝܬܘܢ
ܒܚܪܬܐ ܕܬܗܝܡܢܘܢ ܒܗ.

ܠܓ: ܫܡܥܘ ܐܚܪܢܐ ܡܬܠܐ. ܓܒܪܐ ܚܕ ܐܝܬ ܗܘܐ ܡܪܐ ܒܝܬܐ ܘܢܨܒ ܟܪܡܐ.
ܘܐܚܕܪܗ ܣܝܓܐ. ܘܚܦܪ ܒܗ ܡܥܨܪܬܐ. ܘܒܢܐ ܒܗ ܡܓܕܠܐ. ܘܐܘܚܕܗ
ܠܦܠܚܐ. ܘܐܙܠ.

ܠܕ: ܟܕ ܕܝܢ ܡܛܐ ܙܒܢܐ ܕܦܐܪܐ. ܫܕܪ ܠܥܒܕܘܗܝ ܠܘܬ ܦܠܚܐ ܕܢܫܕܪܘܢ ܠܗ ܡܢ
ܦܐܪܐ ܕܟܪܡܗ.

ܠܗ: ܘܐܚܕܘ ܦܠܚܐ ܠܥܒܕܘܗܝ. ܘܐܝܬ ܕܡܚܐܘܗܝ ܘܐܝܬ ܕܪܓܡܘܗܝ. ܘܐܝܬ
ܕܩܛܠܘܗܝ.

ܠܘ: ܘܬܘܒ ܫܕܪ ܥܒܕܐ ܐܚܪܢܐ ܕܣܓܝܐܝܢ ܡܢ ܩܕܡܝܐ. ܘܗܟܘܬ ܥܒܕܘ ܠܗܘܢ.

ܠܙ: ܐܚܪܝܬ ܕܝܢ ܫܕܪ ܠܘܬܗܘܢ ܠܒܪܗ ܟܕ ܐܡܪ: ܢܒܗܬܘܢ ܡܢ ܒܪܝ.

ܠܚ: ܦܠܚܐ ܕܝܢ ܟܕ ܚܙܐܘܗܝ ܠܒܪܐ. ܐܡܪܘ ܒܢܦܫܗܘܢ: ܗܢܘ ܝܪܬܐ. ܬܘ
ܢܩܛܠܝܘܗܝ ܘܢܚܘܕ ܝܪܬܘܬܗ.

ܠܛ: ܘܐܚܕܘ ܐܦܩܘܗܝ ܠܒܪ ܡܢ ܟܪܡܐ. ܘܩܛܠܘܗܝ.

ܡ: ܡܐ ܕܐܬܐ ܗܟܝܠ ܡܪܗ ܕܟܪܡܐ. ܡܢܐ ܢܥܒܕ ܠܦܠܚܐ ܗܢܘܢ.

ܡܐ: ܐܡܪܝܢ ܠܗ: ܕܒܝܫܐ ܒܒܝܫ ܢܘܒܕ ܐܢܘܢ. ܘܟܪܡܐ ܢܘܚܕ ܠܐܚܪܢܐ ܦܠܚܐ ܐܝܠܝܢ
ܕܝܗܒܝܢ ܠܗ ܦܐܪܐ ܒܙܒܢܝܗܘܢ.

42. Jesus said to them: Have you never read in the book that the stone which the builders had rejected, that very one became the cornerstone; this was from the LORD and it is a wonder in our eyes.[16]

43. Because of this I say to you, that the kingdom of God will be taken from you and shall be given to a people who produce fruits.

44. And anyone who falls on this stone shall be broken but anyone it falls upon, it shall shatter him.[17]

45. And when the high priests and Pharisees heard his parables, they knew he spoke about them.

46. So they wanted to arrest him but they were afraid of the crowds because they regarded him as a prophet.

---

16 Ps. 118:22-23.
17 Any form of resistance to the Messiah and his kingdom would eventually be broken or crushed.

ܡܒ: ܐܡܪ ܠܗܘܢ ܝܫܘܥ: ܠܐ ܡܡܬܘܡ ܩܪܝܬܘܢ ܒܟܬܒ̈ܐ: ܕܟܐܦܐ ܕܐܣܠܝܘ ܒܢ̈ܝܐ.
ܗܝ ܗܘܬ ܠܪܫܐ ܕܙܘܝܬܐ. ܡܢ ܠܘܬ ܡܪܝܐ ܗܘܬ ܗܕܐ ܘܐܝܬܝܗ ܬܕܡܘܪܬܐ ܒܥܝ̈ܢܝܢ.

ܡܓ: ܡܛܠ ܗܢܐ ܐܡܪ ܐܢܐ ܠܟܘܢ: ܕܬܫܬܩܠ ܡܢܟܘܢ ܡܠܟܘܬܗ ܕܐܠܗܐ.
ܘܬܬܝܗܒ ܠܥܡܐ ܕܥܒܕ ܦܐܪ̈ܐ.

ܡܕ: ܘܡܢ ܕܢܦܠ ܥܠ ܟܐܦܐ ܗܕܐ. ܢܬܪܥܥ. ܘܟܠ ܡܢ ܕܗܝ ܬܦܠ ܥܠܘܗܝ.
ܬܕܪܝܘܗܝ.

ܡܗ: ܘܟܕ ܫܡܥܘ ܪ̈ܒܝ ܟܗܢܐ ܘܦܪ̈ܝܫܐ ܡܬܠܘܗܝ. ܝܕܥܘ ܕܥܠܝܗܘܢ ܐܡܪ:

ܡܘ: ܘܒܥܘ ܠܡܐܚܕܗ. ܘܕܚܠܘ ܡܢ ܟܢܫܐ ܡܛܠ ܕܐܝܟ ܕܠܢܒܝܐ ܐܚܝܕܝܢ ܗܘܘ ܠܗ.

CHAPTER 22

THE PARABLE OF THE MESSIANIC BANQUET

1. And Jesus answered again by parables and said:

2. The kingdom of heaven is like a man, a king[1] who prepared a banquet[2] for his son.

3. And he sent his servants to call those guests who were invited to the banquet but they did not want to come.

4. Then again he sent other servants and said, Tell the guests, behold, my banquet is ready and my steers and my fat sheep are slaughtered and everything is ready. Come to the banquet!

5. But they did not care and went away, one to his field and the other to his business.

6. And the rest seized his servants and insulted them and killed them.

7. Now when the king heard it, he became angry and sent his armies and destroyed those murderers and burned their city.[3]

8. Then he said to his servants, The banquet is ready and those who were invited were undeserving.

9. Now you go to the main roads and all those you find, invite them to the banquet.

10. And those servants went out into the roads and gathered together all whom they could find, the good and the bad, and the banquet house was filled with guests.

11. Then the king went in to see the guests and he saw a man there that was not dressed in a banquet garment.

12. And he said to him, My friend, how did you enter here when you do not have a banquet garment?[4] But he was silent.

---

1 The term "king" in this passage refers to a lord who owns a great deal of property, vast estates.
2 An aspect of the kingdom is compared to a banquet; i.e., the messianic banquet derived from Isa. 25:6-8.
3 This declaration was fulfilled under Prince Titus in 70 A.D. when the Roman armies besieged and destroyed the Holy City.
4 Not having a banquet garment symbolizes an individual who does not practice his faith.

ܩܦܠܐܘܢ: ܟܒ.

ܐ: ܘܥܢܐ ܬܘܒ ܝܫܘܥ ܒܡܬܠܐ. ܘܐܡܪ:

ܒ: ܕܡܝܐ ܡܠܟܘܬܐ ܕܫܡܝܐ ܠܓܒܪܐ ܡܠܟܐ ܕܥܒܕ ܡܫܬܘܬܐ ܠܒܪܗ.

ܓ: ܘܫܕܪ ܠܥܒܕܘܗܝ ܕܢܩܪܘܢ ܠܙܡܝܢܐ ܠܡܫܬܘܬܐ. ܘܠܐ ܨܒܘ ܠܡܐܬܐ.

ܕ: ܬܘܒ ܫܕܪ ܥܒܕܐ ܐܚܪܢܐ ܘܐܡܪ: ܐܡܪܘ ܠܙܡܝܢܐ. ܗܐ ܫܪܘܬܝ ܡܛܝܒܐ.
ܬܘܪܝ ܘܦܛܡܝ ܢܟܝܣܝܢ. ܘܟܠ ܡܕܡ ܡܛܝܒ. ܬܘ ܠܡܫܬܘܬܐ.

ܗ: ܗܢܘܢ ܕܝܢ ܒܣܘ ܘܐܙܠܘ. ܐܢܫ ܠܩܪܝܬܗ. ܘܐܢܫ ܠܬܐܓܘܪܬܗ.

ܘ: ܫܪܟܐ ܕܝܢ ܐܚܕܘ ܠܥܒܕܘܗܝ ܘܨܥܪܘ ܘܩܛܠܘ.

ܙ: ܟܕ ܫܡܥ ܕܝܢ ܡܠܟܐ ܪܓܙ ܘܫܕܪ ܦܠܚܘܗܝ. ܐܘܒܕ ܠܩܛܘܠܐ ܗܢܘܢ.
ܘܠܡܕܝܢܬܗܘܢ ܐܘܩܕ.

ܚ: ܗܝܕܝܢ ܐܡܪ ܠܥܒܕܘܗܝ: ܡܫܬܘܬܐ ܡܛܝܒܐ. ܘܗܢܘܢ ܕܩܪܝܢ ܗܘܘ ܠܐ ܫܘܝܢ
ܗܘܘ.

ܛ: ܙܠܘ ܗܟܝܠ ܠܡܦܩܢܐ ܕܐܘܪܚܬܐ. ܘܟܠ ܡܢ ܕܡܫܟܚܝܢ ܐܢܬܘܢ ܩܪܘ
ܠܡܫܬܘܬܐ.

ܝ: ܘܢܦܩܘ ܥܒܕܐ ܗܢܘܢ ܠܐܘܪܚܬܐ. ܘܟܢܫܘ ܟܠ ܕܐܫܟܚܘ. ܒܝܫܐ ܘܛܒܐ.
ܘܐܬܡܠܝ ܒܝܬ ܡܫܬܘܬܐ ܣܡܝܟܐ.

ܝܐ: ܘܥܠ ܡܠܟܐ ܕܢܚܙܐ ܣܡܝܟܐ. ܘܚܙܐ ܬܡܢ ܓܒܪܐ ܕܠܐ ܠܒܝܫ ܠܒܘܫܐ
ܕܡܫܬܘܬܐ.

ܝܒ: ܘܐܡܪ ܠܗ: ܚܒܪܝ. ܐܝܟܢܐ ܥܠܬ ܠܟܐ. ܟܕ ܠܒܘܫܐ ܕܡܫܬܘܬܐ ܠܝܬ ܠܟ. ܗܘ
ܕܝܢ ܫܬܩ.

13. Then the king said to his servants, Tie his hands and his feet and throw him outside in the dark; there will be weeping and gnashing of teeth.

14. Because many are invited and few chosen.

JESUS ANSWERS THE HERODIANS

15. Now then, the Pharisees went away and took counsel as to how they might trap him by a word.

16. So they sent their disciples with the Herodians[5] saying to him: Teacher, we know you are true and you teach the path of God in truth and you do not favor anyone[6] and are not guided by human appearances.

17. Now tell us how does it appear to you? Is it lawful to pay head tax to Caesar[7] or not?

18. But Jesus discerned their cunningness and said: Why do you test me? Hypocrites!

19. Show me that head tax dinara. So they brought him a dinara.

20. And Jesus said to them: And whose image is this and inscription?[8]

21. They replied: Caesar. He said to them: Then, give to Caesar what is of Caesar and to God what is of God.

22. And when they heard it they were surprised; so they left him and went away.

JESUS ANSWERS THE SADDUCEES

23. That same day the Sadducees approached him and said to him: Do the dead live again? So they questioned him,

---

5 Probably friends and supporters of Herod Antipas. They were not a sect or political party.
6 Idiom which describes an impartial individual who accepts no bribes and aids the underprivileged.
7 A poll tax that had to be paid in Roman coin on which the image of Caesar had been inscribed. During the time of Jesus this tax would apply in Judea which was controlled by Rome but it would not apply in Galilee, which was ruled by Antipas.
8 The inscription on the dinara was Caesar's. The acceptance and use of this coin by the religious authorities and Herodians had placed them under Caesar's authority and jurisdiction. Thus, the attempted entrapment of Jesus by their questions was meaningless.

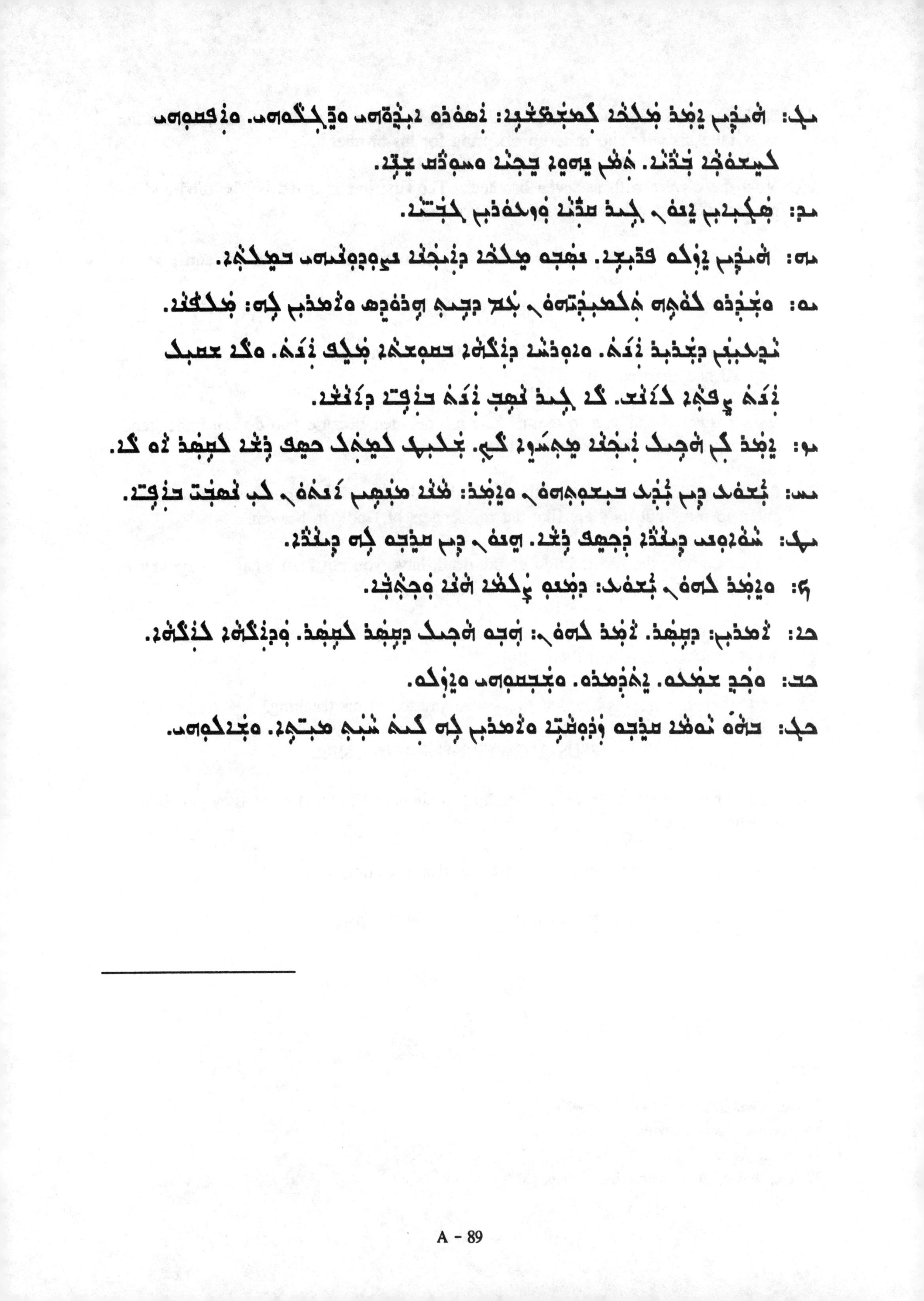

24. Saying to him: Teacher, Moses tells us that if a man dies without sons, his brother must take his wife and raise up offspring for his brother.[9]

25. Now there were with us seven brothers. The first one married but he died and had no sons. So his wife was left for his brother.

26. The same thing also with the second and also with the third up to the entire seven.

27. Then after all of them, the woman herself also died.

28. Now at the resurrection to which of those seven will she be the wife, because they all had married her?

29. Jesus answered and said to them: You are deluded because you do not understand the scriptures nor the power of God.

30. Because at the resurrection of the dead, they do not take women nor are women given to men; but they are like the messengers of God[10] in heaven.

31. But concerning the resurrection of the dead, have you not read what was spoken to you by God when He said:

32. I am the God of Abraham, the God of Isaac, the God of Jacob?[11] Now He is not the God of the dead but of the living![12]

33. And when the crowds heard it they were amazed at his teaching.

JESUS ANSWERS THE PHARISEES

34. Then when the Pharisees heard that he had silenced the Sadducees, they gathered together.

35. And one of them who knew the law, asked him testing him:

36. Teacher, which is the greatest commandment in the law?

---

9 See Gen. 38:8-10 and Deut. 25:5-10.
10 Spiritual beings, Godlike.
11 Exod. 3:6.
12 I.e., "living," "their spirits live," "immortal."

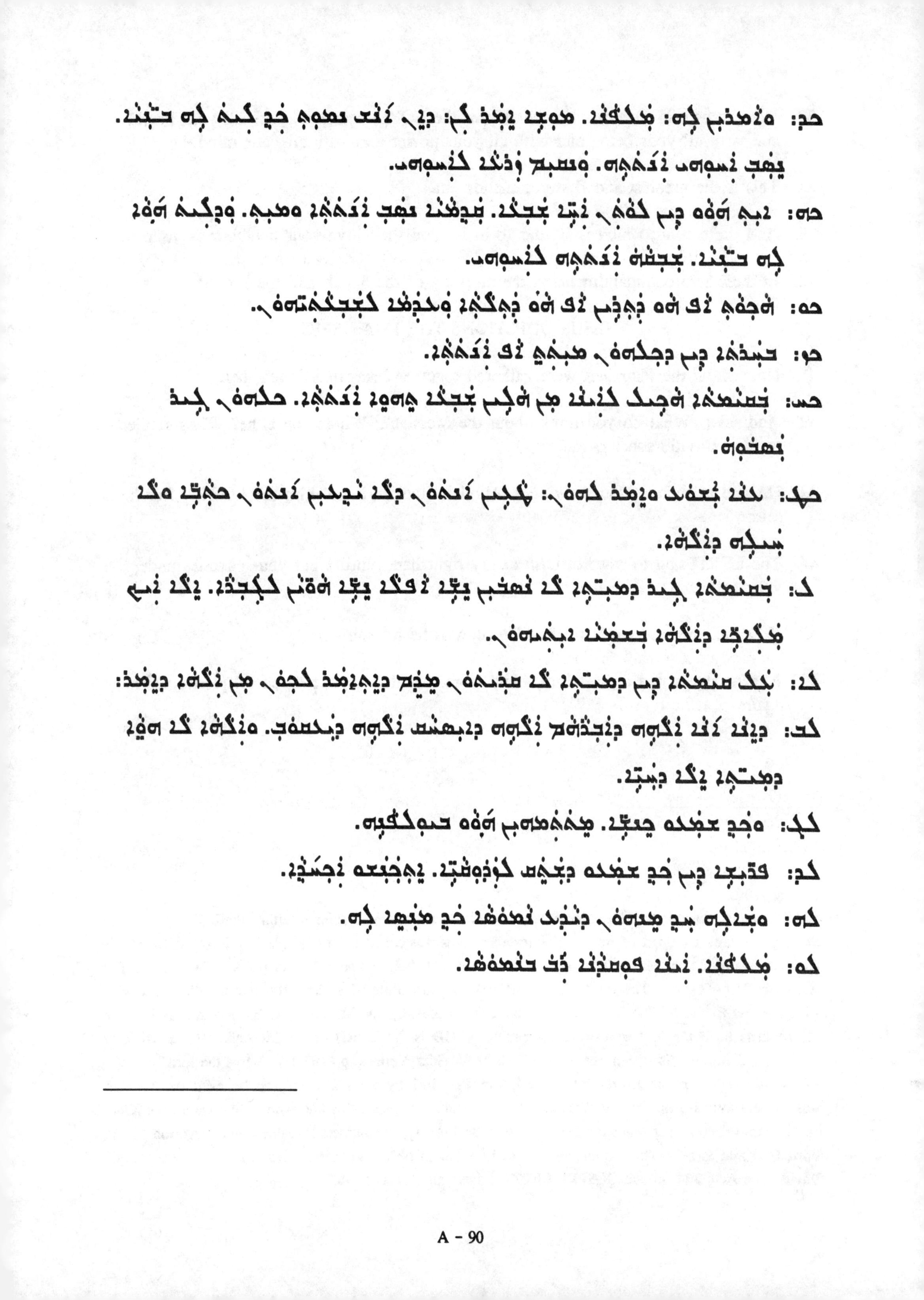

ܟܕ: ܘܐܵܡܪܝܼܢ ܠܹܗ: ܡܲܠܦܵܢܵܐ. ܡܘܼܫܹܐ ܐܸܡܲܪ ܠܲܢ: ܕܐܸܢ ܐ̱ܢܵܫ ܡܵܐܹܬ ܟܲܕ ܠܲܝܬ ܠܹܗ ܒܢܲܝܵܐ.
ܢܸܣܲܒ ܐܲܚܘܼܗ̈ܝ ܐܲܢ̱ܬ݁ܬ݂ܹܗ. ܘܲܢܩܝܼܡ ܙܲܪܥܵܐ ܠܐܲܚܘܼܗ̈ܝ.

ܟܗ: ܐܝܼܬ ܗ̱ܘܵܘ ܕܹܝܢ ܠܘܵܬܲܢ ܫܲܒܥܵܐ ܐܲܚܹ̈ܐ. ܩܲܕܡܵܝܵܐ ܢܸܣܲܒ ܐܲܢ̱ܬ݁ܬ݂ܵܐ ܘܡܝܼܬ. ܘܡܸܛܠ ܕܠܲܝܬ ܗ̱ܘܵܘ
ܠܹܗ ܒܢܲܝܵܐ. ܫܒܲܩܵܗ̇ ܐܲܢ̱ܬ݁ܬ݂ܹܗ ܠܐܲܚܘܼܗ̈ܝ.

ܟܘ: ܗܵܟ݂ܲܢܵܐ ܐܵܦ ܗܵܘ ܕܬܪܹܝܢ ܐܵܦ ܕܬܠܵܬ݂ܵܐ ܘܥܕܲܡܵܐ ܠܫܲܒܥܲܬܲܝܗܘܿܢ.

ܟܙ: ܒܚܲܪܬܵܐ ܕܹܝܢ ܕܟܠܗܘܿܢ ܡܝܼܬܲܬ ܐܵܦ ܐܲܢ̱ܬ݁ܬ݂ܵܐ.

ܟܚ: ܒܲܩܝܵܡܬܵܐ ܗܵܟܝܼܠ ܠܐܲܝܢܵܐ ܡܸܢ ܗܵܠܹܝܢ ܫܲܒܥܵܐ ܬܸܗܘܹܐ ܐܲܢ̱ܬ݁ܬ݂ܵܐ. ܟܠܗܘܿܢ ܓܹܝܪ
ܢܣܲܒܘܼܗ̇.

ܟܛ: ܥܢܵܐ ܝܼܫܘܿܥ ܘܐܸܡܲܪ ܠܗܘܿܢ: ܛܵܥܹܝܢ ܐܢ̱ܬ݁ܘܿܢ. ܕܠܵܐ ܝܵܕ݂ܥܝܼܢ ܐܢ̱ܬ݁ܘܿܢ ܟܬ݂ܵܒܹ̈ܐ. ܘܠܵܐ
ܚܲܝܠܹܗ ܕܐܲܠܵܗܵܐ.

ܠ: ܒܲܩܝܵܡܬܵܐ ܓܹܝܪ ܕܡܝܼܬܹ̈ܐ ܠܵܐ ܢܵܣܒܝܼܢ ܢܸܫܹ̈ܐ ܘܠܵܐ ܗܵܘܝܵܢ ܠܓܲܒܪܹ̈ܐ. ܐܸܠܵܐ ܐܲܝܟ
ܡܲܠܐܲܟܹ̈ܐ ܕܐܲܠܵܗܵܐ ܒܲܫܡܲܝܵܐ ܐܝܼܬܲܝܗܘܿܢ.

ܠܐ: ܥܲܠ ܩܝܵܡܬܵܐ ܕܹܝܢ ܕܡܝܼܬܹ̈ܐ ܠܵܐ ܩܪܲܝܬܘܿܢ ܡܸܕܸܡ ܕܐܸܬ݂ܐܡܲܪ ܠܟ݂ܘܿܢ ܡܸܢ ܐܲܠܵܗܵܐ ܕܐܵܡܲܪ:

ܠܒ: ܕܐܸܢܵܐ ܐܸܢܵܐ ܐܲܠܵܗܹܗ ܕܐܲܒܪܵܗܵܡ ܐܲܠܵܗܹܗ ܕܐܝܼܣܚܵܩ ܐܲܠܵܗܹܗ ܕܝܲܥܩܘܿܒ. ܘܐܲܠܵܗܵܐ ܠܵܐ ܗ̱ܘܵܐ
ܕܡܝܼܬܹ̈ܐ ܐܸܠܵܐ ܕܚܲܝܹ̈ܐ.

ܠܓ: ܘܟܲܕ ܫܡܲܥܘ ܟܸܢܫܹ̈ܐ. ܡܸܬ݂ܕܲܡܪܝܼܢ ܗ̱ܘܵܘ ܒܝܘܼܠܦܵܢܹܗ.

ܠܕ: ܦܪ̈ܝܼܫܹܐ ܕܹܝܢ ܟܲܕ ܫܡܲܥܘ ܕܣܲܟ݂ܲܪ ܠܙܲܕܘܼܩܵܝܹ̈ܐ. ܐܸܬ݂ܟܲܢܲܫܘ ܐܲܟ݂ܚܕܵܐ.

ܠܗ: ܘܫܲܐܠܹܗ ܚܲܕ ܡܸܢܗܘܿܢ ܕܝܵܕܲܥ ܢܵܡܘܿܣܵܐ ܟܲܕ ܡܢܲܣܸܐ ܠܹܗ.

ܠܘ: ܡܲܠܦܵܢܵܐ. ܐܲܝܕܵܐ ܦܘܼܩܕܵܢܵܐ ܪܲܒ ܒܢܵܡܘܿܣܵܐ.

37. Now Jesus said to him: You shall love the LORD your God with all your heart and with all your being and with all your power and with all your mind.[13]

38. This is the greatest and first commandment.

39. And the second, which is similar to it, is, You shall love your neighbor as yourself.[14]

40. In these two commandments is the meaning of the Torah and the Prophets.

JESUS QUESTIONS THE PHARISEES

41. Now while the Pharisees were gathered together Jesus questioned them,

42. And said: What do you think about the Messiah? Whose son is he? They replied to him: David's son.

43. He said to them: Then how does David by the spirit call him the LORD? For he said:

44. The LORD said to my Lord, Sit at my right hand until I put your enemies under your feet.[15]

45. If David, then calls him the Lord,[16] how is he his son?[17]

46. And no one could answer him. And from that day no one dared to question him again.

---

13 Deut. 6:5
14 Lev. 19:18.
15 Ps. 110:1.
16 When the Aramaic word ܡܪܝܐ, מריא, Mariah is used it may refer to either the LORD God or to the highest ranking Lord of lords. For instance Jesus was called by the people "my lord" ܡܪܝ, Mar - from the word ܡܪܐ, Mara, lord, master, sir. See Mt. 8:2, footnote 1; also pp A - 28 and 29, The Aramaic Term "Lord." The term Mariah-LORD was substituted for the Hebrew word יהוה, Yahweh, which refers to the LORD God only, but on a few occasions the Messiah is called Mariah (as in verse 45) because he is the highest Lord among men. (GOD is the LORD of the Messiah.) For a scholarly and detailed Semitic discussion, see JESUS THE JEW, Geza Vermes, pp 103-128, "Jesus the lord."
17 Jesus challenges the literal interpretation of Ps. 110:1 by the Pharisees who believed the Messiah was to be David's progeny. In Aramaic "David's son" can also mean one who is like David the King, not in looks but in certain characteristics such as bravery, zealousness, greatness and devotion to the Lord God and Israel. These qualities and traits were to be found in the Messiah, thus a true son of David. See Acts 2:34-36 and GOSPEL LIGHT, Lamsa, pp 127-128.

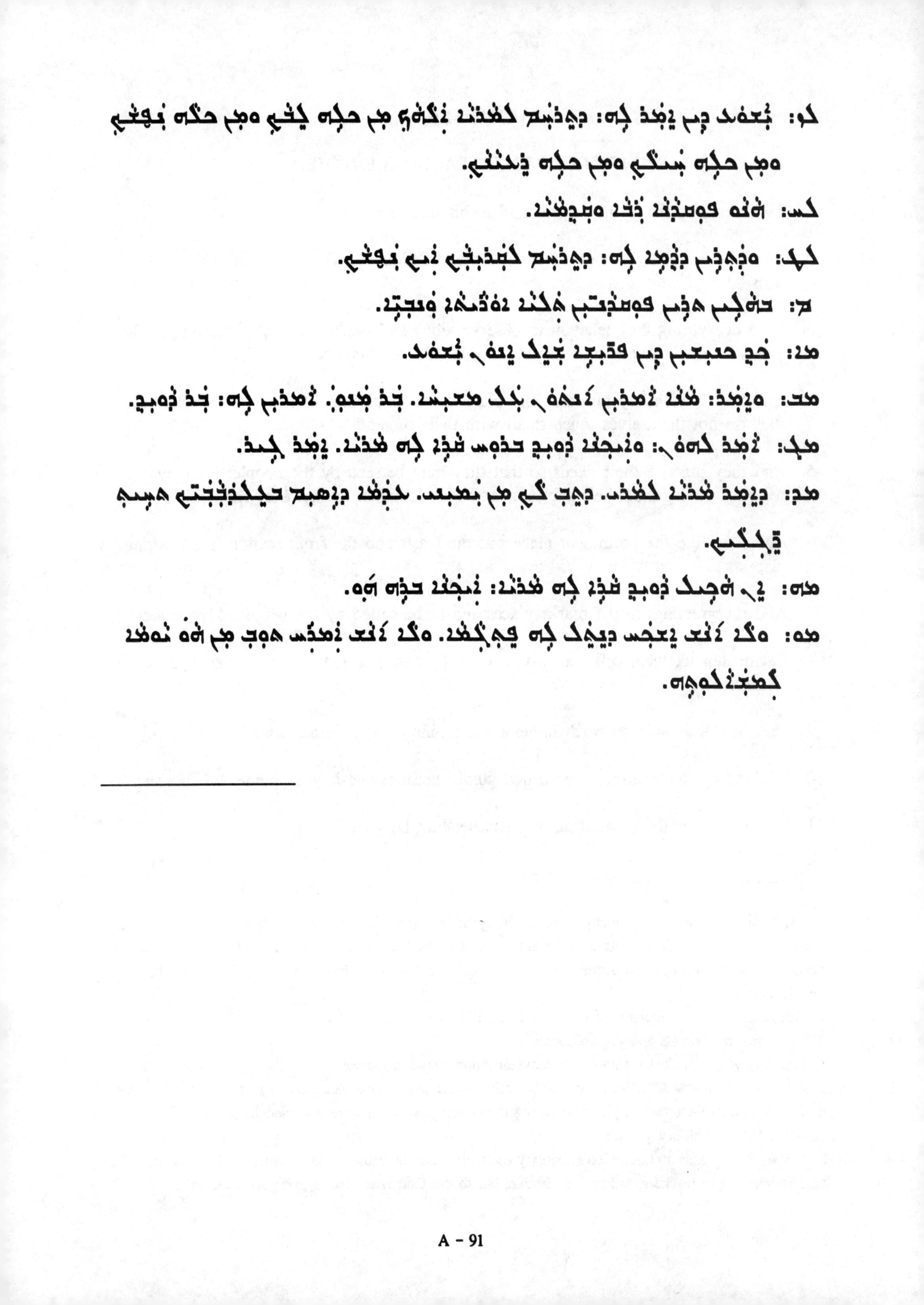

كو:

CHAPTER 23

HYPOCRITICAL TEACHING EXPOSED

1. Then Jesus spoke to the crowds and to his disciples.

2. And said to them: About the Pharisees and Sadducees who sit in the chair of Moses,[1]

3. Now everything they tell you to observe, obey and practice it[2] but according to their deeds do not practice, because they say but do not practice.

4. And they bind heavy burdens[3] and place them on the shoulders of the people; but they do not themselves touch them with their finger.[4]

5. And they practice their deeds so that they may be seen by the people; for they widen the fringes of their garments and they lengthen the hems of their robes.

6. And they like the prominent places[5] at the feasts and the front seats in the meeting places.[6]

7. And the greetings in the marketplaces and to be called by the people, My teacher.[7]

8. But do not let them call you, My teacher; because one is your teacher and you are all brothers.

9. Do not call anyone on earth father because one is your Father who is in heaven.[8]

10. And do not let yourselves be called guides because one is your guide, the Messiah.

11. But he who is the greatest among you, let him be your servant.

---

1 Metaphor for Moses' authority; i.e., carrying on the tradition. It was also a special seat in the ancient synagogues. The congregation sat on stone benches or on mats. The elders sat facing the people with their backs to Jerusalem. Presumably, the seat of Moses was reserved for the most distinguished elder.
2 Obeying religious authorities is based on Deut. 17:9-10.
3 Enact severe precepts and prohibitions.
4 I.e., they would not lift a finger to remove any oppressive ordinance.
5 ܪܝܫ ܣܡܟܐ, ריש סמכא, Resh smakeh, literally - *head seats, front seats, the best seats.*
6 The best seats were on the platform facing the congregation and were occupied by scholars.
7 ܪܒܝ, רבי, Rabbi. *my great one.*
8 Verses 8-9. Jesus stresses God's priority over all teachers, fathers and leaders. It does not mean to be disrespectful to teachers, fathers and leaders but to put God first, that is, over all leadership.

ܩܦܠܐܘܢ: ܟܓ.

ܐ: ܗܝܕܝܢ ܝܫܘܥ ܡܠܠ ܥܡ ܟܢܫܐ ܘܥܡ ܬܠܡܝܕܘܗܝ

ܒ: ܘܐܡܪ ܠܗܘܢ: ܥܠ ܟܘܪܣܝܐ ܕܡܘܫܐ ܝܬܒܘ ܣܦܪ̈ܐ ܘܦܪ̈ܝܫܐ.

ܓ: ܟܠ ܡܕܡ ܕܢܐܡܪܘܢ ܠܟܘܢ ܕܬܛܪܘܢ. ܛܪܘ ܘܥܒܕܘ. ܐܝܟ ܥܒ̈ܕܝܗܘܢ
ܕܝܢ ܠܐ ܬܥܒܕܘܢ. ܐܡܪܝܢ ܓܝܪ ܘܠܐ ܥܒܕܝܢ

ܕ: ܘܐܣܪܝܢ ܡܘܒܠܐ ܝܩܝܪܐ. ܘܣܡܝܢ ܥܠ ܟܬܦܬܐ ܕܒܢܝܢܫܐ. ܗܢܘܢ ܕܝܢ
ܒܨܒܥܗܘܢ ܠܐ ܨܒܝܢ ܕܢܩܪܒܘܢ ܠܗܘܢ.

ܗ: ܘܟܠܗܘܢ ܥܒ̈ܕܝܗܘܢ ܥܒܕܝܢ ܕܢܬܚܙܘܢ ܠܒܢܝ̈ ܐܢܫܐ. ܡܦܬܝܢ
ܓܝܪ ܬܦܠܝܗܘܢ. ܘܡܘܪܟܝܢ ܬܟܠܬܐ ܕܡܪܛܘܛܝܗܘܢ.

ܘ: ܘܪܚܡܝܢ ܪܝܫ ܣܡܟܐ ܕܒܚܫܡܝܬܐ ܘܪܝܫ ܡܘܬܒܐ ܒܟܢܘܫܬܐ

ܙ: ܘܫܐܠܬ ܫܠܡܐ ܒܫܘܩܐ. ܘܕܢܬܩܪܘܢ ܡܢ ܒܢܝ̈ ܐܢܫܐ ܪܒܝ.

ܚ: ܐܢܬܘܢ ܕܝܢ ܠܐ ܬܬܩܪܘܢ ܪܒܝ. ܚܕ ܗܘ ܓܝܪ ܪܒܟܘܢ. ܐܢܬܘܢ ܕܝܢ ܟܠܟܘܢ
ܐܚ̈ܐ ܐܢܬܘܢ.

ܛ: ܘܐܒܐ ܠܐ ܬܩܪܘܢ ܠܟܘܢ ܒܐܪܥܐ. ܚܕ ܗܘ ܓܝܪ ܐܒܘܟܘܢ ܕܒܫܡܝܐ.

ܝ: ܘܠܐ ܬܬܩܪܘܢ ܡܕܒܪ̈ܢܐ. ܡܛܠ ܕܚܕ ܗܘ ܡܕܒܪܢܟܘܢ ܡܫܝܚܐ.

ܝܐ: ܗܘ ܕܝܢ ܕܪܒ ܒܟܘܢ ܢܗܘܐ ܠܟܘܢ ܡܫܡܫܢܐ.

12. Now anyone who exalts himself shall be humbled; and anyone who humbles himself shall be exalted.

MORE HYPOCRITICAL PRACTICES AND TEACHINGS OF THE PHARISEES AND SCRIBES EXPOSED

13. Woe to you scribes and Pharisees, hypocrites! For you embezzle the property of widows with the pretense that you make long prayers; because of this you shall receive a greater judgment.

14. Woe to you scribes and Pharisees, hypocrites! For you close off the kingdom of heaven from the people because you yourselves do not enter and those who would enter, you do not permit them to go in.

15. Woe to you scribes and Pharisees, hypocrites! For you travel sea and land so that you may make one proselyte, and when he becomes one, you make him the son of Gehenna twice more than yourselves.[9]

16. Woe to you blind guides! For you say that anyone who swears by the temple, it is nothing; but anyone who swears by the gold that is in the temple he is guilty.

17. Fools and blind ones! For which is greater the gold or the temple which consecrates the gold?

18. And anyone who swears by the altar, it is nothing; but anyone who swears by the sacrifice that is on it, he is guilty.

19. Fools and blind ones! For which is greater the sacrifice or the altar which consecrates the sacrifice?

20. And anyone who swears by the altar, he swears by it and everything that is on it.

21. And anyone who swears by the temple, swears by it and by Him who lives in it.

22. And anyone who swears by heaven, swears by the throne of God and by Him who sits on it.

---

9 An Aramaic idiom: You make the new convert more corrupt than yourselves.

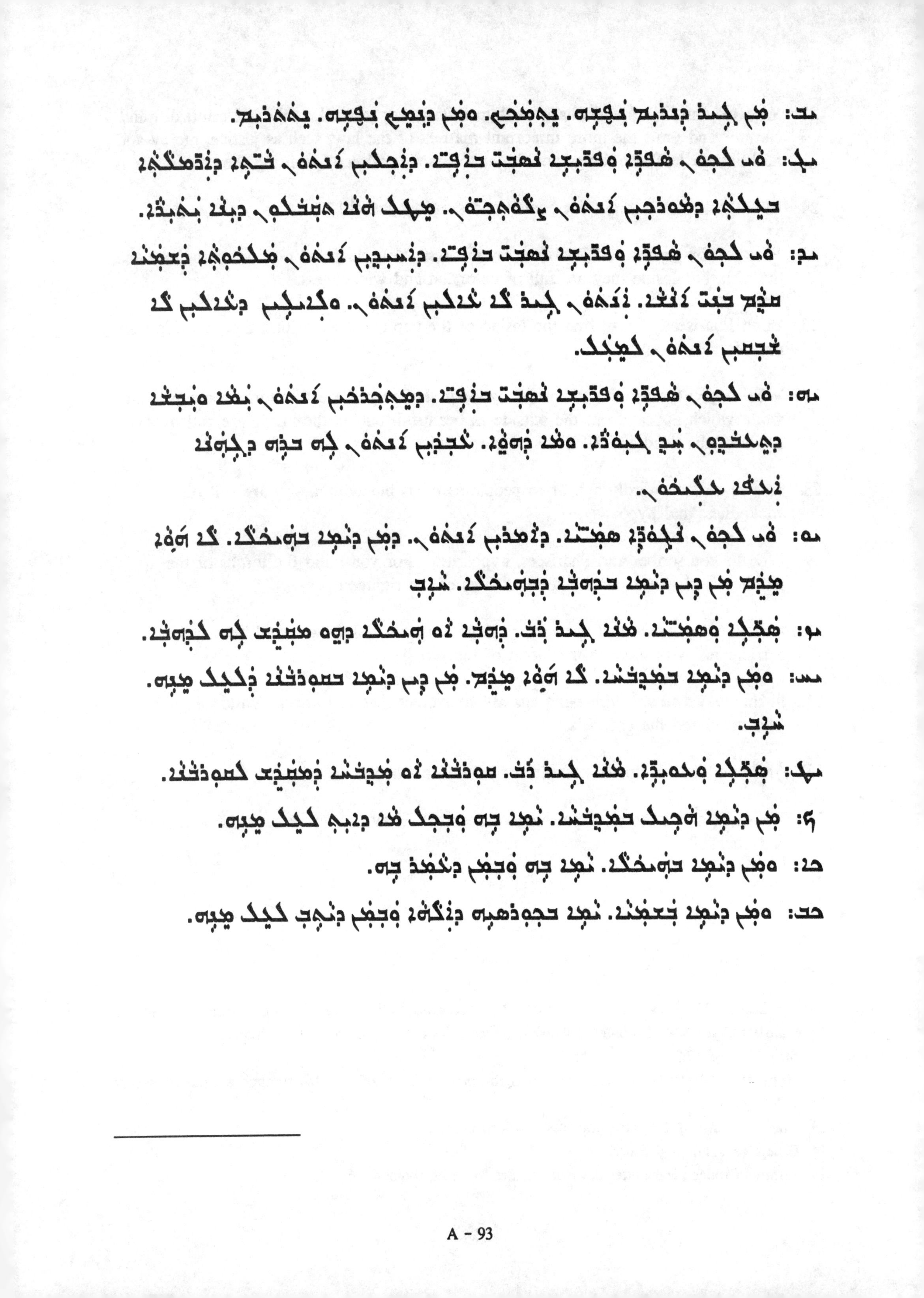

A - 93

23. Woe to you scribes and Pharisees, hypocrites! For you take tithes of mint, dill and cumin[10] and omit the more important matters of the law, such as justice, mercy and faithfulness.[11] These things you ought to practice without omitting the others.

24. Blind guides who strain out gnats[12] and swallow camels!

25. Woe to you scribes and Pharisees, hypocrites! You clean the outside of the cup and the dish, but inside they are full of extortion and wickedness.

26. Blind Pharisees! Clean first the inside of the cup and dish so that their outside also may be clean.

27. Woe to you scribes and Pharisees, hypocrites! For you are like tombstones painted white which appear from the outside as beautiful, but on the inside are full of the bones of the dead and all kinds of putrification.

28. So you also outwardly appear to people as pious but within, you are full of wickedness and hypocrisy.

29. Woe to you scribes and Pharisees, hypocrites! For you build the tombs of the prophets and you decorate the sepulchres of the righteous;

30. And you say, If we had been in the days of our ancestors we would not have been participants with them in the blood of the prophets.

31. In this way you are witnessing against yourselves that you are the children of those who murdered the prophets.

32. And you also fill up the measure of your forefathers.[13]

33. You snakes and brood of poisonous serpents![14] How can you escape the judgment of Gehenna![15]

---

10 See Lev. 27:30, Num. 18:12, Deut. 14:22-23. According to the Mosaic law only grain, wine, and oil were subject to the law of tithing; rabbinically, vegetables and greens were also included.
11 Mic. 6:8, Zech. 7:9.
12 Hyperbole. "Strain out gnats" refers to the practice of straining wine through a cloth or wicker basket.
13 You carry on with the same practices as your forefathers.
14 Deceptive, subtle and dangerous.
15 An idiom which means utter destruction. See Mt. 5:22, footnote 26.

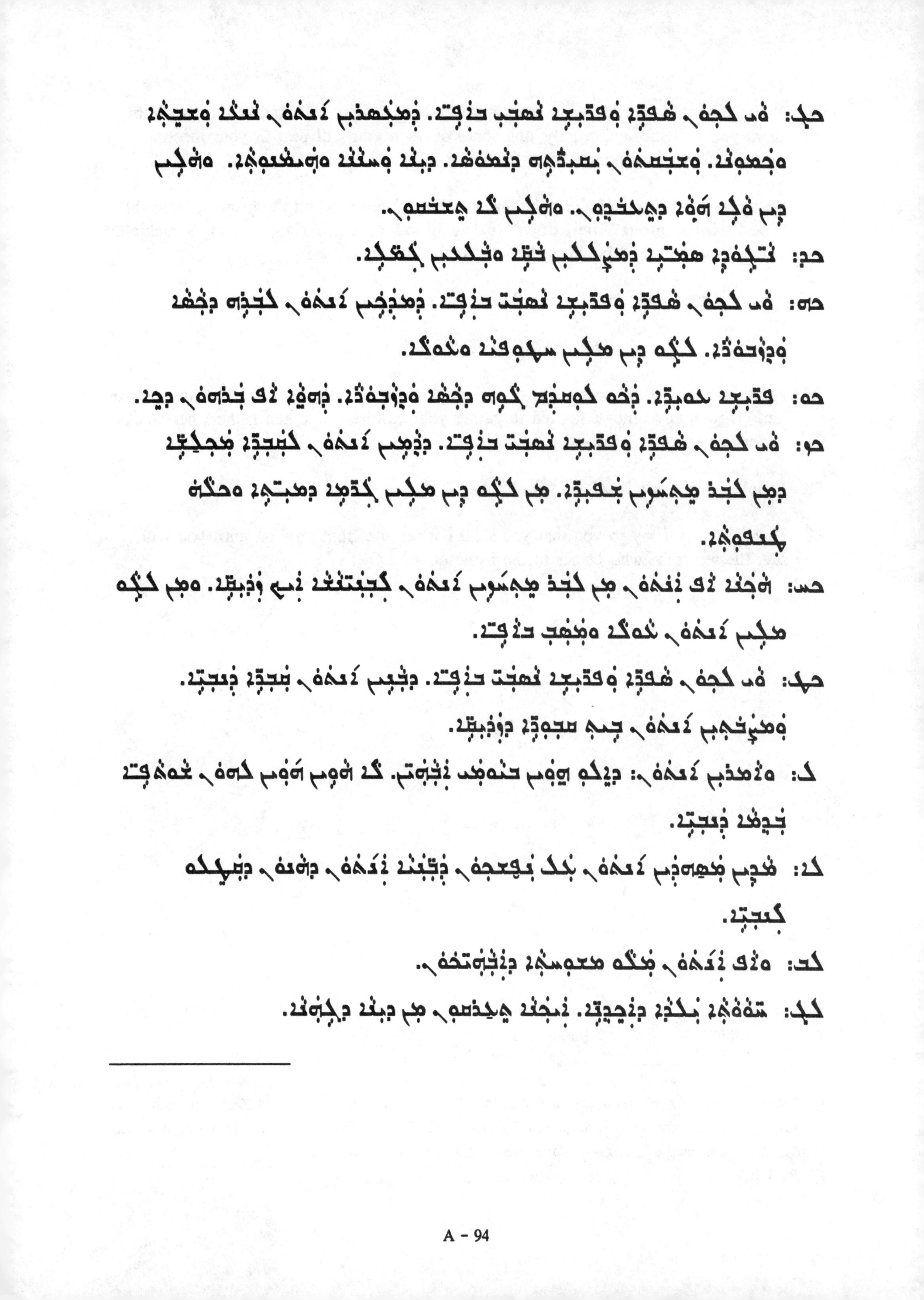

ܟܓ: ܘܝ ܠܟܘܢ ܣܦܪ̈ܐ ܘܦܪ̈ܝܫܐ ܢܣܒ̈ܝ ܒܐܦ̈ܐ. ܕܡܥܣܪܝܢ ܐܢܬܘܢ ܢܢܥܐ ܘܫܒܬܐ ܘܟܡܘܢܐ. ܘܫܒܩܬܘܢ ܝܩܝܪ̈ܬܗ ܕܢܡܘܣܐ. ܕܝܢܐ ܘܚܢܢܐ ܘܗܝܡܢܘܬܐ. ܗܠܝܢ ܕܝܢ ܘܠܐ ܗܘܐ ܠܡܥܒܕܘܢ. ܘܗܠܝܢ ܠܐ ܠܡܫܒܩܘܢ.

ܟܕ: ܡܕܒܪ̈ܢܐ ܣܡܝ̈ܐ ܕܡܨܠܠܝܢ ܩܠܡܐ ܘܒܠܥܝܢ ܓܡܠܐ.

ܟܗ: ܘܝ ܠܟܘܢ ܣܦܪ̈ܐ ܘܦܪ̈ܝܫܐ ܢܣܒ̈ܝ ܒܐܦ̈ܐ. ܕܡܕܟܝܢ ܐܢܬܘܢ ܠܒܪܗ ܕܟܣܐ ܘܕܦܝܢܐ. ܠܓܘ ܕܝܢ ܡܠܝܢ ܚܛܘܦܝܐ ܘܥܘܠܐ.

ܟܘ: ܦܪ̈ܝܫܐ ܣܡܝ̈ܐ. ܕܟܝ ܠܘܩܕܡ ܠܓܘܗ ܕܟܣܐ ܘܕܦܝܢܐ. ܕܢܗܘܐ ܐܦ ܒܪܗ ܕܟܝܐ.

ܟܙ: ܘܝ ܠܟܘܢ ܣܦܪ̈ܐ ܘܦܪ̈ܝܫܐ ܢܣܒ̈ܝ ܒܐܦ̈ܐ. ܕܕܡܝܢ ܐܢܬܘܢ ܠܩܒܪ̈ܐ ܡܚܘܪ̈ܐ ܕܡܢ ܠܒܪ ܡܬܚܙܝܢ ܫܦܝܪ̈ܐ. ܡܢ ܠܓܘ ܕܝܢ ܡܠܝܢ ܓܪ̈ܡܐ ܕܡܝ̈ܬܐ ܘܟܠܗ ܛܢܦܘܬܐ.

ܟܚ: ܗܟܢܐ ܐܦ ܐܢܬܘܢ. ܡܢ ܠܒܪ ܡܬܚܙܝܢ ܐܢܬܘܢ ܠܒܢܝ̈ܢܫܐ ܐܝܟ ܙܕܝܩ̈ܐ. ܘܡܢ ܠܓܘ ܡܠܝܢ ܐܢܬܘܢ ܢܟܠܐ ܘܡܣܒ ܒܐܦ̈ܐ.

ܟܛ: ܘܝ ܠܟܘܢ ܣܦܪ̈ܐ ܘܦܪ̈ܝܫܐ ܢܣܒ̈ܝ ܒܐܦ̈ܐ. ܕܒܢܝܢ ܐܢܬܘܢ ܩܒܪ̈ܐ ܕܢܒܝ̈ܐ. ܘܡܨܒܬܝܢ ܐܢܬܘܢ ܒܝܬ ܩܒܘܪ̈ܐ ܕܙܕܝܩ̈ܐ.

ܠ: ܘܐܡܪܝܢ ܐܢܬܘܢ: ܕܐܠܘ ܗܘܝܢ ܒܝܘܡܝ ܐܒܗ̈ܝܢ. ܠܐ ܗܘܝܢ ܗܘܝܢ ܠܗܘܢ ܫܘܬܦ̈ܐ ܒܕܡܐ ܕܢܒܝ̈ܐ.

ܠܐ: ܗܝܕܝܢ ܡܣܗܕܝܢ ܐܢܬܘܢ ܥܠ ܢܦܫܟܘܢ. ܕܒܢܝ̈ܐ ܐܢܬܘܢ ܕܗܢܘܢ ܕܩܛܠܘ ܠܢܒܝ̈ܐ.

ܠܒ: ܘܐܦ ܐܢܬܘܢ ܡܠܘ ܡܫܘܚܬܐ ܕܐܒܗ̈ܝܟܘܢ.

ܠܓ: ܚܘܘ̈ܬܐ ܝܠܕܐ ܕܐܟܕ̈ܢܐ. ܐܝܟܢܐ ܬܥܪܩܘܢ ܡܢ ܕܝܢܗ ܕܓܗܢܐ.

34. Because of this, behold, I am sending you prophets, wise men and scribes; some of them you will kill and crucify; and some of them you will beat in your meeting places and you will pursue them from city to city;

35. So that all the blood of the righteous which has been shed on the ground, from the blood of the pious Abel, down to the blood of Zachariah, son of Barachiah,[16] whom you murdered between the temple and the altar.

36. Truly I say to you that all these things will come upon this generation.

THE LAMENT OVER JERUSALEM

37. Jerusalem, Jerusalem, murderess of the prophets, and stoner of those who are sent to her! How many times I wanted to gather your children, as a hen gathers her chicks under her wings, yet you would not.

38. Behold your house is left to you desolate!

39. Because, truly I say to you that you shall not see me from now on until you will say, Blessed is he who comes in the name of the LORD![17]

---

16 There are three Zachariahs mentioned in the Hebrew Bible. In Isa. 8:2 and Zech. 1:1 both these Zachariahs are the sons of Barachiah. In 2 Chron. 24:20-21, this Zachariah is the only one who was murdered. Hence, the phrase "son of Barachiah" was an addition to the text.
17 Ps. 118:26.

ܠܕ: ܡܛܠ ܗܢܐ ܗܐ ܐܢܐ ܫܕܪ ܐܢܐ ܠܘܬܟܘܢ ܢܒܝܐ ܘܚܟܝܡܐ. ܘܣܦܪܐ. ܡܢܗܘܢ
ܩܛܠܝܢ ܐܢܬܘܢ ܘܙܩܦܝܢ ܐܢܬܘܢ. ܘܡܢܗܘܢ ܡܢܓܕܝܢ ܐܢܬܘܢ ܒܟܢܘܫܬܟܘܢ.
ܘܬܪܕܦܘܢ ܐܢܘܢ ܡܢ ܡܕܝܢܐ ܠܡܕܝܢܐ.

ܠܗ: ܐܝܟܢܐ ܕܢܐܬܐ ܥܠܝܟܘܢ ܟܠܗ ܕܡܐ ܕܙܕܝܩܐ ܕܐܬܐܫܕ ܥܠ ܐܪܥܐ. ܡܢ ܕܡܗ
ܕܗܒܝܠ ܙܕܝܩܐ ܘܥܕܡܐ ܠܕܡܗ ܕܙܟܪܝܐ ܒܪ ܒܪܟܝܐ ܗܘ ܕܩܛܠܬܘܢܝܗܝ ܒܝܬ
ܗܝܟܠܐ ܠܡܕܒܚܐ.

ܠܘ: ܐܡܝܢ ܐܡܪ ܐܢܐ ܠܟܘܢ. ܕܢܐܬܝܢ ܗܠܝܢ ܟܠܗܝܢ ܥܠ ܫܪܒܬܐ ܗܕܐ.

ܠܙ: ܐܘܪܫܠܡ ܐܘܪܫܠܡ. ܩܛܠܬ ܢܒܝܐ ܘܪܓܡܬ ܠܐܝܠܝܢ ܕܫܠܝܚܝܢ ܠܘܬܗ. ܟܡܐ
ܙܒܢܝܢ ܨܒܝܬ ܕܐܟܢܫ ܒܢܝܟܝ ܐܝܟ ܕܟܢܫܐ ܬܪܢܓܘܠܬܐ ܦܪܘܓܝܗ ܬܚܝܬ
ܓܦܝܗ. ܘܠܐ ܨܒܝܬܘܢ.

ܠܚ: ܗܐ ܡܫܬܒܩ ܠܟܘܢ ܒܝܬܟܘܢ ܚܪܒܐ.

ܠܛ: ܐܡܪ ܐܢܐ ܠܟܘܢ ܓܝܪ: ܕܠܐ ܬܚܙܘܢܢܝ ܡܢ ܗܫܐ ܥܕܡܐ ܕܬܐܡܪܘܢ: ܒܪܝܟ ܗܘ
ܕܐܬܐ ܒܫܡܗ ܕܡܪܝܐ.

CHAPTER 24

THE DESTRUCTION OF THE TEMPLE – THE SIGNS OF THE COMING

1. So Jesus left the temple to go away. And his disciples approached him showing him the structure of the temple.

2. Then he said to them: Behold do you not see all these? Truly, I say to you that there will not be left here a stone upon a stone that shall not be taken down.[1]

3. And when he sat down on the Mount of Olives, his disciples approached, saying among themselves and to him: Tell us when will these things happen, and what is the sign of your coming, and the end of the world?[2]

4. Jesus answered and said to them: Be careful that no one deceives you.

5. Because many will come in my name and say, I am the Messiah; and they will deceive many.[3]

6. Then you will hear of revolutions and rumors of wars; see to it that you are not troubled because all these things must occur but the end is not yet.

7. For nation will rise against nation and kingdom against kingdom, and there will be famines and plagues and earthquakes in different places.

8. But all these things are only the beginning pains of labor.

9. Then they shall put you in distress and kill you; and all the nations shall be hating you because of my name.

10. Then many will stumble and they shall hate one another and betray one another.

11. And many false prophets will rise up and shall deceive a great many.

---

1 The temple was destroyed by Prince Titus in 70 A.D. Later around 135 A.D. the Emperor Hadrian uprooted Jerusalem from its foundations and built a new city, naming it Elia Helipolis.
2 "The end of the world" refers to the reconstitution of the world in accordance with the highest ethical ideals predicted by the Hebrew prophets. Jesus knew this could only come about through an inner revolution of the entire being of humankind. But he also knew certain national events were to occur. The following sayings of Jesus refer to two events: 1) the destruction of the Temple and the Holy City, 2) the final and glorious triumph of the Messiah at the very end of all things.
3 For an account of the fulfillment of these predictions, especially verses 5-8 and 15-22, see JEWISH WARS by Flavius Josephus.

ܩܦܠܐܘܢ: ܟܕ.

ܐ: ܘܢܦܩ ܝܫܘܥ ܡܢ ܗܝܟܠܐ ܠܡܐܙܠ. ܘܩܪܒܘ ܬܠܡܝܕܘܗܝ. ܡܚܘܝܢ ܗܘܘ ܠܗ ܒܢܝܢܗ ܕܗܝܟܠܐ.

ܒ: ܗܘ ܕܝܢ ܐܡܪ ܠܗܘܢ: ܠܐ ܗܐ ܚܙܝܢ ܐܢܬܘܢ ܗܠܝܢ ܟܠܗܝܢ. ܐܡܝܢ ܐܡܪ ܐܢܐ ܠܟܘܢ: ܕܠܐ ܬܫܬܒܩ ܗܪܟܐ ܟܐܦ ܥܠ ܟܐܦ ܕܠܐ ܬܫܬܪܐ.

ܓ: ܘܟܕ ܝܬܒ ܝܫܘܥ ܥܠ ܛܘܪܐ ܕܙܝܬܐ. ܩܪܒܘ ܬܠܡܝܕܘܗܝ ܘܐܡܪܝܢ ܒܝܢܝܗܘܢ ܠܗ: ܐܡܪ ܠܢ ܐܡܬܝ ܗܠܝܢ ܢܗܘܝܢ. ܘܡܢܘ ܐܬܐ ܕܡܐܬܝܬܟ ܘܕܫܘܠܡܗ ܕܥܠܡܐ.

ܕ: ܥܢܐ ܝܫܘܥ ܘܐܡܪ ܠܗܘܢ: ܐܙܕܗܪܘ. ܠܐ ܐܢܫ ܢܛܥܝܟܘܢ.

ܗ: ܣܓܝܐܐ ܓܝܪ ܢܐܬܘܢ ܒܫܡܝ ܘܢܐܡܪܘܢ: ܕܐܢܐ ܐܢܐ ܡܫܝܚܐ. ܘܣܓܝܐܐ ܢܛܥܘܢ.

ܘ: ܥܬܝܕܝܢ ܐܢܬܘܢ ܕܝܢ ܠܡܫܡܥ ܩܪ̈ܒܐ ܘܫܡܥܐ ܕܩܪ̈ܒܐ. ܚܙܘ ܠܐ ܬܬܕܠܚܘܢ. ܘܠܐ ܓܝܪ ܕܢܗܘܝܢ ܟܠܗܝܢ. ܐܠܐ ܠܐ ܥܕܟܝܠ ܫܘܠܡܐ.

ܙ: ܢܩܘܡ ܓܝܪ ܥܡܐ ܥܠ ܥܡܐ. ܘܡܠܟܘܬܐ ܥܠ ܡܠܟܘܬܐ. ܘܢܗܘܘܢ ܟܦܢ̈ܐ ܘܡܘ̈ܬܢܐ ܘܙܘ̈ܥܐ ܒܕܘܟܐ ܕܘܟܐ.

ܚ: ܗܠܝܢ ܕܝܢ ܟܠܗܝܢ ܪܫܐ ܐܢܝܢ ܕܚܒ̈ܠܐ.

ܛ: ܗܝܕܝܢ ܢܫܠܡܘܢܟܘܢ ܠܐܘܠܨܢܐ ܘܢܩܛܠܘܢܟܘܢ. ܘܬܗܘܘܢ ܣܢܝܐܝܢ ܡܢ ܟܠܗܘܢ ܥܡܡܐ ܡܛܠ ܫܡܝ.

ܝ: ܗܝܕܝܢ ܢܬܟܫܠܘܢ ܣܓܝܐܐ. ܘܢܫܠܡܘܢ ܚܕ ܠܚܕ ܘܢܣܢܘܢ ܚܕ ܠܚܕ.

ܝܐ: ܘܢܒܝ̈ܐ ܕܓܠܐ ܣܓܝܐܐ ܢܩܘܡܘܢ. ܘܢܛܥܘܢ ܠܣܓܝܐܐ.

12. And because of the growth of wickedness the love of many shall cool.

13. But anyone who holds out to the end, shall have life.

14. And this joyful assurance of the kingdom shall be proclaimed throughout the world for a testimony to all nations; and then the end shall come.

15. Now when you see the unclean sign of desolation,[4] which was spoken by the prophet Daniel, piling up in the holy place, then he who reads will know.[5]

16. Then let those who are in Judea escape to the mountains.

17. And he who is on the roof let him not come down to take things out of his home.[6]

18. And anyone who is in the field should not turn back to take his clothes.

19. But how terrible for a pregnant woman and for those who breast feed in those days.[7]

20. Now pray that your flight may not occur in the winter nor on Saturday.[8]

21. Because then there will be tremendous suffering such as never happened from the beginning of the world until now, and never will be.

22. And if those days should not be shortened, no human being would remain alive;[9] but because of the chosen ones those days will be shortened.

23. Now if anyone says to you, Behold, here is the Messiah or over here, do not believe it.

---

4 See Dan. 9:27 and Lk. 21:20.

5 Understand.

6 The flat roof of an Eastern home is reached by a staircase from the court near the gateway; so that a person escaping in great haste need not go through any of the rooms of the house and he may run from one rooftop to another since the structures are adjacent to each other.

7 During an invasion women with infants and pregnant women would have a very difficult time fleeing for safety. The invading troops generally raped and killed pregnant women and women with infants.

8 Fleeing for safety during the Sabbath might violate the holy day especially if the adherents would have to go beyond the prescribed distance permitted by the religious law. Winter would be an extremely difficult time to take flight. In other words, they were to pray that there would be no natural (winter) and legal (Sabbath) impediments to their flight.

9 The slaughter of the people during the invasions of Titus and Hadrian was so terrible that the entire Jewish nation was nearly exterminated and had the invasion been prolonged, "no human being" would have remained alive.

_____

A - 97

24. Because there will rise false messiahs and false prophets and they shall demonstrate tremendous signs that they may deceive, if possible, even the chosen.

25. Behold I have told you ahead of time.

26. Now if they say, Behold he is in the desert, do not go out; or behold, he is in an inner room, do not believe it.

27. Because even as lightning comes out of the east and is seen even in the west, such will be the coming of this Human Being.

28. Then wherever the body may be, there shall the vultures be gathered.

29. Immediately, then, after the suffering of those days, the sun will be darkened and the moon will not reveal its light and the stars will fall from the heavens and the powers of the universe will be shaken.[10]

30. And then the warning of this Human Being will be seen in the sky, and then all the tribes of the earth shall mourn, and they shall see this Human Being coming on the clouds of the sky[11] with power and tremendous glory.

31. And he will send his messengers with a large trumpet,[12] and they will gather his chosen from the four winds from one end of the universe to the other.[13]

THE PARABLE OF THE FIG TREE

32. Now from the fig tree learn a parable; as soon as its branches become tender and it shoots forth its leaves, you know that summer has arrived.

33. So even you, when you see all these things, know that it has arrived at the door.

---

10 Poetic figures of speech which describe tremendous upheavals politically, (stars falling from the sky), wars, (sun and moon darkened), all governmental systems failing and great calamity everywhere.
11 Once again, many of these figures of speech must not be understood in literal terms. "Clouds" are symbolic of God's presence, success, high exaltation, extreme honor and praise.
12 "Large trumpet," metaphor meaning a universal announcement.
13 I.e., from all over the earth.

حد:
حه: .

حو:
حز:
حط: .

حك:

34. Truly I say to you that this generation[14] shall not pass away until all these things occur.[15]

35. Even heaven and earth will pass away, but my words shall never pass away.[16]

36. But concerning that very day and that very hour no one knows not even the messengers of heaven, but the Father only.

37. Now even as it was in the days of Noah such will be the coming of this Human Being.

38. For as before the flood, they were eating and drinking, marrying and giving in marriage until the day Noah entered the ark,

39. And did not know, until the flood came and took them all away; such will be the coming of this Human Being.

40. Then two will be in the field, one shall be carried off and the other left.[17]

41. And two will be grinding at the hand mill, one shall be carried off and the other left.[18]

42. Be alert, then, since you do not know at what hour your lord comes.

43. But know this, that if the owner of the house had known at what time the thief would come, he would have been awake and would not let his house be plundered.

44. Because of this you also be ready because this Human Being shall come at an hour when you do not expect him.

---

14 ܫܪܒܬܐ, שרבתא, Sharbtha, *generation, family, tribe, nation*. Some translators read the text as follows, "Truly I say to you that this *race* shall not pass away . . ."
15 Jesus refers to the fall and destruction of the Temple and the Holy City which occurred about 40 years later. Many of his disciples and people of that generation lived to see those things happen.
16 Aramaic idiom: What is said must come true.
17 Easterners generally work in a team of two; a shepherd and his assistant, two men plowing in the field, sometimes father and son or a master and his servant. One holds the plow and the other works with the oxen in front. During an invasion the youngest and strongest is taken captive and the older one is left in the field.
18 Again, as stated above, Easterners work in pairs. Two women grind wheat; two women bake bread, generally an older woman with a younger woman. When the town is attacked the younger are taken captive and the older ones are left.

كد:
كה: .

كو: .
كز: .

كح:
كט:
ל: .

לא: .

לב: .

לג: .
לד:

45. Who, then, is that faithful and wise servant whom his lord has appointed over his household to give them food in due time?[19]

46. Blessed is that servant when his lord comes and finds him so doing.

47. Truly I say to you he will appoint him over all that he has.

48. But if that bad servant will say in his heart, My lord delays his coming;

49. And begin to beat his fellow servants and be eating and drinking with drunkards,

50. The lord of that servant shall arrive on a day which he does not expect and at an hour he does not know.

51. And he shall severely punish him and give him his portion with the hypocrites;[20] there will be weeping and gnashing of teeth.[21]

---

19 Mt. 24:1-44 deals with the destruction of the Temple and the Holy City and the glorious climactic coming of Jesus. But Mt. 24:45 through Mt.25:30 records three parables of Jesus which do not refer to the end of an age but to the end (death) of each individual's life. These parables were given to encourage his disciples to practice the principles of the kingdom so when the unexpectedness of death comes, they would be prepared to meet their Lord without regrets.

20 I.e., the servant will receive a meager wage for his services and then he will be discharged as an unreliable worker.

21 Idiom: Overwhelming disappointment and regret.

ܡܗ: ܡܢܘ ܟܝ ܐܝܬܘܗܝ ܥܒܕܐ ܡܗܝܡܢܐ ܘܚܟܝܡܐ ܕܢܩܝܡܝܘܗܝ ܡܪܗ ܥܠ ܒܢܝ ܒܝܬܗ.
ܕܢܬܠ ܠܗܘܢ ܣܝܒܪܬܐ ܒܥܕܢܗ.

ܡܘ: ܛܘܒܘܗܝ ܠܥܒܕܐ ܗܘ ܕܢܐܬܐ ܡܪܗ ܢܫܟܚܝܘܗܝ ܕܥܒܕ ܗܟܢܐ.

ܡܙ: ܐܡܝܢ ܐܡܪ ܐܢܐ ܠܟܘܢ: ܕܥܠ ܟܠ ܕܐܝܬ ܠܗ ܢܩܝܡܝܘܗܝ.

ܡܚ: ܐܢ ܕܝܢ ܢܐܡܪ ܥܒܕܐ ܗܘ ܒܝܫܐ ܒܠܒܗ ܕܡܘܚܪ ܡܪܝ ܠܡܐܬܐ.

ܡܛ: ܘܢܫܪܐ ܠܡܡܚܐ ܠܟܢܘܬܗ. ܘܢܗܘܐ ܐܟܠ ܘܫܬܐ ܥܡ ܪ̈ܘܝܐ.

ܢ: ܢܐܬܐ ܡܪܗ ܕܥܒܕܐ ܗܘ ܒܝܘܡܐ ܕܠܐ ܣܟܐ ܘܒܫܥܬܐ ܕܠܐ ܝܕܥ.

ܢܐ: ܘܢܦܠܓܝܘܗܝ. ܘܢܣܝܡ ܡܢܬܗ ܥܡ ܢܣܒܝ ܒܐܦ̈ܐ. ܬܡܢ ܢܗܘܐ ܒܟܝܐ ܘܚܘܪܩ
ܫܢ̈ܐ.

CHAPTER 25

THE PARABLE OF THE TEN VIRGINS

1. Now then, the kingdom of heaven is likened to ten virgins who carried their lamps[1] and went out to greet the bridegroom and the bride.

2. Now five of them were wise and five foolish.

3. And those foolish ones took their lamps but did not take oil with them.

4. But those wise ones took oil in containers with their lamps.[2]

5. And while the bridegroom delayed, they all dozed and slept.[3]

6. And at midnight there was a cry: Behold, the bridegroom is coming, go out to greet him![4]

7. Then all those virgins arose and took care of their lamps.

8. And the foolish ones were asking the wise ones, Give us some of your oil, behold, our lamps have gone out.

9. The wise ones answered saying, Why, there would not be enough for us and for you; but go to those who sell and buy for yourselves.

10. And while they went to buy, the bridegroom came; and those who were ready entered with him into the wedding house and the door was locked.

11. Then finally, the other virgins came, saying, Our lord, our lord, open to us!

12. But he answered and said to them, Truly I say to you that I do not know you.

13. Be alert, then, for you do not know that very day nor the hour.

---

1 Oil lamps and candles are prepared before a wedding takes place. Usually the bridegroom's parents, friends, neighbors and even strangers supply the needed light for the evening wedding.
2 Some wedding feasts continue for three days and nights and sometimes up to seven days and nights. The wise virgins came prepared with extra oil in case they would not be able to obtain more oil.
3 Eastern weddings do not run by the clock. If an evening wedding is announced, it could take place at midnight. It depends on the delays. See verse 6.
4 The wedding procession party with their oil lamps.

ܩܦܠܐܘܢ: ܟܗ.

ܐ: ܗܝܕܝܢ ܬܬܕܡܐ ܡܠܟܘܬܐ ܕܫܡܝܐ ܠܥܣܪ ܒܬܘܠܢ. ܗܠܝܢ ܕܢܣܒ ܠܡܦܝܕܝܗܝܢ ܘܢܦܩ
ܠܐܘܪܥ ܚܬܢܐ ܘܟܠܬܐ.

ܒ: ܚܡܫ ܕܝܢ ܡܢܗܝܢ ܚܟܝܡܢ ܗܘ̈ܝ. ܘܚܡܫ ܣܟܠܢ.

ܓ: ܘܗܠܝܢ ܣܟܠܬܐ ܢܣܒ ܠܡܦܝܕܝܗܝܢ. ܘܠܐ ܢܣܒ ܥܡܗܝܢ ܡܫܚܐ.

ܕ: ܗܠܝܢ ܕܝܢ ܚܟܝܡܬܐ ܢܣܒ ܡܫܚܐ ܒܡܐܢܐ ܥܡ ܠܡܦܝܕܝܗܝܢ.

ܗ: ܟܕ ܐܘܚܪ ܕܝܢ ܚܬܢܐ. ܢܡ ܟܠܗܝܢ ܘܕܡܟ.

ܘ: ܘܒܦܠܓܗ ܕܠܠܝܐ ܗܘܬ ܩܥܬܐ: ܗܐ ܚܬܢܐ ܐܬܐ ܦܘܩܘ ܠܐܘܪܥܗ:

ܙ: ܗܝܕܝܢ ܩܡ ܟܠܗܝܢ ܒܬܘܠܬܐ ܗܠܝܢ. ܘܬܩܢ ܠܡܦܝܕܝܗܝܢ.

ܚ: ܐܡܪ̈ܝ ܕܝܢ ܗܠܝܢ ܣܟܠܬܐ ܠܚܟܝܡܬܐ: ܗܒܝܢ ܠܢ ܡܢ ܡܫܚܟܝܢ ܕܗܐ ܕܥܟܘ
ܠܗܘܢ ܠܡܦܝܕܝܢ.

ܛ: ܥܢܝ̈ ܗܠܝܢ ܚܟܝܡܬܐ ܘܐܡܪ̈ܝ: ܠܡܐ ܠܐ ܢܣܦܩ ܠܢ ܘܠܟܝܢ. ܙܠܝܢ ܠܘܬ
ܐܝܠܝܢ ܕܡܙܒܢܝܢ. ܘܙܒܢܝܢ ܠܟܝܢ.

ܝ: ܘܟܕ ܐܙܠ ܠܡܙܒܢ. ܐܬܐ ܚܬܢܐ. ܘܐܝܠܝܢ ܕܡܛܝܒܢ ܗܘ̈ܝ ܥܠ ܥܡܗ ܠܒܝܬ
ܚܠܘܠܐ. ܘܐܬܚܕ ܬܪܥܐ.

ܝܐ: ܒܚܪܬܐ ܕܝܢ ܐܬܝ̈ ܐܦ ܗܠܝܢ ܒܬܘܠܬܐ ܐܚܪ̈ܢܝܬܐ ܘܐܡܪ̈ܝ: ܡܪܢ ܡܪܢ. ܦܬܚ ܠܢ.

ܝܒ: ܗܘ ܕܝܢ ܥܢܐ ܘܐܡܪ ܠܗܝܢ: ܐܡܝܢ ܐܡܪ ܐܢܐ ܠܟܝܢ. ܕܠܐ ܝܕܥ ܐܢܐ ܠܟܝܢ.

ܝܓ: ܐܬܬܥܝܪܘ ܗܟܝܠ. ܕܠܐ ܝܕܥܝܢ ܐܢܬܘܢ ܝܘܡܐ ܐܦܠܐ ܫܥܬܐ.

THE PARABLE OF THE TALENTS

14. Now, it is like a man who went on a journey who called his servants and put his wealth in their charge.

15. To one he gave five talents,[5] to one two, to another one; to each one according to his ability; and immediately he went on a journey.

16. Then, he who received five talents went and invested them, and he gained five others.

17. And in the same manner the one with two, by investing gained two others.

18. But he who received one went and dug in the ground and hid his lord's money.

19. Then after a long time, the lord of those servants came and took an accounting from them.

20. And he who had received five talents approached and brought five others and said, My lord, you gave me five talents; I have gained, by investing, five others.

21. His lord said to him, Excellent, good and faithful servant! You have been reliable with a little, I will place you over much; enter into your lord's joy.

22. And he of the two talents approached and said, My lord, you gave me two talents; behold, I have, by investing, gained two others.

23. His lord said to him, Excellent, good and faithful servant! You have been reliable with little, I will place you over much; enter into your lord's joy.

24. Then he also who received the one talent approached and said, My lord, I know that you are a hard man, and you reap where you did not sow and gather where you did not scatter.

25. And I was afraid and I went and hid your talent in the ground, behold, you have what is yours.

26. His lord answered and said to him, Bad and lazy servant! You knew me that I reap where I have not sowed and gather where I have not scattered?

---

5 See Mt. 18:24, footnote 10 - Talent.

مد: .

מה: .

מו: .

מז: .

מח: .

מט: .

נ: .

נא: .

נב: .

נג: .

נד: .

נה: .

נו: .

27. Then you should have left my money on the tray and when I returned I would have demanded my own with interest.[6]

28. Take, now, that talent from him and give it to him who has ten talents.

29. Because to him who has, it shall be given and he will have more; but from him who has not, even what he has shall be taken away.

30. And the idle servant they threw out into the outer darkness; there shall be weeping and gnashing of teeth.

THE PARABLE OF THE SHEEP AND GOATS

31. Now when this Human Being comes in his splendor and all his holy messengers with him then will he sit on the throne of his glory.[7]

32. And all the nations will be gathered before him; and he will separate them one by one just as a shepherd who separates the sheep from the goats.[8]

33. And he will place the sheep on his right hand and the goats on his left.[9]

34. Then the king will say to those on his right, Come, you blessed of my Father, inherit the kingdom that was prepared for you from the foundation of the world.

35. Because I was hungry and you gave me to eat; I was thirsty and you gave me to drink; I was a stranger and you sheltered me.

---

6 In the East a lord has a special tray or table where money is left which his servants may take to invest for him. At a later time their lord then may call for the interest on the money loaned.

7 Jesus reassures his followers that, although he is at this time the suffering Messsiah who will die and be raised for the salvation of humankind, they will at the end enjoy seeing him come with splendor as a spiritual ruler. See Dan. 7:13.

8 Jesus had prepared his followers by teaching them about 1) the destruction of the Temple, 2) the siege and fall of the Holy City, Jerusalem, 3) the end of the age, 4) the end of individual, that is, personal lives, and now 5) the final judgment for all nations. This judgment is based on what an individual did not do for his neighbor; i.e., not practicing love and caring for others' needs. See Mt. 25:41-45.

9 Custom: Eastern families keep sheep and goats; sheep supply the wool for clothing and the hair of goats is used for making tents, bags and ropes. Both sheep and goats supply the family with milk which is made into butter and cheese. The shepherds usually separate the sheep from the goats making the sheep pass to the right and on to the roof of the fold (corral). The goats are made to move to the left of the shepherds through a narrow passage into the fold. Thus will it be among the nations separating the just and the unjust.

ܟܙ: ܘܙܕܩ ܗܘܐ ܠܟ ܕܬܪܡܐ ܟܣܦܝ ܥܠ ܛܪܦܝܙܐ. ܘܐܬܐ ܗܘܝܬ ܐܢܐ ܘܬܒܥ ܗܘܝܬ ܕܝܠܝ ܥܡ ܪܒܝܬܗ.

ܟܚ: ܫܩܘܠܘ ܗܟܝܠ ܡܢܗ ܟܟܪܐ. ܘܗܒܘܗܝ ܠܗܘ ܕܐܝܬ ܠܗ ܥܣܪܐ ܟܟܪ̈ܝܢ.

ܟܛ: ܠܡܢ ܓܝܪ ܕܐܝܬ ܠܗ. ܢܬܝܗܒ ܠܗ ܘܢܬܝܬܪ ܠܗ. ܡܢ ܗܘ ܕܝܢ ܕܠܝܬ ܠܗ. ܘܐܦ ܗܘ ܕܐܝܬ ܠܗ ܢܫܬܩܠ ܡܢܗ.

ܠ: ܘܠܥܒܕܐ ܒܛܝܠܐ ܐܦܩܘܗܝ ܠܚܫܘܟܐ ܒܪܝܐ. ܬܡܢ ܢܗܘܐ ܒܟܝܐ ܘܚܘܪܩ ܫܢ̈ܐ.

ܠܐ: ܡܐ ܕܐܬܐ ܕܝܢ ܒܪܗ ܕܐܢܫܐ ܒܫܘܒܚܗ. ܘܟܠܗܘܢ ܡܠܐܟܘܗܝ ܩܕܝܫܐ ܥܡܗ. ܗܝܕܝܢ ܢܬܒ ܥܠ ܟܘܪܣܝܐ ܕܫܘܒܚܗ.

ܠܒ: ܘܢܬܟܢܫܘܢ ܩܕܡܘܗܝ ܟܠܗܘܢ ܥܡ̈ܡܐ. ܘܢܦܪܘܫ ܐܢܘܢ ܚܕ ܡܢ ܚܕ ܐܝܟ ܪܥܝܐ ܕܡܦܪܫ ܐܡܪ̈ܐ ܡܢ ܓܕܝ̈ܐ.

ܠܓ: ܘܢܩܝܡ ܐܡܪ̈ܐ ܡܢ ܝܡܝܢܗ. ܘܓܕܝ̈ܐ ܡܢ ܣܡܠܗ.

ܠܕ: ܗܝܕܝܢ ܢܐܡܪ ܡܠܟܐ ܠܗܢܘܢ ܕܡܢ ܝܡܝܢܗ: ܬܘ ܒܪܝܟܘܗܝ ܕܐܒܝ. ܝܪܬܘ ܡܠܟܘܬܐ ܕܡܛܝܒܐ ܗܘܬ ܠܟܘܢ ܡܢ ܬܪܡܝܬܗ ܕܥܠܡܐ.

ܠܗ: ܟܦܢܬ ܓܝܪ ܘܝܗܒܬܘܢ ܠܝ ܠܡܐܟܠ. ܘܨܗܝܬ ܘܐܫܩܝܬܘܢܢܝ. ܐܟܣܢܝܐ ܗܘܝܬ ܘܟܢܫܬܘܢܢܝ.

36. I was naked and you covered me; I was sick and you visited me; I was in prison and you came to me.[10]

37. Then will those righteous say to him, Our lord, when did we see you hungry and gave you to eat, or thirsty and gave you drink?

38. And when did we see you a stranger and sheltered you? Or that you were naked and covered you?

39. And when did we see you sick, or in prison and visited you?

40. And the king will answer and say to them, Truly, I say to you that inasmuch as you have done it to one of these, my little brothers, you have done it to me.

41. Then he will also say to those on his left, Get away from me, you cursed, into everlasting fire which was prepared for the adversary and his messengers.

42. Because I was hungry and you did not give me to eat; I was thirsty and you did not give me drink.

43. I was a stranger and you did not shelter me; I was naked and you did not cover me; I was sick and in prison and you did not visit me.

44. Then they also will answer and say, Our lord, when did we see you hungry, or thirsty, or a stranger, or naked, or sick or in prison and did not serve you?

45. Then he will answer and say to them, Truly, I say to you that inasmuch as you did not do so to one of these little ones, you also did not do it to me!

46. And these will go into everlasting torment and the righteous into everlasting life.[11]

---

10 Prisoners in the East are usually bound in chains, fed bread and water and beaten once or twice a day. They depend on relatives to bring food and clothing and usually only after the guards have been bribed. There are those whom no one visits. Thus Easterners believe God greatly rewards people who go to prisons and help those unfortunate criminals with food and clothes. Many of the early Christians experienced the life of a prisoner. See verses 39, 40 and 43.

11 Jesus' rewards were not based on extraordinary actions or deeds but on simple acts of mercy and compassion which can be practiced by anyone, anywhere, at anytime.

_____

A - 104

CHAPTER 26

THE CONSPIRACY AGAINST THE MESSIAH

1. And so it was that when Jesus finished all these sayings,[1] he said to his disciples:

2. You know that after two days it is Passover[2] and this Human Being is to be betrayed and crucified.[3]

3. Then the high priests and the scribes and the elders of the people gathered in the courtyard of the High Priest who is named Caiaphas.[4]

4. And they held a counsel concerning Jesus that they might arrest him by trickery and kill him.

5 And they were saying: Not on a feast day,[5] lest there be trouble among the people.

ANOINTED AT BETHANY

6. Now when Jesus was at Bethany, in the home of Simon the leper,

---

1 Meaning the entire teaching ministry of Jesus from the very beginning to the end and linking it with the Passion-Resurrection narrative, Chapterss 26-27.

2 ܦܶܨܚܳܐ, פסחא, Pisḥa, *Passover, Festival of Rejoicing.* The Feast of the Passover was celebrated on the 14th day of Nisan, (see verse 17, footnote 10, for an explanation of Nisan.) Also see Ex. 12:1-6, Num. 9:1-14, Deut. 16:1-8.

3 Crucifixion was the Roman manner of execution. According to Jewish law, criminals were executed by stoning, burning, decapitation or strangulation. Jesus had been tried and convicted under Roman law as a political criminal (treason against Caesar) even though he had been convicted of blasphemy by the High Priest. Jesus was Galilean and therefore subject to Roman capital punishment.

4 Joseph Caiaphas, a Sadducee, was the high priest during Pilate's government. He was son-in-law of Annas, who had been deposed from the high priesthood by the Roman procurator Valerious, but he (Annas) still retained the title and considerable authority.

5 The Roman authorities were always deeply troubled about uprisings during feast days because of the masses of people assembled in the Holy City. This fear would even be more pronounced during Passover which was a celebration of freedom and salvation from Egyptian oppression. The priests for the most part were pro-Roman collaborators.

ܡܬܝ: ܟܘ.

ܐ: ܘܗܘܐ ܕܟܕ ܫܠܡ ܝܫܘܥ ܟܠܗܘܢ ܡܠܐ ܗܠܝܢ. ܐܡܪ ܠܬܠܡܝܕܘܗܝ.

ܒ: ܝܕܥܝܢ ܐܢܬܘܢ ܕܒܬܪ ܬܪܝܢ ܝܘܡܝܢ ܗܘܐ ܦܨܚܐ. ܘܒܪܗ ܕܐܢܫܐ ܡܫܬܠܡ ܕܢܙܕܩܦ.

ܓ: ܗܝܕܝܢ ܐܬܟܢܫܘ ܪܒܝ ܟܗܢܐ ܘܣܦܪܐ ܘܩܫܝܫܐ ܕܥܡܐ ܠܕܪܬܗ ܕܪܒ ܟܗܢܐ ܕܡܬܩܪܐ ܩܝܦܐ.

ܕ: ܘܐܬܡܠܟܘ ܥܠ ܝܫܘܥ ܕܢܐܚܕܘܢܝܗܝ ܒܢܟܠܐ. ܘܢܩܛܠܘܢܝܗܝ.

ܗ: ܘܐܡܪܝܢ ܗܘܘ: ܠܐ ܒܥܐܕܥܐܕܐ ܕܠܐ ܢܗܘܐ ܫܘܓܫܐ ܒܥܡܐ.

ܘ: ܘܟܕ ܗܘܐ ܝܫܘܥ ܒܒܝܬ ܥܢܝܐ ܒܒܝܬܗ ܕܫܡܥܘܢ ܓܪܒܐ.

7. A woman[6] with a jar of perfume[7] which was very expensive approached him, and she poured it on the head of Jesus, while he was reclining.[8]

8. Now his disciples saw it and were displeased and said: Why this waste?

9. Because this could have been sold for a great deal and given to the poor.

10. But Jesus understood and said to them: Why are you bothering the woman? She has done a beautiful deed to me.

11. Now you always have the poor with you, but you will not always have me.

12. But this one who poured this perfume over my body did it as it were for my burial.

13. And truly I say to you that wherever this my joyful message may be preached throughout the world, this thing she has done will be told as a memorial for her.

JUDAS SELLS HIS LORD AND THE CELEBRATION OF PASSOVER

14. Then one of the twelve, named Judas Iscariot, went to the high priests,

15. And said to them: What are you willing to give me if I turn him over to you? Then they promised him thirty pieces of silver.[9]

16. Then from that time on he looked for an opportunity to betray him.

17. Now on the first day of unleavened bread,[10] the disciples approached Jesus and said to him: Where do you want us to prepare the Passover for you to eat?

18. Then he said to them: Go into the city to a certain man and tell him, Our teacher says, my time has come, I will keep the Passover with my disciples at your place.

---

6 According to Jn. 12:1-3, the woman mentioned here by Matthew is Mary, the sister of Lazarus and Martha.
7 Alabaster containers were commonly used for precious ointments. This ointment was prepared from the leaves of spikenard.
8 Eastern custom is to anoint a guest while at the meal.
9 See Ex. 21:32 and Zech. 11:12.
10 The feast of Unleavened Bread begins on the fifteenth day of Nisan. Nisan is the first month of the religious year, seventh month of the civil year. In the books of Moses it is called the month of Abib; i.e., spring. Matthew and Mark describe this event as the Seder*, while John saw it as an ordinary meal. (*Seder in Hebrew means *Order:* Ceremony and supper observed in the Jewish home on the first night of Passover and regulated by rabbinic injunction. Outside Israel, it is celebrated the first two nights of Passover.)

ܙ: ܩܪܒܬ ܠܗ ܐܢܬܬܐ. ܕܐܝܬ ܥܡܗ ܫܛܝܦܘܬܐ ܕܡܫܚܐ ܕܒܣܡܐ ܣܓܝ ܕܝܩܪܐ.
ܘܐܫܕܬܗ ܥܠ ܪܫܗ ܕܝܫܘܥ ܟܕ ܣܡܝܟ.

ܚ: ܚܙܘ ܕܝܢ ܬܠܡܝܕܘܗܝ. ܘܐܬܚܡܬܘ ܠܗܘܢ. ܘܐܡܪܝܢ: ܠܡܢܐ ܐܒܕܢܐ ܗܢܐ.

ܛ: ܡܫܟܚ ܗܘܐ ܓܝܪ ܕܢܙܕܒܢ ܗܢܐ. ܒܣܓܝ. ܘܢܬܝܗܒ ܠܡܣܟܢܐ.

ܝ: ܝܕܥ ܕܝܢ ܝܫܘܥ. ܘܐܡܪ ܠܗܘܢ: ܡܢܐ ܡܠܐܝܢ ܐܢܬܘܢ ܠܗ ܠܐܢܬܬܐ. ܥܒܕܐ
ܫܦܝܪܐ ܥܒܕܬ ܠܘܬܝ.

ܝܐ: ܒܟܠܙܒܢ ܓܝܪ ܡܣܟܢܐ ܐܝܬ ܠܟܘܢ ܥܡܟܘܢ. ܠܝ ܕܝܢ ܠܐ ܒܟܠܙܒܢ ܐܝܬ ܠܟܘܢ.

ܝܒ: ܗܕܐ ܕܝܢ ܕܐܪܡܝܬ ܒܣܡܐ ܗܢܐ ܥܠ ܦܓܪܝ. ܐܝܟ ܕܠܡܩܒܪܢܝ ܥܒܕܬܗ.

ܝܓ: ܘܐܡܝܢ ܐܡܪ ܐܢܐ ܠܟܘܢ: ܕܐܝܟܐ ܕܬܬܟܪܙ ܣܒܪܬܝ ܗܕܐ ܒܟܠܗ ܥܠܡܐ.
ܢܬܡܠܠ ܐܦ ܡܕܡ ܕܥܒܕܬ ܗܕܐ ܠܕܘܟܪܢܗ.

ܝܕ: ܗܝܕܝܢ ܐܙܠ ܚܕ ܡܢ ܬܪܥܣܪ ܕܡܬܩܪܐ ܝܗܘܕܐ ܣܟܪܝܘܛܐ ܠܘܬ ܪܒܝ ܟܗܢܐ.

ܝܗ: ܘܐܡܪ ܠܗܘܢ: ܡܢܐ ܨܒܝܢ ܐܢܬܘܢ ܠܡܬܠ ܠܝ. ܘܐܢܐ ܡܫܠܡ ܐܢܐ ܠܗ ܠܟܘܢ.
ܗܢܘܢ ܕܝܢ ܐܩܝܡܘ ܠܗ ܬܠܬܝܢ ܕܟܣܦܐ.

ܝܘ: ܘܡܢ ܗܝܕܝܢ ܒܥܐ ܗܘܐ ܠܗ ܦܠܚܐ ܕܢܫܠܡܝܘܗܝ.

ܝܙ: ܒܝܘܡܐ ܕܝܢ ܩܕܡܝܐ ܕܦܛܝܪܐ ܩܪܒܘ ܬܠܡܝܕܐ ܠܘܬ ܝܫܘܥ ܘܐܡܪܝܢ ܠܗ: ܐܝܟܐ
ܨܒܐ ܐܢܬ ܕܢܛܝܒ ܠܟ ܕܬܐܟܘܠ ܦܨܚܐ.

ܝܚ: ܗܘ ܕܝܢ ܐܡܪ ܠܗܘܢ: ܙܠܘ ܠܡܕܝܢܬܐ ܠܘܬ ܦܠܢ. ܘܐܡܪܘ ܠܗ: ܪܒܢ ܐܡܪ:
ܙܒܢܝ ܡܛܐ ܠܗ. ܠܘܬܟ ܥܒܕ ܐܢܐ ܦܨܚܐ ܥܡ ܬܠܡܝܕܝ.

19. And his disciples did as Jesus had directed them so they prepared the Passover.

20. Then when it was evening, he reclined with his twelve disciples.

21. And while they were eating he said: Truly I say to you that one from your midst is to betray me.[11]

22. And it made them feel exceedingly sad. Then each one of them began to say to him: Why, is it I, my lord?

23. Then he answered and said: He who dips his hand with me in the dish,[12] that one will betray me.

24. And this Human Being will go just as it is written about him. But how miserable is the man through whom this Human Being is arrested. It would have been better for that man if he had not been born!

25. Judas, the traitor, answered and said: Maybe it is I, my teacher? Jesus said to him: You have said that![13]

---

11 Easterners are never afraid to let their emotions show, be it joy, sorrow or deep disappointment. Jesus giving vent to his emotions during the entire supper is typical Eastern temperament. See Lk. 22:15.
12 Custom: In the East men generally eat their fraternal feasts as they sit or recline in something like a circle and eat out of a few large dishes which the group share. It is not unusual for one to take food from the dish of another sitting next to him. The food is eaten with small "shreds" of thin bread and even liquid food is sometimes "dipped up" with pieces of bread formed like the bowl of a spoon. The phrase "He who dips his hand with me in the dish," has been construed to mean Judas only, but this is not true to the normal custom although possible. *"The fact is that according to custom on such occasions each of the few large dishes contains a different kind of food. Each one of the guests is privileged to reach to any one of the dishes and dip his bread in it. From this it may be safely inferred that several or all of the disciples dipped in turn in the dish which was nearest to Jesus. (See Mk. 14:17-20.) The fact that the other disciples did not know whom their Master meant by his saying that one of them should betray him, even after he had said, "He that dips with me in the dish," shows plainly that Judas was eating in the same fashion as all the other disciples were.*

The saying, "He that dips with me," etc., was that of disappointed love. It may be thus paraphrased: "I have loved you all alike. I have chosen you as my dearest friends. We have often broken bread and sorrowed and rejoiced together, yet one of you, my dear disciples, one who is now eating with me as the rest are, intends to betray me!" Rihbany, THE SYRIAN CHRIST, pp 60-61.
13 Aramaic style of speech meaning "You said it, not I." See verse 64, footnote 34 and Mt. 27:11, footnote 4.

ܝܛ: ܘܬܠܡܝܕ̈ܘܗܝ ܥܒܕܘ ܐܝܟܢܐ ܕܦܩܕ ܠܗܘܢ ܝܫܘܥ. ܘܡܛܝܒܘ ܦܨܚܐ.

ܟ: ܘܟܕ ܗܘܝܐ ܪܡܫܐ. ܣܡܝܟ ܗܘܝܐ ܥܡ ܬܪܥܣܪ ܬܠܡܝܕ̈ܘܗܝ.

ܟܐ: ܘܟܕ ܐܟܠܝܗܘܝ. ܝܡܪܐ: ܫܪܝܪ ܐܡܪܢ ܐܢܐ ܠܟܘܢ: ܕܚܕ ܡܢܟܘܢ ܡܫܠܡܠܗ ܠܝ.

ܟܒ: ܘܟܪܝܠܗ ܠܗܘܢ ܛܒ. ܘܫܪܝܠܗܘܢ ܠܡܐܡܪܐ ܠܗ ܚܕ ܚܕ ܡܢܗܘܢ: ܠܡܐ ܝܠܐ ܐܢܐ ܡܪܝ.

ܟܓ: ܗܘ ܕܝܢ ܥܢܐ ܘܝܡܪܐ: ܡܢ ܕܨܒܥ ܐܝܕܗ ܥܡܝ ܒܩܠܩܠܬܐ. ܗܘ ܡܫܠܡܠܝ.

ܟܕ: ܒܪܗ ܕܐܢܫܐ ܝܙܠ ܐܝܟܢܐ ܕܟܬܝܒܐ ܒܝܠܗ. ܘܝ ܠܗ ܕܝܢ ܠܓܒܪܐ ܗܘ ܕܒܐܝܕܗ
ܒܪܗ ܕܐܢܫܐ ܡܫܬܠܡ. ܦܫܝܛ ܗܘܝܐ ܠܗ ܠܓܒܪܐ ܗܘ ܐܠܘ ܠܐ ܝܠܝܕ.

ܟܗ: ܥܢܐ ܝܗܘܕܐ ܡܫܠܡܢܐ ܘܝܡܪܐ: ܕܠܡܐ ܝܠܐ ܐܢܐ ܪܒܝ. ܐܡܪ ܠܗ ܝܫܘܥ: ܐܢܬ
ܝܡܪܬ.

26. Then while they were eating Jesus took the bread[14] and blessed it and broke it and gave it to his disciples and said: Take, eat, this is my body!

27. And he took the cup[15] and gave thanks, then he gave it to them and said: Take and everyone of you drink from it.

28. This is my blood of the new covenant[16] which, on the behalf of many, is shed for the release of sins.

29. Now truly I say to you that from now on I will not drink from this fruit of the vine until the day in which I will drink it anew with you[17] in my Father's kingdom.[18]

---

14 In the East, bread is considered as more than just life sustaining. Usually, Easterners will not tell a lie when there is bread present on the table. The bread and salt covenant is a strong bond of friendship. To be unfaithful to a bread and salt covenant and to lie when there is bread on the table is to be stigmatized as a base ingrate and untrustworthy person. Among Easterners bread has always been eaten with a deep sense of sacredness. There are many sayings in Scripture which testify to this fact; i.e., "Bread and salt," "bread and wine," "Christ the bread of life," "For we, being many, are one bread" and "Give us this day our daily bread."

15 *To us the one cup meant fellowship and fraternal communion. The one who gives drink fills the cup and passes it to the most honored member of the company first. He drinks the contents and returns the cup to the one who poured, who fills it again and hands it to another member of the group, and so on, until all have been served once. Then the guests drink again by way of nezel. (A word difficult to translate into English, some say "treating" but this falls short of expressing the affectionate regard which the nezel signifies.) The one guest upon receiving the cup wishes for the whole company "health, happiness, and length of days." Then he singles out one of the group and begs him to accept the next cup that is poured as a pledge of his affectionate regard. The pourer complies with the request by handing the next cup to the person thus designated, who drinks it with the most effusive and affectionate reciprocation of his friend's sentiments. It is also customary for a gracious host to request as a happy ending to the feast that the contents of one cup be drunk by the whole company as a seal of their friendship with one another. Each guest takes a sip and passes the cup to the one next to him until all have partaken of the "fruit of the vine." See Mk. 14:23.* Rihbany, THE SYRIAN CHRIST, pp 62-63. At Seder, four cups of wine are drunk, each representing a redemptive word connected with the Exodus, two before the meal and two after the meal. Evidently this was the last cup of the Seder; hence, Jesus' final statement, "From now on I will not drink from this fruit of the vine until the day in which I will drink it anew with you in my Father's kingdom." See verse 29.

16 "The blood of the covenant" is an ancient Eastern covenant and connected with rite of circumcision and the Passover, Ex. 12:48, 24:8. Jesus' blood of the covenant refers more to Lev. 17:11.

17 A Semitic expression of speech meaning, "I shall not be fully joyful again till we are all together once more"; in this case, at the banquet and celebration of the kingdom of God. See Mt. 22:1-2. ܚܡܪܐ, חמרא, Ḥmara, *wine* also means metaphorically "joy, teaching and inspiration."

18 See Mt. 8:11.

ܟܘ: ܟܕ ܕܝܢ ܐܟܠܝܢ. ܢܣܒ ܝܫܘܥ ܠܚܡܐ. ܘܒܪܟ ܘܩܨܐ. ܘܝܗܒ ܠܬܠܡܝܕܘܗܝ
ܘܐܡܪ: ܣܒܘ ܐܟܘܠܘ. ܗܢܘ ܦܓܪܝ.

ܟܙ: ܘܢܣܒ ܟܣܐ ܘܐܘܕܝ. ܘܝܗܒ ܠܗܘܢ ܘܐܡܪ: ܣܒܘ ܐܫܬܘ ܡܢܗ ܟܠܟܘܢ.

ܟܚ: ܗܢܘ ܕܡܝ ܕܕܝܬܩܐ ܚܕܬܐ. ܕܚܠܦ ܣܓܝܐܐ ܡܬܐܫܕ ܠܫܘܒܩܢܐ ܕܚܛܗܐ.

ܟܛ: ܐܡܪ ܐܢܐ ܠܟܘܢ ܕܝܢ: ܕܠܐ ܐܫܬܐ ܡܢ ܗܫܐ ܡܢ ܗܢܐ ܝܠܕܐ ܕܓܦܬܐ ܥܕܡܐ
ܠܝܘܡܐ ܕܒܗ ܐܫܬܝܘܗܝ ܥܡܟܘܢ ܚܕܬܐ ܒܡܠܟܘܬܗ ܕܐܒܝ.

30. And they sang praise[19] and went out to the Mount of Olives.

31. Then Jesus said to them: Tonight all of you will stumble because of me for it is written I will strike the shepherd and the sheep of his flock will scatter.[20]

32. But after I am risen, I will go to Galilee ahead of you.

33. Peter answered and said to him: Though everyone doubts you, I will never doubt you.

34. Jesus replied to him: Truly I say to you that tonight before the rooster crows, you will deny me three times.

35. Peter said to him: If I were to die with you, I would never deny you! Then all the disciples also said the same thing.

JESUS' AGONY IN THE GARDEN

36. Now Jesus went with them to a place which is called Gethsemane,[21] and he said to his disciples: Sit down here while I go and pray.

37. And he took Peter and the two sons of Zebedee and he began to feel sad and to feel grieved.

38. And he said to them: I feel sad even to the point of death. Wait for me here and watch with me.

39. And he went a little distance and he bowed with his face to the ground and was praying and saying: My Father, if it is possible, let this cup[22] pass from me, but not as I wish it but as you desire.

40. Then he came to his disciples and found them dozing, and he said to Peter: So, you were not able to watch with me for one hour?

41. Stay awake and pray that you may not enter into temptation. The spirit is prepared but the body is not strong.[23]

---

19 The praises which his disciples sang are Psalms 112 - 117.
20 See Zech. 13:7.
21 ܓܕܣܡܢ, גדסמן, Gadseman - Gethsemane, *an olive press*. Gethsemane was located in the Valley of Kidron at the foot of the Mount of Olives.
22 Metaphor. Often called the cup of death or the cup of poison, it is the symbol of pain and suffering. See Ezk. 23:32-34.
23 Indeed Jesus' spirit was ready (prepared) for the coming ordeal but the body protested.

كد: .

كה: .
كו: .

كז:
كח: .
كט:
كי:
كיא: .

كיב: .
كיג: .
كיד:
كיה: .

─────────
A - 109

42. Again he went away a second time, prayed and said: My Father if it is not possible for this cup to pass, but I must drink it, let it be as you wish.

43. And he came again and found them dozing, for their eyes were heavy.[24]

44. And he left them and went to pray again for the third time, and he said the same word.

45. Then he came to his disciples and said to them: Sleep from now on and rest! Behold, the hour has arrived and this Human Being is handed over to sinners.

46. Rise up and let us go; behold, he who betrayed me has come.

THE KISS OF BETRAYAL AND JESUS ARRESTED

47. And while he was speaking, behold, the traitor Judas, one of the twelve, arrived and with him a large crowd with swords and clubs, from the high priests and elders of the people.

48. And the traitor Judas had given them a sign and he said: He whom I kiss, that very one is he, arrest him!

49. And right away he approached Jesus and said: Peace, my teacher! Then he kissed him.[25]

50. Then Jesus said to him: Is it about this that you have come, my friend?[26] Then they approached and seized Jesus and arrested him.

51. And behold one of those who was with Jesus stretched out his hand and drew a sword and struck a servant of the high priest and cut off his ear.[27]

52. Then Jesus said to him: Return the sword to its place; because all those who use the sword will die by the sword.

---

24 I.e., the Apostles were extremely weary from the mental and emotional exhaustion of the surprising events of Passover week. They were also physically tired from their long journey to Jerusalem.

25 Judas' treasonable kiss was the greatest sign of hypocrisy and perversion of an ancient, deeply cherished and common Eastern custom. When friends of the same social rank greet each other, especially after being gone for a while, they do so with a kiss on both cheeks, sometimes, as it is said, with very noisy profusion.

26 The use of the term "friend" by Jesus is because Judas greeted him with the kiss of friends. See above footnote.

27 According to Jn. 18:10, the person with the sword is Peter.

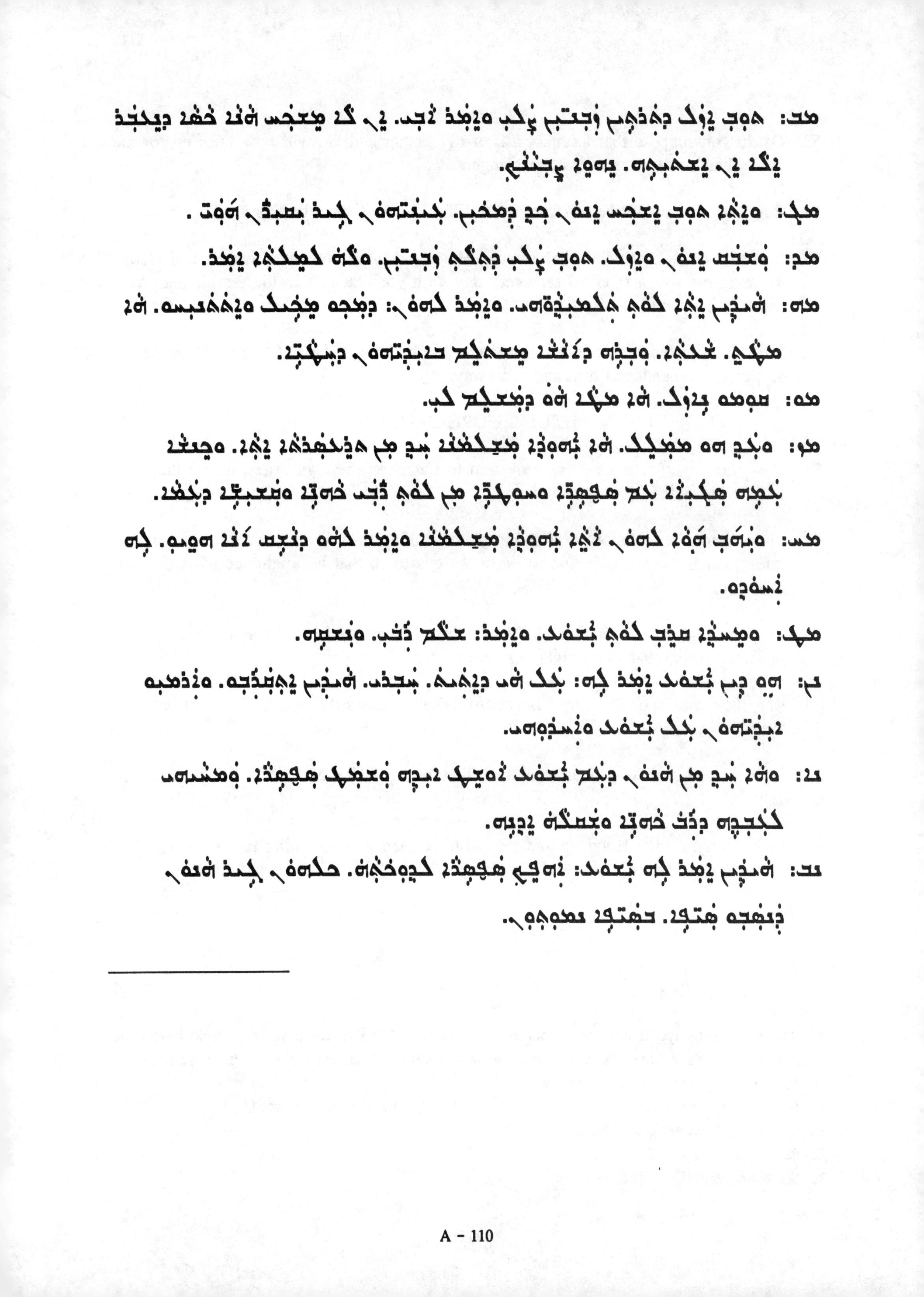

53. Or do you suppose that I cannot ask of my Father and He will now raise up for me more than twelve legions[28] of messengers?[29]

54. But how then could the scripture be fulfilled?[30] So it must be this way!

55. Immediately Jesus said to the crowds: Have you turned out with swords and clubs to arrest me like a thief? I sat every day with you teaching in the temple and you did not arrest me.

56. But this occurred that the writings of the prophets might be fulfilled.[31] Then the disciples all abandoned him and ran away.

JESUS BEFORE CAIAPHAS

57. Now those who arrested Jesus took him to Caiaphas, the high priest, where the scribes and elders were gathered.

58. Then Simon Peter followed after him from afar up to the courtyard of the high priest; and he went inside and sat with the guards so that he might see what was going on.

59. Now the high priests and the elders and the entire group looked for witnesses against Jesus so that they might put him to death.

60. And they could not find any. But many false witnesses did come. Then, at last, two came forward,[32]

61. Saying: This man says I can demolish the temple of God and rebuild it in three days.

62. And the high priest stood up and said to him: Are you not going to give any answer to these men who testify against you?

---

28 The number twelve is used as a contrast; i.e., instead of twelve disciples, Jesus could have more than twelve legions of angels. The Romans commonly kept at least one legion in Palestine, consisting of about 6,000 infantry and 600 cavalry.
29 See Ps. 91:11. Rabbinic literature often refers to "legions of messengers" (angels).
30 See Isa. 53:7, the suffering Messiah.
31 See Isa. 53:2, 12.
32 See Num. 35:30; Deut. 17:6, 19:15.

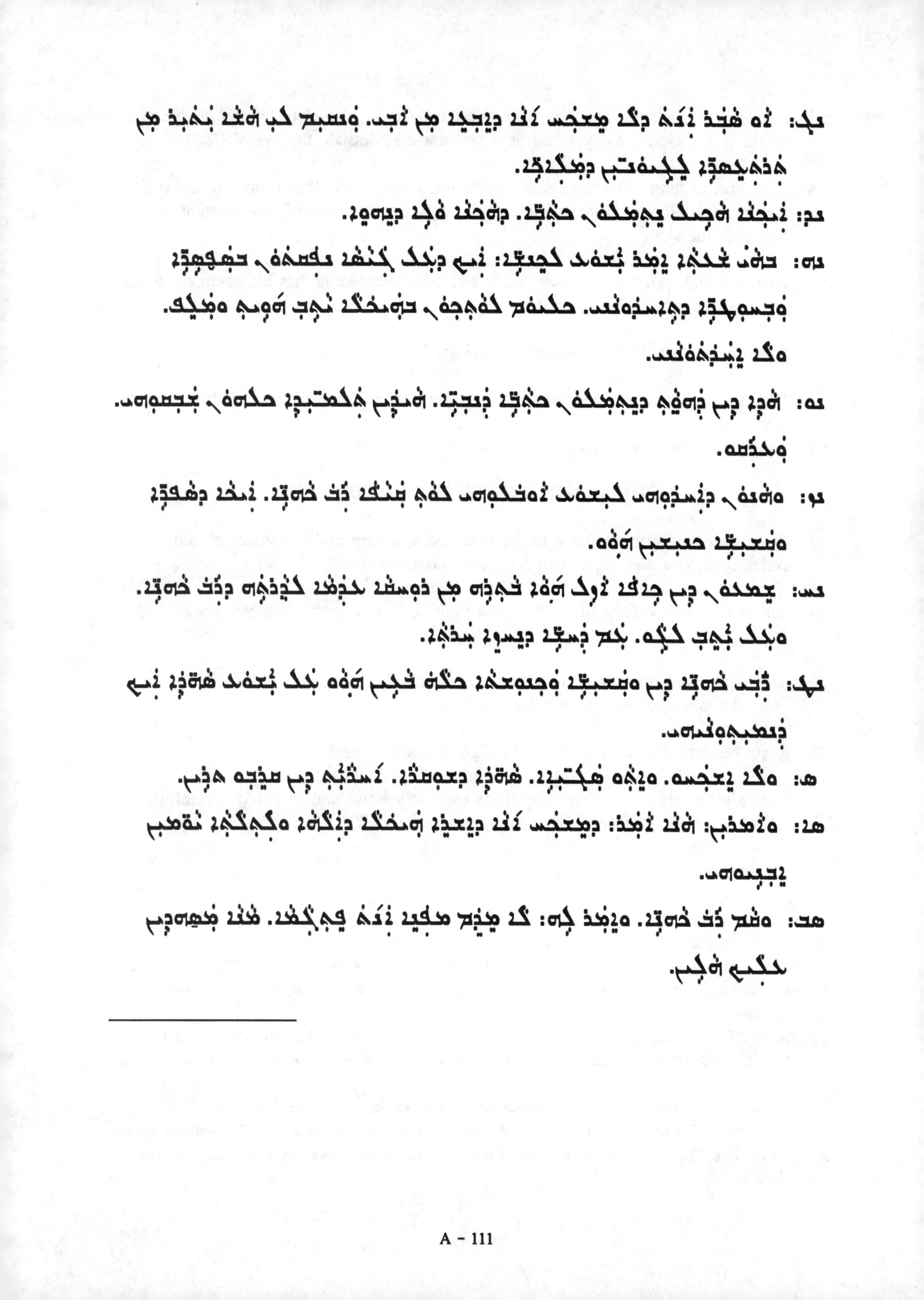

63. But Jesus was silent. Then the high priest answered and said to him: I charge you by the living God[33] that you tell us if you are the Messiah, the son of God?

64. Jesus said to him: You have said that![34] But I say to you that from now on you shall see this Human Being[35] sitting at the right hand of power[36] and coming on the clouds of the sky.[37]

65. Then the high priest tore his clothes[38] and said: Behold, he has blasphemed! Behold you have now heard his blasphemy!

66. What do you want? They answered saying: He deserves death!

67. Then they spat on his face and struck him on his head and others were beating him,

68. Saying: Prophesy to us, Oh you Messiah, who is it that struck you?

THE APOSTLE SIMON DENIES HIS LORD

69. Now Peter was sitting outside in the yard and a certain maid approached him, exclaiming: You, too, were with Jesus the Nazarene!

70. But he denied it before all of them and said: I do not know what you are talking about!

71. And as he went out to the porch another one saw him, and she said to them: This man was also there with Jesus, the Nazarene.

72. Again he denied it with an oath: I do not know the man!

73. Then after a while, those standing there approached and said to Peter: Truthfully, you also are one of them, even your speech proves it.[39]

---

33 Once this was said Jesus had to answer the High Priest.
34 Aramaic expression: "You have said so, not I" or "This is what you say." See verse 25, footnote 12.
35 Breh dnasha, *ordinary human being, commoner*. See Mt. 4:4, footnote 6 and Mt. 8:20, footnote 12.
36 Figurative speech: Complete authority.
37 Idiom: Triumphant, success assured, highest honors. See Mt. 24:30, footnote 11. It may be paraphrased: *But I am telling you that from now on you will see this commoner triumphant with total authority.*
38 Custom: A high priest may tear his garments when he hears blasphemy. See 2 Ki. 18:37.
39 Peter, being from Bethsaida in Galilee, spoke the northern dialect of Aramaic. The southern dialect of Aramaic was Chaldean. People recognized the northern dialect spoken by Peter which proved he was a Galilean.

ܣܓ: ܝܫܘܥ ܕܝܢ ܫܬܝܩ ܗܘܐ. ܘܥܢܐ ܪܒ ܟܗܢܐ. ܘܐܡܪ ܠܗ: ܡܘܡܐ ܐܢܐ ܠܟ ܒܐܠܗܐ
ܚܝܐ ܕܬܐܡܪ ܠܢ. ܐܢ ܐܢܬ ܗܘ ܡܫܝܚܐ ܒܪܗ ܕܐܠܗܐ.

ܣܕ: ܐܡܪ ܠܗ ܝܫܘܥ: ܐܢܬ ܐܡܪܬ. ܐܡܪ ܐܢܐ ܠܟܘܢ ܕܝܢ: ܕܡܢ ܗܫܐ ܬܚܙܘܢ
ܠܒܪܗ ܕܐܢܫܐ ܕܝܬܒ ܡܢ ܝܡܝܢܐ ܕܚܝܠܐ. ܘܐܬܐ ܥܠ ܥܢܢܝ ܫܡܝܐ.

ܣܗ: ܗܝܕܝܢ ܪܒ ܟܗܢܐ ܨܪܐ ܢܚܬܘܗܝ. ܘܐܡܪ: ܗܐ ܓܕܦ. ܡܢܐ ܡܬܒܥܝܢ ܠܢ
ܣܗܕܐ. ܗܐ ܗܫܐ ܫܡܥܬܘܢ ܓܘܕܦܗ.

ܣܘ: ܡܢܐ ܨܒܝܢ ܐܢܬܘܢ. ܥܢܘ ܘܐܡܪܝܢ: ܚܝܒ ܗܘ ܡܘܬܐ.

ܣܙ: ܗܝܕܝܢ ܪܩܘ ܒܐܦܘܗܝ. ܘܡܩܦܚܝܢ ܗܘܘ ܠܗ. ܐܚܪܢܐ ܕܝܢ ܡܚܝܢ ܗܘܘ ܠܗ.

ܣܚ: ܘܐܡܪܝܢ: ܐܬܢܒܐ ܠܢ ܡܫܝܚܐ. ܡܢܘ ܗܘ ܕܡܚܝܟ.

ܣܛ: ܟܐܦܐ ܕܝܢ ܝܬܒ ܗܘܐ ܠܒܪ ܒܕܪܬܐ. ܘܩܪܒܬ ܠܘܬܗ ܐܡܬܐ ܚܕܐ. ܘܐܡܪܐ ܠܗ:
ܐܦ ܐܢܬ ܥܡ ܝܫܘܥ ܗܘܝܬ ܢܨܪܝܐ.

ܥ: ܗܘ ܕܝܢ ܟܦܪ ܩܕܡ ܟܠܗܘܢ. ܘܐܡܪ: ܠܐ ܝܕܥ ܐܢܐ ܡܢܐ ܐܡܪܐ ܐܢܬܝ.

ܥܐ: ܘܟܕ ܢܦܩ ܠܬܪܥܐ. ܚܙܬܗ ܐܚܪܬܐ. ܘܐܡܪܐ ܠܗܘܢ ܕܬܡܢ ܗܘܘ: ܐܦ ܗܢܐ ܥܡ
ܝܫܘܥ ܢܨܪܝܐ.

ܥܒ: ܘܬܘܒ ܟܦܪ ܒܡܘܡܬܐ: ܕܠܐ ܝܕܥ ܐܢܐ ܠܗ ܠܓܒܪܐ.

ܥܓ: ܡܢ ܒܬܪ ܩܠܝܠ ܕܝܢ ܩܪܒܘ ܗܢܘܢ ܕܩܝܡܝܢ. ܘܐܡܪܘ ܠܟܐܦܐ: ܫܪܝܪܐܝܬ ܐܦ
ܐܢܬ ܡܢܗܘܢ ܐܢܬ. ܐܦ ܡܡܠܠܟ ܓܝܪ ܡܘܕܥ ܠܟ.

74. Then he began to curse and to swear: I do not know the man! Immediately the rooster crowed.

75. And Peter remembered Jesus' words which he had said to him: Before the rooster crows, you will deny me three times. Then he went outside and cried bitterly.

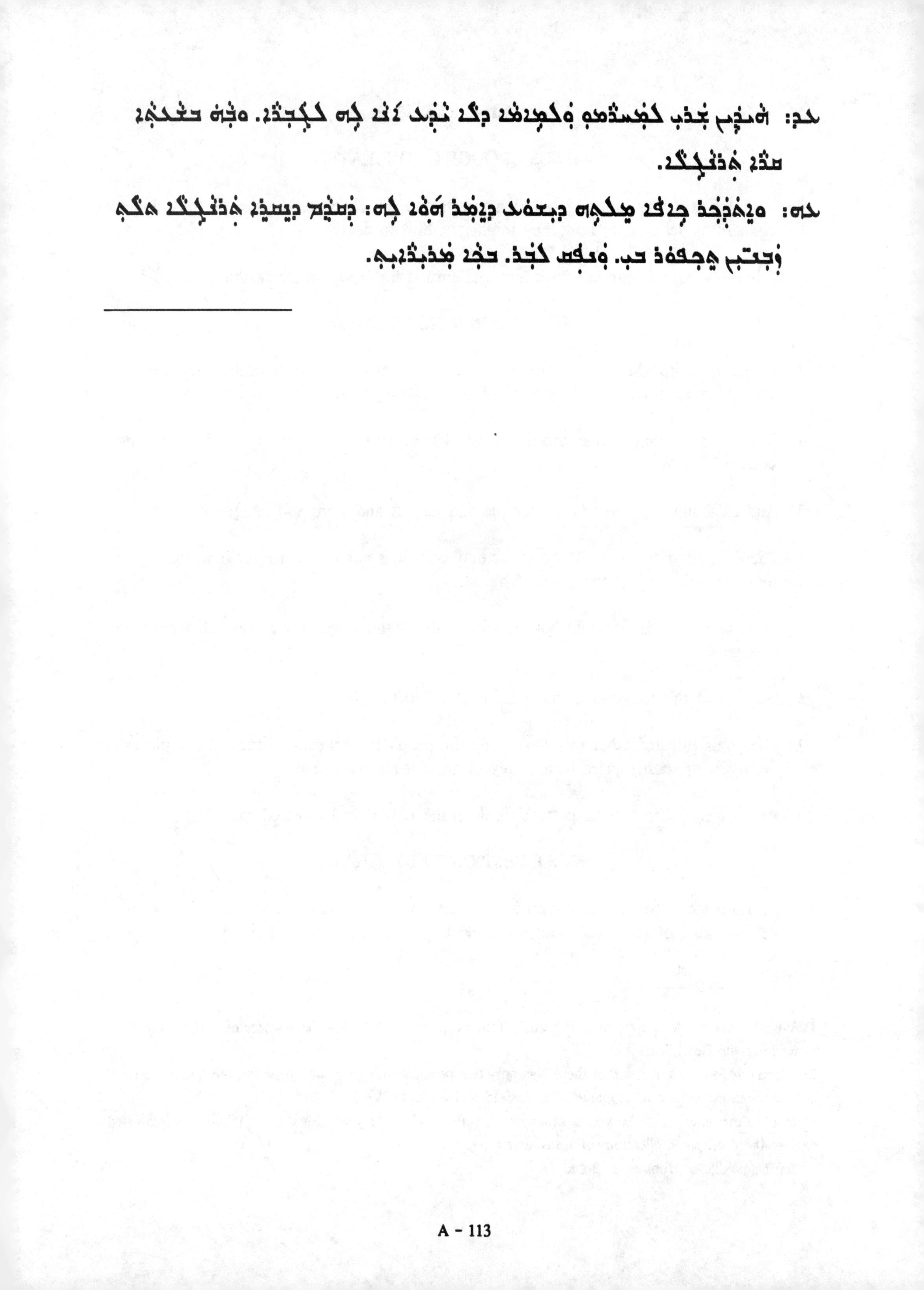

CHAPTER 27

JESUS BROUGHT TO PILATE

1. Now when it was morning the high priests and the elders of the people took counsel concerning Jesus as to how they might put him to death.

2. And they bound him and took him and turned him over to Pilate the governor.[1]

JUDAS COMMITS SUICIDE

3. Then the traitor Judas, when he saw that Jesus was convicted, became sorry and went and returned those thirty pieces of silver to the high priests and elders.

4. And he said: I have done wrong because I have betrayed innocent blood. Then they said to him: What is that to us?

5. And he flung the silver in the temple and he left and went and hanged himself.

6. Then the high priests took the silver and said: It is not lawful to put it in the treasury because it is the price of blood.

7. And they took counsel and bought with it the potter's field for a place to bury strangers.

8. Because of this it is called the field of blood to this day.

9. Then was fulfilled what was spoken by the prophet[2] who said: I took thirty pieces of silver, the costly price which they of Israel have bargained.

10. And I gave them for the potter's field, as the LORD had directed me.

JESUS QUESTIONED BY PILATE

11. So Jesus stood before the governor, and the governor asked and said to him: Are you the king of the Jews?[3] Jesus replied to him: You have said that![4]

---

1 Tiberius Caesar had appointed Pontius Pilate as governor of Judea the borders of which were from Samaria to the Dead Sea.
2 Although Matthew states that there was only one prophet who gave the prophecy, the quotation itself is a combination from two prophets: Jer. 32:6-15 and Zech. 11:12-13.
3 Double meaning: (1) "Are you a king; i.e., a ruler?" (2) "Are you a Messiah?" Pilate was interested only in the political implications of Jesus' arrest.
4 See Mt. 26:25, 64, footnotes 13 and 34.

ܦܨܚܬܐ: ܟܘ.

ܐ: ܟܕ ܕܝܢ ܗܘܐ ܨܦܪܐ ܡܠܟܐ ܢܣܒܘ ܥܠ ܝܫܘܥ ܟܠܗܘܢ ܪ̈ܒܝ ܟܗ̈ܢܐ ܘܩܫܝ̈ܫܐ
ܕܥܡܐ ܐܝܟ ܕܢܡܝܬܘܢܝܗܝ.

ܒ: ܘܐܣܪܘܗܝ. ܘܐܘܒܠܘܗܝ. ܘܐܫܠܡܘܗܝ ܠܦܝܠܛܘܣ ܗܓܡܘܢܐ.

ܓ: ܗܝܕܝܢ ܝܗܘܕܐ ܡܫܠܡܢܐ ܟܕ ܚܙܐ ܕܐܬܚܝܒ ܝܫܘܥ. ܐܬܬܘܝ ܘܐܗܦܟ ܗܠܝܢ
ܬܠܬܝܢ ܕܣܐܡܐ ܠܪ̈ܒܝ ܟܗ̈ܢܐ ܘܠܩܫܝ̈ܫܐ.

ܕ: ܘܐܡܪ ܚܛܝܬ ܕܐܫܠܡܬ ܕܡܐ ܙܟܝܐ. ܗܢܘܢ ܕܝܢ ܐܡܪܘ ܠܗ: ܠܢ ܡܐ ܠܢ. ܐܢܬ
ܝܕܥ ܐܢܬ.

ܗ: ܘܫܕܝܗܝ ܣܐܡܐ ܒܗܝܟܠܐ ܘܫܢܝ. ܘܐܙܠ ܚܢܩ ܢܦܫܗ.

ܘ: ܪ̈ܒܝ ܟܗ̈ܢܐ ܕܝܢ ܫܩܠܘܗܝ ܠܣܐܡܐ. ܘܐܡܪܘ: ܠܐ ܫܠܝܛ ܕܢܪܡܝܘܗܝ ܒܝܬ
ܩܘܪܒܢܐ. ܡܛܠ ܕܛܝܡܝ ܕܡܐ ܗܘ.

ܙ: ܘܢܣܒܘ ܡܠܟܐ. ܘܙܒܢܘ ܒܗ ܐܓܘܪܣܐ ܕܦܚܪܐ ܠܒܝܬ ܩܒܘܪܐ ܕܐܟܣܢ̈ܝܐ.

ܚ: ܡܛܠ ܗܢܐ ܐܬܩܪܝ ܐܓܘܪܣܐ ܗܘ ܩܪܝܬܐ ܕܕܡܐ ܥܕܡܐ ܠܝܘܡܢܐ.

ܛ: ܗܝܕܝܢ ܐܬܡܠܝ ܡܕܡ ܕܐܬܐܡܪ ܒܝܕ ܢܒܝܐ ܕܐܡܪ: ܕܢܣܒܬ ܬܠܬܝܢ ܕܣܐܡܐ ܕܛܝܡܗ
ܕܝܩܝܪܐ ܕܦܣܩܘ ܡܢ ܒܢ̈ܝ ܐܝܣܪܝܠ.

ܝ: ܘܝܗܒܬ ܐܢܘܢ ܠܐܓܘܪܣܐ ܕܦܚܪܐ. ܐܝܟ ܕܦܩܕ ܠܝ ܡܪܝܐ.

ܝܐ: ܝܫܘܥ ܕܝܢ ܩܡ ܩܕܡ ܗܓܡܘܢܐ. ܘܫܐܠܗ ܗܓܡܘܢܐ ܘܐܡܪ ܠܗ: ܐܢܬ ܗܘ
ܡܠܟܐ ܕܝܗܘܕ̈ܝܐ. ܐܡܪ ܠܗ ܝܫܘܥ: ܐܢܬ ܐܡܪܬ.

12. And while the high priests and elders were making accusations, he gave no reply to the matter.

13. Then Pilate said to him: Do you not hear how much they testify against you?

14. But he gave him no answer, not even one word; and Pilate was exceedingly puzzled by this.

15. Now on every feast day it was the custom of the governor to set one prisoner free for the people, anyone whom they wanted.

16. And they[5] had in bonds an infamous prisoner known as Baraba.[6]

17. And when they gathered, Pilate said to them: Whom do you want me to set free for you, Baraba, or Jesus who is called the Messiah?

18. For Pilate knew that it was because of jealousy they had arrested him.

19. Now when the governor was sitting on his judgment seat,[7] his wife sent to him saying: Have nothing to do with that just man; because I have suffered a great deal today in my dreams because of him.

20. But the high priests and elders urged the crowds to free Baraba and to destroy Jesus.

21. And the governor answered and said to them: Which of these two do you want me to set free for you? Then they said: Baraba!

22. Pilate replied to them: Then what shall I do with Jesus who is called the Messiah?

23. They all said to him: Let him be crucified! Pilate said to them: But what is it that he has done that is so wrong? But they shouted even more and said: Let him be crucified!

24. Now when Pilate saw that he was getting nowhere but the rioting was increasing, he took water and washed his hands before the people[8] and said: I am not responsible for the death of this just man. You know that!

---

5 I.e., the Romans.
6 בר אבא, ܒܪ ܐܒܐ, Bar Awa. The name means *one who resembles, or looks like his father*.
7 The judgment seat was on an elevated stand or platform for public meetings for speakers, readers and for holding court.
8 See Deut 21:6. The washing of hands to show innocence.

ܝܒ: ܘܟܕ ܐܟܠܝܢ ܗܘܘ ܩܪ̈ܨܘܗܝ ܪ̈ܒܝ ܟܗܢ̈ܐ ܘܩܫܝ̈ܫܐ. ܡܕܡ ܦܬܓܡܐ ܗܘ ܠܐ ܦܢܝ

ܝܓ: ܗܝܕܝܢ ܐܡܪ ܠܗ ܦܝܠܛܘܣ: ܠܐ ܫܡܥ ܐܢܬ ܟܡܐ ܣܗܕܝܢ ܥܠܝܟ.

ܝܕ: ܘܠܐ ܦܢܝ ܠܗ ܦܬܓܡܐ ܐܦܠܐ ܒܚܕܐ ܡܠܐ. ܘܡܛܠ ܗܕܐ ܐܬܕܡܪ ܛܒ.

ܝܗ: ܒܟܠ ܥܐܕܐ ܕܝܢ ܡܥܕ ܗܘܐ ܗܓܡܘܢܐ ܕܢܫܪܐ ܐܣܝܪܐ ܚܕ ܠܥܡܐ. ܐܝܢܐ ܕܗܢܘܢ
ܨܒܝܢ ܗܘܘ.

ܝܘ: ܐܝܬ ܗܘܐ ܠܗܘܢ ܕܝܢ ܐܣܝܪܐ ܝܕܝܥܐ ܕܡܬܩܪܐ ܒܪ ܐܒܐ.

ܝܙ: ܘܟܕ ܟܢܝܫܝܢ. ܐܡܪ ܠܗܘܢ ܦܝܠܛܘܣ: ܠܡܢ ܨܒܝܢ ܐܢܬܘܢ ܕܐܫܪܐ ܠܟܘܢ.
ܠܒܪ ܐܒܐ. ܐܘ ܠܝܫܘܥ ܕܡܬܩܪܐ ܡܫܝܚܐ.

ܝܚ: ܝܕܥ ܗܘܐ ܓܝܪ ܦܝܠܛܘܣ ܕܡܢ ܚܣܡܐ ܐܫܠܡܘܗܝ.

ܝܛ: ܟܕ ܝܬܒ ܕܝܢ ܗܓܡܘܢܐ ܥܠ ܒܝܬ ܕܝܢܐ. ܫܕܪܬ ܠܗ ܐܢܬܬܗ ܘܐܡܪܐ ܠܗ:
ܠܐ ܠܟ ܘܠܗܘ ܙܕܝܩܐ. ܣܓܝ ܓܝܪ ܚܫܬ ܝܘܡܢܐ ܒܚܠܡܝ ܡܛܠܬܗ.

ܟ: ܪ̈ܒܝ ܟܗܢ̈ܐ ܕܝܢ ܘܩܫܝ̈ܫܐ ܐܦܝܣܘ ܠܟܢ̈ܫܐ ܕܢܫܐܠܘܢ ܠܒܪ ܐܒܐ. ܠܝܫܘܥ ܕܝܢ
ܕܢܘܒܕܘܢ.

ܟܐ: ܘܥܢܐ ܗܓܡܘܢܐ ܘܐܡܪ ܠܗܘܢ: ܠܡܢ ܨܒܝܢ ܐܢܬܘܢ ܕܐܫܪܐ ܠܟܘܢ ܡܢ
ܬܪܝܗܘܢ. ܗܢܘܢ ܕܝܢ ܐܡܪܘ: ܠܒܪ ܐܒܐ.

ܟܒ: ܐܡܪ ܠܗܘܢ ܦܝܠܛܘܣ: ܘܠܝܫܘܥ ܕܡܬܩܪܐ ܡܫܝܚܐ ܡܢܐ ܐܥܒܕ ܠܗ.

ܟܓ: ܐܡܪܝܢ ܟܠܗܘܢ: ܢܙܕܩܦ. ܐܡܪ ܠܗܘܢ ܦܝܠܛܘܣ: ܡܢܐ ܓܝܪ ܕܒܝܫ ܥܒܕ.
ܗܢܘܢ ܕܝܢ ܝܬܝܪܐܝܬ ܩܥܝܢ ܗܘܘ ܘܐܡܪܝܢ: ܢܙܕܩܦ.

ܟܕ: ܦܝܠܛܘܣ ܕܝܢ ܟܕ ܚܙܐ ܕܡܕܡ ܠܐ ܡܘܬܪ. ܐܠܐ ܝܬܝܪܐܝܬ ܫܓܘܫܝܐ ܗܘܐ. ܫܩܠ
ܡܝܐ. ܐܫܝܓ ܐܝܕܘܗܝ ܠܥܝܢ ܟܢܫܐ. ܘܐܡܪ: ܙܟܐ ܐܢܐ ܡܢ ܕܡܗ ܕܗܢܐ ܙܕܝܩܐ.
ܐܢܬܘܢ ܬܕܥܘܢ.

25. And all the people answered and said: We and our children bear the responsibility of his death!

26. Then he set Baraba free for them and had Jesus beaten with whips[9] and handed him over to be crucified.

JESUS MOCKED, CROWNED AND BEATEN

27. Then the soldiers of the governor took Jesus to the Praetorium[10] and the entire group gathered around him.

28. And they took off his clothes and put on him a scarlet[11] military robe.

29. And they wove a crown of thorns and placed it on his head and a reed in his right hand; and they knelt on their knees before him and they made fun of him, exclaiming: Peace, king of the Jews!

30. And they spat on his face and took the reed and hit him on his head.

31. And after they had ridiculed him, they took the robe off him and put his own clothes back on him and took him to be crucified.

32. And as they were going out, they found a man of Cyrene,[12] whose name was Simon, whom they compelled to carry his cross.

THE CRUCIFIXION

33. And they came to the place which is called Golgotha[13] which means the skull.

34. And they gave him vinegar mixed with gall to drink;[14] and he tasted it but would not drink it.

---

9 A Roman custom: Whipping a criminal before the death sentence was carried out.
10 The official residence of a Roman governor; however, in this case, used only during festivals. The actual, official residence was in Caesarea. "Praetorium" also refers to a building where cases were judged by a Roman magistrate. This Latin word has another meaning which does not apply to this scripture, signifying the tent of a Roman general; the headquarters of an encampment.
11 The color scarlet stands for loyalty and a willingness to give one's life.
12 Cyrene was a region of North Africa.
13 ܓܓܘܠܬܐ, נגולתא, Gaghoolta. The knoll was compared to a skull because the top of it was bald, that is, no grass, plants or trees.
14 This drink was given to criminals to lessen the pain. It acted as a narcotic and was offered to deaden awareness. See Ps. 69:21.

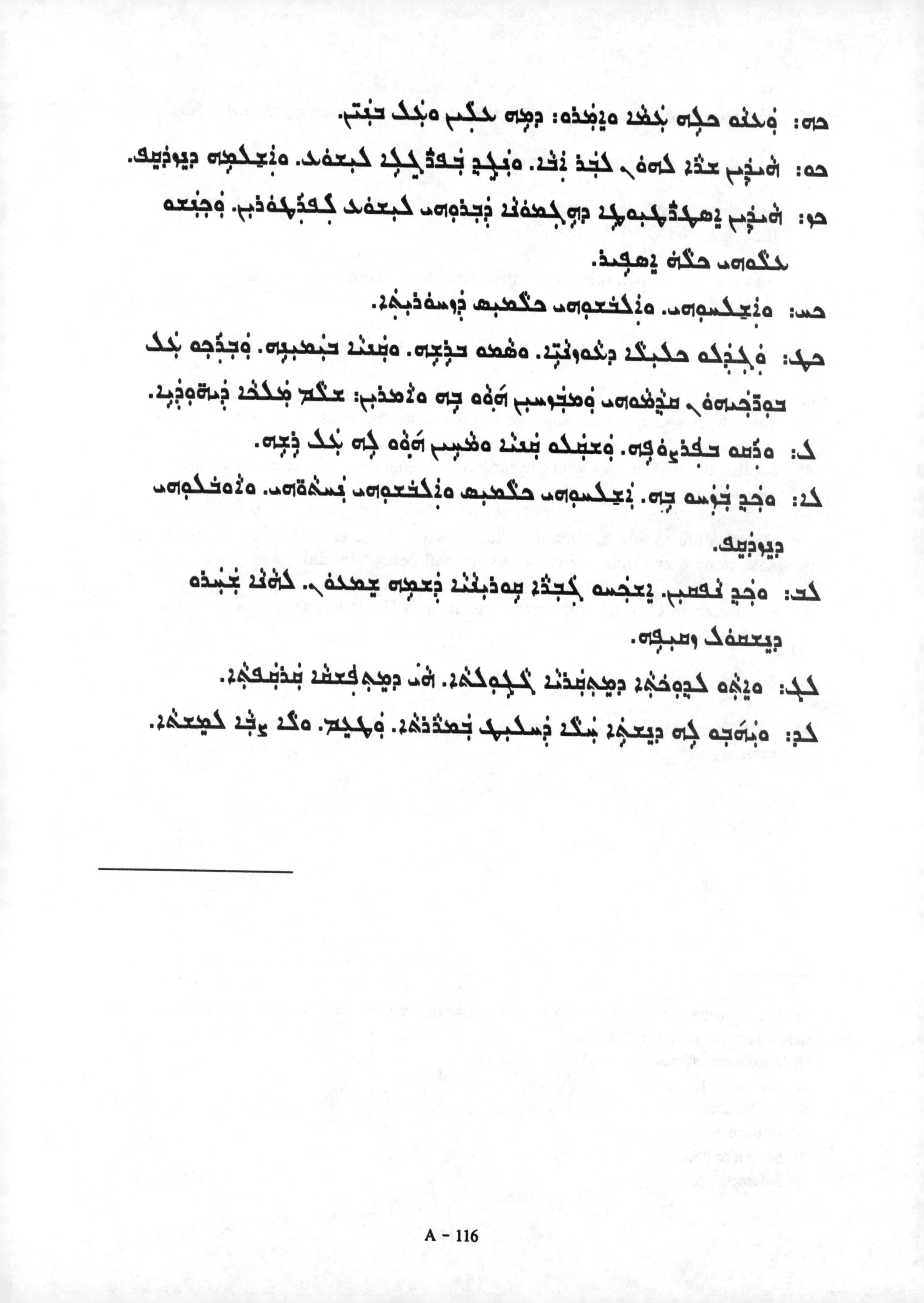

حه: .

35. And when they had crucified him, they divided his clothes by throwing lots.

36. And they were sitting there watching him.[15]

37. And they placed above his head in writing the reason for his death: THIS IS JESUS, KING OF THE JEWS![16]

38. And there were two thieves crucified with him, one on his right and one on his left.[17]

39. Then those who were passing by berated him shaking their heads,

40. Saying: Oh you who tears down the temple and builds it up in three days, save yourself, if you are God's son, come down from the cross.

41. So also the high priests with the scribes and elders and Pharisees were ridiculing him, saying:

42. He gave life to others, himself he cannot save. If he is the king of Israel let him now come down from the cross and we will believe in him.

43. He trusted in God; let Him rescue him if he is His favorite;[18] for he said that I am God's son.

44. So also the thieves who were crucified with him were berating him.

45. Now from the sixth hour[19] there was darkness[20] all over the land until the ninth hour.[21]

---

15 Usual custom for the soldiers to remain and keep a watchful eye lest the friends of the crucified should take the body before death.
16 A political offense.
17 See Isa. 53:12.
18 See Ps. 22:8.
19 12 noon.
20 See Amos 8:9.
21 3 o'clock.

ܠܗ: ܘܟܕ ܙܩܦܘܗܝ. ܦܠܓܘ ܢܚܬܘܗܝ ܒܦܣܐ.

ܠܘ: ܘܝܬܒܝܢ ܗܘܘ ܘܢܛܪܝܢ ܠܗ ܬܡܢ.

ܠܙ: ܘܣܡܘ ܠܥܠ ܡܢ ܪܝܫܗ ܥܠܬܐ ܕܡܘܬܗ ܒܟܬܒܐ: ܗܢܘ ܝܫܘܥ ܡܠܟܐ ܕܝܗܘܕܝܐ.

ܠܚ: ܘܐܙܕܩܦܘ ܥܡܗ ܬܪܝܢ ܠܣܛܝܐ. ܚܕ ܡܢ ܝܡܝܢܗ. ܘܚܕ ܡܢ ܣܡܠܗ.

ܠܛ: ܐܝܠܝܢ ܕܝܢ ܕܥܒܪܝܢ ܗܘܘ ܡܓܕܦܝܢ ܗܘܘ ܥܠܘܗܝ. ܘܡܢܝܕܝܢ ܪܫܝܗܘܢ.

ܡ: ܘܐܡܪܝܢ: ܣܬܪ ܗܝܟܠܐ ܘܒܢܐ ܠܗ ܠܬܠܬܐ ܝܘܡܝܢ. ܦܨܐ ܢܦܫܟ. ܐܢ ܒܪܗ ܐܢܬ
ܕܐܠܗܐ. ܘܚܘܬ ܡܢ ܙܩܝܦܐ.

ܡܐ: ܗܟܘܬ ܐܦ ܪܒܝ ܟܗܢܐ ܡܒܙܚܝܢ ܗܘܘ ܥܡ ܣܦܪܐ ܘܩܫܝܫܐ ܘܦܪܝܫܐ ܘܐܡܪܝܢ:

ܡܒ: ܠܐܚܪܢܐ ܐܚܝ. ܢܦܫܗ ܠܐ ܡܫܟܚ ܠܡܚܝܘ. ܐܢ ܡܠܟܗ ܗܘ ܕܐܝܣܪܝܠ. ܢܚܘܬ
ܗܫܐ ܡܢ ܙܩܝܦܐ. ܘܢܗܝܡܢ ܒܗ.

ܡܓ: ܬܟܝܠ ܥܠ ܐܠܗܐ. ܢܦܪܩܝܘܗܝ ܗܫܐ ܐܢ ܨܒܐ ܒܗ. ܐܡܪ ܓܝܪ ܕܒܪܗ ܐܢܐ
ܕܐܠܗܐ.

ܡܕ: ܗܟܘܬ ܐܦ ܠܣܛܝܐ ܗܢܘܢ. ܕܐܙܕܩܦܘ ܥܡܗ ܡܚܣܕܝܢ ܗܘܘ ܠܗ.

ܡܗ: ܡܢ ܫܬ ܫܥܝܢ ܕܝܢ ܗܘܐ ܚܫܘܟܐ ܥܠ ܟܠܗ ܐܪܥܐ ܥܕܡܐ ܠܫܥܝܢ ܬܫܥ.

AN ANCIENT COMMENTARY

See Mt 27:45–46. There is an ancient commentary written in Aramaic for Mt. 27:46 from the 9th Century C.E. The title of the scroll reads: *The Testimony (Evidence) from the book of Commentaries of Lord Ishodad of Merv, Bishop of Hadatha, Beth Naharain (Mesopotamia) 850 C.E.* The following is my translation of one paragraph: *The explanation of 'EL, 'EL, L'MANA SHAWAKTHANI: Not at all was he forsaken by the Godhead. Not even during suffering nor during death because the Godhead was always with him—in suffering and on the cross and in death and in the grave; and very God Himself raised him in power and in glory as in the psalm of David: "For You have not left my soul in SHEOL, and neither have You allowed Your holy one to see corruption."* (According to ancient Hebrew belief, SHEOL is a place of silence and inactivity for the departed soul.) This comment by Ishodad is reassuring testimony to the comforting power and presence of God and of Jesus' victory over sin, Sheol and death. See verse 46, footnote 23; also GOSPEL LIGHT, Lamsa, pp 151–155 and NEW TESTAMENT LIGHT, Lamsa pp. 80–85.

46. And about the ninth hour, Jesus called out in a loud voice and said: Oh God, oh God,[22] to what an end You have kept me![23]

47. Then some of those who were standing there when they heard it were saying: This man called upon Elijah.

48. And immediately one of them ran and took a sponge and filled it with vinegar and put it on a reed, and gave him to drink.

49. But the rest were saying: Leave him alone! Let us see if Elijah is coming to rescue him.

50. Then Jesus called out again in a loud voice and his spirit departed.

51. And instantly, the curtains of the temple door were torn in two, from the top to the bottom, and the earth quaked and the rocks split open.

52. And the tombs were opened and many bodies of the saints who were sleeping in death stood up,

53. And went out; and after his resurrection, they entered the holy city, and were seen by many.[24]

54. Then the centurion and those who were with him, guarding Jesus, when they saw the earthquake and the things that occurred, were exceedingly afraid and said: Truly, this man is God's son!

55. Now there were many women there who were looking on from a distance, those who followed Jesus from Galilee, and who had served him.

56. One of them was Mary of Magdala[25] and Mary the mother of Jacob and Joses, and the mother of Zebedee's sons.

---

22 ܐܠܗ, אל, El – God, in Aramaic means *Sustainer, Helper, Supporter, One who constantly aids*.
23 Another possible rendering is: "For what a purpose You have kept me!" It is taught that pious Jews before their death recite the 22nd Psalm. Many New Testament authorities believe that Jesus was reciting the 22nd Psalm on the cross. However, others have suggested that if Jesus did recite the 22nd Psalm, Matthew would have said, "So that it might be fulfilled which was spoken by, etc.". Jesus' usual way of referring to God was "my Father" or "our Father." On one or two occasions he did say "my God." See "An Ancient Commentary," p. A - 117.
24 Many scholars believe that verses 52 and 53 were a later addition. Other experts believe it was an embellishment.
25 A small town near Tiberias and mentioned frequently in rabbinic sources.

ܡܘ: ܘܠܐܦܝ ܬܫܥ ܫܥܝܢ ܩܥܐ ܝܫܘܥ ܒܩܠܐ ܪܡܐ. ܘܐܡܪ ܐܝܠ ܐܝܠ ܠܡܢܐ
ܫܒܩܬܢܝ.

ܡܙ: ܐܢܫܝܢ ܕܝܢ ܡܢ ܗܢܘܢ ܕܩܝܡܝܢ ܗܘܘ ܬܡܢ ܟܕ ܫܡܥܘ. ܐܡܪܝܢ ܗܘܘ: ܗܢܐ
ܠܐܠܝܐ ܩܪܐ.

ܡܚ: ܘܒܗ ܒܫܥܬܐ ܪܗܛ ܚܕ ܡܢܗܘܢ: ܘܢܣܒ ܐܣܦܘܓܐ. ܘܡܠܗ ܚܠܐ. ܘܐܪܡܝܗ
ܒܩܢܝܐ. ܘܡܫܩܐ ܗܘܐ ܠܗ.

ܡܛ: ܫܪܟܐ ܕܝܢ ܐܡܪܝܢ ܗܘܘ: ܫܒܘܩܘ ܢܚܙܐ. ܐܢ ܐܬܐ ܐܠܝܐ ܠܡܦܪܩܗ.

ܢ: ܗܘ ܕܝܢ ܝܫܘܥ ܬܘܒ ܩܥܐ ܒܩܠܐ ܪܡܐ ܘܐܫܠܡ ܪܘܚܗ.

ܢܐ: ܘܡܚܕܐ ܐܦܝ ܬܪܥܐ ܕܗܝܟܠܐ ܐܨܛܪܝ ܠܬܪܝܢ ܡܢ ܠܥܠ ܥܕܡܐ ܠܬܚܬ. ܘܐܪܥܐ
ܐܬܬܙܝܥܬ. ܘܟܐܦܐ ܐܨܛܪܝܘ.

ܢܒ: ܘܩܒܪܐ ܐܬܦܬܚܘ. ܘܦܓܪܐ ܣܓܝܐܐ ܕܩܕܝܫܐ ܕܫܟܝܒܝܢ ܗܘܘ ܩܡܘ.

ܢܓ: ܘܢܦܩܘ. ܘܒܬܪ ܩܝܡܬܗ. ܥܠܘ ܠܡܕܝܢܬܐ ܩܕܝܫܬܐ. ܘܐܬܚܙܝܘ ܠܣܓܝܐܐ.

ܢܕ: ܩܢܛܪܘܢܐ ܕܝܢ ܘܐܝܠܝܢ ܕܥܡܗ ܕܢܛܪܝܢ ܗܘܘ ܠܝܫܘܥ ܟܕ ܚܙܘ ܙܘܥܐ ܘܡܕܡ ܕܗܘܐ
ܕܚܠܘ ܛܒ ܘܐܡܪܘ: ܫܪܝܪܐܝܬ ܗܢܐ ܒܪܗ ܗܘܐ ܕܐܠܗܐ.

ܢܗ: ܐܝܬ ܗܘܝ ܕܝܢ ܬܡܢ ܐܦ ܢܫܐ ܣܓܝܐܬܐ. ܕܚܙܝܢ ܗܘܝ ܡܢ ܪܘܚܩܐ. ܗܠܝܢ ܕܐܬܝ
ܗܘܝ ܒܬܪܗ ܕܝܫܘܥ ܡܢ ܓܠܝܠܐ ܘܡܫܡܫܢ ܗܘܝ ܠܗ.

ܢܘ: ܚܕܐ ܡܢܗܝܢ ܡܪܝܡ ܡܓܕܠܝܬܐ. ܘܡܪܝܡ ܐܡܗ ܕܝܥܩܘܒ ܘܕܝܘܣܐ. ܘܐܡܗܘܢ
ܕܒܢܝ ܙܒܕܝ.

THE ENTOMBMENT

57. Then when it was evening, there came a rich man from Ramtha[26] whose name was Joseph, who also was a disciple of Jesus.

58. This man approached Pilate and had asked for the body of Jesus. And Pilate ordered that the body be given to him.

59. And Joseph took the body and wrapped it in a shroud of fine linen;

60. And he placed it in his new tomb which was hewn in a rock, and they rolled a large stone and put it against the door of the tomb and went away.

61. Now Mary of Magdala and the other Mary were there and were sitting opposite the tomb.

62. Then the next day, which is after Friday, the high priests and the Pharisees gathered before Pilate,

63. Saying to him: Our lord, we remember that this deceiver used to say while he was alive that after three days I will arise.

64. Now then, command that the tomb be guarded until the third day, maybe his disciples will come and steal him at night and tell the people that he has risen from the dead; and the last deception shall be worse than the first.

65. Pilate said to them: You have guards, go and guard it as best you know.

66. Then they went and kept a watch at the tomb with the guards, and they sealed that very stone.

---

26 Formerly Ramathaim Zophim, the city of Samuel (1 Sam. 1:1), not far from Jerusalem.

نو: ܀

CHAPTER 28

THE RESURRECTION OF JESUS

1. Now late Saturday night, when the first day of the week began to dawn, Mary of Magdala and the other Mary[1] came to see the tomb.

2. And behold a tremendous earthquake occurred because a messenger of the LORD came down from the sky and went and rolled away the stone from the door and sat upon it.

3. Now his appearance was like lightning; and his clothes were white like snow.

4. And because of the fear of him those who were guarding were trembling and had fainted.

5. Then the messenger answered and said to the women: Do not be afraid because I know that you are looking for Jesus who was crucified.

6. He is not here because he has risen,[2] even as he said, Come, see the place where our lord was laid.

7. Then go quickly, tell his disciples that he has risen from the dead. Now behold, he has gone on ahead of you in Galilee, there you shall see him; Behold, I have told you.

8. So they went quickly from the tomb with fear and great joy, running to tell his disciples.

9. And behold, Jesus met them and said to them: Peace to you! Then they approached and grasped his feet and bowed before him.[3]

---

1 According to Mt. 27:56; Mk. 16:1; Lk. 24:10, this Mary was the mother of Jacob and Joses.

2 ܠܗ ܩܡ, Kam Leh, *He has risen*. This word "Kam" has many meanings in Aramaic, *to stand up, to succeed, to rise*. Metaphorically, *to come through, to awaken*. Thus it may be translated, "He has come through," or "He has awakened."

3 Eastern custom: The greeting of grasping the feet and the bowing showed a very deep affection and respect. Holy men, rulers and dignitaries were greeted by bowing down almost to the ground. When an Easterner takes hold of the feet of a nobleman or holy man, the supplicant reveals his/her humility and submission and pays the highest respect to the one so greeted.

ܦܨܚܠܐܘܢ: ܟܚ.

ܐ: ܒܪܡܫܐ ܕܝܢ ܒܫܒܬܐ ܕܢܓܗ ܚܕ ܒܫܒܐ ܐܬܬ ܡܪܝܡ ܡܓܕܠܝܬܐ ܘܡܪܝܡ ܐܚܪܬܐ
ܕܢܚܙܝܢ ܩܒܪܐ.

ܒ: ܘܗܐ ܙܘܥܐ ܪܒܐ ܗܘܐ. ܡܠܐܟܐ ܓܝܪ ܕܡܪܝܐ ܢܚܬ ܡܢ ܫܡܝܐ. ܘܩܪܒ ܥܓܠ
ܟܐܦܐ ܡܢ ܬܪܥܐ. ܘܝܬܒ ܗܘܐ ܠܥܠܝܗ.

ܓ: ܐܝܬܘܗܝ ܗܘܐ ܕܝܢ ܚܙܘܗ ܐܝܟ ܒܪܩܐ. ܘܠܒܘܫܗ ܚܘܪ ܗܘܐ ܐܝܟ ܬܠܓܐ.

ܕ: ܘܡܢ ܕܚܠܬܗ ܐܫܬܓܫܘ ܐܝܠܝܢ ܕܢܛܪܝܢ ܗܘܘ. ܘܗܘܘ ܐܝܟ ܡܝܬܐ

ܗ: ܥܢܐ ܕܝܢ ܡܠܐܟܐ ܘܐܡܪ ܠܢܫܐ: ܐܢܬܝܢ ܠܐ ܬܕܚܠܝܢ ܝܕܥ ܐܢܐ ܓܝܪ ܕܠܝܫܘܥ
ܕܐܙܕܩܦ ܒܥܝܢ ܐܢܬܝܢ.

ܘ: ܠܐ ܗܘܐ ܗܪܟܐ. ܩܡ ܠܗ ܐܝܟ ܕܐܡܪ: ܬܘ. ܚܙܝܘ ܕܘܟܬܐ ܕܣܝܡ ܗܘܐ ܒܗ
ܡܪܢ.

ܙ: ܘܙܠܝܢ ܒܥܓܠ. ܐܡܪܝܢ ܠܬܠܡܝܕܘܗܝ ܕܩܡ ܡܢ ܒܝܬ ܡܝܬܐ. ܘܗܐ ܩܕܡ ܠܟܘܢ
ܠܓܠܝܠܐ ܬܡܢ ܬܚܙܘܢܝܗܝ. ܗܐ ܐܡܪܬ ܠܟܘܢ.

ܚ: ܘܐܙܠܝܢ ܒܥܓܠ ܡܢ ܩܒܪܐ ܒܕܚܠܬܐ ܘܒܚܕܘܬܐ ܪܒܬܐ. ܘܪܗܛܝ ܕܢܐܡܪܢ
ܠܬܠܡܝܕܘܗܝ.

ܛ: ܘܗܐ ܝܫܘܥ ܦܓܥ ܒܗܝܢ. ܘܐܡܪ ܠܗܝܢ: ܫܠܡ ܠܟܝܢ. ܗܢܝܢ ܕܝܢ ܩܪܒ ܐܚܕ
ܪܓܠܘܗܝ. ܘܣܓܕܝ ܠܗ.

10. Then Jesus said to them: Do not be afraid but you go and tell my brothers that they should go to Galilee and there they shall see me.[4]

11. Now while they were going, some of the guards went into the city and told the high priests everything that had happened.

12. So they gathered with the elders and took counsel; and they gave money, not a little amount, to the guards,

13. Saying to them: You tell that his disciples came and stole him at night while we were sleeping.

14. And if this might be reported to the governor, we will appeal to him and declare you are without fault.

15. Then when they took the money, they did as they were instructed, and this word went out among the Jews to this very day.

JESUS IN GALILEE AND THE GREAT COMMISSION

16. Now his eleven disciples went to Galilee to a mountain, where Jesus had promised to meet them.

17. And when they saw him they bowed to him; but some of them were doubting.[5]

18. Then Jesus approached, speaking to them and said to them: All authority has been granted to me in heaven and on earth. Even as my Father has sent me, I am also sending you.

19. Now, go, disciple all nations, and baptize them in the name of[6] the Father and the son, and the holy Spirit.[7]

20. And teach them to keep[8] everything which I have commanded you. And behold, I am always with you even to the end of the world. ❖ ❖ ❖

---

4 Matthew states that the Apostles saw the apparition of Jesus in Galilee only (See Mt. 28:16–20), but he never mentions any appearance in Jerusalem (See Lk. 24:13–53, Jn. 20:19–29) or by the Lake of Galilee (See Jn. 21). Presumably, the four messages (documents) of Matthew, Mark, Luke and John complement each other, collectively presenting the teachings and deeds of Jesus as accurately as possible.

5 I.e., "uncertain."

6 For the purpose, to the end.

7 The trinitarian formula was a Church precept and was probably added to Matthew's text in the beginning of the second century.

8 ܢܛܪ, נטר, Ntar, *to observe, keep, guard.*

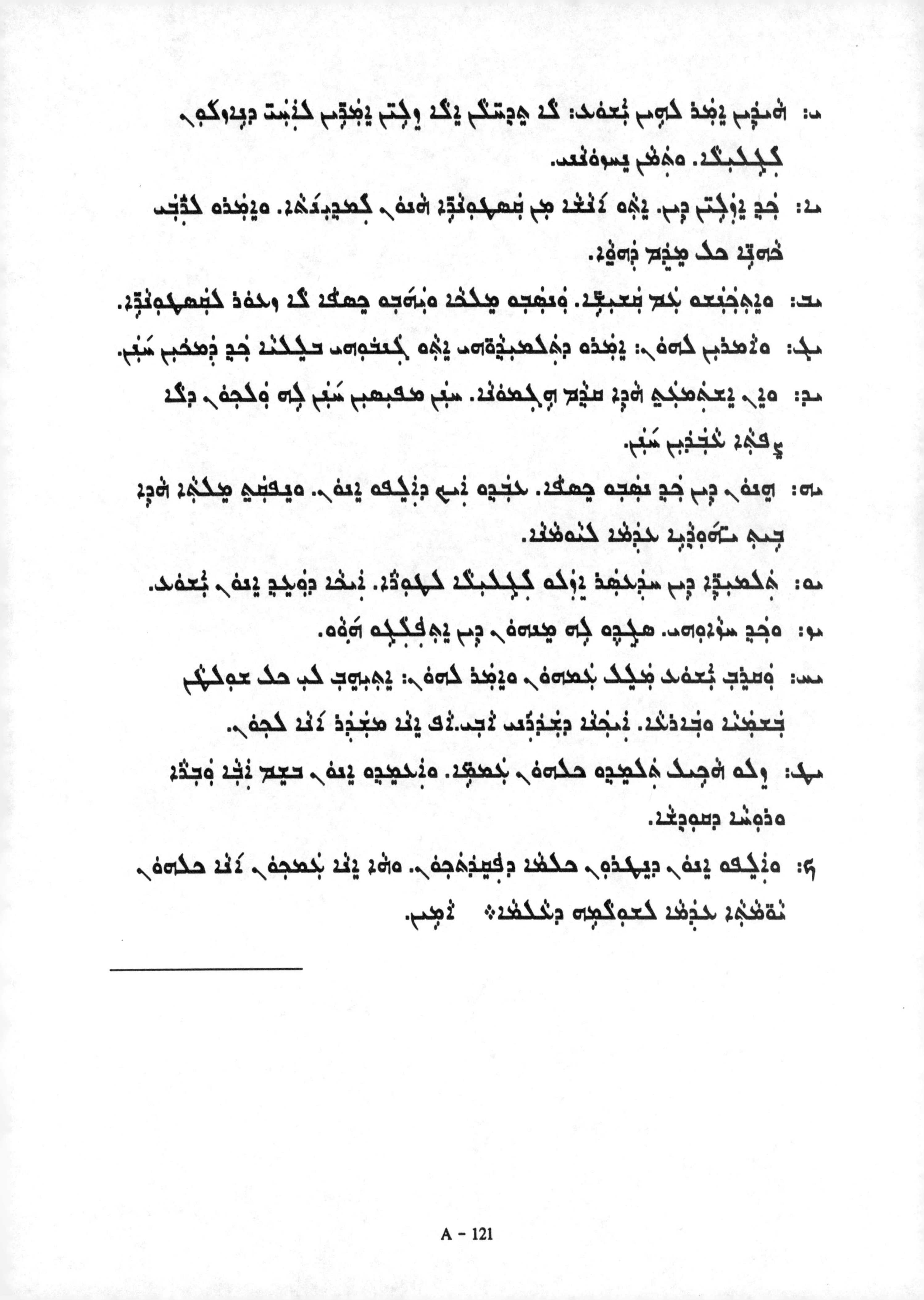

ܝ: ܗܝܕܝܢ ܐܡܪ ܠܗܝܢ ܝܫܘܥ: ܠܐ ܬܕܚܠܝܢ ܐܠܐ ܙܠܝܢ ܐܡܪܝܢ ܠܐܚܝ ܕܢܐܙܠܘܢ ܠܓܠܝܠܐ. ܘܬܡܢ ܢܚܙܘܢܢܝ.

ܝܐ: ܟܕ ܐܙܠܝܢ ܕܝܢ. ܗܐ ܐܢܫܐ ܡܢ ܩܣܛܘܢܪܐ ܐܬܘ ܠܡܕܝܢܬܐ. ܘܐܡܪܘ ܠܪ̈ܒܝ ܟܗ̈ܢܐ ܟܠ ܡܕܡ ܕܗܘܐ.

ܝܒ: ܘܐܬܟܢܫܘ ܥܡ ܩܫܝ̈ܫܐ. ܘܢܣܒܘ ܡܠܟܐ ܘܝܗܒܘ ܟܣܦܐ ܠܐ ܙܥܘܪ ܠܩܣܛܘܢܪܐ.

ܝܓ: ܘܐܡܪܝܢ ܠܗܘܢ: ܐܡܪܘ ܕܬܠܡܝܕܘܗܝ ܐܬܘ ܓܢܒܘܗܝ ܒܠܠܝܐ ܟܕ ܕܡܟܝܢ ܚܢܢ.

ܝܕ: ܘܐܢ ܡܫܬܡܥܐ ܗܕܐ ܩܕܡ ܗܓܡܘܢܐ. ܚܢܢ ܡܦܝܣܝܢܢ ܠܗ ܘܠܟܘܢ ܕܠܐ ܨܦܬܐ ܥܒܕܝܢ ܚܢܢ.

ܝܗ: ܗܢܘܢ ܕܝܢ ܟܕ ܢܣܒܘ ܟܣܦܐ. ܥܒܕܘ ܐܝܟ ܕܐܠܦܘ ܐܢܘܢ. ܘܢܦܩܬ ܡܠܬܐ ܗܕܐ ܒܝܢ ܝܗܘܕܝܐ ܥܕܡܐ ܠܝܘܡܢܐ.

ܝܘ: ܬܠܡܝܕܐ ܕܝܢ ܚܕܥܣܪ ܐܙܠܘ ܠܓܠܝܠܐ ܠܛܘܪܐ. ܐܝܟܐ ܕܘܥܕ ܗܘܐ ܠܗܘܢ ܝܫܘܥ.

ܝܙ: ܘܟܕ ܚܙܐܘܗܝ. ܣܓܕܘ ܠܗ. ܡܢܗܘܢ ܕܝܢ ܐܬܦܠܓܘ ܗܘܘ.

ܝܚ: ܘܩܪܒ ܝܫܘܥ ܡܠܠ ܥܡܗܘܢ ܘܐܡܪ ܠܗܘܢ: ܐܬܝܗܒ ܠܝ ܟܠ ܫܘܠܛܢ ܒܫܡܝܐ ܘܒܐܪܥܐ. ܐܝܟܢܐ ܕܫܕܪܢܝ ܐܒܝ ܐܦ ܐܢܐ ܡܫܕܪ ܐܢܐ ܠܟܘܢ.

ܝܛ: ܙܠܘ ܗܟܝܠ ܬܠܡܕܘ ܟܠܗܘܢ ܥܡ̈ܡܐ. ܘܥܡܕܘ ܐܢܘܢ ܒܫܡ ܐܒܐ ܘܒܪܐ ܘܪܘܚܐ ܕܩܘܕܫܐ.

ܟ: ܘܐܠܦܘ ܐܢܘܢ ܕܢܛܪܘܢ ܟܠ ܡܐ ܕܦܩܕܬܟܘܢ. ܘܗܐ ܐܢܐ ܥܡܟܘܢ ܐܢܐ ܟܠܗܘܢ ܝܘ̈ܡܬܐ ܥܕܡܐ ܠܫܘܠܡܗ ܕܥܠܡܐ܀ ܐܡܝܢ.

APPENDIX 1

PREFACE FROM THE ARAMAIC DICTIONARY BY MAR TOUMA ODDO

Abridged Translation from Syriac into English by Louis Khodabakhsh

Those who invented the art of writing contributed a remarkable service to mankind worthy of high praise. Yet unfortunately, the names of the persons who brought this precious art to light and made it known to the world remain concealed and almost unheard of.

The time of this discovery is not known. However, it is truly believed what nation initiated writing and what people taught it first to the succeeding generations. We frankly state that the Assyrians deserve the pride of priority over all the known people of old times in the invention of the art of writing and passing it on to other nations. It is obvious that all the nations of western and northern Europe received the art of writing from the well-known Romans. It is also known that the Romans learned their writing, science, art and knowledge from the Greeks. The Greeks in turn, who surpassed all others in wisdom, science, art and virtue took the privilege of writing from the Assyrians.

It is stated in the Greek books around 1500-1590 B.C. that a group of the inhabitants of Phoenicia, located on the western centre of Assyria, took the Assyrian characters to Greece. I mention Cadma, called by Greeks Cadmus, who spread the writings of Assyrians in Greece. The Greeks called these characters "Assyrian letters." Contrary to what the Arabs did by taking the Assyrian letters and changing their names, order and system, the Greeks retained the letters and their names in order, making them better than the Assyrians themselves. At the end of the names they added a final "alpha" (a), as the Assyrian did by adding an alep at the end of their names (nouns and adjectives); the Greeks also named their letters alpha, beta, gamma, delta, etc.

Although the Greeks formed their letters similar to those used in Assyria at that time, yet they started to write them from left to right, unlike the Assyrians who wrote from right to left.

The Phoenicians did not have the art of writing; they learned it from the Assyrians and Babylonians. This is so obvious that it needs no proof. History relates that the Phoenicians appeared at a time when the Assyrians and the Babylonians were dominant and possessed mighty kingdoms. Being the most cultivated, they spread first the principles and bases of civilization in the world. This is so, as far as the Western nations were concerned.

The Eastern nations also, without any shadow of a doubt, learned their own writing from the Assyrians. The Hebrews enumerated their alphabets after the order of the Assyrian letters. They used also Abgad, hawaz, hatay etc., as we notice that in the Book of Psalms where the beginning of the verses correspond to the same order of the Assyrian alphabet. The two nations (Assyria and Israel) used the same order of letters. But since the Jews were slaves for many centuries and had no country or educational power except in the time of King David, it is sure that they did not discover the letters but learned them from the Assyrians. It is not reasonable to say that the Jews had at any time their own letters of writing, and then left them and took the Assyrian alphabets. The same is true of the Persians; they too used the Assyrian letters, as the records of antiquity prove.

The Armenians until the 6th century A.D. had no particular letters and were using

Assyrian characters until the time of Mesrop, a well-known Armenian who arranged his letters and called them "Mesrop letters." These characters have been in use until our day.

The Arabs, since 1500 years ago more or less, took their writing from the Arameans. Gradually the style found variations in which you see a diversity of dialects with their origin in the Aramaic language. The shape of the first characters that Arameans used in the beginning are not exactly known. The noticeable change in most of the letters has been done through the course of time and in a variety of places, but we know from the different writings that there is a similarity in them. The manner of the Aramaic writing is the most ancient that has come to us. The Babylonians used it at the time of Cyrus, King of Persia. It is considered the most ancient Aramaic style of writing.

The Jews learned the Assyrian letters during their captivity in Babylon. After returning to their homeland, they continued to use them until today. They called them "Assyrian letters." The Europeans call them "square characters" because most of them are square-shaped and separated from each other similar to the Greek letters mentioned above. These letters are considered holy by the Jews.

From the Babylonian characters emerged, much later, the Estrangela writing which prevailed at the time of the appearance of Christ on earth. This form of writing is the first Assyrian writing known with good qualities and which replaced the Babylonian tongue completely and is still in use today. Yet this system too has been changed into another one with less difficulties and faster writing. This latter we call "common writing," which was known in the first century of the Christian era.

The Estrangela script was chosen for the purpose of writing the New Testament books and other holy scriptures. Probably, this is the reason for calling it "Estrangela," "stra," for "srat," meaning "writing," and "evangeleon" meaning "gospel." However, some think that the word stems from the Greek, meaning "square-shaped;" and still others think that it is related to the name of the person who tried to keep alive such writing and make it known to people, because he thought that the Western Assyrians were inclined to forget it, according to Bar Hebraeus' Chronicles. Moreover, Youhannan (Jean) Bishop of Qartmin at the end of the 10th century A.D. laboured extensively to keep alive the Estrangela script at Toor Awdin close to Merda town. His activities lasted more than a century. So also Emmanuel, the nephew of the said Bishop, wrote more than seventy books with Estrangela letters from the Holy Scriptures that are highly esteemed by Jacobites.

However, through the course of time, this form also split into two streams: the one called "Assyrian," or "East Syriac (Aramaic)," or "Nestorian," used by the Nestorian groups, and the other known as "Western Syriac," or "Jacobite" used in the Maronite and Assyrian books. Through the Maronite scholars, the Western Syriac has been used for printing Assyrian books in Europe during the last three centuries. At the moment almost all Europe employs the Western Syriac characters. The script corresponds to the 16th, 17th and 18th centuries' writing.

The Eastern Syriac (Aramaic) too has been used in the presses of great centres of the world such as New York, London, Rome and Leipzig. Father Bedjan Paul Lazarist, native of Salmas (Salamas, Khosrawa), spread in the East and West the Eastern Syriac through his printed books that are well known. Such a person ought to be thanked and honoured for a job well done. Also, the Dominican Fathers in Mosul, the American Presbyterian Mission in Urmia and the Church of England in Great Britain have printed books with Eastern Syriac characters.

In addition to these two types of writing, there is a third one which stems from the first common writing mentioned above and is as old as Eastern and Western Syriac. It is the writing of the Assyrians who follow the liturgy of Constantinople since the 8th century A.D. and usually known as Greek or Imperial Rome (Melkite). There is a theological reason for labeling it thus: all the Greeks and others who followed Emperor Marcian and the royal throne of Rome and adopted the doctrine of monophysitism were excommunicated at the Council of Chalcedon. These groups adopted this third kind of writing, which is rarely used today.

The time of the origin of these three types of writings cannot be precisely detected. They do not have the same beginning. However, it is evident from the books transmitted to us from the past centuries that the writing employed by the Western Assyrians goes back to the time before the era of Bar Hebraeus who lived in the 13th century. We cannot say that the writing practiced by the East Assyrians or Nestorians is younger than the Western Assyrian writing. This writing was propagated by the Alqosh writers of the last centuries. They edited many books, especially ecclesiastical ones. Two families who spread the art of East Syriac writing must be mentioned: The family of Father Israel, also known as Bet Rabba, and the family of Father Homo.

In the beginning, the Aramaic writing had no vowels and vocalization points; the reader had to supply the vowels and pronounce the consonants to form the meaning of the word as is done in Arabic, Persian and even in Assyrian because they did not want to bother themselves by putting the necessary vowel-points in their writing.

When the Greeks learned the writing from the Arameans, they faced difficulties in reading it. Hence, they chose six of the Arameans letters and used them as vowels: alap, he, waw, het, yod and a, corresponding to six Greek letters: A, N, E, I, O, Y. From thence, the usage of vowels began in all the European writings. All the European letters became divided into two categories: vowels and consonants.

When the Arabs spread the Moslem religion and culture in the world in the 8th century, they too, adopted vowels for their own writing. The Hebrews did the same thing. In the 9th century they added on the Babylonian writing, vowel-points which they had learned from the Assyrians and are still in use. The vowels are:

qamus	=	sqapa
patah	=	ptaha
seri	=	zlama
sigol	=	zlama qishya
hirig gadol	=	long khawasa
holem	=	rwaha
shoorik	=	rwasa
hirik qaton	=	regular zlama
qamus hatop	=	rwaha
kebos	=	rwasa

The Arameans, who for centuries were writing without vowels, started using some big points on or under the letters in order to avoid confusion in similar words used by the Western Assyrians as well as by the Eastern Assyrians. These big points can be seen in the old books. However, the Eastern Assyrians abandoned them after discovering the small vowel points. It is not known at what time the usage of these bigger points started. We only know that in the fourth century they were used. Yakoo Urhaya (Jacob the Edessene) in the seventh century wrote about them.

However, these big points were not adequate when reading, writing and learning increased among people. Therefore, the Assyrian writers started looking for some more definite signs to distinguish the syllables in the language. Bar Hebraeus mentions that Yakoo Urhaya (Jacob the Edessene, or Jacob of Edessa) was the first to initiate this process. He started putting some signs--small points on or under, or sometimes on and under a letter marking the vocalization of a consonant. This system gradually developed, became more intelligible and is used even today among the Eastern Assyrian groups.

Only Western Assyrians have used the Greek vowel-signs. It is not clearly known which of these two kinds of vowels, small points or Greek signs was first used; however, it is believed that the Greek letters were in use around the 8th century by the Jacobites monks of Dor d'toor Audin, called the Monastery of the Skull. But we are sure that before the 8th century the Eastern and Western Assyrians, the Hebrews, the Arabs and the rest of the Semitic peoples were not using any vowel-signs in their writings. Still further, we are sure that Assyrian was the language of a strong and important people. Eastern countries, such as Syria, Mesopotamia, Babylon, Sin'ar and Assyria, and the countries mentioned in the Old Testament, called by the Jews "Aram," were speaking and writing Aramaic, because Aram, son of Shem and his descendants had dominated these lands. That is the reason why the Assyrian language in the Old Testament is called Aramaic. The Assyrians themselves called their language Aramaic also.

The word "Syriac" or "Assyrian" can be seen only in the Greek and the Roman writings before Christ. When the Christian religion started in Beth Aram, Syria was a powerful nation. Antioch was its capitol, a flourishing town where the disciples were called "Christians" for the first time (Acts 11:26). Therefore, all those who turned toward the Christian faith were called "Syrians" or "Assyrians." When the Aramean nation as a whole, before any other nation, followed Christ and embraced His teaching, gradually the name "Aramean" disappeared. The whole nation with its tribes and off-shoots were called Assyrians or Syrians, and the language came to be known as "Syriac," or "Assyrian" until today.*

The Assyrian language was spoken by the descendants of Shem who are: Hebrews, Assyrians, Arabs, Cushites (Ethiopians) and others. The most important is the Arabic language. Knowing this language is valuable to anyone who wants to learn adequately other Semitic languages.

Our Aramean language (i.e. Assyrian) has undergone some changes by the passage of time just as it happens to any human language. The Assyrian language has been divided into several dialects according to the locations where the Assyrians live. However, besides the changes of different intervals, the first Aramean language with the Mesopotamian letters which was used at the time of Christ is still is use. Since that time, the same language, with

---

*The word "Syria" and "Syrian" defined by famous scholars such as Renan the Frenchman, is a matter of two letters, Atoor and (Atooraya) Atoorian. The Greeks made the mistake of changing "T" to "S" for their convenience, and said "Assyria" and "Assyrian," corresponding to the kingdom of "Atooria" and "Atoorian." The Assyrians were ruling Mesopotamia, the present Syrian countries and even spread to Egypt and Cush (Ethiopia). This is the reason for different nominations of "Atoorian," or "Asoorian."

some few variations has been employed by the Assyrians. And all the books existing now in the hands of the Assyrians were absolutely written in this language. Yet unhappily, because of the continual trouble and confusion in the Assyrian nation, it could not keep all the books or scrolls written before the time of Christ. On the contrary, other people such as Greeks, Jews, etc., possess the writings of our fathers. Thus being deprived of the heritage of our former language, our nation does not know the history of its ancestors, kings, battles, customs and all that concerns that nation. If an Assyrian wants to know something about himself, he is forced to search minutely into the writings of foreigners, especially of the Jews and Greeks. Without their writings we know nothing about the situation of the ancient Arameans and their dwellings until the coming of Christ.

The Assyrian language known today falls into two categories: the Eastern and the Western. The Eastern dialect is called "Chaldean," the Western, the "common Syriac." The Eastern dialect was indeed the dialect of Assyria and Babylon and the eastern countries of Mesopotamia. Today, this dialect is used by the Eastern Assyrians (although not fluently) in their liturgy and writings.

The Western dialect is used ecclesiastically by the Assyrian Catholics, Jacobites and Maronites. A part of Jacobites today living close to the Merda town and Zebedeen Island speak it colloquially. This dialect is also called "Edessean" (Urhaya), because the Edessa town at that time was flourishing in Aramaic language; whereas the Eastern is called "Sowaya," academic, because in Nesebis (Nsebin) there was a university for the Eastern Assyrians where the Nestorians got their education. That University produced doctors and illustrious masters who wrote Eastern dialect more beautifully than any other.

The difference between these two dialects was not radical. The pronunciation of some vowel-signs and letters already mentioned was the only difference. There was no major change in the works of the scholars; some little variations were normally seen at different places.

I want to make it clear that the Eastern dialect is not properly called Chaldean. It is very close to the real Aramaic language and has precedence over the Western. The Eastern and the Western dialects existed together since the 8th century. The major difference started when the vowel-signs were borrowed from the Greek letters. Mar Gregoreus Bar Hebraeus (Bar Ewraya), the great master, at this point found himself a failure when he abandoned the Eastern dialect and chose the Western due to the circumstances and location. It is easy to understand the fact that those who introduced the Assyrian language into the European schools made the mistake by adopting the Western Syriac and spreading it in these schools. They should have chosen the Eastern Assyrian dialect for its value and ingenuity.

The Assyrian language has excellent characteristics which distinguish it from other languages. *First,* as it has been pointed out, it is the language of the inspired scripture. Parts of the book of Daniel, parts of the book of Ezra and of Nehemiah of the Old Testament were written in the Assyrian language. The Gospel of Matthew claimed as being written first in the Assyrian language. *Second,* Christ and the Virgin Mary and His Apostles spoke this language. It should be noted that the Jews in the time of Christ spoke the Assyrian language and not Hebrew, the language of their fathers. They had learned this language in Exile in Babylon and continued to use it after their return to their homeland. Jewish scholars called their language Aramaic, Suryaya (Syriac) and sometimes Assyrian. Yet this language today is called Hebrew. It has been so called because the Jews were speaking it, not because it was the real Hebrew language. The Europeans called it Chaldean. They relate it to Chaldeans known then by the land of Babylon. *A third* characteristic that distinguishes this language from others is that it was the language of liturgy honoured by the Christian Church. It became next to Greek in administration of Church liturgy. The first congregation that the Apostles built, after our Lord's ascension, was in Jerusalem. The Jerusalemites at that time spoke Assyrian, a little different from the present Assyrian. At that time the Assyrian language was the liturgical language of the greater part of the Christians of the East. *Fourth,* Assyrian was the third language used by the doctors of the Church after Greek and Latin. All the scribes of the Church were using either Greek, Latin or Assyrian. That is why this language is more approved of than its cognates, and this is the reason why the scholars respected it. At the present time many European schools teach it next to Hebrew and Greek. If these Western schools were not teaching it, it would have fallen into oblivion.

We mentioned earlier that the Assyrian language was, at one time, the language of several strong nations in the East. But when the Mohammedan power emerged, this language started to decline due to the decreasing power of the Assyrian nation which was the result of persecutions and similar difficulties plus the intrusion of other languages such as Arabic, Turkish, Persian, and Kurdish. Today the surviving dialect is spoken only by a few in the region of Mesopotamia. In the fourth, fifth and sixth centuries A.D. this language reached its zenith, especially at the two universities of Edessa (Urhai) and Nesibis (Nesiwin).

At that time and at those two centers of education, illustrious writers acquired skill in all branches of science and knowledge. After that period, two skilled writers emerged, Gregorius Bar Habraeus (Bar Ewraya), a productive scholar in the 13th century from among the Western Assyrians, and Mar Audishoo of Soba in the 14th century from among the Eastern Assyrians. Since their time, no one has truly been an expert in the Assyrian language. Perhaps we can say that this language was almost buried with these two prominent scholars.

We hope that in the years to come this language will be resurrected and cleansed from its swathe. In Mosul we hear that our Assyrian people are teaching it. Probably, the books and writings that come into the hands of people through the presses of the East and West may call for its resurrection. We can say for sure, that if the Assyrian language were not the liturgical language, it would have been forgotten in the East a long time ago.

Submitted to the Metropolitan Cell in Urmia, Persia on the first day of the blessed year, 1886 by Mar Touma Oddo.

Assyrian (Aramaic) Dictionary reprinted by Edwards Brothers Inc., Ann Arbor, Michigan, 1978.

Preface reprinted with special permission granted by Mr. Louis Coda aka Mr. Louis Khodabakhsh for THE MESSAGE OF MATTHEW.

APPENDIX 2

THE ARAMAIC LETTERS, VOWELS AND THEIR ENGLISH EQUIVALENTS

The Alphabet: There are 22 letters in the Aramaic alphabet. Please note that the Aramaic letters are read from the right to the left.

ARAMAIC	ENGLISH
ܐ	A*
ܒ - ܒ̄	B - W
ܓ - ܓ̄	G - GH
ܕ - ܕ̄	D - DH
ܗ	H
ܘ	W
ܙ	Z
ܚ	Ḥ
ܛ	Ṭ
ܝ	Y
ܟ - ܟ̄	K - KH
ܟ݂	final K
ܠ	L
ܡ	M
ܡ	final M
ܢ	N
ܢ	final N
ܣ	S
ܥ	A̤*
ܦ - ܦ̄	P - W
ܨ	Ṣ
ܩ	Q
ܪ	R
ܫ	SH
ܬ - ܬ̄	T - TH

The letters ܐ and ܥ - A* are silent unless a vowel appears above or beneath them. When a vowel is used on these letters then they take the sound of that particular vowel.

The Vowel Points: There are seven vowel points in Aramaic. They are named as follows: Zqapa, Pthaḥa, Zlama Psheeqa, Zlama Qashya, Rwaḥa, Rwaṣa and Ḥwaṣa.

The first vowel ܆ Zqapa. It is usually pronounced *AH* as in F**a**ther. It always appears as two points over a letter as in ܐ̈ - ah, ܒ̈ - bah, ܓ̈ - gah, etc.

129

The second vowel ◌ֽ Pthaḥa. It is usually pronounced as a short *A* as in verb<u>a</u>l, ment<u>a</u>l, loc<u>a</u>l or rent<u>a</u>l. It always appears with one point above and below a letter as in ܐ - Ah, ܒ - bah, ܓ - gah, etc. (Remember the sound in short and almost closed.)

The third vowel ◌ Zlama Psheeqa. It is pronounced as a short *I* as in s<u>i</u>t and h<u>i</u>t. It always appears as two points beneath a letter as in ܐ - i, ܒ - bi, ܓ - gi, etc.

The fourth vowel ◌ Zlama Qashya. It is pronounced *EH* as in b<u>ea</u>r, p<u>ea</u>r. It is like <u>ey</u> in English th<u>ey</u> without the final I or Y glide. It always appears as two slanted points beneath the letter as in ܐ - eh, ܒ - beh, ܓ - geh, etc.

The fifth vowel ܘ݁ Rwaḥa. It is pronounced *OH* as in p<u>o</u>le, h<u>o</u>le. It always appears as the letter waw - ܘ with a point above it ܘ݁ and becomes the vowel O as in ܐܘ݁ - oh, ܒܘ݁ - bo, ܓܘ݁ - go, etc.

The sixth vowel ܘ݂ Rwaṣa. It is pronounced *OO* or *U* as in p<u>oo</u>l, f<u>oo</u>d. It always appears as the letter waw - ܘ with a point beneath it ܘ݂ and becomes the vowel OO as in ܐܘ݂ - oo, ܒܘ݂ - boo, ܓܘ݂ - goo, etc.

The seventh vowel ܝ݂ Ḥwaṣa. It is pronounced as a long *EE* as in b<u>ee</u>, s<u>ee</u>. It always appears as the letter yodh - ܝ with a point beneath it ܝ݂ as in ܐܝ݂ - ee, ܒܝ݂ - bee, ܓܝ݂ - gee, etc.

PALESTINIAN ARAMAIC LETTERS

A	א	ל	L
B	ב	מ	M
G	ג	נ	N
D	ד	ס	S
H	ה	ע	Ạ
W	ו	פ	P
Z	ז	צ	Ṣ
Ḥ	ח	ק	Q
Ṭ	ט	ר	R
y	'	ש	SH
K	כ	ת	T

BIBLIOGRAPHY

Aland, Kurt and Barbara. *The Text of the New Testament,* translated by Erroll F. Rhodes. Grand Rapids, MI: William B. Eerdmans, Second Edition, Revised and Enlarged 1989.

Bauman, Clarence. *The Sermon on the Mount: The Modern Quest for its Meaning.* Macon, GA: Mercer University Press, 1985.

Black, Matthew. *An Aramaic Approach to the Gospels and Acts.* Oxford: Clarendon University Press, 3rd edition 1967.

Bowden, John. *Jesus: The Unanswered Questions.* Nashville: Abingdon Press, 1989.

Brown, Raymond E., Fitzmyer, Joseph A. and Murphy, Roland E., Editors in Chief. *The New Jerome Biblical Commentary.* Engelwood, NJ: Prentice Hall, 1990.

Charlesworth, James H. *Jesus Within Judaism: New Light from Exciting Archaeological Discoveries.* New York: Doubleday, 1988.

Comfort, Philip W. *Early Manuscripts & Modern Translations of the New Testament: How 20th Century Discoveries of the Earliest New Testament Manuscripts Have Influenced Modern English Translations.* Wheaton, IL: Tyndale House Publishers, 1990.

Eisenberg, Azriel. *The Synagogue through the Ages.* New York: Bloch Publishers, 1990.

Errico, Rocco A. *The Ancient Aramaic Prayer of Jesus*: *The Lord's Prayer.* Los Angeles: Science of Mind Publications, 1978.

——————. *Let There Be Light: The Seven Keys.* Marina del Rey, CA: DeVorss & Co., 1985.

——————. *Treasures from the Language of Jesus.* Marina del Rey, CA: DeVorss & Co., 1987.

Fitzmyer, Joseph A. *Essays on the Semitic Background of the New Testament.* Chico, CA: Scholars Press, 1974.

——————. *A Wandering Aramean: Collected Aramaic Essays.* Chico, CA: Scholars Press, 1979.

Gibson, Margaret D. *The Commentaries of Isodad of Merv.: The Gospel of Matthew (Aramaic).* London: Cambridge University Press, 1911.

Hitti, Philip K. *The Near East in History.* Princeton: D. Van Nostrand Co., 1960

Jeremias, Joachim. *New Testament Theology.* New York: MacMillian, 1971.

Lach, Samuel Tobias. *A Rabbinic Commentary on the New Testament.* Hoboken, NJ: KTAV Publishing House Inc., 1987.

Lamsa, George M. *Gospel Light.* Philadelphia: A. J. Holman Co., 1939. (Presently published by Harper & Row, 1981.)

———. *More Light on the Gospels.* Garden City, NY: Doubleday & Co., 1968. (Presently entitled: *New Testament Light*, San Francisco: Harper & Row, 1983.)

———. *A Key to the Original Gospels.* Phildelphia: A. J. Holman Co., 1932. (Presently published by Harper & Row, 1983.)

———. *My Neighbor Jesus.* Philadelphia: A. J. Holman Co., 1932.

———. *New Testament Origin.* Irvine, CA: Noohra Foundation, 1976.

———. *The Holy Bible: From the Ancient Eastern Text*, San Francisco: Harper & Row, 1981.

Marxsen, Willi. *Jesus and Easter: Did God Raise the Historical Jesus from the Dead?* Nashville: Abingdon Press, 1990.

———. *The Resurrection of Jesus of Nazareth.* Philadelphia: Fortress Press, 1979.

Metzger, Bruce M. *The Early Versions of the New Testament: Their Origin, Transmission and Limitations.* New York: Clarendon University Press, 1977.

———. *The Text of the New Testament: Its Transmission, Corruption, and Restoration.* New York: Oxford University Press, 1968.

Montefiore, C. G. *The Synoptic Gospels,* 2 vols. New York: KTAV, 1968.

Neusner, Jacob. *Judaism in the Beginning of Christianity.* Philadelphia: Fortress Press, 1984.

Patai, Raphael. *The Messiah Texts.* New York: Avon Books, 1979.

Prabhu, George M. Soares. *The Formula Quotations in the Infancy Narrative of Matthew: An Enquiry into the Tradition History of Mt. 1-2.* Rome: Biblical Institute Press, 1976.

Rihbany, Abraham M. *The Syrian Christ.* Boston: Houghton Mifflin, 1916.

Robinson, John A. T. *The Priority of John.* Oak Park, IL: Meyer Stone Books, 1987.

Roth, Cecil and Wigoder, Geoffrey, Editors in Chief. *The New Standard Jewish Encyclopedia.* Garden City, NY: Doubleday & Co., 1970.

Sevenster, J. N. *Do You Know Greek?: How Much Greek Could the First Jewish Christians Have Known?* Leiden: E. J. Brill, 1968.

Stendahl, Krister. *The School of St. Matthew: And Its Use of the Old Testament.* Ramsey, NJ: Sigler Press, 1990.

Torrey, Charles Cutler. *The Four Gospels: A New Translation.* New York: Harper & Publisher, 1947.

Vermes, Geza. *Jesus the Jew.* Philadelphia: Fortress Press, 1981.

—————. *Jesus and the World of Judaism.* Philadelphia: Fortress Press, 1983.

Wigram, W. A. *The Assyrians and their Neighbors.* London: G. Bell & Sons, 1929.

Wright, Fred H. *Manners and Customs of Bible Lands.* Chicago: Moody Press, 1953.

Young, Brad H. *Jesus and His Jewish Parables: Rediscovering the Roots of Jesus' Teaching.* New York: Paulist Press, 1989.

Zeitlin, Irving M. *Jesus and the Judaism of His Time.* London: Polity Press/Basil Blackwell, 1988.

—————. *Ancient Judaism.* London: Polity Press, 1984.

BIBLICAL TEXTS AND MANUSCRIPTS

The Hebrew Bible, Masoretic Text, Biblia Hebraica (BHA). Stuttgartensia, 1983.

The New Testament, Peshitta Text, Classical Eastern (Assyrian-Chaldean) Aramaic script. Mosul-Bagdad, 1950.

The Gospel of Matthew, Peshitta Aramaic Text of the New Testament (Estrangela script) 6th century C.E., photocopy from the Freer Gallery of Art, Smithsonian Institute, Washington, D.C. - No. 37.41.

Khaboris Aramaic Manuscript of the New Testament. Estrangela - 10th century C.E.

NOTES

NOTES

NOTES

NOTES

NOTES

NOTES

NOTES

NOTES

Rocco A. Errico, founder and president of the Noohra Foundation Inc., a non-profit biblical-religious educational organization and pastor of the Church of Daily Living (non-denominational, non-sectarian), both in Irvine, California, is a lecturer, author, Bible authority, translator, specialist in the Aramaic language, educator and pastoral counselor.

For ten years Dr. Errico was taught intensively by and traveled with the late George M. Lamsa, Th.D., world renowned Assyrian biblical scholar and translator of the Holy Bible from ancient Aramaic (Peshitta) texts. He was accredited by Dr. Lamsa to teach the ancient Near Eastern Aramaic branch of biblical studies.

He is proficient in Aramaic and Hebrew exegesis, Old and New Testaments, and in the biblical customs, idioms, psychology, symbolism and philosophy of the Semitic peoples. He is also fluent in the Spanish language and has translated the four gospels, Matthew, Mark, Luke and John into Spanish from the English - Peshitta version by Dr. Lamsa.

Dr. Errico holds a Doctor of Philosophy degree from the College of Christianity, Los Angeles. In addition he has received several honorary doctorates, a Doctor of Divinity from St. Ephrem's Institute, Sweden, a Doctor of Sacred Theology from the College of Christianity, Los Angeles.

He serves as professor of biblical studies in schools of ministry for many denominations and is a regular feature writer for several religious publications. He formerly served as an editor and writer for *Light for All*, a religious magazine. He has held advisory positions with many boards of ecumenical religious organizations. Dr. Errico has over 25 years of pastoral experience in non-denominational churches. He travels extensively throughout the country and is widely known for his numerous radio and television appearances.

Under the auspices of the Noohra Foundation, Dr. Errico continues to lecture for colleges, civic groups and churches of various denominations.

Publications:

The Ancient Aramaic Prayer of Jesus - 1975
The Mysteries of Creation - 1979
Let There Be Light: The Seven Keys - 1985
Treasures from the Language of Jesus - 1987
Classical Aramaic: Elementary Book 1 - 1989

Spanish Publications:

El Sermon del Monte - 1966
El Evangelio Segun San Juan - 1967

For further information and for a free catalog of Aramaic Bible translations, books, audio and video cassette tapes and for brochures of classes, retreats and seminars, write or call:

Noohra Foundation
18022 Cowan St., Suite 100-B
Irvine, CA 92714

PH: 714/975-1944